Woody Allen
on
Woody Allen

REVISED EDITION

D0177113

Woody Allen
on
Woody Allen

IN CONVERSATION WITH STIG BJÖRKMAN

Revised Edition

faber and faber

First published in England in 1995
by Faber and Faber Limited
Bloomsbury House, 74-77 Great Russell Street, London WC1B 3DA

This revised edition first published in 2004

Originally published in Sweden in 1993
as Woody om Allen
by Alfabeta Bokförlag

Printed and bound by CPI Group (UK) Ltd, Croydon, CR0 4YY

A CIP record for this book is available from the British Library

ISBN 978-0-571-22317-6

Contents

List of Illustrations

Acknowledgements

My thanks first and foremost to Woody Allen for the trust and great confidence he showed during all the work on the book and for the generosity he showed in allowing me to acquaint myself with all his work.

Many thanks not least to Lauren Gibson, Woody's personal assistant, who indefatigably and with great friendliness used her great talents for organization in keeping in order all the threads of meetings and agreements and all kinds of practical problems during the work with the first edition of this book. And the same warm thanks to her successor Sarah Allentuch, who to the same extent has helped me with information and advice during the continued work. Also to some of Woody's closest co-workers, Kay Chapin, Carlo Di Palma, Jack Rollins and Juliet Taylor, who made themselves available for personal interviews. Again to Susan E. Morse for many illuminating comments and to Carl Turnquest Jr who gave his service in running a number of films at the Manhattan Film Center.

Finally a thank you to Holger and Thyra Lauritzen's fund for film research. The working grant I received from the fund has been of great value in making this book possible.

Foreword

When I was asked to write this book I had only met Woody Allen on one occasion. It was in the Spring of 1986. *Hannah and Her Sisters* had been invited to be shown 'hors concours' at the Cannes film festival. Woody Allen, who does not like to leave New York and is even more unwilling to make public appearances in connection with his films, did not intend to be present at the screening. So, if Woody Allen would not come to the festival, the festival had to come to Woody Allen.

The festival commissioned Jean-Luc Godard to make a filmed interview with Allen in New York about his film. By chance, I was present at this interview. I happened to know the producer who had arranged the filming, Tom Luddy, and he hired me on the spot as still photographer. Both Allen and Godard agreed to this, but on one condition from Woody – he was to approve which picture or pictures I could use.

The filming took place in the private cinema in Woody's office, the Manhattan Film Center in New York. It is a quite bare and unfurnished place. There was just a sofa standing there, with a couple of armchairs and a low table. Along one of the longer walls there was a couple of metres of shelves with part of Woody's record collection, together with an old piano. The cinema screen on one of the shorter walls was concealed by a black curtain.

The conversation between these two celebrated directors – both almost equally shy – went on for a good hour. When the shooting was finished Allen and Godard posed for my camera. Then I handed the rolls of film over to Woody.

After that I kept up a very sporadic correspondence with him until the summer of 1991, when I contacted him with a proposal for a possible book of interviews concerning his career as writer, entertainer, actor and – above all – film-maker. After a while came the reply, friendly, rather evasive: the time was not right. Woody was – as usual – preparing a new film. But he left open the option of taking up the project again.

In January 1992 I was invited to New York for an interview in connection with *Shadows and Fog*, which was soon to have its première. I saw the film in the projection room of Columbia Films. The next day I had my meeting with Woody as one of several film critics who have come there from Europe. The friendly, but breathless, press lady informed me that I had 45 minutes at my disposal. 'Mr Allen is a very busy man!'

I am back again in the private cinema in Woody's office. It hadn't changed. The same spacious room. The same wide soft armchairs. Perhaps the record collection, from which Woody gets inspiration and music for his films, has grown quite a bit since last time. Beneath the shelves of records are stacks of sound cassettes for the newly shot film, which will be called *Husbands and Wives*. Woody is right in the middle of editing this film.

I am rather early, or perhaps Woody is a bit late. As I am setting up the recorder I suddenly hear a discrete cough and a 'Sorry, I'm a bit late.' It is Woody. He has made his entrance completely unnoticed and in silence. He seems to have suddenly materialized from a dark corner of the room. An illusionist's act in the style of those performed in *Oedipus Wrecks* or, for that matter, in *Shadows and Fog*. Or perhaps he has quite simply stepped down from the silver screen like the film hero in *The Purple Rose of Cairo*.

We start to talk, primarily about *Shadows and Fog*, but also about Woody's first film experiences and about his early film career. Time passes very quickly. Suddenly Woody's secretary looks in to say that 45 minutes have passed. But Woody waves her away. We continue our conversation for about another half hour.

Before we part I return to the book project. Woody cannot give an answer yet. He asks me to take it up again later in the spring. Then, after some further correspondence, an answer comes at the beginning of June. Woody will be able to cooperate for a few weeks in July–August, before he gets under way with his new film, which will be *Manhattan Murder Mystery*.

Chronologically – but with spontaneous digressions and with no pre-conceptions – we go through Woody's career. Before we begin, I assure Woody that he can put limits to what he wants to talk about. If there were questions he did not want to answer, of course, he would decline. But this was never the case. Woody's only request or stipulation about the book was that it should have a nice cover.

Our meetings usually take place in the morning. We sit and talk with a tape recorder in a corner of the cinema at the Manhattan Film Center, about two hours at a time. Concurrently, Woody is occupied with the preparations for *Manhattan Murder Mystery*.

On 13 August the newspaper placards and the front pages of the New York press trumpet out the news that Woody Allen and Mia Farrow are separating and that they have both brought suits about the custody of their common children. The private lives and personal affairs of this otherwise very retiring couple are thrown open to public inspection in a completely ruthless way.

The events naturally mean an unwelcome intrusion into Woody Allen's life – his private as well as his professional life. I fear that our work will have to be postponed, but the delay is only temporary. Two days later Woody resumes our meetings, but this time we meet at his home, in the penthouse he lives in close to Central Park.

Ironically enough, we have just got as far as *A Midsummer Night's Sex Comedy* and *Zelig*, two films which Woody worked on at the same time and in both of which Mia Farrow began her long association with him. To the unavoidable question of how they both met and began their fruitful association, Woody answers as openly and willingly as to everything else with which I have confronted him.

Nevertheless, because of the circumstances around Woody's private concerns and because of the ever more time-consuming preparation for *Manhattan Murder Mystery*, we are compelled to make a break in our talks. We make a temporary stop after going through *Hannah and Her Sisters*. I return to Sweden, also to begin a first review of the already very copious interview material.

In January 1993 the conversations resume – in the same way as before, alternating between the Manhattan Film Center and Woody's home. Some of the more comprehensive and intensive conversations, like the chapters about *September* and *Crimes and Misdemeanours*, took place in Woody's home. Perhaps the isolation and quiet there offered greater concentration and frankness. The study of *Radio Days*, on the contrary, took place in more chaotic conditions, in Woody's trailer, between takes during one of the last shooting days of *Manhattan Murder Mystery*.

During these January days I also got the opportunity to follow the filming. What impressed me most of all was the ease and lightheartedness which marked the work. Shooting a film is a complicated and unwieldly undertaking, but here there was none of the stress which normally prevails in this context. Then, of course, Woody has for a long time surrounded himself with the same fellow workers in most of the vital posts behind the camera. Everyone knows each other, knows each other's working routine. Communication takes place almost without words. A gesture, a look, nothing more is needed.

The following year I get the opportunity to watch Woody at work again, now with *Bullets Over Broadway*. What strikes me then is the respect and the total trust that characterizes the collaboration with the actors. When Woody, if ever, directs them, it is almost invisibly. A total concentration in the recording moment, but between the takes Woody seems more or less absent. Several actors have confirmed that they haven't felt really directed by Woody. And this just might be the secret behind his personal instructions. Woody totally relies on the actors' professional skills, on their ability to interpret the characters in their own way. He offers them a free scope that includes both freedom and responsibility. In all, a collaboration built on trust. Most likely, this is the reason why so many renowned actors seem to line up to get the opportunity to take part in a Woody Allen film.

In fall 2001 I meet Woody again to continue our conversations on film and life, art and music. As usual, Woody has been very busy. The overwhelming incidents in his private life have in no way affected his creativity and work. Since the work with the first edition of this book, he has written and directed nine more films, written a number of theatre plays and acted in a number of films. His latest film, *Hollywood Ending*, which is not to come up until April 2002, is already finished.

Maybe this latter part of his production is characterized by a bigger looseness, as if to balance the drama that has marked his life beside the film work. Like a bigger openness. It is no longer so difficult to get to interview Woody. He moves more often than before from the shielded bunker that Manhattan for a long time has seemed like. He has even visited the Oscars Award Ceremony and the Cannes Festival.

Yet everything is still the same when we meet again at the Manhattan Film Center. The same shabby couch and armchairs are in the exact same positions in the showroom where our conversations take place. I even think that we place ourselves in the exact same places as before, Woody in a corner of a couch and I in an armchair with the tape recorder between us. Some of his co-workers have been replaced by others, but the new-comers also seem the loyal kind. Most likely, they will follow Woody on his new film odysseys for several years. When the last sentence has been said in our conversations in April 2002, Woody is at work with the preparations for the film that goes under the name 'Woody Allen Spring Project'. Probably the manuscript for his next film is already lying finished in a drawer.

Woody Allen's position in the film world is unique. He has a contract with his producers which guarantees him complete freedom to write and direct one film a year – at least. The contract means unlimited control on Woody's side over choice of subject, script, actors and team members, final cut and so on. The only condition is that he keeps within the economic boundaries fixed for the project.

The Woody Allen I learned to know during the work on this book bears no great resemblance to the *film persona* we are familiar with on the screen, the lone wolf and the incurable neurotic, to all the suffering and, not least, the self-pity as a welcome basis for all the shortcomings which he seems to want to reveal with almost masochistic enjoyment: the hypochondria, self-absorption, indecisiveness and other more or less definable phobias. Instead, there was the disciplined working man and decision-maker, a serious and conscious artist who makes far-reaching demands on himself and refuses to compromise his art and vision.

His private life is a shielded sector, the official life reduced to a minimum. One exception is the Monday evenings at Michael's Pub where Woody, practically every week, appears as clarinettist in a group of trad jazz musicians. Now the gigs have been moved to the Café Carlyle but the time is the same: each Monday night when Woody is not occupied with film work. Music is perhaps one of the most important sources of inspiration for Woody. This and other sources of inspiration and creativity are considered in the following pages.

Stockholm, May 2002

CHAPTER I

Beginnings

FAT MAN: Have you studied film-making in school?
SANDY: No, no, I didn't study anything in school. They studied me.

(From Stardust Memories)

STIG BJÖRKMAN: *Since we are going to be talking about your career in films, we should go through it chronologically. But we should, as well, be open to a kind of flow of consciousness, going back and forth in time, using a kind of flashback-technique.*

The last thing I did before leaving Stockholm was to see the beginning of Alice. It's a film I like very much, having seen it several times before. And I expected the film to open with the morning scene with Alice, her husband and the kids . . . but that's not how the film starts. It starts with a scene in the aquarium between Alice and her lover-to-be. So, this taught me that one's memory isn't always to be trusted and that one has to be very careful about details.

WOODY ALLEN: Right, right, one often remembers films differently.

SB: *But it also showed the kind of flow of consciousness which your films express, the great liberty in their structuring. So, I would like to hear your comment on this.*

WA: Well, film is wonderful that way. It's like prose writing. There are no limits, no physical limits to what you can do with time. It's a wonderful, wonderful thing.

So, there are people that think in a narrative linear mode all the time and make wonderful movies that way. And there are people that think in a way that is less linear and more digressive. I tend to do that more. I tend to move around at times. Not deliberately, just instinctively.

SB: *And these digressions, are they already in the script?*

WA: Mostly. Every now and then an idea emerges in the editing room or when I'm shooting, but generally speaking that kind of thing is inherent in the basic structure of the film.

SB: *Making use of a flashback now – what are your first memories of film, which was the first film you ever saw?*
WA: It's hard to say. It was probably *Snow White* or something like that. Probably some Disney film, I guess. What I remember most vividly are the years 1940–41–42. From then on I was a frequent movie-goer.

SB: *You were five–six–seven years old then . . .*
WA: Yeah, I was born December 1st in '35. They started to take me to movies when I was five years old or so. And I got very entranced by films. I lived in a lower middle-class section of Brooklyn, and there were about 25 movie-theatres to go to within walking distance of my home. So, I spent endless time at the movies. In those days the studios were making many, many pictures every year, and in the space of one month one would see pictures with James Cagney and Humphrey Bogart and Gary Cooper and Fred Astaire and pictures by Disney and . . . it was just astonishing, the abundance.

SB: *I became a frequent movie-goer as well, but I started late. I saw my first film when I was eleven years old. But to me this first visit to a movie-theatre was a kind of revelation, an almost religious experience. It was an MGM musical and I immediately fell in love with the leading actress, Jane Powell. And then I started watching movies almost every day.*
WA: Was it *A Date with Judy* you saw?

SB: *No, it was Luxury Liner. Your parents didn't oppose your great interest in films? They never protested or tried to prevent or prohibit you from seeing films?*
WA: No. When I was at that very young age, an older cousin of mine used to take me to the movies once a week. But as I got older . . . the other kids in the neighbourhood, their parents did discourage them from going. They used to say, if it was summertime, 'Go out and play in the fresh air, go and play in the sun, get some exercise, go swimming.' There were many myths in those days that films were bad for your eyes and things like that. My parents didn't bother about that or try to force me to do other things. And I always hated the summertime, I hated the hot weather, I hated the sunshine. So I used to go into an air-conditioned movie-house. And sometimes, you know, I would go four, five, six times a week or every

single day, for as much money as I could scrape together. There was always a double-feature to see. And I loved it! But in the wintertime, when there was school, it was a different matter. You could only go on the weekends. But usually I went Saturday and Sunday, and sometimes on Friday afternoon, after school.

SB: *Did you just see everything they happened to show, or were you in any way selective? Were you more interested in some specific kind of films, genre films?*

WA: At first I saw everything and whatever there was. And then, when I got a bit older, I liked romantic comedies very much, sophisticated comedies. And I liked the Marx Brothers very much, and murder mysteries.

SB: *The Marx Brothers must have been a bit advanced in terms of taste for a young kid, weren't they?*

WA: I think that I've always had a relatively sophisticated taste in comedy. Because even as a child, I was not very crazy about slapstick comedy. I never liked clowns – unlike Fellini. And this may be because what we get as clowns in the United States is radically different from European clowns. I've never enjoyed circus clowns. And I never really enjoyed slapstick movies very much. I was drawn, instantly, to a more sophisticated kind of comedy. I liked Preston Sturges and some of the early 1940s sophisticated comedies. Those were more my favourites. The Marx Brothers are in a special category, because they were broad and clownlike, but highly, highly sophisticated as well. Highly cerebral and witty. You know, to this day I've never really gotten much fun out of Laurel and Hardy. Everybody I know, all my contemporaries, all my friends, just love them. They think they're great, and often try to show me what I'm missing. It's not that I hate Laurel and Hardy, but they've never really meant anything to me. I've just never had a big tolerance of broad comedy.

SB: *I like* The Music Box *a lot. That's a small masterpiece, I think.*

WA: Sure, there are moments when they are quite funny. But in general, the silent slapstick comedies didn't interest me much. Chaplin himself interested me, because I think he was a hilariously funny man. I think he was wonderfully funny, malicious and direct. I did not think that Buster Keaton was particularly funny. I think his movies are superb. They are masterpieces; his work is beautifully crafted, flawless. But he himself never makes me laugh very much. Whereas, when Chaplin comes down the street, there's a mischievous and malicious streak in him. He wipes his face with the man's beard and kicks him in the ass. I don't warm to Keaton as much. Objectively, if you're to just judge movies by craft, Keaton's are superior; but if you judge them by feeling and by their impact on the audience, I find Chaplin's much more fun and much more interesting. I'm much more involved with *City Lights* than any Keaton film. Even though, when I see *Steamboat Bill* or *The General*, I can see they're great. There's no question about it. It's great film-making, first-rate work.

SB: *There is such a precision in his work.*
WA: Yeah, it's masterful. I admire and enjoy it, but it's not the same for me as the personal involvement I get with Chaplin and his personal, psychological relationship to the men and women he's dealing with.

SB: *And what was it in the Marx Brothers that attracted you?*
WA: Their wit is so wonderful. The surrealism, the nonsensity and the unexplainable, unmotivated craziness is so fantastic. And, of course, the guys were talented! That's what it is. Chico was talented, Harpo was extremely talented and Groucho was the best of them all. They just had a great gift. Everything they did had a certain funniness to it. It was built into them, like it was in the genes or the cells or something. I've often made this comparison, that if you get someone like Picasso and he draws a little rabbit, a simple rabbit, and then the kids in class draw the same rabbit, there's just something in his line. He doesn't have to do anything fancy, no explosive idea. But it's just something in his line, the feeling in his line on the paper that's so beautiful. It's the same thing if someone is playing a great violin, if they just play up and down the scale, the feeling, the intonation is so beautiful. It's the same with someone like Groucho. If you had dinner with Groucho, just in conversation with him, it was funny. It was not that he was trying to be funny, it was not the content of what he said. Just something in his rhythm, in the intonation of his voice, was built-in 'funny'. So I was a great, great fan of theirs and their movies were full of energy and preposterous craziness.

SB: *Did you go and see their movies again and again?*
WA: Yes, whenever they played in the neighbourhood, I did, sure. I always see movies again and again. I'm never tired of the movies I like. I'm never tired of seeing them year after year.

SB: *And you came to know Groucho well?*

WA: Yes, I came to know him fairly well. I spent a reasonable amount of time with him, and I found him very nice. Of course people said to me that at the time I got to know him he had mellowed, that he had been a terror in his early years. This may be true, I don't know. When I met him though, he was very nice and full of anecdotes; he was an admirer of mine and I was a worshipper of his. In certain ways he reminded me of the kind of uncle that one meets at a family affair, or a family reunion, who is full of wise-cracks. Most of the uncles you meet are not good enough to be professional, but they are always saying something sarcastic or amusing. Groucho could just have been someone who had shown up at a family wedding or funeral or party or something, and he would have fit right in. He would have been the funny uncle at the buffet-table taking some chicken and some rice and, you know, making some funny remarks.

SB: *At the time when you got to know Groucho, were the other brothers already dead?*

WA: No, I met Harpo. But I didn't know Chico. Or the other two, Gummo and Zeppo. Harpo came to see me when I played in a cabaret once.

SB: *At the beginning of* The Purple Rose of Cairo *Cecilia (Mia Farrow) and her sister talk about movies and movie-stars. They seem to be interested not only in the films but also in the life of the stars of the screen. Did you share a similar interest when you were young and started to see films?*

WA: I was only moderately interested in the stars and in their lives. As a very young child I could identify everybody in the movies. By the time I was eight or nine years old there was not a movie actor that I couldn't identify, because I saw so many films and I studied the movie magazines. But I wasn't very caught up in the gossip of it.

SB: *And were you aware of the people behind the films as well? The people who had made the films, the directors etc.?*

WA: That came later. When I grew up it was the time of the star system. In the United States, in particular, there was not an emphasis on directors. It was only later that I started to realize what the directors were doing.

SB: *Apart from the Marx Brothers, were there other movie-stars you looked forward to seeing on the screen?*
WA: Oh yes, all the time! I loved Fred Astaire and Humphrey Bogart and James Cagney and Edward G. Robinson. All the ones that everybody loved: Jimmy Stewart, Gary Cooper, Alan Ladd and right down the list. I loved them all, I loved watching them.

SB: *When did you grow more conscious about the directors and the role of the director?*
WA: As I got older, as I got into my teens – it was not until my teens – I started to realize that certain directors were better than other directors. When I was about fifteen or so, a few foreign film houses opened up in my neighbourhood. You couldn't see very many foreign films during the war. But then, after the war, I started to see the really great European masterpieces. Because they only imported the finest European films to the States. Then I became very conscious of the Italian directors and of the French cinema and of some of the German cinema. And at some point I saw a film of Ingmar Bergman's. But that was a little later.

SB: *Do you remember which of his films this was?*
WA: It was *Summer with Monika*. It was wonderful! Absolutely wonderful. And then I saw *The Naked Night*. And that was the one that completely captivated me. It was tremendous. Then there was a rush of Bergman's films in the United States. *Wild Strawberries* came over and *The Seventh Seal* and *The Magician*. And he made a very big reputation in the art houses here. This was in the fifties.

SB: *And when you compared these foreign films with the American films you were used to seeing, what was your reaction?*
WA: They were, of course, very different; my friends and I took an instant love to the foreign cinema because it was so much more mature than the American cinema. The American cinema was basically entertainment and escapism. The European cinema – or at least those European films that we saw here – was much more confrontational and much more grown up. European films were not those silly little cowboy movies or silly little entertainment movies where boy meets girl, then loses girl and in the end gets girl again. So, we loved them. They were very impressive to us. It was a wonderful, eye-opening experience. They made us more interested in directors and in film history as well.

SB: *You say you and your friends. Was this the older cousin you mentioned before?*

WA: No, she took me to see the American films when I was small. By the time I was a teenager I went with my friends from school. We were very devoted to the foreign films, and found foreign comedies very funny as well.

SB: *Like which?*

WA: I remember a number of them, like *Fanfan, la tulipe* or the early Jacques Tati films. And we saw some British movies that were quite amusing. And the René Clair films! I was so impressed when I saw *A nous la liberté* the first time. I thought it was wonderful. But, of course, the serious films were really the ones that were so impressive to us – *The Bicycle Thief*, for instance – those were tremendous experiences. And the Jean Renoir films were overwhelming too: *The Rules of the Game* and *La Grande Illusion*, and that wonderful short one, *Une Partie de campagne*. And at this time the early Fellini films reached us as well. I don't remember having seen the very early Bergman films. To me the Bergman style started to gel with *Summer with Monika*. Before that the films he was making were, to me, like very good American films. They were in the style of American films. But there seemed to be some kind of break with that Harriet Andersson film, and after that it drifted into the emergence of that great poetic style.

SB: *You know, Bergman started his career in films as a script-writer. He has given very vivid accounts about his time as a kind of script slave for the most important Swedish production company at the time, in the early and middle forties. He and his colleagues had to see a lot of American films and they were supposed to study and copy the American way of script-writing. That's what the producers of that time expected and wanted from them. So this influence must therefore be very obvious in his early films as a director as well. But did your very vivid interest in films at this time lead you into the idea of one time being able to work with films?*

WA: No, but it occurred to me even as a young child while once watching, of all things, a pirate picture. And I thought to myself, 'Gee, I could do that, I could make a film like that.' This was at the age of seven or eight. It was just some dream deferred that I didn't think about.

SB: *Do you remember which film this was?*

WA: Yes, it was *The Black Swan* with Tyrone Power. I don't know why or what it was in the film that made me think like this, because I saw so many films at the time. But maybe it was more colourful or fun or exciting than the others. I really wanted to become a writer, and a writer for the theatre. I would not have known how to get into films or what to do. I just wanted to be a playwright.

SB: *You started very early to write: material for other comedians, stories for newspapers, pieces for television, etc. When, at what age, did you start to write? I mean, before sending it to anybody to read or use or publish?*
WA: I could always write. Even as a little child. I could make up good stories before I could even read. I've always said that I could write before I could read. Then I was hired to write when I was sixteen, when I was still in school. They hired me to write funny jokes and amusing anecdotes. And then I wrote for radio and television and cabaret comedians. And then I wrote for myself as a cabaret comedian. And then I wrote that film script and ultimately I directed.

SB: *Has writing always been a pleasure for you. Or do you experience* angst *in front of the white and empty paper as well?*
WA: No, in that way I feel like Picasso, who once said that when he sees an empty space, he has to fill it. And I feel the same way. Nothing makes me happier than to tear open a big big ream of yellow or white paper. And I can't wait to fill it! I love to do it.

SB: *When did you start to write short stories? In the beginning, I guess, your writing consisted merely of jokes and sketches for yourself and other comedians.*
WA: I started with that a couple of years after I started writing. I fooled around trying to write plays, not doing very well at it. I was not very good at it.

SB: *Why not, do you think?*
WA: I just had not yet developed enough craft. I was not educated enough. I was ejected from school, at an early term. And I was not that literate, not that familiar with literature, not an habitual reader. It took me a while to absorb things, to read a lot, to see a lot of theatre. But then I would go away during the summer and write sketches to be played on stage in summer theatres. And I would watch the reactions. I learned a lot from it. And gradually, as I grew up and matured, I started to get better at it.

SB: *When you ask writers how they learnt their craft, how they learnt their job, they usually answer 'by reading'. And we learnt the craft of film-making by seeing a lot of films. Nowadays there are film schools, there are courses in creative writing and so on. Do you believe more in learning by oneself through experience rather than in schools, when it comes to training yourself to a creative occupation or profession?*

WA: Absolutely. It's socratic. It enters through a different opening in your body. For instance, in order to be a jazz musician, you have to listen and listen and listen to a lot of jazz. And that's an act of love. You don't think, I'm listening to study it. You just listen because you love it. And you love it, and love it ... and gradually you learn. You really learn everything valuable through osmosis. It's the same with play-writing or movie-directing or acting. You love either reading or watching films or plays or listening to music. And in some way, over the years, without making any attempt, it gets into your blood, into the fibre of your body or something. The business of studying it where it becomes a chore and a discipline is wrong. For instance, some actors would watch Marlon Brando when he first started in films. They just loved watching his movies, they'd watch and watch. And when they went to act, they acted like Marlon Brando. They didn't try to, but his acting style became absorbed in them. You find the same thing with music all the time. Someone listens to Charlie Parker. And he listens and listens and loves him and learns to play the saxophone – and he sounds like him! Then he has to break off from that and develop his own style. But it all comes from a very personal and passionate interest. If you want to teach someone film-directing, you could almost say, 'Just keep going to the movies, and it will pass into your body.'

SB: *You said that you started to read literary works late in life. But when you started to read, which authors or which books caught your attention?*

WA: When I first started to read, I read Ernest Hemingway, William Faulkner, F. Scott Fitzgerald, John Steinbeck, those writers.

SB: *And this was in what period of your life?*

WA: I didn't start reading until I was in my late teens, because I never liked to read. I still read a lot. But I have never read a lot for pleasure. I read because it's important to read. Every now and then something gives me pleasure, but mostly it's a chore for me to read.

SB: What's New, Pussycat? *was your first film script. Was it more or less by chance that you got involved in that project?*

WA: Yes, I was in a cabaret, and some people came in and liked me and thought, 'Gee, he writes all his own cabaret material. He'd be very good to maybe write a script.' So they hired me. And I wrote it, and I wrote what I thought was a good script. But they didn't know what to do with it. They didn't know how to make it. They made it into a film that I was very unhappy with. I didn't like it at all. And I vowed at that time that I would never write another film script, unless I could be the director of the film.

SB: *At that time did you have any ideas about directing films? Did you want to direct* What's New, Pussycat?, *for instance?*

WA: No. Only out of self-defence. I felt that nobody seemed to understand what to do with the film. The director, Clive Donner, was a very good director. But he had no power, because all the studio people were sitting on him and the stars were badgering him and forcing him to do things. If it wasn't for him, I would really have had a bad time.

SB: *At that time he was one of the more interesting and promising young British directors. Had you seen any of his films prior to* Pussycat?

WA: I had seen *Nothing But the Best*. I liked it and I liked him personally. And I thought he was trying his best, but they were hemming him in all over the place. They wouldn't give him any freedom.

SB: *What was it in* What's New, Pussycat? *that you didn't like? In what way would you have liked to change it?*

WA: I had written what I felt was a very off-beat, uncommercial film. It was not a factory-made kind of film. And the producers I turned it over to were the quintessential Hollywood machine. They undertook to execute this project with everything that everyone hates about Hollywood films. People that had no sense of humour deciding what's funny and what's not. People putting their girlfriends in roles. People writing special roles just to accommodate stars, whether those roles worked or not. The worst nightmare one could think of. And just about every creative decision made was incorrect. For example, I would write a scene where a man would stop an elevator between floors and make love to a woman. Now, if you're in a busy office building in New York, that can be funny. But the producers went out and found a building in Paris with an elevator that was so beautiful that it looked like the bridal suite of a hotel. And, suddenly, there was no joke anymore. To stop and make love in that elevator was

1   Woody Allen and Peter Sellers in *What's New, Pussycat?*

meaningless! The producers never understood the script, not any of it at any point. And, of course, I had no say over anything. I could only raise my voice, and they would dismiss it or throw me out. So, I didn't like the experience and didn't like the film.

SB: *I understand that a small war was going on between you and the producer, Charles Feldman. But didn't you and Clive Donner try to form a pact or something similar to fight him and his influence?*
WA: Yes, we tried. We did as much as we could. But there are different kinds of movie-making. There's movie-making that's serious movie-making – whether the film is funny, musical or serious. And then there are people that use the movies for a life-style. They spend a year meeting with writers and going to lunch and meeting with actors and actresses and going to lunch and doing screen-tests with pretty actresses and sleeping with them and having social meetings and bringing in new writers and so on . . . They spend a year, two years doing all these things, and then when they make the movie, they have dinners with the cast and dinners with the director and with the writers and they bring their friends by and they interfere with a work they don't know anything about. A producer can come in and say, 'I need a close-up of that actress the first time we see her.' And everybody argues with each other. The stars argue with each other, because they think the other actors have a bigger or more important part or funnier lines to say. This goes on and on. And it is not movie-making. Just once in a great, great while – in spite of everything – it works. But 99 per cent of the time it's a disaster. It's a terrible way to make movies! It's all social. It's partying.

SB: What's New, Pussycat? *offered you your first acting experience in films. How was this experience?*
WA: Shaky. I didn't know whether I should do a lot or do a little. It was hard. It was not such that I could look at myself in the dailies and then say, 'OK, now I know what to do. I'll go back tomorrow and do that properly.' That didn't happen. I got one chance to do it and no chance to redo it. I was doing the best I could, but I was unconfident.

SB: *Actors are not always allowed to see the dailies, but could you in your capacity as script-writer go and see the dailies?*
WA: Yes, I went to the dailies. I was allowed to see them. But I didn't like any of them. I always used to say, 'This is terrible!' And they always said, 'Keep quiet!'

SB: *In* Pussycat *you act opposite one of my favourite actresses, Romy Schneider. What were your impressions of her as an actress and co-star?*

WA: Well, I had liked her in other movies. When I met her on *Pussycat*, I had very little contact with her. She was pleasant, but our stations were so far apart. I had never been in a film before, and she was a big star. I was so far beneath her that we had very little contact. But when I worked with her, she certainly was pleasant.

SB: *Was your next venture into films,* Casino Royale, *a similar experience for you?*

WA: Well, there I was just an actor. I was offered quite a lot of money and it was a very small part. But my manager said, 'Why not? It could become a big movie, and it will keep you going in cinema. And it's lucrative.' So I went to London. And I was on a good salary and a good expense account, per diems. But they didn't get to film me for six months! I stayed in London at their expense for six months. That's only one example of how utterly wasteful the project was.

SB: *So what did you do in London during all these six months?*

WA: I wrote a play, *Don't Drink the Water*. I socialized, I played cards, I gambled. I enjoyed London. Then finally, six months down the line, they called me in to do my miniscule amount of shooting. And I went home! I thought it was a moronic enterprise from start to finish, that everything about it was a stupidity and a waste of celluloid and money. It was another dreadful film experience.

SB: *During the time of these two films you did other kinds of writing, such as short stories.*

WA: Yes, I used to write short stories for the *New Yorker Magazine*. And I was very thrilled to be published by them, because it was an extremely high-grade literary magazine in the United States, and everybody I knew wanted to be published in the *New Yorker*. And the first thing I sent them, they published.

SB: *When was that?*

WA: It was around the time of *What's New, Pussycat?* Around the mid-sixties, I guess. They kept publishing me and I kept writing for them and I enjoyed it.

2   Woody Allen and friend in *Casino Royale*

SB: *And these are the same stories which later on have been published in book form?*

WA: Yes, in *Getting Even, Side Effects* and *Without Feathers.*

SB: *Then you made your first film – which wasn't your film to begin with – What's Up, Tiger Lily? This was a Japanese film which you dubbed into English, completely changing the original story on the way.*

WA: Right, that was another dreadful experience. Somebody purchased a Japanese film and asked me to put words into the Japanese actors' mouths. I had my friends with me, and we went to a dubbing studio, watched the Japanese actors on the screen and dubbed their voices into English. It was a very stupid enterprise; stupid and juvenile. Just before the movie came out I sued the producer to try to keep the movie from coming out. He made changes to it that I thought were terrible. And while the suit was getting under way the movie opened and got very good reviews from the critics. So I dropped the suit, because I thought that I wouldn't have much of a case. But I never thought that the film was anything but insipid. It was a sophomoric exercise.

SB: *Do you know how the people who originally made the film reacted?*

WA: No, I don't know anything about that.

Take the Money and Run

OG, THE SPACEMAN: We enjoy your films.
Particularly the early funny ones.
(From *Stardust Memories*)

STIG BJÖRKMAN: *But anyway, this leads to your first directing experience with* Take the Money and Run.
WOODY ALLEN: Yeah, that's really where I feel my career in films began. Before that it was all reasons not to go into the cinema.

SB: *And what was the origin of this film?*
WA: I wrote *Take the Money and Run* with my friend Mickey Rose. We thought it was a funny idea. And I gave the script to the British director Val Guest, because I thought he might like to direct it. He had directed the part of *Casino Royale* where I was acting. I didn't think that anyone would give me a chance to direct it. Guest said that he would love to do it, but the film company didn't want him to do it. Then I gave it to Jerry Lewis, who was a comedy director of great experience. He was also very interested in directing it. But the film company still didn't want to do it. So the project was just hanging around.

SB: *You asked Jerry Lewis to direct it. You had, of course, seen some of his films?*
WA: I had seen his films, and I thought that they had some very funny moments. I can't say that I was a fan of his films *per se*, but I thought that he was a hilariously talented man. I thought that if I could have him direct me in the film, it would be great. In every one of his films, no matter how askew the film went, there were always a couple of sequences that were wonderful, because he was such a natural talent himself, such an energetic talent.

3   Woody Allen as a bankrobber in *Take the Money and Run*

SB: *I very much liked his early films as a director. I think he had a great visual talent as well, a talent for composing and structuring his films.*
WA: Yes, his films were good, had good craftsmanship. But they were always too infantile for me. But his own work was quite good.

SB: *But the film was made, eventually.*
WA: Yes, then this new film company was formed, Palomar Pictures. It was a small company with no big name directors connected to it. They were trying to get started. And they asked if I could make the film on a small budget, which was less than a million dollars. I said 'yes', and they decided to take a chance on me, because I had written *What's New, Pussycat?*, I had written for the theatre and I had written the material for my cabaret acts. I seemed intelligent enough to them. I didn't seem irresponsible, that I would gamble their money away. So they said, 'OK, we'll take a chance with you.' And they did. They were very enlightened and gave me no problems at all. It was strictly *carte blanche*. They allowed me my freedom in working. They never bothered me. I got final cut, everything I wanted to do. It was a very pleasant experience. And from that day on I never ever had any problems in the cinema from the point of view of interference in any way.

SB: *You wrote* Take the Money and Run *and also your next film,* Bananas, *together with Mickey Rose. Who is he?*
WA: He's an old friend of mine from school. We grew up together, went to school together, played on the same baseball team. Then he moved out to California. I speak to him on the phone, once or twice a year now.

SB: *Was he a writer at the time?*
WA: Yes. He is very, very funny. So it was fun collaborating with him.

SB: *When you co-write a film together with another writer, how do you proceed? Do you sit together and write or do you write separately and then bring your individual writings together?*
WA: In those days, when I wrote those two scripts with Mickey, we worked together. We kept a typewriter in the room and we were both there and we went line by line. Years later when I collaborated with Marshall Brickman [on *Annie Hall* and *Manhattan*], I did it differently. Marshall and I spoke and spoke and worked out the plot and worked out the details. Then he went away and I wrote the draft. Then he would see it and make comments on it, tell me what he liked and what he disliked. We went over

the draft together. It was quicker with just one of us going all the way and writing it. And I did it, because I was the one who would have to speak it. So it was easy for me to do it.

SB: *I gather that your way of writing scripts has changed over the years, but is there anything general in your way of writing that you could comment on? For instance, do you write very rapidly, during a concentrated time, or do you go around with the project and the ideas in your head for a long time before writing the script?*
WA: No, no, I write rapidly. Very rapidly. Sometimes an idea will occur to me, like say today. But I can't write now, because I'm in preproduction for another film. Then, when that film's over and I start writing the new script, you could say, that this idea has been kept in my head. But sometimes it happens that one film ends and I have no ideas at all for a new film. And I just go into my workroom in the morning and I start thinking and I force myself into work.

SB: *But do you make notes for projects to come?*
WA: No. If I get an idea today for a joke or a story, I might write it down quickly and throw it in a drawer. But I don't make notes when I write. I prefer to write the script.

SB: *So once you've decided that now you have the time to write, then do you just sit down and do it in one go?*
WA: Yes. I get the idea, and then think about the idea a lot. I make sure that it's a whole idea, that it's got development. And then I sit down and write it. I don't like to write a treatment or a synopsis or notes or anything like that. I write the script.

SB: *Do you have any yet-unrealized scripts in your drawers?*
WA: I have a couple, yeah. A few scripts that I wrote and then didn't think were worth doing, for one reason or another.

SB: *Before the production of* Take the Money and Run *started, did you talk to any other more experienced film-makers for advice or to prepare yourself for work as a director?*
WA: Well, to tell you the truth, it never occurred to me for a second that I wouldn't know what to do. I was guided by the fact that I knew what I wanted to see. So it seemed to me elementary how to get to see it. There was no trick at all. I know that a man was to come into a room, he pulls a

gun out, etc. And it doesn't require any great brilliance to know how to do that. I did go to lunch with Arthur Penn, whom I didn't know and who was very nice. I tried to see if I could get any information from him. And I did. He provided me with some information, but it was more of a practical kind. Like, when he made his first film, he would order a hundred extras. But then on the set he would use only ten of them. And he felt guilty, because he had ordered a hundred and the company was paying for them. So he tried to figure out some way of getting them all in. But, he told me, after a while he realized he shouldn't do that. So he just used the ten and let the other ninety be an expense. He told me little things like that. And he spoke to me about colour correcting the film, important details like that. But there wasn't really much. I never for a second thought that there would be any problem with the film. I just thought it would be funny.

SB: *You didn't discuss any specific technicalities with Penn? Like how to proceed when you want to cross-cut a scene or things like that?*
WA: No, it just seemed to me that, if I knew I wanted this character to speak and then that character, then I knew what I had to do. It was common sense, because I knew what I wanted to see on the screen.

SB: *How did you choose the collaborators for the film, for instance the cameraman and other members of the technical crew? I mean, this was your first film, so did you pick them or were they chosen for you by the producer?*
WA: Everything was chosen for me except for a few people. I chose the costume designer, the cameraman and the art director. But I didn't know what I was doing. I just did the best I could at the time. I had no idea what the real problems were. But soon I discovered. Because I fired the cameraman and I fired the costume designer.

SB: *And the cameraman who came in is the one who is credited on the film?*
WA: Yes, he was fine. He was professional.

SB: *Had you seen any of his work before?*
WA: No, he was all I could get quickly, after I'd fired the first one. I'd never heard of him. When I first made that film, ironically, I sent a telegram to Carlo Di Palma. And he has kept it to this day. I wrote, 'Can you come and shoot my first movie?' But he couldn't. It was only twenty years later that I got a chance to work with him.

4   Gordon Willis at work on *Stardust Memories*

SB: *You had seen his work with Antonioni then?*

WA: Yes, I had seen *Blow up* and I had seen *Red Desert*. And I liked them. When he was not available, I tried to get a Japanese cameraman who had worked with Kurosawa – can't remember his name. So I had very grandiose ambitions. But when it came down to it, I hired absolute hacks. And I'm glad I did, because years later I started to work with Gordon Willis, who is a great cameraman, truly great. If I had hired him or Carlo Di Palma for my first movie, I think that would have been a mistake. I would not have known how to utilize them. I would have gotten into arguments with them. Because I knew exactly what I wanted. And that's what I did and that's what I got. And that's the way it was for a number of films. So when I did *Annie Hall*, which was my first collaboration with Willis, I was more confident. Gordon was so brilliant. He would say to me, 'Look, it doesn't matter if it's very, very dark there and you don't see anything. They'll still think it's funny.' And I took a chance. I had some confidence, because I had done four, five films already. And suddenly I realized, that the person who is speaking doesn't have to be on camera. Really, my maturity in films began with my association with Gordon Willis. The films I made before Gordon were, I think, fun and exuberant and the best I could do. But I didn't really know what I was doing, I was just learning. And everything there was dependent on funniness. If the movie was funny, it was successful. If it was not funny, it wasn't. And I could always be funny. That I had control over. So everything was subjugated to *the joke*. The films were a series of jokes. But it was not until later, when I did *Annie Hall*, that I became more ambitious and started to use the cinema a little bit. Then I could refrain from too many jokes; I tried to make the film more dimensional and searched for other values. That's how I developed.

SB: *But there are traces of things to come in some of your earliest films. There are, for instance, scenes in* Bananas *between you and Louise Lasser that reminds me a lot of later scenes in* Annie Hall. *I'm not only thinking of the dialogue. The staging of the scenes share an affinity.*

WA: I'm sure. Because those are things I know from life. You know, apartments, restaurants, sidewalks. I know city life. *Bananas* was also a fun picture to make, but there everything was subjugated to the joke.

SB: *We were talking about the cinematographer and his importance. I guess, that he's your closest collaborator behind the camera.*

5   Woody Allen and Carlo Di Palma at work on *Radio Days*

WA: Sure! Because what is a film? It's photography. So it's very, very important to be in sync with your cinematographer.

SB: *You worked for a long time with Gordon Willis, but then mainly with European cameramen.*
WA: Well, Gordon Willis is one of the great American photographers, and I worked with him for ten years. Then we diverged. He was not available for a production. Then I made a film with Carlo Di Palma, and when that film was finished Gordon was on another film. But I would work with him again. He's great. So I worked with Carlo, and I love working with him. And then he had a stomach operation and was not able to work for about two years. Then I had the opportunity to work with Sven Nykvist. And I've always loved his work. So we did two and a half pictures together.

SB: *I wondered if there was something specific in European photo-graphy, in the way of lighting, that interested you.*
WA: Yes, there is. I think that the European photographers on the whole have been better than the American photographers. There's Gordon, of course, and there might be two or three other good ones. But he's in a class by himself. To me, the European shooting of a film and the style of European films has always been more interesting than American films. Basically, 98 per cent of American films are factory-made films. Whereas in the European films they don't have too much money, so they have to use more innovation. Also, they have a greater respect for the director and the artist in a film. The whole European phenomenon of making films has always been much superior. I like very much the style of European films.

SB: *European cinematographers on the whole, I think, are more sparse when it comes to lighting. They show a greater interest in the interplay of light with shadow and darkness. In many American films you see this very flat light. The whole scene, the whole set is lit up.*
WA: You never see that with Gordon, though. He is a master of shadows, the master of chiaroscuro. Fortunately, he's been an influence on many American cameramen, so there's a greater tendency to appreciate shadow and dimension now. But for years it has been as you described it: everything had to be lit and flat and you had to see all the faces.

SB: *Do you remember your first day of shooting on* Take the Money and Run?

WA: Yes, I remember it very clearly. I was excited, not nervous at all. I was excited for a number of reasons. One, because it was my first day. And two, because I was going to be filming in prison, in the San Quentin prison in California. The thought of going into that famous big prison was enormously exciting to me. So when I was shaving, I cut my nose. If you look at the prison scene in *Take the Money and Run*, you can see the cut on my nose from that very first morning. That was probably the first shot I made in that movie. But I didn't have one moment's apprehension. I just thought it will be easy. I'll go into the prison, and I know exactly what I want to see. For the joke to be funny, the camera has to be here. It's common sense. But I remember my excitement, and I thought it was great fun. And the convicts, the inmates were very nice. They were very cooperative. Everybody enjoyed it.

SB: *Do you remember how many takes you managed to shoot that first day? And how effective you considered your work as a director to be?*
WA: I think I did a lot of takes, because somewhere in my mind there was the thought that a good director probably does a lot of takes. He's a perfectionist and meticulous. In the first films I did, I did do a lot of takes and I printed a lot. Because I was insecure. Now I don't do that. Now I do long, long takes, and I have much more confidence. In those days I also did a lot of coverage. I would reshoot the scene from many different angles. Now I haven't done coverage for, I don't know, ten years or something. When I worked with the editor of *Take the Money and Run*, he said, 'Always take a lot of coverage, because then we can do everything we want here, in the editing room.' So, on *Bananas* and *Everything You Always Wanted to Know About Sex . . .* and *Sleeper* I did a lot of coverage all the time – for security. But then I stopped. It seemed silly to me.

SB: *Were you married to Louise Lasser when you made* Take the Money and Run?
WA: Yes . . . I think I was.

SB: *But the co-star in the film was Janet Margolin. Did you ever consider Louise Lasser for the female lead?*
WA: No, probably she wasn't well enough known to be able to get that. She probably didn't have the qualifications yet with the studio. But she's in the film! She has a small part towards the end of the film.

SB: *The structure of the film, this semi-documentary or rather false documentary attitude, was that already conceived at the script stage?*
WA: Yes, I wanted to make it in black-and-white and make it look like a real documentary. Something I did later in *Zelig*. But at that time I wasn't allowed to make it in black-and-white. I did the best I could, but – yes – the documentary style was written and conceived that way.

SB: *I guess it's not by chance that the parents, when being interviewed in the film, are both disguised as Groucho Marx.*
WA: Well, we saw those masks in a store, and they were funny-looking things, so we bought two of them and put them on the actors.

SB: *But of course it also works as a reference.* Take the Money and Run *is filled with different kinds of references to other films or film phenomena.*
WA: Yes, I used to do that a lot.

SB: *Your film persona was already formed in the two earlier films which you didn't direct,* What's New, Pussycat? *and* Casino Royale. *Here it's more developed.*
WA: Well, it seemed to me like a very standard film persona for a comedian. Someone who is a physical coward, who lusts after women, who is good-hearted but ineffectual and clumsy and nervous. All standard things that you've seen in different various disguises. In Charlie Chaplin or W. C. Fields or Groucho Marx there's the same things but in different forms. But the structural underbase was the same thing, as I view it.

SB: *As I understand, one of the comic actors you like and admire a lot is Bob Hope. What in his film persona or his films is it that you like?*
WA: You know, when I tell this to people, they always think I'm crazy. But there was a time when he was still appearing in films where he was quite wonderful. The films are not always so wonderful. Sometimes they're good, but he's always a very funny man in them. Then, when he went on to television years later, he was not so funny. So there are many people who only know him from television and think, 'What are you talking about? He's very unfunny.' But if you look at *Monsieur Beaucaire*, for instance, he's very, very funny. There are a number of films where he's allowed to show his brilliant gift of delivery, his brilliant gift of comic speech. He had a very breezy attitude, he was a great man with a quip. Those one-liners and witticisms, they're just like air. He does them so lightly. When somebody else tries to do them, they're so leaden. It's hard to

6 Bob Hope in *Monsieur Beaucaire*

counterfeit his work and describe it. At times, I even prefer him to Groucho. The 'Road' pictures are not my favourites. But in pictures like *Monsieur Beaucaire* or *The Great Lover* he's just wonderfully funny. This often happens to comedians: their movies are not very good, but they are wonderful. So the movies become pot-boilers for them to show their wares. This happened to W. C. Fields. The movies themselves are not very good, but he's wonderful in them and the moments are great. Chaplin had a good sense of story, he was more interested in that. But the early two-reelers are silly little stories. They're not very interesting, but it's fun to watch him.

SB: *Just prior to my going to New York I saw an old Bob Hope film on Swedish television. I don't recall the title, but it's a kind of take-off on* The Big Sleep *and similar films where he dreams of becoming a detective.*
WA: *My Favourite Brunette!* It's very funny. Where he has a gun and the bullets fall on the floor, and they put him in an insane asylum.

SB: *There is usually an anachronistic quality to his comedy and jokes. In* Monsieur Beaucaire *he executes jokes that are contemporary within a historical setting.*
WA: Yes, he does that and it's fine. You don't care. He does that in *The Princess and the Pirate* and in *Fancy Pants* and in any of his period movies. He's wonderfully funny in *Casanova's Big Night*, with Joan Fontaine and Basil Rathbone. It's exactly that. He's anachronistic and hilariously funny.

SB: *I don't know if he's been an inspirational source for you, but you work with similar kinds of jokes in, for instance, the first episode of* Everything You Wanted to Know About Sex . . . *or* Love and Death.
WA: Yes, sure, I was very anachronistic. It didn't bother me at all. If you do a certain kind of picture, and then you abandon all believability, you have a certain gain and a certain loss. You gain great freedom to do funny jokes, but you lose legitimate audience involvement in the movie. The viewer knows it's not really real, and so he waits from funny line to funny line. When you see some of these comedies that are made today, like *Airplane* or *The Naked Gun*, you go moment to moment, joke to joke. And to the degree that they can sustain many funny things, the pictures succeed. They do sustain them and that's fine. And those pictures deserve to succeed. So in a period comedy your choice is either to be less funny and go for more human values to engage the audience in the story or to be very funny and just not care about anything and abandon

audience involvement. Bob Hope abandons audience involvement. You know he's not going to die, you don't really care about his fate. It's almost like an elongated sketch.

sb: *What do you think then of a comedian like Danny Kaye, who appeared somewhat later than Bob Hope?*

wa: When I was a boy I liked Danny Kaye very much, and I like some of the movies he made. As a boy I was very impressed with *Up in Arms*. The first time I saw that I was completely destroyed. He was so terrific in that. And he was very good in *The Secret Life of Walter Mitty* and *The Court Jester* and *Knock on Wood*. I think he was quite good in a small group of pictures, and then, after that, he kind of disappeared from the scene. Now when you go back and see these films, they're not very good pictures. But he was a wonderful talent of a certain kind, and an original. He was unlike anybody else.

sb: *He had a great musical talent as well.*

wa: Yes, that was his strength, I think. Much more than anything else.

sb: *In Eric Lax's biography of you, you mention a comedian who is not very well known outside the United States but who apparently meant a lot to you, Mort Sahl. Could you tell me something about him and his influence on you?*

wa: There was a cabaret tradition in the United States with stand-up comedians, who worked on TV, who worked on the Borscht circuit. The Borscht circuit is the Jewish summer resorts in the Catskill Mountains, where all the Jewish families used to go. They all had borscht, so they used to call them the Borscht circuit. And lots of comedians played there. Everyone played there: Danny Kaye, Sid Caesar, just every comedian you could think of went up there and entertained. And apart from that there was TV and there were night clubs. All these comedians were very, very formula. They'd all come out in a tuxedo and they would say, 'Good evening, ladies and gentlemen,' and there was no sincerity to any of it. And they would do silly little jokes. They joked about Eisenhower when he was president. They would do golf jokes, because the president played golf. And suddenly in this small cabaret, this comedian comes along, Mort Sahl. He was just wearing slacks and a sweater and a *New York Times* folded under his arm. He was a nice-looking guy in a certain way, very intelligent. And highly, highly energetic, like hypermanic. And a spectacular phrasemaker, but of an intellectual type. He came out on stage and just killed the audience. None of that 'Good evening, ladies and gentlemen' business. He'd come out and start to talk about culture and politics and people in the arts and relationships, but in a totally fresh way so that each joke he made was not just a golf joke, for instance, but a genuine insight into politics, into social relationships between men and women. He was absolutely like nothing anybody had ever seen before. And he was so natural that the other comedians became jealous. They used to say, 'Why do people like him? He just talks. He isn't really performing.' But his jokes came out as a stream of consciousness, in a kind of jazz rhythm. And he would digress. He would start to talk about Eisenhower and then he would digress from that to the FBI and mention something that happened to him and then something about electronic surveillance and then he would talk about hi-fi equipment and women and then come back to his point about Eisenhower. It was a spectacular format and it was all natural with him. I mentioned to Eric Lax, it was like when Charlie Parker came along, it was just like an automatic revolution in jazz. So suddenly, with Mort Sahl, the whole face of comedy changed completely. He was quite a sensation for a while. He was on the cover of *Time Magazine*. The thing that hurt him eventually was, that, in spite of his success he had great personal problems. I guess you can't be a genius without having personal problems, and they affected him.

SB: *Has he disappeared from the entertainment scene now?*
WA: No, he's still around. He shows up every now and then, and he's still great. But he was such a sensation years ago. And he's still wonderful, but strictly cabaret. He didn't do movies. I think he appears in one or two films for a minute or two not doing anything special. But he's a great great wit, like Mark Twain.

SB: *How did you come into contact with him? Did you see him perform?*
WA: Someone sent me to see him. I saw him perform and thought it was about the greatest thing I'd ever seen.

SB: *Did he inspire you in any way, when you started as a stand-up comedian?*
WA: Yes, completely. I would never have been a cabaret comedian at all, if it hadn't been for him. I was a writer. I had no interest in being a performer. But when I saw him, it was inspirational. It felt like something

worth doing. He had sort of opened a door. I realized that you didn't have to be one of those cliché formula type of comedians. You could do things more authentic. There was such an authenticity about him.

SB: *And what about Lenny Bruce? Did you see him and did you like him? Did he in any way influence you?*

WA: I was not a great fan of his. Now, I think he was very good, but he didn't mean much to me personally. I adored Mort Sahl. I adored Mike Nichols and Elaine May. And I adored Jonathan Winters. I thought they were three – actually four – genius comedians. Lenny Bruce I thought was ... OK. Decent, but not great. I think that many middle-class people and squares followed him very avidly, because he was – at a time when it was forbidden – talking dirty, and clearly on dope. And a huge amount of his audience were straight middle-class people who thought they were doing something wicked, that they were suddenly 'in the know', that they were suddenly hip or rebellious. And they tittered and snickered at all the marihuana references as if they knew just how it was and they were souls in common with him. I found him talented, but pretentious. Sometimes funny. I don't mean to put him down completely. I think he was a good and talented comedian, but nowhere near in the class of these others.

SB: *You worked as a cabaret artist and stand up-comedian many years prior to your working in films. The character you acted in your early films – is he a continuation of the character you created for yourself as a stand up-comedian?*

WA: Yes, I usually just went up and talked as myself. The standard fare of all comedians. No different than Bob Hope. You know, insecurity in life, nervousness and insecurity towards women, inability in having good relationships, fear, cowardice – all the things that Charlie Chaplin played or Buster Keaton played. It's a standard material of the comedian.

SB: *Those cabaret performances of yours, were they improvised?*

WA: No, I wrote them. I wrote my material and then did it. There was very rarely any improvisation. Sometimes there had to be, because it's a live act. But usually it was prepared routines.

SB: *I'd like to go back to your first film again. We talked briefly about your collaboration with the two producers, Jack Rollins and Charles H. Joffe, who are still producing your films. This apparently is quite a unique collaboration. Could you tell me something about how it has developed and changed over the years?*

WA: When I first started, they were my managers. I was a writer, and they were managing my affairs. And I told them once, that I sometimes thought about getting up on stage like Mort Sahl and being a comedian. They seized on that and did not let me put that idea aside. They pushed me and badgered me and got me up on stage.

SB: *Were you hesitant about this, about getting on stage?*

WA: Oh yes, I felt a great hesitation. I had great ambivalence about it. I was a little frightened of getting up on a stage, because I had been a writer in a quiet room for years. Then I got out on stage, and I was successful as soon as I started doing it. And they wouldn't let me stop. Many times I said, 'This is not really for me.' But they came every night with me to the cabaret, and they pushed me and pushed me. And they said that once you emerge as a performer, everything else will follow. And they were right. I got more offers to write and, later on, direct, because I was a performer. It showcases you in a certain way.

SB: *Where did you start as a performer?*

WA: The very first time I ever went on a cabaret stage was at 'The Blue Angel' in New York. A very famous place. Another place where I learned my craft was upstairs at 'The Duplex'. There's a wonderful woman named Jane Wallman who ran it, and she used to push me out on stage every night and comfort me. There used to be a comedian, a singer, new talents. I worked there for a long time with no salary. And shortly after that I performed at a place called 'The Bitter End', which was in Greenwich Village, and there I really made my reputation. The press started to come, and I started to emerge as a comedian. Then, when I started making films, we thought it would be a good idea that my two managers would be the producers. This would further contribute to my self-contained quality. So I didn't have to have strange producers or anything. So Rollins and Joffe came on as producers.

SB: *At the start of your film career, did you discuss your projects with them? Did they suggest certain projects?*

WA: Yes, I used to discuss my cabaret material with them. Every night we sat and talked about it. They spent a lot of time talking with me – and me with them. Then when I started making films, I suggested things to do with them. They never suggested any projects. Nowadays I don't have to talk as much about my projects with them. I mean, we've remained friends and colleagues at work. But now, over the last decade, when I finish a film, I don't feel the need to give it to somebody else to say, 'What do you think about this?' I do it, if I want to do it. But when the film is finished, I always want them to see it. I'm interested in their comments on it.

SB: *But initially they were more involved in the films during production?*
WA: No, never during production! Not even for my first film. They were involved at the beginning. I would show them a script and ask, 'Do you think I should make this into a movie? Do you think that I could direct it?' And we would talk about that. Then I would show them another script and ask them about that, whether they found it dull or not. But as my own confidence started to form and grow, I grew less and less dependent on them. Jack Rollins has often said that it's a tragedy of a manager's job that the more successful the manager becomes doing what he's doing, the less the client needs him. At first the client is like a baby chick, completely helpless. Then as he builds strength and the person gets more well known and wealthier and job offers keep coming in and experience builds and the person gets more artistically confident, you have less and less need for the manager. He makes himself obsolete, and in many cases in show-business managers get left. It's a very famous thing.

SB: *But there exists, I presume, a very strong confidence from both sides. From you towards them, the two producers, and from them towards you.*
WA: Right. That's true.

SB: *But I understand you had some trouble with* Take the Money and Run *when it reached the editing room. Could you comment on that?*
WA: Yes, I started to cut the film with an editor. I knew exactly what I wanted, but I didn't realize how unfunny things look in the editing room, that are, indeed, quite funny in reality. And so I kept cutting the film down, shorter and shorter; throwing things away, throwing things away. Finally I had no film. So the production manager of the film said, 'Let's bring in Ralph Rosenblum, who is a very renowned editor, very gifted. Maybe you need a fresh mind. You've been working on this for months.' And Ralph came in. He was very nice, and he looked at all the material.

The material I'd cut out as well. And he said, 'This stuff is great. What are you doing? You're throwing away all your good jokes.' And he helped me with the film. I worked with him for a few years, and I really learned an awful lot from him. He's a great editor.

SB: *Could you give any example of this, when you felt that a joke or a scene didn't work. Was it the construction of the joke that didn't work? I mean, the way it was built up in filmic terms?*

WA: A scene would look very unfunny to me, and Ralph would say, 'Look, what you have to do is to put in the sound effects in the scene. You don't think it's funny because you're not hearing anything. When you hit the lamp with your billiard cue, you don't hear anything. But if you hear a "smash" and then music comes in, the whole thing will come to life!' Then he put a record behind it and the whole thing was suddenly alive. I was just so inexperienced. This happened to me any number of times: I would put a scene in in the laborious way that I wrote it, and he would say, 'Why are you wasting your time with all that? Just use the first cut and the last cut and throw out the middle. You don't have to watch the character progressively go. You just cut right in.' Ralph showed me many, many things. Not the least of which was that I was never editing with any music at all. I just edited the film. But he said, 'When you edit, take a couple of records, put them on tape and – it doesn't have to be the final music for the film – throw them in behind the scenes.'

SB: *In* Take the Money and Run *the music is composed by Marvin Hamlish.*

WA: Right, in the first couple of movies I felt that it was just a cliché. Everybody used somebody to score their movies. So I thought, here is this kid, he's very talented. And I used him and he scored my first couple of films. Then, a little bit further down the line, I started to realize that every time I edit, I stick these records behind the scenes. And I like it better that way. I like the sound of the records. I can control it, I can do the music myself, right here in this room. There are all my records over there. I just pick up the world's great music and melodies, and I can choose whatever I want. And I need no finesse. I can turn it up when I want to. I can turn it off when I want to. So I started doing that, and I never stopped.

SB: *Has it ever happened to you that you haven't been able to use some music or songs that you've chosen for a film?*

WA: Yes, it happens to me every so often, but then we get something else. Also, once in a great while I will, for special reasons, use scoring. For instance, I wanted to use scoring in *Manhattan*, because I wanted to use the Philharmonic and I had a certain sound in mind. And also in *The Purple Rose of Cairo*. But, generally speaking, I don't using scoring. In all of my twenty-what films I might have used scoring in maybe five of them. Six at the most. The most recent one, *Husbands and Wives*, is records. The one I'm working on now is records.

SB: *You say, 'The one I'm working on now is records.' Have you already planned the music before you even shoot the film?*
WA: Yes, I have some songs that I think will be right for it.

SB: *Is this because in some way you want to base the feeling of the film, or parts of the film, on some specific music?*
WA: Yes, sometimes I do that. Sometimes I know in advance. When I made *Manhattan*, for example, I knew I was going to use this Gershwin music. There I filmed scenes that in themselves might not mean anything, but I knew that later, when I put the music behind it, the combination would be good.

SB: *Have you ever used music on the sets while shooting?*
WA: On the set, no. Unless it was direct playback at the time.

SB: *You know, Fellini often used music on the set, to create certain feelings he wanted to induce in certain scenes.*
WA: Well, Fellini never used direct sound, so he could do that.

SB: *Do you use direct sound in your films or do you do a lot of post-synchronization?*
WA: I never post-synchronize. I don't do any of what we call looping, because I don't believe in it. Over the course of the many years that I've made films there've been maybe one or two words here and there that I had to get in this way, because of some really disastrous thing. But, in general, I never do any post-synching.

SB: *In* Take the Money and Run *there is already a psychoanalytical touch to the story. The main character, Virgil Rockwell, is not on the analyst's couch yet, but there is an analyst being interviewed in the film about the problems and behaviour of Virgil. You yourself started in*

analysis at quite an early age. What was your reason for this?
WA: Well, I went because I felt there were problems that I had when I was younger that I wanted to see if I could deal with. And I've flirted with psychoanalysis and psychotherapy over the years, every now and then. I've gone in and out and above and back. Sometimes I feel that it can be helpful, sometimes I feel that I get less out of it. You know, mixed reactions.

SB: *Has your interest in psychoanalysis also led you into reading about the subject? For instance, have you studied the theories of people like Ronald Laing or David Cooper or Alice Miller?*
WA: No, I'm not interested in it as a student. Of course everybody who studies or gets an education reads Freud, and I've read some psychiatric literature. But I never wanted to be a doctor. I'm just happy being a patient.

SB: *After* Take the Money and Run, *wasn't there a project which you never got the chance to do, called* The Jazz Baby?
WA: Yes, there was.

SB: *What was this project about and why wasn't it made into a film?*
WA: I was signed to a contract with United Artists right after my first film, and they said, 'Just write what you want to write and do what you want to do.' This has always been my blessing. And I wrote a film called *The Jazz Baby*. The executives at United Artists read the script and they were stunned, because they expected a comedy like *Take the Money and Run* or something like that. They were shocked, because it was very serious. They were very worried and told me, 'We realize that we signed a contract with you and you can do anything you want. But we want to tell you that we really don't like this. It took us all by surprise.' So I said, 'Look, this is my first film with you people, and if you don't like it, I will not force you to do it just because I've a contract. I don't want to make a film where you people are out there hating it every second of the way. Let me have it back, and I will write another film and we will do that. And maybe somewhere down the line things will change and we'll see.' And I went back and very quickly wrote *Bananas*. It took me no time at all.

SB: The Jazz Baby, *was that a contemporary story?*
WA: No, it was a period jazz story. But probably too ambitious.

sB: *Jazz was an early interest of yours.*
WA: Yes, it's a passion of mine.

sB: *When did you start to listen to jazz, and when did you start to play an instrument yourself?*
WA: I started to listen to jazz in my teens. But, of course, I'd heard jazz before. When I grew up, popular music was Benny Goodman and Artie Shaw and Tommy Dorsey, swing music. But then, in my teens, when I was fourteen, fifteen – fourteen maybe – I heard Sidney Bechet. On record. And I was very, very taken with it. And this gradually introduced me to more jazz recordings. I listened to Bunk Johnson and Jelly Roll Morton. And I got very, very interested in jazz. I loved it. I bought myself a soprano saxophone and tried to learn it. And I did learn it. But I knew that I could never be really very good. It was just not a talent of mine. But I enjoyed playing very much, and then I sort of switched a little bit to the clarinet, which is a logical progression. At first I only played along with records. Then, when I was playing 'The Hungry I', a cabaret in San Francisco – where Mort Sahl started as a matter of fact – I used to go around the corner to a jazz joint and listen. Turk Murphy played there. He was a great trombone player and he had a great traditional jazz band there. So I used to listen to him, and he saw me sitting there all the time and said, 'Why don't you come in and play?' And I told him that I played the clarinet, but that I never could do that. But he just would not take no for an answer. He insisted and insisted and was so nice to me and made me play with them. He just made me comfortable and pushed me and prodded me. So gradually I played more and more. Then when I came back to New York I felt that I wanted to play with other musicians. So I got together with a few others and we started to play. And now we've been playing for over twenty years, on Monday evenings.

sB: *So, today is Monday. And you will play tonight?*
WA: Yes, sure!

sB: *Last time we met you didn't play that Monday night.*
WA: Right, when I'm shooting or when something special is happening, I don't. But I miss very few Mondays in a year. Maybe not even a half dozen.

sB: *And you've been playing with the same group of people over the years?*
WA: Yes, pretty much. There've been some changes because one person left us and another person died. But they're basically the same.

7 Woody Allen playing clarinet with Herb Hall

CHAPTER 3

Bananas

STIG BJÖRKMAN: *Your second film,* Bananas *(a satire on a revolutionary situation in a fictitious Latin American country), was made in 1971, during a period when these kind of revolutionary uprisings were a fact in many Latin American countries. It was also the time of the Vietnam war. What were your own political ideas at this time, and how have they developed and changed over the years? Do you consider yourself a political person?*

WOODY ALLEN: No, I don't think I'm a political person. I'm basically – you could say to 99 per cent – a liberal democrat. That's pretty much what I was; I was against the war, as everyone I knew was. I'm basically not very political. I've campaigned for certain politicians. Like show people sometimes do.

SB: *Which people have you supported in this way?*

WA: Originally, when I was younger, I campaigned for Adlai Stevenson and George McGovern and Eugene McCarthy. All those guys who have lost. I campaigned for Lyndon Johnson when he ran against Barry Goldwater. I've campaigned for Jimmy Carter, for Michael Dukakis. And now I've given my name to the Clinton people. I'm basically a democratic liberal.

SB: *I wanted to pose this question also, because in later films, like* Annie Hall *or* Manhattan, *you make ironical remarks about left-wing intellectuals, a group of people of which I presume you count yourself as a member.*

WA: Yes, and which I observe.

SB: *In the beginning of* Bananas *we hear quite ironical remarks on the American influence on other countries and specially on the Latin American countries. In the big crowd of people that has gathered outside the parliament building there is someone who is forcing himself through the crowd claiming he is a representative of American television.*

8   Sylvester Stallone and Woody Allen in *Bananas*

WA: Well, in the United States it has huge power. I don't know how it is abroad, but in America it's gigantic. From our point of view the governments of Latin America have never seemed to work too well. The United States of America, relatively speaking, has always had a stable government. So it's always seemed strange to us how unstable these countries were. They've changed leaders and policy so frequently.

SB: *But there has also been the very strong and devastating influence of the United States upon these countries. On countries like Chile and Argentina, in particular.*
WA: Yes, without a question. The American influence has been severe, with enormous exploitation.

SB: *There is an ironical comment towards the end of the film where you address another part of the world, our part of the world. One character quotes Kierkegaard and says, 'Scandinavians have such an instinctive feeling for the human condition.' And later on it's stated that the official language for the new republic of San Marco will be Swedish. Your strong feelings for Scandinavia and, particularly, Sweden is manifested here.*
WA: Yes, I've always liked the Scandinavian countries and, of course, Sweden led the pack, because my interest in Sweden originally came through Swedish cinema. But I like that part of the world. I like the way it looks, I like the weather. There's just something about it that's interesting to me.

SB: *You've read Strindberg, of course, but are you acquainted with anybody else in Scandinavian literature or with Scandinavian art?*
WA: I'm acquainted with that which everyone is acquainted with, the paintings of Edvard Munch, the music of Sibelius or Allan Pettersson – those things we all know. I do enjoy Scandinavian culture to a certain degree, but we only get a certain amount of it here. And the best, most generous, and most important was, of course, the Bergman films. There you see Swedish life. You get a very good feel for Scandinavian culture through those films. With Strindberg it's something else. You read his plays or go and see one of them at the theatre – *Dance of Death*, for instance – and it might be a good production, but you don't get the same feel from it. With Bergman you see the Swedish settings, the cities, the countryside, the churches and the people. It's different.

sb: *Bananas* is one of your most stylized films. Did you feel a stronger confidence as a film-maker this time, making your second film?

wa: Yes, I felt more confident, definitely. But not nearly as much as later on. The big break for me came when I made *Annie Hall*. But prior to that, yes, I felt confident, because I had one film under my belt and I knew what to do to avoid mistakes that I felt I had made on *Take the Money and Run*. Something I had learnt through that film was that, no matter how fast a scene is played, you always want it faster in comedy. That's a golden rule. There is a wonderful story about . . . I believe it's René Clair. He would shoot a scene and finally, after the third or fifth take, get it perfect. And he'd say, 'This was just perfect, the actors perfect, everything was exactly right on cue. It couldn't be more perfect. But now, before we go, let's just have one more take – very fast.' And he would do that. And always use the fast one. I understand that completely, because no matter how fast you think you're going, when you see it on the screen later, it slows up.

sb: *I think speed is one of your characteristics. It definitely distinguishes your films from other films. I couldn't escape noticing this when looking through most of your films once more prior to seeing you for this conversation. They are all very tight, very concentrated in time, and fairly short. A film like* Zelig, *for instance, is just an hour and a quarter, but most of your other films are five-reelers – which means they are about one and a half hours long. But still they are very dense in content, whether they are comedies or dramas.*

wa: Right. I feel that has to do with the natural biological rhythm of the film-makers. Certain people feel things in certain phrases. It just seems to me, that without trying to make my films shorter, trying to make them any special length, my body feels that the length they're made is right. I thought about this when I made a film with Paul Mazursky recently, *Scenes from the Mall*. His body rhythm is longer. Scorsese's body rhythm is longer. I don't mean that their films are not well-paced. It's just another type of temperament.

sb: *Yes, Scorsese's films are also well paced, even if they are six or seven reels long mostly.*

wa: Right, they are wonderfully paced and they are wonderful films. And he likes a two-hour story or a two-hour-ten-minute story. But for me, if I make a film which is one hour forty minutes, it's long. I just run out of story impetus after a certain time. Film-makers reflect their own rhythms, their own metabolism.

SB: *I guess* Hannah and Her Sisters *is one of your longest films, and* Hannah *is about one hour forty minutes.*

WA: Yes, and I think *Crimes and Misdemeanours* and *Husbands and Wives* are close to that. The ensemble story ones tend to be longer. The snappy ones tend to be shorter. But again, if you look at the Marx Brothers' movies, W. C. Fields' movies and others, they are mostly shorter than mine.

SB: *In some of your films, take* A Midsummer Night's Sex Comedy *as an example, you have very abrupt beginnings. There you have José Ferrer walking into a close-up in the very first image of the film and he starts talking. It's a very effective opening.*

WA: I think the way you begin a film is important. This comes probably from my cabaret training. It's important for the beginning and the ending to have a special quality of some sort, a special theatrical quality, or something to arrest the audience instantly. So I think all my films begin in some unusual, or if not unusual, some special way. The first image on the screen is important to me.

SB: *I agree totally. Most of the time you can tell from the first three or five minutes of any film whether it's going to be a good film, an interesting film or not.*

WA: I couldn't agree more with you. You get the feeling in the first three or five minutes that you are in good hands or not. That the film-maker has lifted you up or not. I feel that's absolutely true.

SB: *And this has nothing to do with efficiency. It could be a very, very slow beginning as well. But you get a certain feeling that this film-maker knows how to bring us into his or her story or personal universe or not.*

WA: Yes, it should be before you know it. You see the first couple of minutes, the first scene or two of the film, and before you know it, you don't think about it, but you're involved. That's an important thing to do.

SB: *And where do you think this initial charge is created? Is it already in the script?*

WA: Yes, it's done in the script in my case. When I write a script I *almost* always know what the first *kind* of image is going to be. It might be changed when I go and see the location, but the basic kind of shot I know. Now, sometimes I start a script without knowing that. I don't know what the first image will be. But I always stop and try and make a good one. A certain kind that's arresting.

SB: *Yes, like the first scene in* Alice; *the scene with Mia Farrow and Joe Mantegna in the aquarium is arresting because we have no idea of what it means or stands for at the start of the film. It really draws you into the picture. And then it takes quite a while before Mantegna appears in the picture again.*

WA: Yes, you know that something is up. That this woman, Alice, is dreaming about another guy. That something else is on her mind. So, when you sit through that early expository material, it's not so painful, because you already know that even though Alice seems rich and happy, something is wrong someplace. So it helps your audience become interested in the material.

SB: *Yes, we keep this scene as a kind of mental image.*
WA: Right.

SB: *One interesting thing, seeing the whole body of your work within such a limited time as I did, was the coherence of your work. I know – and you know – that critics and other people have often pointed out the different influences present in your films, influences from Bergman or Fellini or Keaton or other comedians. But even if your films differ a lot, in content as well as in style, being sometimes comedies and sometimes dramas, there is a coherence about them, not unlike that which unites the many different films by François Truffaut.*
WA: I loved the work of Truffaut!

SB: *I mean, he changed subject very much from film to film. He made very personal, semi-biographical films, like the series of films about Antoine Doinel. He made thrillers, comedies, romantic dramas. He made films about children, like* Pocket Money *which reminds me a bit of* Radio Days. *It's not exactly that your films reminded me of his films, but there are resemblances in your works.*
WA: Because we both made a number of films about very different subjects?

SB: *Yes, but there's also a question of feeling. There is a similar kind of feeling which generates from all of your films; you can experience a similar sensation when you see a couple of Truffaut films in a row. He, like you, showed a similar interest in experimenting, in changing styles as well as subjects.*

WA: Well, I like his films very much. I think he was a wonderful, charming film-maker. There are a number of his films that I find terrific. Someone said something similar, I think it was Vincent Canby in *The New York Times*, that there are certain film-makers that, no matter what their subject-matter, you can tell it's their film. There is some kind of philosophical or emotional sensibility, some kind of thing that permeates the material, and you just *feel* that it's one of their pictures. In my case it could also be because it's the same person writing the films. It's like a signature. It's hard to shake that handwriting.

SB: *So, to return to* Bananas *again, one notices a new kind of security in the way the film is made. Also, a certain kind of joy in parodying other film genres or film-makers. For instance, the almost cartoon-like editing of the scenes from the camp. Or the very romantic, melodramatic love scene between you and the rebel girl, Yolanda, by the sea.*

WA: *Bananas* was still a film where I only cared about being funny. That was my main thing. After *Take the Money and Run* I felt I didn't want to make any of the same mistakes I'd made on that first film. I wanted to make sure that everything was funny and fast-paced. That was really what I was concentrating on. So if I shot or edited certain scenes almost cartoon-like, it was for that reason. And I started to feel that there are certain films I make that are best described as cartoons, because people don't bleed and nobody dies really. They're just fast-moving and joke-joke-joke-joke and onto the next thing.

SB: *Cartoons also have the same principle of something happening in the beginning and something in the middle and something in the end, but there are big chunks of story-telling missing.*

WA: Right, which you don't need.

SB: *This was also very true of the farces made by Frank Tashlin or Jerry Lewis, for instance. They worked very much in the same way. Was Tashlin a director you recognized or liked?*

WA: No. I mean, I saw some of his films, but I don't know them that well.

SB: *Then the end of* Bananas, *the trial scene, is almost like a Marx Brothers film.*

WA: Right. It's funny how these things happen. I needed a climax for the film, and I didn't have the money for the traditional chase. So I made it a trial. It's always much cheaper.

SB: *So in a way the end is traditional, but in another tradition.*
WA: Right.

SB: *In this end scene you have the J. Edgar Hoover character played by a black actor. This is one of the very few parts in your films portrayed by a black. There is, for instance, the black sergeant in* Love and Death, *put there as a kind of anachronistic figure, and there is a black character in* Sleeper *and the black maid in the film within the film in* The Purple Rose of Cairo. *But apart from that there are almost no black people in your films. Why?*
WA: Do you mean in principal roles or in general?

SB: *In general. We almost never see any black extras in the films even.*
WA: Well, usually there are two different situations when it comes to extras. One is that we just call up the extra people and say, 'Send over a hundred extras or twenty extras or something.' And they usually send over a mixture of people. I mean, if it's a street in New York, they usually send over a mixture of hispanics, black and white people. But that's just something we call up and order for background. I mean, we don't buy them by the pound. Then for principal roles, I don't know the black experience well enough to really write about it with any authenticity. In fact, most of my characters are so limited locally. They're mostly New Yorkers, kind of upper-class, educated, neurotic. It's almost the only thing that I ever write about, because it's almost the only thing I know. I just don't know enough about these other experiences. I have, for instance, never written anything about an Irish family or an Italian family, because I don't really know enough about it.

SB: *I've also noticed this, because in Hollywood films from the last decade or so black actors or black characters have been given more parts in the movies. This is maybe especially true with the cop films, where there is often a white cop working together with a black cop, and the black guy has taken over the classical 'buddy' part. It has almost become a pattern.*
WA: Yes, one does tend to get more blacks in the film business. But, for instance, when I did *Hannah and Her Sisters,* I was writing about a

milieu that I know quite well. And I made the maid black because in those families 90 per cent of the time the maid is black. I got a lot of criticism from black people who wrote me letters and said, 'You never use blacks, and when you use one, it's in a menial job.' Now, I'm not thinking of that when I write the character. In my political life – whatever that is – I'm always very pro all those candidates who want the most generous accommodation for blacks. I've marched with Martin Luther King in Washington. But, when I'm writing, I don't believe in equal opportunity or affirmative action. You can't do that. So when I was trying to draw a picture accurately, it just seemed to me that those families on the upper West Side almost always had black help. So that's the way I did it. But I did get criticized for it. I'm just trying to depict the reality as I experience it, my own authenticity. In the same sense, if I was depicting the kind of Jewish family that I grew up in, I would depict them, accurately, with that which is flattering and that which is unflattering. I've also had an enormous amount of criticism from Jewish groups who feel that I have been very harsh or denigrating or critical. So there's a lot of sensitivity always on these matters. But the only thing I try to let guide me is the authenticity of the scene.

CHAPTER 4

Play It Again, Sam

STIG BJÖRKMAN: *Then you wrote and acted in the play* Play It Again, Sam. *I believe this was your only stage appearance in a play. How was this experience?*

WOODY ALLEN: It was fun. I liked Diane Keaton and Tony Roberts, and we had a good time doing it. The play was successful. And the director who directed it for the stage, Joe Hardy, did a good job. Once the play opened, it was a *very* easy job. There is no easier job than being in a play. I mean, you have the whole day off and you do whatever you want. You can write, you can relax, whatever you want. You just drop over to the theatre at eight o'clock at night. I would walk over there with Diane. I lived within walking distance and we could take a nice stroll down Broadway. Then you go in. There's no nervous tension. The play is running. You're onstage with your friends. Curtain goes up. You play it. It's about an hour and a half. And two hours later you're in a restaurant having dinner with your friends. It's the easiest job in the world! So it was very pleasurable.

SB: *You didn't find it at all difficult, having written the play and being directed by somebody else?*

WA: No, not at all. I have never really wanted to direct in the theatre. So I didn't really care about it. And Joe Hardy was fine. I don't mind being directed by other people. I enjoy my experiences.

SB: *Later, when the play was filmed, it was directed by Herbert Ross. Didn't you ever think of directing it yourself?*

WA: No, I never wanted to make *Play It Again, Sam* into a film. But then, my agents sold the play to the movies, and I was glad of that. When they sold it I was not significantly well-known enough to play in it. I was not eligible as a movie star. They tried to get other people to play in it. And these people turned it down. Finally, I became more well-known from doing my own films, and they said, 'OK, we will take a chance with

9   Woody Allen in *Play It Again, Sam*

him.' And they used the original cast. I was very happy that Herb Ross directed *Play It Again, Sam*. I didn't want to make it into a movie. I was more interested in making *movies*. Tennessee Williams said years ago, that, when a writer finishes something, he transcends it. And it's a shame you have to go on and put the play on. It would be nice to write it and just throw it into the drawer. I felt the same way. I wrote the play, I transcended it, and then it was old history. I didn't want to spend a year making it into a movie. I thought that was a kind of thing you could hire somebody else to do, and somebody would come very fresh. I mean, for Herb Ross it was all new territory, so it would be more fun for him.

SB: *The movie was also made four years after the Broadway production.*
WA: That too. Yes, it was already an old thing for me.

SB: *The theme of* Play It Again, Sam *is daydreaming, which takes up a great part of our lives. What importance do you give to films regarding this? The character in the play – and movie – tries to turn films or filmic situations into his own contemporary life.*
WA: It has been said, that if I have any one big theme in my movies, it's got to do with the difference between reality and fantasy. It comes up very frequently in my films. I think what it boils down to, really, is that I hate reality. And, you know, unfortunately it's the only place where we can get a good steak dinner. I think it comes from my childhood, where I constantly escaped into the cinema. I was quite an impressionable boy and I grew up during the so-called 'Golden Age of Cinema', when all those wonderful films were coming out. I remember when *Casablanca* came out and *Yankee Doodle Dandy* – all those American films – the Preston Sturges films, the Capra films ... I was always escaping into those films. You would leave your poor house behind and all your problems with school and family and all that and you would go into the cinema, and there they would have penthouses and white telephones and the women were lovely and the men always had an appropriate witticism to say and things were funny, but they always turned out well and the heroes were genuine heroes and it was just great. So, I think that had such a crushing influence, made such an impression on me. And I know many people my age who've never been able to shake it, who've had trouble in their lives because of it, because they still – in advanced stages of their lives, still in their fifties or sixties – can't understand why it doesn't work that way, why everything that they grew up believing and feeling and

wishing for and thinking was reality was not true and that reality is much harsher and much uglier than that. When you sat in those movie theatres, you thought it was real. You didn't think, well, that's just the way it is in the movies. You thought, well, I don't live that way. I live in Brooklyn and a poor place, but there are many people in the world who have a home like this, and they do horseback-riding and they meet beautiful women and they have cocktails at night. It's just a different life. Then that gets corroborated by the fact that you read the newspapers and see that there are people whose lives are different and happy like in the movies. It's just such a crushing thing and I've never surmounted it. And I know many people who have never surmounted it. And it appears in my work all the time. The sense of wanting to control reality, to be able to write a scenario for reality and make things come out the way you want it. Because what the writer does – the film-maker or the writer – you create a world that you would like to live in. You like the people you create. You like what they wear, where they live, how they talk, and it gives you a chance for some months to live in that world. And those people move to beautiful music, and you're in that world. So in my films I just feel there's always a pervasive feeling of the greatness of idealized life or fantasy versus the unpleasantness of reality. You know, there was an article in *The New York Times* about Susan Sontag and her novel, *The Volcano Lover*. And one of the things she was saying was, when she had given her book to the publisher, she came home and felt bereft of her characters.

SB: *Yes, you create your characters and you make up different worlds for them. And then their lives end with the last scene and the last image of your film. But have you ever reflected over what might happen to them after this? Have you ever thought of making a sequel to any of your films, telling more about one or more of the characters in a specific film?*

WA: I did think once – I'm not going to do it – but I did think once that it would be interesting to see Annie Hall and the guy I played years later. Diane Keaton and I could meet now that we're about twenty years older, and it could be interesting, because we parted, to meet one day and see what our lives have become. But it smacks to me of exploitation, of sequelism, and I wouldn't like to fall into that. It has become an annoying thing. I don't think Francis Coppola should have done *Godfather III* because *Godfather II* was quite great. When they make a sequel, it's just a thirst for more money, so I don't like that idea so much.

SB: *I can understand if you've considered the possibility of following up the lives of Annie Hall and Alvy. One could also wonder about the subsequent lives of Hannah and her sisters.*

WA: Yes, I've thought that about any number of characters in my movies. Not enough to want to continue with them, but I certainly do always think: what happens at the end of the movie, what's going to happen with these people? What impressions am I leaving the audience with? I do think about that.

SB: *I guess, it was during the Broadway production of your play* Play It Again, Sam *that you first met Diane Keaton?*

WA: Yes. That's right.

SB: *How did she come to influence your life and, in particular, your creative life?*

WA: She has had a definite influence on me. First of all, she has flawless instincts. She is very lucky. She's a very gifted person. She was very beautiful. She could sing, she could dance, she could draw, she could paint, she could take photographs. She could act. I mean, she had so much talent. And quite good in every department. And she was an eccentric dresser. And wonderfully funny. Very much her own person. I mean, it didn't matter to her if she'd be watching Shakespeare. If she didn't like what he was doing, she'd say so and she knew why she didn't like it. There was no pretentions, there was no baggage in the way. It was all very clear. And her taste was quite good. There was only one area that we ever differed on in all our years, and that was popular music, music from the sixties and seventies. She liked it, likes it. I could never stand it. But apart from that, we seldom disagreed. I remember, taking her to see the rough cut of *Take the Money and Run* up in a small projection room somewhere. And she said, 'You know, this is good. It's funny. It's a funny film.' I somehow knew at that moment, at that second, that it was going to be OK with the audience. Her imprimatur was very meaningful to me, because I felt she was in touch with something deeper than I was in touch with. So over the years we went out together, we lived together and we've remained great friends to this day. And I always rely on her. It's always perhaps the most important screening I have of any of my movies, when she's in town and I can get her to see it.

SB: *Do you show it to her before it's finished then? In rough cut form?*

WA: Well, if she's in town, I would ask her before it's finished. But she's

10   Diane Keaton and Woody Allen in *Play It Again, Sam*

living in California now, so I don't always get that opportunity. But her words carry great weight with me. If she likes something or doesn't like something, it influences me. And there are many things in life I've seen through her eyes. She's always had a visual filter as well. She has a cerebral and musical filter, but in addition to that she has a visual one. I got to look at things through her eyes very frequently, and it really upgraded and broadened my perception. She has been a major influence on me. I've also influenced her a lot too. I was from New York, very urban. Liked the streets of New York, liked basketball, liked jazz, had read a lot. She was from California, liked visual things, photographic things, paintings, colours. She had her feelings about movies, I had mine. And over the years there was a healthy interaction. I introduced her to things. I showed her films that she had not seen, that I thought were great, ranging from certain Bergman films to . . . I remember the first time I showed her *Shane*, the George Stevens film, how great she thought that was, never thinking she'd think a western was great. I just recently, about four weeks ago, had her here and showed her a Billy Wilder film she'd never seen, *Ace in the Hole*. This has always been one of my favourite films of his. A fantastic piece of work. It was completely unsuccessful in the United States, but a wonderful movie. I showed it to her, and she was very taken with it. And the next day we both saw, for the first time, *The More the Merrier*, the George Stevens film with Charles Coburn, Jean Arthur and Joel McCrea. It's a wonderful comedy. So over the years there has been this creative interaction between the two of us. And as I say, once I make a film, if *she* likes it, then I feel I have accomplished my goal and it becomes utterly irrelevant to me whether anybody else in the world does. It just doesn't mean a thing to me whether the critics like it, whether the public likes it, no matter what. Now you can say to me, has she ever *not* liked a film of mine? Well yes, she is polite, but I can tell by her degree of enthusiasm or from what she says, what she really thinks. So that's a very important opinion for me.

SB: *I guess Diane Keaton wants to become a film-maker as well? She has already made a couple of short films and she directed a couple of episodes of* Twin Peaks.

WA: I think she'll get a chance to direct. She will be a very good director. She will be nervous at first, because she's very unconfident and self-effacing. And of all people to be nervous and self-effacing, she's so full of talent. That is so ironic. But she is very good and she will be a wonderful director, if she's given a chance.

SB: *Have you seen her film* Heaven?

WA: Yes, I saw *Heaven*. And she made a very interesting television film, Wildflower, recently. She is just very good.

SB: *You have been married to or you've lived together with actresses like Louise Lasser and Diane Keaton and Mia Farrow. In what way have they inspired you or influenced you – or, rather, have they in any way inspired you when you've written your films, when you've written the female portraits for your stories?*

WA: Well, Diane and Mia and I, we've never been married. I've lived with Diane, but I've never lived together with Mia. We always lived separately. They all have been helpful to me, in many ways. And yes, they've often been in mind when I've created certain characters for the films. Very often over these last years I've had Mia in mind for these parts.

SB: *And how have you been thinking? That, for instance, now she has made this and this character, but she has never played this kind of character before, so it would be interesting or fun to draw a portrait like this?*

WA: Yes, that's exactly right. There are times when exactly that has happened. Like *Broadway Danny Rose*. I thought to myself, she has always wanted to play this kind of character, but she never has. And I wrote a story with a part in it which would be fun for her to do.

SB: *There are some parts I've imagined being more close to her and her own character, like the part she had in* Hannah and Her Sisters . . .

WA: No, not so much. She had trouble with that character. It was very difficult for her. We couldn't find a clear handle on it. I could never decide whether Hannah was good or bad. It was very hard for me to know whether Hannah was a good sister or a bad sister.

SB: *But that's what's interesting with that character, I think.*

WA: Yes, it's interesting, but that's a happy accident, because I wanted to try and figure out, is Hannah a good sister to these people. If she's the basic, good, nourishing person in the story or if she isn't really so good. And the two of us could never figure out what it was. So it came out more interesting this way.

SB: *And now, in retrospect, have you made up your mind yet?*
WA: Well, in retrospect, I think she's not so nice. If you look closely, she's not as nice as you imagine.

CHAPTER 5

Everything You Always Wanted to Know About Sex . . .

STIG BJÖRKMAN: *Sex is one of the more pronounced subjects or themes in your films. When you were growing up, was sex more or less a forbidden subject?*
WOODY ALLEN: Oh yes, completely. It was not talked about, nobody even practised it.

SB: *So then the cinema was even more important. To be able to see sex being practised . . .*
WA: Well, you never saw it in the cinema in the United States. There was always the joke about foreign films. In foreign films they accepted sex in a different way than Americans. Americans always had a laughable attitude towards it.

SB: *But when you were growing up, what were the most important things you wanted to know about sex, but were too afraid to ask?*
WA: Really just, where was it available? And how fast? That's all I cared about in relation to it. Quantity and accessibility.

SB: *In the titles of the film you point out that the script is based on a book by Dr David Rueben. What kind of a book was that?*
WA: I was thinking about my next film and didn't know what to do. And I came home one night with Diane Keaton, we'd been to a basketball game. And we got into bed and turned on the television set for a moment, and there was this doctor who had written this very popular book called *Everything You Always Wanted to Know About Sex and Were Afraid to Ask*. It was questions and answers, and it presumed that nobody knew anything about sex. The questions people asked were like: 'Can you become pregnant during a woman's period?' 'How is the best way of doing this?' Millions of questions all over the place. And I thought to myself, 'Gee, that would make a funny movie.' To get the rights to that book and make little short things. Questions and then a little sketch or

something. Just purely for fun. So I asked United Artists, and they told me that the rights had already been purchased by Elliot Gould. But he wasn't doing anything with it, so my office called his and asked about it. And he said, 'Oh sure, if you want to do something, go ahead. We'll sell it to you, and you do it.' And he did, and I made the movie. I know that the doctor who wrote the book hated the movie. I don't know why. I guess he just thought it was trivial or foolish or silly. But, you know, this book was silly also, and if he had really cared about it, he wouldn't have sold it to the movies. It could have fallen into worse hands than mine. It was fun to make a movie with just a couple of short pieces in it. Just for amusement's sake.

SB: *But did you use any of the material from the book?*
WA: I used the questions. Only the questions. Like 'What happens during orgasm?' That was a question in the book. And I gave my version of it with the sperms. I would use his questions but add my answers.

SB: *In the first episode, 'Do aphrodisiacs work?', you have two British actors, Lynn Redgrave and Anthony Quayle. You seem to have a certain flair for English actors. Later on you have worked with other British actors like Charlotte Rampling, Michael Caine, Denholm Elliot, Ian Holm, Claire Bloom and an actress I like a lot who is not English but Australian, Judy Davis.*
WA: Oh yes, I love her. She's such a great actress. She's a genius! The British film and theatrical community is great and has always been great. They have a much wider variety of performers than we have. Of course, in that particular movie I used them because I was doing a Shakespearian kind of thing and I wanted that authenticity. But, in general, the United States, for the most part, usually produces a certain kind of male star. You know, gunfighters and tough guys. Whereas in England you can get real men. Just regular, normal men. Vulnerable men. So I've relied on English actors a number of times, because I couldn't find the American actors to do what I wanted.

SB: *And the actresses? Like Charlotte Rampling or Claire Bloom?*
WA: Well, Charlotte Rampling has always been a favourite of mine, so *Stardust Memories* was finally a chance to get to work with her. I didn't need an English woman, but I've just always loved her quality, and as for Claire Bloom I wanted a very dignified wife in *Crimes and Misdemeanours*. But it's easier to find women in the United States than men.

There's a much greater variety of types of women for films than there are men. So I don't really have to resort to English women very much.

SB: *A character actor like Denholm Elliott meant a great deal to September.*
WA: It's hard to find Americans like him.

SB: *You've worked with just a few actors from other countries, like Max Von Sydow in* Hannah and Her Sisters *or Marie-Christine Barrault in* Stardust Memories. *You've never considered working with other actors from foreign countries?*
WA: Yes, I have. It's just, when they fit, it's fine. I would not hesitate to work with any Swedish actors or actresses. Sometimes some European actors can't speak English, but the Swedes can. With the French it's a tougher problem, they don't speak English as well and they have a much heavier accent. So it's not easy. Swedes have a tendency to speak a truly good English. So I wouldn't hesitate for a second to use them. I wish I had material that would be good for them. It's just hard; if you portray a family and half the family is American you can't make the other half Swedish or from some other European origin.

SB: *Ingmar Bergman, you know, has worked with actors from other countries, like Liv Ullmann who is Norwegian.*
WA: So, when Swedes watch Liv Ullmann in *Persona* or *A Passion*, they are hearing a Norwegian accent?

SB: *Yes, a slight accent. She speaks very good Swedish, but there is a noticeable accent.*
WA: But the characters she played could be of Norwegian origin, right?

SB: *Yes, there's maybe just one film where this fact becomes slightly strange, and that's* Autumn Sonata, *where she is supposed to be the daughter of Ingrid Bergman, who speaks perfect Swedish.*
WA: But nobody minds, nobody comments about it, right? We've had the same thing here in the States with English actors, for instance. There could be a family, and the father would be James Mason. And he would speak English, he would speak British. But I always feel funny about that. I mean, in *Crimes and Misdemeanours* it's never defined where Claire Bloom is from. Or Michael Caine in *Hannah*; he could be someone that has moved to New York from London. But if it's a father-son

11   Woody Allen and Lynn Redgrave in *Everything You Always Wanted to Know About Sex* . . .

or a similar relationship, then I would have a problem with it. And probably in this country you would get comments.

SB: *In the first episode of* Everything You Wanted to Know About Sex . . . *you play the part of a court jester. This, of course, is a kind of continuation of your role as a stand-up comedian.*
WA: Yes, absolutely. I wanted that to be.

SB: *A couple of years ago you played the part of the jester in Jean-Luc Godard's* King Lear *as well. How was this experience?*
WA: That was a unique experience, because I love Godard's work. I never saw that movie. But he asked me, he was here, came into this room and asked me if I would like to be in his *King Lear*. For him I would have done anything because he's one of the really great masters. And he said it would only take a few hours in the morning. So I went over to the place where they were filming, and he was in his bathrobe, with his cigar, directing. He had a very small crew, like three people or something. One cameraman, one sound person and somebody else. It couldn't be more sparse. And he asked me to do certain things, which I did, because he asked me. And I felt while I was doing it, this is going to be a *very* silly movie. A very foolish movie. But I thought, this is for Godard. And I got a chance to meet him. Then I left and I've never heard about the movie since. I never saw it.

SB: *I saw it last year for the first time. I'm a great admirer of Godard as well, but I must say that* King Lear *is one of his strangest films, one of his most incomprehensible films.*
WA: Yes, he's gotten more and more incomprehensible over the years, so experimental.

SB: *Yes, but some of his later films, like* Nouvelle Vague *or the one he made in Germany with Eddie Constantine,* Germany Nine Zero, *are very beautiful. Visually stunning and with a most personal poetic touch to them.*
WA: Good. That's nice.

SB: *Well, talking of* Everything You Wanted to Know About Sex . . . , *I found a quotation from your piece 'My Speech to the Graduates' where you say: 'We live in far too permissive a society. Never before has pornography been this rampant. And those films are lit so badly!' Do you*

think there is a kind of 'double morality' in the American view of sex?
WA: We sometimes refer to something called a double standard, which means that what's agreeable for men is not permissible for women. But the American view of sex is infantile.

SB: *A puritanical attitude.*
WA: Absolutely.

SB: *And I guess this is what you're after in this quotation and with your film?*
WA: Yes, you grow up with this attitude here. It's a silly attitude, but we're influenced by it.

SB: *Do you feel this attitude has changed in recent years? I mean, at a superficial level we can see there are changes. But basically, do you think it has remained the same?*
WA: Overall in the United States I think it's still a subject of titillation. In more sophisticated circles there's been some progress made, but in general in this country it's still this silly attitude. You can see, for instance, how the majority elects our leaders. These leaders have to reflect this kind of old-fashioned morality, or they'll have a hard time being elected.

SB: *To us in Europe it seems extremely ridiculous, or upsetting, when these candidates to major positions have to have their family lives scrutinized. If they've been involved in extra-marital affairs, etc....*
WA: That's because America is a very hypocritical country.

SB: *The second episode of* Everything You Wanted to Know About Sex, *'What is Sodomy?', is very funny, and I think you presented Gene Wilder with the best part in the film. How come you chose him and how do you regard him as an actor?*
WA: He's a wonderful comic actor. I didn't want to be in all of the sequences, I just wanted to be in a few of them. And so I was looking to get the best people I could for the sequences that I was not in. I think Gene Wilder is terrific.

SB: *I also thought he's brilliant in this very intense little story. One thing I specially noticed here is his very personal timing. He uses very long and expressive pauses in his acting. Is this something specific for him, or did you ask him to perform in this way?*

12   Gene Wilder in *Everything You Always Wanted to Know About Sex . . .*

WA: No, that's his own rhythm. He has said at times that he felt he was working in a more subtle vein in the film we did together than he often does. But no, it's all his own timing. It's his natural feel. If I have somebody like Gene Wilder and he's doing something funny, I'll get out of his way. Only if he does something that I can see is really wrong for the character or the script, would I comment on that. Otherwise I don't see any point in hiring a great actor like Gene Wilder or like Gene Hackman or anybody comparable to them and then hovering over them and bothering them. They have a good instinct for what they do. They read the part. If they have any questions, they ask me. Very often they don't ask me anything. They understand what it is. They do it, and they do it very well. Sometimes I don't have to say anything to them at all. Sometimes I only have to ask them to do it a little faster. There is a scene, for instance, between Max Von Sydow and Barbara Hershey in *Hannah and Her Sisters*. They have a big fight scene. And they had rehearsed it themselves without me. Then, when I saw them do it, it was twice as long as it appears in the movie. They were *so slow*. And all I had to do in their case was to tell them, 'You have to do this much faster, you can't take that long to do the scene.' But their instincts on what to do were their own. They were great.

SB: *Do you think this slower pace might come from the fact that Max is Swedish and that we usually act and react in a slower way, that we're more used to a slower pace in life?*
WA: I have a feeling that actors – all actors – take a slower pace, because they are enjoying what they're doing at the time and they like it and they don't realize that when you watch it, it's not as interesting to other people. And when you film it, it becomes twice as slow. I don't think they understand that. It's a hard concept. Since they're having such a good time, they think the audience is too. But I will say that the European rhythm, in general, is a much slower rhythm than the American rhythm. Ours is much more nervous. Outside of those early Godard films, like *Breathless* or *A Woman Is a Woman* and others, the rhythm of European films is a much slower one.

SB: *Yes, I've noticed the same thing, that the actor's concept of screen-time is sometimes non-existent. This is especially true with actors who mainly work in the theatre.*
WA: Sure, it's hard enough for the director to feel it. But for the actors, they just take forever. With Gene Wilder, though, I didn't have that

problem. He understood the character and the part and did it naturally. I had to do very little with him. To me it's very important to have a spontaneous response from the actor. I watched Liv Ullmann on television the other night, she was being interviewed. She was talking about how annoying it is with certain directors that they don't do their homework. They're insecure, they're unprepared on the set. She talked in connection with directing her own movie. But I'm of the exact opposite point of view. I just backtracked once, when I did this film with Paul Mazursky. I was amazed how much preparation he had done. He went to the set, to the locations and looked at them. He brought the actors to every location, so we could look at it before the film started. He knew where the camera was going to be. He did a lot of homework. Everything went very smoothly for him and it was fun. But I don't do that. I find the location with the art director. We agree on it, that's it. The cameraman goes there and I talk to him about it for a few minutes, a month before we go there, a few weeks before we go there. Just so we've decided that this is the right thing. Then I never think about it again, I keep it out of my mind. And the morning when I show up on the set, I have no idea of what I'm going to be filming, in what way I'm going to be filming. I like it to be spontaneous at that time. I walk about the set, by myself and with the cameraman. We throw some ideas back and forth and then I plan how the actors are going to be. And we get the place lit. Then, and only then, I call the actors in. And I tell them how to move in the scene, where to go. Not too precisely, just in general. Then we start to shoot. And then, sometimes, the very first thing we shoot is the best. It's never better after that. And sometimes it takes us a while. The actors have to get more used to it, and the third take or the tenth take is the best one. But there's never any rehearsal or any preparation. After I'm through writing the script – I rewrite it once before I'm sure everything's OK – then I practically never look at the script again before the production. I don't memorize my part. I just give a fast look at the script ten minutes before I do it. Very, very often, and on most films, I don't even have a script. I distribute the script to the people, and they print them up and everyone gets one. But I don't have a script of my own in my home or any place. The less I study it, the fresher it is to me.

SB: *Then, when you shoot, how many takes do you average? I gather it differs a lot from film to film or rather from situation to situation.*

WA: I try not to do so many. As an average, probably about four. But if I can just do two, I'm happy. One, plus one for protection. But there have been times when I've done more. In *Broadway Danny Rose* I did fifty takes at one point. But that's very rare.

SB: *The third sequence in* Everything You Wanted to Know About Sex ... *is the semi-Italian episode, where you and Louise Lasser are talking some kind of pidgin Italian.*
WA: Yeah, we learned that by phonetics.

SB: *Of course, this sequence is a take-off on Italian movies. Did you have any specific film or specific film-maker in mind when you made this episode?*
WA: No, I was just in a slight Antonionish mood. Originally we thought of doing the sequence as peasants and being in that very familiar cliché that you see in early Fellini or De Sica. But then we said, 'Why don't we make them rich and sophisticated people and do that kind of Italian approach?' So we did that.

SB: *Over the title sequence of the film, the scenes with all the rabbits, you put this beautiful song by Cole Porter, 'Let's Misbehave'. Cole Porter seems to be one of your favourite composers. His music appears in many of your films.*
WA: In fact, he is responsible for the title music and the end music to *Husbands and Wives*. Yes, you can say I'm addicted to Cole Porter. In *Husbands and Wives* I use 'What Is This Thing Called Love'. A very good version of it. A very, very old version with Bubber Miley, a great black cornet player who played with Duke Ellington and Jelly Roll Morton.

CHAPTER 6

Sleeper

MILES: I'm always joking. It's a defence mechanism.
(From *Sleeper*)

STIG BJÖRKMAN: *How did you get the idea for* Sleeper?
WOODY ALLEN: Well, I had this idea, and I went to United Artists with it and said that I wanted to make a very big, expensive film. Four hours long. It would be a New York comedy and at the end of this comedy, after two hours, I accidentally get frozen in a cryogenic machine. Then there would be an intermission, and the audience can leave the theatre and buy their candy and popcorn, and after the intermission they come back to Act 2 of the film. There in Act 2 I wake up, and it's New York 500 years in the future. And there comes a second movie. The people at United Artists loved the idea. But it was such a big job to write it that way, that I decided that I would just use the idea for the second part of the film. I called Marshall Brickman and asked him if he wanted to join the project, and he said, 'Sure!' And we wrote it together.

SB: Sleeper *has a double meaning, hasn't it? It means a very successful movie as well?*
WA: Yes, it means a successful thing that you didn't expect to be successful. But I had not thought of this double meaning. I just wanted to have a short title on the film, a one-word title.

SB: *The music in* Sleeper *is by your own band, the Ragtime Rascals. It's a music which gives the film a kind of slapstick quality.*
WA: We played the score, yes. I didn't know what kind of music to use. And then I thought, since it was the future, I wasn't going to use any futuristic music, as that's unpleasant and strange to listen to. And since it was a slapstick movie, I wanted to use that kind of music. The most fun I had on the movie was playing the score.

SB: *How was the music composed and played to the scenes?*
WA: It was classical New Orleans jazz. I listened to a whole lot of New Orleans music from which I chose. I gave myself a library.

SB: *Diane Keaton appears for the first time in a film of yours in* Sleeper; *I guess that her part was specially designed for her.*
WA: Right. I tried to make her into a Buster Keaton-like heroine, someone who is funny and who is always getting the hero into trouble. And she did that well.

SB: Sleeper *has probably more visual gags than most of your other films. Do you remember how you came to construct these gags for the film?*
WA: Well, I wanted to make a kind of slapstick-style movie, a visual movie in that sense. Mostly I found it very easy. *Sleeper* was a quite inexpensive film. It cost less than three million dollars.

SB: *Do you find it harder to find visual gags than verbal ones?*
WA: They're not hard to think of. They just require a lot of work to film.

SB: *There's a scene with you shaving in front of a mirror which recalls some jokes from the Marx Brothers' films. I guess this was intentional?*
WA: So, so. I mean, it's a different kind of an idea, because there's another person in the scene as well. The visual jokes in the film are mainly based on the futuristic context.

13 Woody Allen and Diane Keaton in *Sleeper*

CHAPTER 7

Love and Death

STIG BJÖRKMAN: Love and Death *was shot by Ghislain Cloquet. Was the film made in France?*
WOODY ALLEN: It was shot in France and Hungary, in Budapest and Paris. I had to make the film abroad for obvious reasons, because it was a European story. And the producers wanted me to do the big scenes in Hungary, because it was much less expensive there. So I went over there, and I had a wonderful French crew. I met many French cameramen and looked at their work, and the one whose work I liked the best was Cloquet's. I can't remember what films of his I saw, because I just saw one reel of many films.

SB: *Was this the first time you had casting by Juliet Taylor?*
WA: Well, Juliet Taylor was the assistant to Marion Dougherty who did my casting right from my first film. Then when Marion went to California to work for the Studios, Juliet became the head. But I had always worked with Juliet before.

SB: *How do you work together? Do you have conferences and she suggests possible actors and actresses for the parts . . . ?*
WA: Yes, I let her read the script, and generally don't tell her anything. She prefers me not to. Then she meets with me, and she always has a big list of possibilities for each role. Then we have endless conversations, and I say, 'No, I hate that actor!' and she suggests another one. And we just go on and on and on. And very gradually we select someone for each role.

SB: *Is this procedure true both for the main actors and the supporting actors? You've never chosen any of the main actors yourself beforehand?*
WA: No, no, we choose every single person for the film together.

SB: *The music for* Love and Death *is Prokofiev.*
WA: Originally I wanted it to be Stravinsky. But I found that when I put

Stravinsky behind the scenes, it made it unfunny. It was just so heavy. And in addition to that – but this was not the reason – Stravinsky was very expensive to obtain and Prokofiev was not. But the real reason was that Stravinsky was far too heavy. Ralph Rosenblum, the editor, would say, 'Why don't we forget about Stravinsky? He's not working. Why don't we try Prokofiev?' And we did, and it was just fine. It lightened the whole mood, it was brilliant and gay, whereas Stravinsky was always strange and offputting and disturbing.

SB: *Somewhere at the beginning of the film, Sonya (Diane Keaton) asks Boris (played by you): 'Isn't nature incredible?' And you answer: 'To me nature is, I don't know, spiders eating bugs and big fishes eating little fishes and plants eating plants. It's like an enormous restaurant. That's how I see it.' What is your attitude towards nature as opposed to urban life? I guess maybe your attitude is not of a Rousseau-like kind?*

WA: It's deeper than that, because certainly in terms of the contrast between urban life and rural life I fall into the urban life personality. This kind of dichotomy in artists has existed for many years. I mean, Dostoyevsky was clearly an urban person where Tolstoy was quite rural. Turgenev was particularly rural. But it has no relationship to the quality of the work or the depth of the work. I prefer the city to the country. I don't mind driving in the country or being in the country for one day now and then. But, in this context, I meant 'nature' overall, city and country. I mean, when you look at natural beauty you look at a beautiful pastoral scene. If you look closely, what you will see is pretty horrible. If you really could look closely, you would see violence and chaos and murder and cannibalism. But when you look at the broad picture, a Constable painting, it looks quite beautiful.

SB: *Yes, and that goes for the urban landscape as well.*

WA: Yes, if you look at the city, you can see a picture of urban beauty. But when you come in close, you can see the bacteria and what happens between man and his fellow man. It's a pretty miserable, ugly, horrifying thing.

SB: *Love and Death, compared to your later films, is still a more loosely told story. And sometimes, like in your earlier films, the dialogue is mere wisecracking. A typical example of this is the scene between Boris and Sonya in the attic.*

WA: Sure, I used to always want my character to speak in jokes, like

Groucho Marx or Bob Hope. So there is always a witticism rather than behavioural dialogue.

SB: *In your book* Side Effects *you have written a couple of short stories which are pastiches or parodies on specific literary styles. There's one story in particular which I like a lot, called 'The Condemned'. It's a kind of take-off on French existentialist writings in the tradition of Sartre or Camus. There are similar traits in* Love and Death.

WA: Right, everyone has his own favourite areas to tease and to satirize and to poke fun at. I have great affection for those writers and those subjects. It would be as if I made a parody of Ingmar Bergman, it would be done out of affection.

SB: *And* Love and Death *has traces of that – parodies of Bergman, of Eisenstein, of certain French directors.*

WA: Sure, because I was dealing in that area. I knew I would have a good time in that whole philosophical world. Penelope Gilliatt, reviewing the movie, wrote that 'we're not in the world of Russia here, we're in the world of Russian literature.' And that's really what it is. It's almost literary parody.

SB: *So, what inspired you to write this film?*

WA: It's an interesting little story, maybe. I had just done *Sleeper*, which I had shot in Colorado and California. And I wanted to make a picture in New York City. I wrote a murder mystery. But when I'd finished it, I didn't want to do a murder mystery. I didn't think it strong enough for me, so I put it aside. Then I got a sudden wish to do a Russian thing, with a lightly philosophical theme, so I wrote *Love and Death*. And I did it. After that I came back to the murder mystery, and I took some of that plot, some of the characters in it, and I made it into *Annie Hall*. The characters were Annie and Alvy and the murder mystery, and there were many things that were exactly the same. But I dropped the murder part. But for *Manhattan Murder Mystery*, I came back to the murder mystery.

SB: *That same story?*

WA: Pretty much – I adapted it a little bit – but pretty much. So with *Love and Death* I surprised everybody, because they all expected a film in New York, a contemporary New York film. But that was some of the most fun I had, making that film. I like that area. It was fun working in Paris. I liked the French people and I loved being in France. Budapest was a little rough at that time for me, because it was cold.

14   Woody Allen in *Love and Death*

SB: *We talked about references before, filmic references. Bergman, of course, is a strong one. You have the character of Death collecting the dead, for instance. But there is also a startling image at the end of the film, reminding me of Persona. There is a close-up of Diane Keaton and Jessica Harper which cannot be an accidental reference.*

WA: Sure, we just used anything we wanted in those days. We took Russian books and Swedish films and French films and Kafka and French existentialists. Whatever gave us an amusing time, we did.

SB: *Did you come upon these things while you were writing the script? Or did you collect different elements with pastiche-like qualities to put into the script, into the film?*

WA: It came as I was writing. I just started to write it and I came upon something and thought, 'This would be funny.' And one thing led to another.

CHAPTER 8

Annie Hall

ALVY: The universe is expanding.
(From *Annie Hall*)

STIG BJÖRKMAN: *Then came* Annie Hall, *which is the kind of city film everybody expected you to do.*
WOODY ALLEN: Right, I really feel it was a major turning point for me. I had the courage to abandon . . . just clowning around and the safety of complete broad comedy. I said to myself, 'I think I will try and make some deeper film and not be as funny in the same way. And maybe there will be other values that will emerge, that will be interesting or nourishing for the audience.' And it worked out very well.

SB: Annie Hall, *like* Sleeper, *was written by you and Marshall Brickman. Who is he? Is he a writer by profession?*
WA: Marshall and I used to appear in cabaret together. He was with a musical act. He played the bass and the guitar. And we got friendly, we used to talk. And then we decided we would try and write something together for fun. So we wrote, and we liked it. We wrote *Sleeper* and then *Annie Hall* and then *Manhattan* together. I like him. He's been a friend and very nice. He has also directed several films.

SB: *How was your collaboration? Did you meet daily to write together, or . . . ?*
WA: No, we walked the streets together, we had lunch together, dinner together. We sat in a room together. We talked, talked, talked. And then, when all the talking was done, I went and wrote the script. Then I showed it to Marshall, and he made his comments: 'This seems quite good, but this scene is weak, why don't we try this instead.' He provided new points of view and ideas, but I felt that I had to be the one to actually write it down. Because I had to say it, I wanted it written down the way I'm comfortable saying it.

SB: Annie Hall *starts in total silence, in contrast to many of your other films, where you usually set the mood with a piece of music. Why did you want to do without music here? Was it to prepare the audience for another kind of film of yours, a new kind of film where you wanted to give more emphasis, more importance to the dialogue?*

WA: In those days I was sort of still groping for a musical approach. I had used classical music in *Love and Death*. In *Sleeper* I had played the music myself, me and my jazz band. I wasn't sure yet what I really wanted to do musically, so I was trying this film without music. The only music in *Annie Hall* is source music. There's no scoring at all. It's either coming from a car radio or a party or something. But there is no music in the movie. I don't know, I was just experimenting, seeing what it would be like. To be very, very sparing with the music. I was so uncompromising in my feeling. I didn't care if the audience liked it or not. I just wanted to do what I wanted to do there, make some turning point. If I did that same film today, it would probably be full of music. There's also another possibility – I remember Bergman never used music, and I was so taken with his film-making in those days, I may have thought to myself, 'Perhaps he's right about the use of music.' But over the years I came to a different feeling about music.

SB: *I've thought of another possible influence from Bergman a propos* Annie Hall. *Here you use the kind of very simple and clean title logotype which you've continued to use for all your films since. Bergman also kept to one and the same logo for all his films over the years.*

WA: I didn't know that, I hadn't thought about that. Originally, my intent was different. I had done some fancy titles on *Bananas* and *Everything You Always Wanted to Know About Sex* ..., and then I thought to myself, 'It's silly to spend money on titles! It's a very American stupid habit. I'm going to get the cheapest titles I can, just a plain announcement.' And I picked the typeface that I liked, and I never changed it after that. Because, what do titles mean? It's just simple information.

SB: *Right. But your titles have become a trademark for your films.*

WA: Yes, now they've been on fifteen films, or something. And I think it's just fine. It costs no money at all. It really got out of hand in the United States. There was a time during the sixties, when the titles got to be like *The Pink Panther*. The producers would put aside $250,000 for the title sequence. It would be one of the main things in the movie. I also wanted to go against making it a special event when my films came out. I just want to make a lot of films and keep putting them out. And I don't want it to be: 'Oh, it's the new Woody Allen film! Two years we've waited for it!' I just want to turn them out – and that's it! I like to work a lot, and I've made a deal with the film company, so that the minute I pull out the script from the typewriter and it's finished, the next day I'm in production. The deal is already there, I don't have to worry about that. And that's how I like it. I don't want to finish a script, show it to someone, meet for lunch, get the money and so on.

SB: *Did you feel, by the time of making* Annie Hall, *that you had reached or obtained the freedom to express whatever you liked, economically as well as artistically? And that's why you could make* Annie Hall *the way you did.*

WA: Well, two things happened on *Annie Hall*. One was that I reached some kind of a personal plateau where I felt I could put the films that I had done in the past behind me. And I wanted to take a step forward toward more realistic and deeper films. The other thing was that I met Gordon Willis. And Gordon was a very important teacher to me, from a technical point of view. He's a technical wizard. He's also a great artist. He showed me things about camera and lighting; it was a real turning point for me in every way. From then on, I really count *Annie Hall* as the first step toward maturity in some way in making films.

SB: *It has a total freedom in structure as well.*

WA: I've always had that in the writing. I've always felt free and open in the chronology of a film, the structure of it.

SB: *The film starts very abruptly with you addressing the audience with two witticisms. One is about the two old ladies at a spa in the mountains and one of them says, 'The food in this place is really terrible.' And the other one answers, 'Yeah, I know, and there are such small portions!' The other joke is attributed to Groucho Marx whom you're paraphrasing: 'I would never wanna belong to any club that would have someone like me for a member.' This gives the film a touch of immediacy and directness.*

WA: Right, it sets up the idea of the film. I felt instinctively that a picture where I addressed the audience directly and talked about myself personally would interest them, because I felt many of the people in the audience had the same feelings and the same problems. I wanted to talk to them directly and confront them.

SB: *At the start of the film you say that Alvy Singer was brought up under the roller-coaster in Brooklyn. The picture of a roller-coaster is a recurrent image in a couple of your films, like* Stardust Memories, The Purple Rose of Cairo *and* Radio Days.

WA: Right. I grew up in Brooklyn, not completely near, but not very far from Coney Island which was a major amusement park, a legendary amusement park. It was fairly broken down by the time I was a child, but it was still there. And I spent a lot of time there. I used to go there with my friends all the time. We'd go swimming, we'd go on the boardwalk. You see some of it in *Radio Days*. I was brought up by the beach, by the water. A portion of my childhood I did live by the ocean, though the greater portion I did not. But the one portion I did was significant. So originally, when I wrote *Annie Hall*, I didn't have myself brought up at the amusement park, I had myself brought up where I was really brought up, that is a few miles from it. But when we were driving around Brooklyn, looking for locations, Gordon Willis, the art director Mel Bourne and I saw this roller-coaster, and I saw the house under it. And I thought, we have to use this. So I shifted his provenance to that house. It's such a strong image.

SB: *And what about your early childhood, the Alvy/Woody childhood?*
WA: That was accurate. I did live in a place like that, I went to a school with those blue-haired teachers, very, very strict and very unpleasant.

SB: *And in connection to this you say, 'I have a certain difficulty, some trouble between reality and fantasy.'*
WA: Yes, this is the main theme of my films. I remember my childhood in certain ways. Sometimes I remember it unpleasantly, other times I remember it more pleasantly than it was. It's hard to remember it exactly, accurately.

SB: *In* Annie Hall *there are some, what one could call, interludes of confidential conversation between you and the kind of buddy character you have in the film, played by Tony Roberts. In the beginning of the film there is a long scene where you walk together on a sidewalk, towards the camera. It's a very long, unbroken scene. At first we hardly see you at the end of the street, and then you come closer and closer towards the camera, and then the camera follows you two along the street. There are similar scenes in other films by you staged in the same way. They are quite long and you just let them continue in this way while the people are*

talking. Do you like to present these kind of reflections in this way?
WA: Someone was criticizing me for this once in *Manhattan*. But this is what city life is. It's verbal communication. City life is cerebral. You're not up in the morning like the Tolstoy peasant cutting the hay. And it's not the silent rituals like with the family in Bergman's *The Virgin Spring*.

SB: *I like these kind of commentary scenes precisely because they are presented in this way, in one long unabridged take.*
WA: I started with that in *Annie Hall*, and then I've done an enormous amount of movies in just a few takes. So for some pictures we, my editor Susan Morse and I, could put the whole picture together in just one week, starting from scratch, because there are just master-shots. Forty master-shots, and then it's finished. Most of my latest pictures are just built up on long, long master-shots. I got away from shooting any kind of coverage years ago. It just seems more fun and quicker and less boring for me to do long scenes.

SB: *This scene reminded me, both in structure and content, of a film like Mike Nichols'* Carnal Knowledge, *which is also a comedy of manners of sorts.*
WA: Yes, maybe. I saw that film years ago. I think it's one of his best films.

SB: *In* Annie Hall *Annie and Alvy are going to see Bergman's* Face to Face, *and I presume not by chance they've chosen this film. But Alvy refuses to go into the cinema, as the film has already started.*
WA: Right, that was the first scene of the murder mystery. I'm waiting at the movie theatre, and Annie comes and then we go some place, and then the murder happens. But in *Annie Hall* I'm just waiting there, and I don't want to see Bergman's movie after it's begun.

SB: *Then there's the discussion with a man in line outside the cinema. He starts a quarrel and quotes Marshall McLuhan incorrectly and you produce McLuhan from behind a poster to correct the man.*
WA: Well, I tried many people, and McLuhan finally agreed to do it. He was not my first choice. My first choice was Fellini, because it would be more natural if people were standing in line talking about movies, that they would be talking about Fellini. But Fellini didn't want to come over to the United States to do this, which is OK. So I got Marshall McLuhan.

SB: *Did you ever think of Bergman?*
WA: No, Bergman didn't seem the type to ever want to do a thing like that. All you heard about him was how reclusive he was, on his island, Farö.

SB: *Did you have any contact with him at this time?*
WA: No, I never had any contact with Bergman until I was filming *Manhattan*. And Liv Ullmann, whom I had met and who knew how much I liked Bergman, said that he would be in town in a week. She suggested that she, I, Bergman and his wife had dinner together. And she assured me that he wanted to as well. So I went to Bergman's hotel room, and we had dinner there. We had a long, long conversation and it was very pleasant. We talked about many, many things. I was very surprised that many of the trivial things that I went through, he had also gone through at the exact same time. And we talked. But last time I was in Stockholm I couldn't go, because I had too many children there. But we had a long conversation on the phone, maybe for one to two hours. He's very amusing in his conversation. We've had several conversations over the phone like this, but the only time I've been in contact, in physical contact with him, was that evening at the hotel in New York. It was very pleasant. But it was funny to me how many silly things happen to all film-makers, I guess it's universal. He said to me that when a film of his comes out, the production people call him immediately and report. 'Well, the first showing was full and we predict it's going to make more money than any film of yours has done.' And this happens to me too. The same kind of predictions. It all looks great, and after five days it all vanishes, all the optimistic predictions. And the same with him.

SB: *Do you have these kind of optimistic feelings for your films while you're making them? For instance, when you've finished a script and you start directing the film?*
WA: Commercially, no. Artistically, yes. I always think that the next film I do is just going to be great artistically. But commercially, I'm always pessimistic. When I did *September* or *Another Woman* or *Interiors* or *Stardust Memories*, I knew when I was making them that nobody was going to go and see them. Even if I made them artistically and worked hard and they came out good, I *knew* that there wouldn't be an audience for them. You can feel that. Whereas when I make a picture like *Annie Hall* or *Sleeper*, I can feel that, if I do it well, there will be a reasonable audience.

SB: *But this knowledge, of course, has never stopped you from making the pictures you want to make.*

WA: It doesn't stop me, no. The more surprising thing is that it never stopped the studio. If you said to me, you will always have money to make your films, then it's irrelevant to me. I make any film I want. I don't care if the public likes it, the critics like it. I mean, I would like them to. But if they don't, they don't. I make films for my own enjoyment. But unfortunately the realities are that after a while the studio will say, 'Look, you've made ten films and we've lost so much money.' But so far that hasn't happened to me. It's lucky.

SB: *It's ironic, as I think some of the films you just mentioned, like* Stardust Memories *and* September *and* Another Woman, *are among your best works. It's maybe not strange that they don't appeal to the public, but it's a sad fact.*

WA: I think so too, but there's never – or not very often – a correlation between one's best work and one's commercial work. *What's New, Pussycat?* was a huge hit, which I think is shameful. Sometimes you get lucky, sometimes you make a good film and people also come and see it. But very often not. I'm not one to judge which are good films or which are not for other people. The only thing that I can ever judge is, was I able to execute my own idea to my satisfaction? So a film that's always been a favourite of mine – and it made no money at all in the United States – was *The Purple Rose of Cairo.* That to me has always been a favourite, because I had an idea, and I got that idea on the screen as I wanted it. When it was finished, I said, 'Yes I had a script and an idea – and there it is!' I managed to express myself the way I wanted. The film was very, very well critically received, but it had a *very* small audience. Some people have suggested that perhaps if they had married at the end, Cecilia and the movie star, the film would have had a bigger audience. There was such a feeling of unhappiness or melancholy when he left her at the end. But that was the whole reason I was doing the film, that was the whole point of the film. But other films of mine have had similar destinies. *Zelig,* for instance, was a tremendous critical success, but nobody came to see it. *Radio Days* was a critical success that nobody came to see. And these are accessible films. *Broadway Danny Rose,* which was a real old-fashioned comedy, was a similar case. Over the years people have said to me, 'Oh, that's my favourite film of yours. I laughed and laughed!' But nobody came to see it at the time.

SB: *I think the European reaction has not been similar to the American.*
WA: No, Europe has saved my life in the last fifteen years. If it wasn't
for Europe, I'd probably not be making films. Films that were commercially unsuccessful in this country, made their money in Europe, or at
least made enough in Europe, so the loss was minimal. My early films
were not so popular in Europe – though I think France went crazy over
Bananas. That was a big, big opening for me in Europe. And then Italy
followed very quickly. Then, after a while, I started to build a European
audience. Now I'm completely dependent on the European audiences.
Shadows and Fog is a perfect example. Nobody went to see it in the
United States at all, but in Europe it did nicely.

SB: *You mentioned Fellini before, and he, of course, has been one of
your inspirational film-makers.*
WA: Yes, I think his *The White Sheik* is perhaps the best sound comedy
ever made. It's hard for me to think of a comedy with dialogue that's
better. I think maybe there's one Preston Sturges film that's quite good,
Unfaithfully Yours. And there are two films of Lubitsch that are quite
wonderful. *The Shop Around the Corner* which is a tremendous film, and
Trouble in Paradise, which is quite a funny film. But in terms of actual
talking comedies – and then I don't count the Marx Brothers' films,
because they're really a record of the Marx Brothers' work – it's hard for
me to think of a comedy that's better than *The White Sheik*. It's as good
as I can think of as a total comedy. Surprisingly enough, one of the
script-writers was Antonioni. You wouldn't think it, because he's such a
dour character.

SB: Annie Hall *again! In the film you do something which has been
more or less 'forbidden' in films, when you're directly addressing the
audience with comments on the story and the characters. It has a kind of
Brechtian or Godardian touch. There are traits of this in your early
comedies as well, but there these viewpoints are more like side-remarks
in the Bob Hope tradition.*
WA: Right, like Groucho or Bob Hope. This was more for the development of the story than for the joke. I wanted the audience to experience
this *with me*. That was the impetus for doing the picture to begin with.

SB: Annie Hall *is one of the few films where we see you active in sports.
Is that a field where you have some interest or no interest at all?*
WA: No, quite the opposite. I was always a good athlete as a boy.

People never think that of me, but I was always a good athlete. And I grew up with a great love of sports as a spectator. So I like sports very much to this day. Very often I lament the fact that the theatre cannot achieve the tension that a good sporting event can achieve. I love many, many sports as a spectator now.

SB: *Like which?*
WA: Many. Baseball, basketball, boxing, football, tennis, golf . . . There are very few sports I don't like. When I was in London, I had no problem watching cricket, which is a sport that Americans never can understand. But I was interested instantly in that.

SB: *Do you watch them on TV or do you prefer to see them live?*
WA: Depending on the convenience of going to the place, most of them I watch on TV, because it's much easier. But many, many times I'm at the basketball games. I used to never miss a prize fight. I don't go to baseball games much. I watch them on television, because it's much harder to go to baseball games. There are fifty thousand people, not fifteen thousand. So the access is more difficult, it's difficult getting in and out. Basketball is much easier for me. It's also here in Manhattan. I can get a taxi and within ten minutes or less I'm there. The baseball game is 45 minutes to get to – Yankee Stadium – out by the airport.

SB: *But you do regularly go and see different sport games?*
WA: Yeah, depending on if I'm shooting or not. There were times when Diane Keaton and I used to go to basketball games every single night there was one. We never missed one.

SB: *A propos Diane Keaton,* Annie Hall, *is that her real name?*
WA: Yes, Diane Hall is her real name. She had to change it to Keaton, which is her mother's maiden name, because there was a Diane Hall in Actor's Equity, and so there couldn't be two of them.

SB: *So that's why the movie was called* Annie Hall?
WA: Yes, it just seemed like a good name to me.

SB: *You talked before about Diane Keaton and her very personal way of dressing. Her style in dressing in* Annie Hall *became a kind of fashion at that time.*
WA: Yes, that was her way. She came in, and the costume lady on the

15   Diane Keaton and Woody Allen in *Annie Hall*

picture, Ruth Morley, said, 'Tell her not to wear that. She can't wear that. It's so crazy.' And I said, 'Leave her. She's a genius. Let's just leave her alone, let her wear what she wants. If I really hate something, I'll tell her. Otherwise she can choose for herself.'

sb: *There is a remark in the film on her way of dressing, with her trousers and vest and tie and hat. You say, 'Were you brought up in a Norman Rockwell painting?' But there's another American painter who sometimes comes to my mind when watching your films, and that's Edward Hopper.*
wa: Well, I love Hopper of course. All Americans love Hopper. He's got a certain melancholy that I like.

sb: *Are there other American artists you like or feel influenced by?*
wa: I don't feel influenced by any painters, but I do like all the abstract expressionist painters, De Koonig and Pollock and Frank Stella. And I love a lot of stuff by Andy Warhol and a lot of stuff by Rauschenberg and Jasper Johns. Yes, I love contemporary American painting.

sb: *Diane Keaton is acting in the film in a way that could be described as 'absent-minded'. Sometimes it's slightly defensive, she's very often backing into the scenes. Was this deliberate from her side or your side?*
wa: No, that's her! Diane wakes up in the morning and apologizes. That's just her personality. It's very self-effacing. She's like all very smart people; *extremely* modest, *extremely* self-effacing. She's got that quality.

sb: *So, when you wrote* Annie Hall, *you had Diane Keaton in mind for the main part?*
wa: Yes, definitely! It was tailored for her.

sb: *After Alvy's and Annie's first night together there is a scene in a book-store where Alvy confesses that he has a rather pessimistic view on life: 'Life is divided into the horrible and the miserable. Those two categories.' Do you share Alvy's view on life?*
wa: Oh, yes. That's a reflection of my own feelings. Be happy that you're just miserable.

sb: *So, you modelled the character of Annie Hall very much on Diane Keaton. But does your character in the film, Alvy Singer, reflect a lot of yourself as well? Is he the character in your films that comes closest to yourself, do you think?*

WA: Oddly enough, no. People have asked me this question a lot. Paddy Chayevsky said years ago that all the characters are the author. And I found that true. I identified a great deal with Cecilia in *Radio Days*, with the mother in *Interiors*, as well as with Alvy. I find myself all over the place. It's very hard for me to pick out one more than the other. They all reflect me. You disguise yourself in many forms. It can be either gender or age. Pauline Kael, writing about *Interiors*, felt that the character that most personified me was Mary Beth Hurt. But she was basing it on the clothing. That was not it at all. There might have been some elements of my feelings in the character Mary Beth Hurt played, Joey. But Joey's problem was that she had feelings but no artistic talent to express them. And I felt I'd been lucky that I had had some talent, so I didn't have that particular problem. But the one I had identified with was the mother-figure, Geraldine Page.

SB: *In what way?*
WA: I just felt that she reflected me. I have a certain part of my personality that has got that rigid, obsessive coldness. Everything has to be perfect and in perfect order.

SB: *Life needs an order?*
WA: Yes. And everything in earth-tones and soft tones. And just the right amount of furniture. Very obsessive.

SB: *Colleen Dewhurst, who plays Annie's mother in the film, is the first in a line of portraits of very strong mothers.*
WA: I picked her not only because she's a fine actress, but she also looks like Diane's mother. Diane's mother has that real American pioneer look, very classic. And Colleen not only had the look, but she's such a wonderful actress.

SB: *But it's not by chance that you have this succession of strong mother-figures in your films. Like Geraldine Page in* Interiors, *Maureen O'Sullivan in* Hannah, *Elaine Stritch in* September *or Gwen Verdon in* Alice.
WA: When I first started writing, I could only write from the man's point of view. And I was the man. Every situation was from a male point of view. But somewhere along the line – I don't know why or what happened – it switched. And suddenly, for some reason, I started to write basically from the woman's point of view all the time. There came all

these women portraits. If you look at the women's parts I've had over the last fifteen years – the mothers and sisters, in *Interiors* and *Hannah and Her Sisters* and *September*; the roles I wrote for Diane Keaton; the roles I wrote for Mia Farrow, there's always women in the central parts. I don't know how that happened or why or when, but something turned around.

SB: *Could it be the influence of Bergman? I mean, he has very strong female parts in his films as well.*
WA: I don't know, but I don't think so. It doesn't seem to me the kind of thing that could be externally motivated. It's more likely a change in the person. One could say, Bergman writes beautiful portraits of women, but I can't do it, because I don't feel the woman's psychology. But then it changed in me, inside me. Maybe it had to do with psychoanalysis, maybe it had to do with my interpersonal relationship with Diane. I mean, Annie Hall was the first good woman's role I ever wrote. A really good one. And from then on there were good women's roles. Very often better than the men's roles. In *Husbands and Wives* I think the women's roles are superior.

SB: *Could it also be because you're more interested in working with certain actresses? You talked before about the difficulty in finding good American actors for the male parts in your films. Maybe in some unconscious way you've found it more interesting to write parts that can be created by some good and gifted actresses?*
WA: I think so. I've always wanted to make a movie with all my favourite women in it. With Mia and Diane Keaton and Dianne Wiest and Meryl Streep and Judy Davis. I mean, there are so many very gifted women. I've just mentioned a few of them. We have some fantastic actors as well, of course, like Gene Hackman or Robert De Niro. But you have to put them in more virile situations. You can't put these men in weak situations. They can't play that. The same kind of parts that Emil Jannings used to play in Germany, or Edward G. Robinson or Fredric March sometimes here in the States. Robert De Niro or Jack Nicholson or Gene Hackman or Al Pacino – to name the greatest actors here – cannot play Willy Loman. They would have to force it. They're too virile, too attractive for that kind of part. Dustin Hoffman could play him, though he was a bit young. He could play the part when he's sixty. Dustin is maybe the only one who has that quality. But there are English or Swedish actors who possess this quality.

SB: *It was very interesting, though, to see Gene Hackman in* Another
Woman.
WA: But that was a more virile part. And yes, you couldn't get anybody
better.

SB: *But there was a softness expressed in his acting in this film.*
WA: More than usual, because he was playing romantic and he very
rarely does that. But even here he's still virile. Hackman's borderline, he
can go either way a little more than the others. I'm thinking of him in *The
Conversation*. He had a certain amount of that in there. He could go
both ways. But it's rare. George C. Scott used to be able to do both.
Others like Redford and Newman are great, but they are very heroic.
They are tremendous actors both of them, but they're not the man next
door.

SB: *When you have Alvy and Annie visiting their respective analysts,
why did you choose to present that on split screen?*
WA: Because I thought it was an interesting thing how two people
report the same phenomenon differently. I thought the point was most
theatrically made that way.

SB: *In* Annie Hall *there are ample occasions for reflections, but still the
film and the story is told with quite a fast pace. It's very dense and rich in
this way. There is, for instance, a scene where Annie and Alvy are
quarrelling in the street which then cuts to a scene with Alvy washing
dishes, and the quarrel continues on the soundtrack. Then suddenly
Annie walks into the frame and into this new location and we're in a new
situation. Do you remember this?*
WA: I don't remember it too clearly, because I never see these films. But
I do remember that kind of device. Here I tried to make it more introspec-
tive, so you're in Alvy's mind a lot of the times. I've tried this twice in
films. The one film that I finally got into the mind completely was
Stardust Memories. That was all taking place in the mind, so anything
could happen. But in *Annie Hall* I was trying this for the first time.

SB: *Alvy passes through existence with memories and experiences from
the past present all the time. This gives the film a very improvised feeling,
and I guess that initially this was your intention as well.*
WA: Sure, because what I like with films is that I can do what I want. It's
a very free feeling.

16 Diane Keaton and Woody Allen with their analysts in *Annie Hall*

SB: *In the film* Alvy *makes a visit to Los Angeles to see his friend Rob (Tony Roberts) who has now become a television star. They visit the TV studio with the laughing machine much to Alvy's contempt. And somewhere towards the end of his stay, he utters, 'I'm getting my chronic LA nausea.' What are your personal views on that town and the film industry there?*

WA: Well, the film industry is, of course, not great. Because it's an industry which, for the most part, makes pretty expensive, junky films and very little of any quality comes out of there. It is aimed towards a mass market and young people, so most of the stuff that comes out is junk. And the good people are always struggling to get their works done properly. But Los Angeles is fine. It's just not to my taste. People think that I hate it, but that's not really so. I have many friends out there. I just don't like that kind of light. I don't like sunshine. And I don't like it where everything is spread out and you need a car to go to every place. It doesn't have a cosmopolitan feeling or a cosmopolitan quality, the type that I'm used to, like London or Paris or Stockholm or Copenhagen or New York. There it's more a suburban feeling. So I'm not comfortable. I like to be able to walk out of my house and have the whole city around me, pavement to walk on and stores and places to go to. Once you're used to New York or Paris or something, it's very hard to get used to a city like Los Angeles. That's why I always tease it. Also between the television industry and the film industry so much of what comes out of there is in bad faith. It's done for the sake of exploitation. It's not that bad things don't come out of every place, of course. But so much of what goes on there is related to low ambitions – money, fame and things like that.

SB: *Juliette Lewis says in* Husbands and Wives *that 'Life doesn't imitate art, it imitates bad television.'*

WA: Yes, I think that's true.

SB: *Do you think that this kind of non-metropolitan city creates the kind of pictures that are being made there? LA is also quite an impersonal city and people seem to live a more superficial life there.*

WA: Yes, I think that in the United States there are only a handful of film-makers that are really in the serious business of making movies. The others are doing what they call 'projects'. It takes them a long time to do them. They are preceded by lots of meetings, lunch meetings and dinner meetings and meetings with writers, meetings with directors, meetings with actors. Their life centres around the pre-production ceremonies. And finally they make the picture, and it's usually commercial nonsense. There are few film-makers there who are serious and who are trying to make interesting films and to take risks where the primary concern is not to make money.

SB: *Well, some of the most gifted and interesting among contemporary American film-makers do live in other places than Los Angeles and also tell stories from those places, like you and Martin Scorsese here in New York, or Gus Van Sant who makes films in Portland or David Mamet in Chicago. A director like Barry Levinson started out in Baltimore, making films from and about that town, which is his native town.*

WA: Yes, and Francis Coppola is working in San Francisco. The films by these people are more hand-made as opposed to the factory feeling you get from the films made in California. Not all the time, but mostly. John Cassavetes, of course, was an exception, but he also had to struggle hard to get his films made.

SB: *How come you chose Paul Simon, the singer, for an acting part in* Annie Hall*?*

WA: I was looking for a fresh look. Somebody interesting that you didn't see acting very often. I think even that it might have been Marshall Brickman who suggested Paul Simon for the part. And it seemed a very good idea.

SB: *During the visit to Los Angeles you have Alvy say, 'They just give out lots of awards, I can't believe that. "The greatest fascist-dictator: Adolf Hitler"!'* Annie Hall *got awarded a couple of Oscars. What do you think of the Academy Awards and other kind of awards?*

WA: It's hard to imagine competition between books or films or works of art. Who's to say which is better? I think it would be better if the film industry met each year and in a dignified way just said, 'These are our favourite films of the year! We're all voting and these are our five favourite films.' Not *the* best film. Because all the films nominated are so different, each in its own way. The Academy Awards are particularly grubby, because people pressure you to vote for them and their friends. Films and candidates are campaigned for and ads are taken. There isn't any Best Film of any year. There is no integrity or credibility.

SB: *But apparently it has a great importance for the film industry.*
WA: Commercially, yes. But it's of a momentary commercial importance. An actor wins an Academy Award and he's hot for a year. Then he
does a picture and that picture doesn't do that well . . . he's finished! All
the heat is off.

SB: *It's very seldom that a film of yours is in a foreign festival. Is that a
choice you've made?*
WA: I sometimes show them at festivals, but I've never, ever had one in
competition. I don't feel that I want to compete with them. They're not
made for competition, they're just made for people to enjoy or not. So
I'm happy to send them to Cannes or to Venice and various other film
festivals. I've never been to any of these festivals, but I understand that
they've gotten very political. It's like what happened with the Olympics.
What started out as a very pure, good idea has degenerated into an
opportunity for exploitation.

SB: Annie Hall *ends with a resumé. Why did you choose that ending?*
WA: Because the editor, Ralph Rosenblum, and I tried to think how to
best end the film. And we thought that what felt best was a tie-up,
bringing it up to where it began. And that's what we did. But that's
something that we added later. It was not in the script. Actually it was in
the original murder mystery script which became *Annie Hall*.

SB: *But then you end the film very beautifully with about thirty seconds
of empty street scenery.*
WA: Right, after Annie and I depart from one another.

SB: *Do you remember why you wanted this ending for the film?*
WA: Well, I was shooting that scene with Diane Keaton, and when
you're shooting on natural locations in the street and you're doing a
momentous moment in a movie, like the opening shot or the closing shot
or something that's really significant for a film, I used to look at the scene
and see what would be the most I can get out of it for a dramatic or
emotionally satisfying ending. And here it seemed to me, since all I had
was the street and the little café, was to let the two of them vanish and
just let the street life flow on. It was some instinctive sense that I had. I
felt that it sucked the audience up and gave an intensified feeling. And
later when I saw it with the music, it seemed correct, so I left it that way.

SB: *In* Annie Hall *we very briefly see a couple of actors for the first time who later have become very well-known. One is Sigourney Weaver whom we see from a distance as Alvy's new date outside the movie theatre. Another one is Jeff Goldblum who appears at the Hollywood party. This brings to mind one actor who appeared in* Bananas, *probably for the first time in films as well, an actor who later on became very famous and popular, Sylvester Stallone. Isn't he the hood on the subway train? Is this a mere chance that these actors had their first small parts in films of yours?*

WA: Well, Sigourney was good immediately. When I saw her she was a young actress and she was instantly very good and I wanted to use her. Sylvester Stallone was a different matter entirely. I wanted two tough guys, and these two guys come. One is Sylvester Stallone and one is another. And I looked at them and said, 'This is not what I want. These guys are not very dangerous-looking.' But they said, 'No, please, give us a chance! Let us change our costume, let us change our hair. Please!' So I said OK. It took five minutes. They came back and they looked great. I never forgot that, because my own lack of prescience would have done me in there, had they not showed me the correct way.

SB: *But I guess that must have been his first acting part.*

WA: I'm sure it was. Now when you see that film playing in small towns, it says: *Bananas* with Woody Allen and Sylvester Stallone.

CHAPTER 9

Interiors

ALVY: You know, I'm, I'm obsessed with death, I think. Big subject with me, yeah.

ANNIE: Yeah?

ALVY: I've a very pessimistic view of life. You should know this about me if we're gonna go out, you know. I feel that life is divided up into the horrible and the miserable. Those are the two categories. The horrible would be like, I don't know, terminal cases, you know? And blind people, crippled . . .

ANNIE: Yeah.

ALVY: I don't know how they get through life. It's amazing to me. You know, and the miserable is everyone else. That's all. So when you go through life you should be thankful that you're miserable, because that's . . . You're very lucky . . . to be . . . to be miserable.

ANNIE: U-huh.

(From *Annie Hall*)

STIG BJÖRKMAN: *This, I believe, was a film that you had planned for a long time. Did it meet with resistance or difficulties, because it was a serious story, a drama?*

WOODY ALLEN: From the studio? No. I was working for very enlightened and very liberal people. Arthur Krim was the head of United Artists at that time. He just said, 'You've made some funny films, and now you feel like you want to try something else. You've earned it. Go ahead!'

SB: *Maybe the success with* Annie Hall *and the Academy Awards helped?*

WA: Right. So they allowed me to do the film, and I did. It was a mixed critical success here. It opened up, and there were some critics that liked it very much. But this was also the first time that I came up with a significant amount of negative press.

SB: *Why do you think? Was it because* Interiors *was such an unexpected venture of yours? That you'd made a dramatic film?*

WA: Yes, people were so shocked and so disappointed with me that I broke my contract with them, my implicit deal with them. And particularly this kind of a drama. It's not the kind of drama Americans like very much anyhow. You know, what passes for drama in the States anyhow. What passes for drama in America is something, more television style, soap opera kind of things. *Interiors* was not the usual kind of affair. So not only were people annoyed at me – their lovable comic figure – for having the pretension to try something like this, but giving them *this kind of a drama* as well. They felt there was a solemnity to it, which I like in films. And then, let's not forget, this was the first time I did a drama, so my lack of skill and experience didn't help me. I'm not saying that *Interiors* is any Shakespearean masterpiece. It was my first one. But they were not charitable. There were people who accused me of bad faith.

SB: *What was your reaction towards this?*

WA: *Interiors* was what I wanted to do and the best I could do at the time. I wanted to start to work in dramatic films a little bit. I didn't want to work in them most of the time, but I wanted it to be part of my production. And I was not going to start off with any half-hearted measure. I was not going to do a little bit of a drama or a conventional drama or a commercial drama. I wanted to go for the highest kind of drama. And if I failed, I failed. That's OK. But what I was aiming for, if I had made it, would have been very, very significant. I'm not saying I made it, but the ambition was good, the ambition was high. So that's the way I felt about it and I was sorry that people didn't accept it, that it received as much criticism as it did.

SB: *But did you feel hurt or disappointed over the reaction at that time?*

WA: I felt it was a shame.

SB: *Do you usually read the reviews of your films?*

WA: No. I used to read them all the time, when my first four or five films came out. I just thought that was the thing to do, and I had to find the quotes for the ads and so on. And then I started to think, that the less I know about what people think of my work, the better off I am. I should just keep my nose to the grind-stone and do the films I want to do. And put them out there. If people like them – great! It does not mean that I'm a genius, just because some newspaper writer says, 'This is a work of genius!' And it doesn't mean that I'm an idiot, if he says I'm an idiot. Just forget about what people say! I told the studio, 'Don't call me on the phone and tell me who's coming and how many people. I don't care!' And that's what I've done for many years now. I finish a film, it's over, and then – goodbye. I remember when *Manhattan* opened, I wasn't even in New York. The downside to that is that you don't quite get a fulfilled, finished feeling. Other people finish a film. It's over and it's successful. They read the reviews. They have a party. There's some kind of relief. For me it's like stamping out cookies. I finish a film and I go on to the next one.

SB: *But then, I presume, you have people close to you who can forward similar reactions and feelings to you. You talked before about Diane Keaton and how much her judgements meant to you. But I guess there are others that you trust and rely upon in a similar way?*
WA: Yes, and that happens before the film comes out usually.

SB: *Then, nowadays, you are usually already at work on a new film when a film of yours comes out.*
WA: Yes, that happens to me all the time. I'm even thinking of my *next* film, when I have some spare time during shooting. I already think about what would be interesting to do next. I'm interested in the work. I'm not interested in the immediate reception. The rewards come automatically. The salary comes.

SB: Interiors *starts very beautifully and suggestively with the empty picture of the house by the beach and the rooms of the villa, which gives the film a base of reflection. These images are like still-life pictures.*
WA: Yes, I wanted to set a certain rhythm at the beginning.

SB: *Then, when the acting scenes start, we see scenes with the sisters by a window. And the film ends with similar compositions with the sisters by a window. These twin images provide the film with an elliptic structure.*
WA: At one point we thought of calling the movie *Windows*. And Gordon Willis, when he directed his own first film, called it *Windows*.

SB: *Then comes this very unexpected picture of the father (E. G. Marshall) by his office window with his back towards us giving a kind of very short resumé of the story. At what stage did you decide to put him there in the film?*
WA: That scene was to come much later in the film. But when I was

editing the film, the editor Ralph Rosenblum and I were looking at it, and we thought, 'Wouldn t it be interesting to stick it right in the front? It might give us an interesting effect.'

SB: *Do you remember why? Was it out of a psychological reason, or...?*

WA: It just got the film off to an interesting start for some reason. I remember when we thought of it, we just said that that scene would really be great if it played the third or fourth cut of the picture. We put it there and we looked at it there, and thought, 'Well, what will that do to the end of the picture?' But then we found that it was no problem, so we left it there. That's happened to me before on other films, where a scene meant for another part of a picture is moved elsewhere. I just get a sudden idea. I could be walking down the street while I'm editing, and suddenly rearrangements like this enter my mind. And it's great. It gives a certain extra vitality, because it's spontaneous.

SB: *Much of the story revolves around the mother, Eve. Even when she's not there, her presence in the life and actions of the others is very strong. Her husband, Arthur, says about her: 'She'd created a world around us that we existed in ... where everything had its place, where there was always a kind of harmony. A great dignity ... It was like an ice palace.'*

WA: Yes, she's definitely the central character.

SB: *She is a very domineering mother figure, and in many of your films you've had a succession of very strong mothers. Why does she occupy such a great interest in your films? Is this, do you think, a specific American phenomenon?*

WA: No, the fathers are strong American dramatic figures as well. I've just been more comfortable in recent years with female characters. So mothers have loomed more potently in my films. But I wouldn't mind writing a film about a strong father.

SB: *Was your mother a very strong figure in your life as well?*

WA: No. She's alive. She was fine. She is pleasant. I'm friendly with her. Both my father and my mother live very near me. I guess you can say, she was a very typical mother. A little too strict maybe, but basically nice.

SB: *Here in* Interiors *the mother is impersonated by Geraldine Page.*
WA: She was at that time our greatest actress in that age group. And she seemed perfect for the part. She's very dynamic and expressive and very refined. In general, I like to trust the actors; when an actor is doing something that's good and meaningful, I just like to leave the camera on them and let them be there and not bother them. And Geraldine Page was that kind of an actress, somebody to trust.

SB: *Her environs are also very important and they reflect her character to a great deal.*
WA: I wanted the Geraldine Page character to have everything harmonious and cool. And just the right amount of furniture. No more. And when this poor man who has been living with her for years finally breaks out, he picks a completely different kind of wife. A much more vital one. I felt that the daughter Joey played by Mary Beth Hurt was in the worst predicament of all, because Joey had no talent. She was full of feelings, but she had no way of expressing them. She is a victim of this terrible mother. I had a feeling myself, when the mother died at the end and Joey got this kiss of life from this other mother, that she was reborn and that there would be more hope for her in the future.

SB: *There is a scene where Joey unconsciously addresses Pearl, the father's new wife, played by Maureen Stapleton and says, 'Mother'. And Pearl answers, 'Yes. You said "Mother" and I said "Yes".' This of course foreshadows the end.*
WA: Yes, at that point Pearl is becoming the mother.

SB: *Then you also present Maureen Stapleton all the time in very vivid colours. For instance, she wears a flamboyant red dress when she's introduced to the family the first time.*
WA: Right. She likes to eat steak and she does magic tricks and things like that. I think I could remake that film now and make it a success.

SB: *But are you unhappy with the film?*
WA: No, I'm not unhappy with it, but I think after seeing it, I would have done different things. Just from a technical point of view, a structural point of view. Just out of pure writer's instinct now I would have brought Maureen Stapleton into the story earlier. I could have figured out how to do that.

SB: *When the father decides to break the news about leaving the family, it's quite a violent revelation. He does it openly at the breakfast table. Why did you choose this violent confrontation between him and all the members of the family at the same time?*

WA: I had heard of an incident like that, where a husband at the breakfast table, just very nicely, in a very gentlemanly way, said that he was finally going to leave. And the mother left the table and went to her room and killed herself. Now in *Interiors* I didn't want to take it that far. But I was imitating that incident.

SB: *It reminds me of the opening of* Husbands and Wives, *where the one couple, Sally and Jack, very casually inform their friends that they are going to divorce. The interesting thing of course is how Judy reacts there.*

WA: In *Husbands and Wives* I tried to make the characters always contradicting themselves. Always saying one thing, but doing something else. Or pretending to feel one way, but you see that they don't feel that way.

SB: *Most of the characters in* Interiors *are intellectuals. The sisters, apart from the youngest one, who is a soap opera actress, as well as their husbands. And they all have different hang-ups and neuroses. Did you think that this was (or still is) typical of New York intellectuals?*

WA: No, and I didn't think of this as a generically New York film. I was more interested in the symbolic story. This is one of those things that takes place more metaphysically. I mean, I didn't locate this in New York in any way that exploited the city. I wanted it to be in the realm of the subconscious and the unconscious.

SB: *We talked about Maureen Stapleton and her colourful appearance. There is a scene in the film in a church where Geraldine Page suddenly sees a lot of red candles and she smashes them. Did you see this as a kind of symbolic action where she tries to smash the other woman out of her life?*

WA: No, that was just a gesture of great upset. I had not seen that as anything beyond her becoming very emotionally upset.

SB: *In* Interiors *there are three sisters. In* Hannah *as well. Is this by chance or are you interested in these kinds of big family set-ups and their close relationships?*

WA: Yes, I'm interested in the relationships that women have with other women. When Sidney Lumet made *The Group*, I couldn't wait to go and see that film. I was looking forward to it so much. I also like *Cries and Whispers* for this reason. I love the relationship of women to women.

SB: *Then they could be of different kinds, friends as well as relatives?*
WA: Yes, they could be friends, but the relationship between sisters is also very interesting to me.

SB: *In* Interiors *the middle sister, Joey, is the most complex character. Why did you choose Mary Beth Hurt for this part?*
WA: Juliet Taylor introduced me to her, and the minute she walked into the room, the second I set eyes on her, she was exactly what I envisioned. Juliet just knew her, and she's a wonderful actress.

SB: *You mentioned before that many critics saw her as your alter ego in the film. Why, do you think?*
WA: I think because they dressed her in my kind of clothing, in tweed jackets and grey sweaters, things that I wear a lot. I couldn't see any other reason.

SB: *Also, she is very much in the centre of the action. When Pearl is being introduced, for example, you concentrate very much of the attention on Joey.*
WA: Right, because she's competitive.

SB: *Joey's been 'Daddy's favourite' and now he's got a new favourite.*
WA: Yes, but Pearl is the breath of spring in the movie. She represents vitality and life and vibrancy. And it turns out that Joey is the one that Pearl saves. She saves her from the water in the end and gives her mouth-to-mouth resuscitation.

SB: *And do you think that Joey's life can change after this?*
WA: Hopefully. She's the one that I think has a chance. The others, I think, are too far gone. One is a superficial actress and the other one a cold artist who hides behind her talent. And Joey is potentially real, having no big talent but human feelings. If Joey had had a different mother, she'd been fine. What they're all lacking is some warmth. So, yes, I think she gets a new mother in the end, and this mother is going to make a difference in her life.

SB: *Pearl also becomes a critic of this family's life. During the discussion of the Algerian play at the dinner table, for instance, her remarks are very direct and uncomplex.*

WA: Yes, she's vulgar. In the best sense. Her son paints those terrible pictures in Las Vegas, those clowns on black velvet. But she also willingly admits that these paintings are trash. She's a vulgarian, but alive. Very natural, very real. Everybody else is very superior and supercilious, very ordered.

SB: *Interiors was the first film where you don't have a part. Did you ever consider acting in the film? I mean, you could have played any of the parts which Richard Jordan or Sam Waterston play.*

WA: No, I didn't consider that for a second.

SB: *Was this because of the character of the film?*

WA: Yes, because I'm a comedian, a comic actor and I don't know if I could do that kind of thing. I think the audience would have laughed as soon as they saw me. It just never occurred to me.

SB: *There is almost no music in* Interiors. *Instead you have more of a kind of atmospheric soundtrack, the sound of the waves, of the wind, and so on.*

WA: Again, I was in that period, just coming off *Annie Hall*, where I still was not firm about the musical direction that I wanted to go in. So in *Annie Hall* I used no music and I didn't do that in *Interiors* either. At that point I was in a transitional phase from composed music to the recordings of 'my kind of music'. So I felt, as this picture is a serious picture, it didn't need any music. But there's ambience in it throughout anyway.

SB: *The scene with the mother's suicide has a dream-like quality. One wonders, is this really happening or is it a dream we're witnessing?*

WA: I wanted it real, but I wanted her state of mind to be disassociated. I wanted to get something that fit that bill. She actually does commit suicide, but I also wanted us to get a sense of her state of emotions at the time.

SB: *We've talked about Joey, but Renata, the oldest sister, who is played by Diane Keaton, is quite a complex character as well. At some point, she expresses her anxiety over the risk of becoming like her mother. She seems to be the very stable one in the film, the one who Joey adores and looks up to. But she's not that kind of person.*

17   Diane Keaton, Kristin Griffith and Mary Beth Hurt in *Interiors*

WA: No. She's talented. But she's also selfish like her mother. Her talent is not the saving grace that people think it is.

SB: *But what do you think of her? Is she a positive and nice person and sister, or is she a not so nice sister, especially in connection to Joey?*
WA: Renata is lucky, because she has her talent and she has what Joey doesn't have, that is, a means of expressing all these painful things that trouble us in life. But she's selfish. Because to me, artists frequently are selfish. They need time alone, they need discipline and they need sometimes to behave with people in ways that are important for them but are not really very nice for other people. And Renata has come to the realization early on that her art is not going to save her, and it's bothering her. I sometimes feel that art is the intellectual's religion. Some artists think that art will save them, that they will be immortalized through their art, they will live on through their art. But the truth of the matter is, art doesn't save you. Art to me has always been entertainment for intellectuals. Mozart or Rembrandt or Shakespeare are entertainers on a very, very high level. It's a level that brings a great sense of excitement, stimulation and fulfilment to people who are sensitive and cultivated. But it doesn't save the artist. I mean, it doesn't profit Shakespeare one iota that his plays have lived on after him. He would have been better off if he was alive and his plays were forgotten.

SB: *Do you feel this conflict yourself to a great extent, the need for isolation and withdrawal from other people?*
WA: Well, I don't have the problem, because I *am* in isolation. But I have felt the same problem Renata has felt, that when you're younger, you think, I will be an artist and it will save me. Maybe you don't think in those words, but the thought is there somehow. In *Stardust Memories* I used the term 'Ozymandias Melancholia'. That's a symptom I've invented that describes that phenomenon specifically, the realization that your works of art will not save you and will mean nothing down the line. Eventually, there won't be any universe, so even all the works of Shakespeare and all the works of Beethoven will be gone. And I've experienced that and Renata is experiencing that, the sense of 'What's it going to mean?'

SB: *In the film Renata says to Joey that 'Creation is very delicate. It needs isolation.' Do you share this view?*
WA: I gave her that line, because I wanted her to be selfish. But I don't

18   Maureen Stapleton and E. G. Marshall in *Interiors*

share that, because to me it's not so delicate. I think there are artists for whom it's delicate. For instance, take someone like Kafka. He couldn't stand any noise. It was a very delicate muse that he had. There are other people like Fellini who thrive in chaos. There's nothing delicate about it at all. He has hundreds of people around him all the time, and out comes a beautiful work of art. So, it's different. But with Renata it's delicate, because she's selfish and she doesn't care about Joey, she doesn't care about her husband. She cares about . . . herself.

SB: *But she's anguished as well. I'm thinking about her visions, the dream she has. The dream with the entwining and menacing branches of the tree.*

WA: Yes, but she's only afraid for herself, of her own mortality. Here comes also my view upon nature, that when you look close at nature, you find that nature's not your friend. It's marked by murderous and cannibalistic competition. So Renata is having these deep visions toward nature and seeing what nature really is and what life really is and that her art is not going to save her. It's not going to protect her. Later in the film Renata and her youngest sister, Flyn, are talking about Flyn's old movies appearing again on television, where there is a kind of pseudo-sense of immortality, when in fact those films and Flyn's appearance in them don't mean a thing. I've made this joke before, that I'm not interested in living on in the hearts of my countrymen, I'd rather live on in my apartment! And that's really what I feel about it. In *Interiors* that theme occurs a few times. That really what we're all talking about is the tragedy of perishing. Ageing and perishing. It's such a horrible, horrible thing for humans to contemplate, that they don't contemplate it. They start religions, they do all kinds of things not to contemplate it. They try to block it out in every way. But sometimes you can't block it out. And when you can't block it out, you can either go the route that Renata goes, where she tries to express certain things in poetry. But if you're not lucky, if you're someone like Joey, you don't know what to do. You can never find yourself. But even someone like Renata, who is luckier than Joey, eventually comes to yet another conclusion, that even though she's an artist and she has some ways of expressing these painful ideas, even the art is not going to save her. She's going to perish like everybody else. Even if her poems are read a thousand years from now.

SB: *This, I think, is a very recurrent theme in your films, this fear of perishing. Maybe that's a reason why you've inhabited your films with so*

many people of different ages, never excluding the old ones.
WA: There is no other fear of significant consequence. All other fears,
all other problems one can deal with. Loneliness, lack of love, lack of
talent, lack of money, everything can be dealt with. In some way, there
are ways to cope. You have friends that can help you, you have doctors
that can help you. But perishing is what it's all about. I firmly believe the
ideas in *The Denial of Death*, the book by Ernst Becker that I recommended to Diane Keaton's Annie in *Annie Hall*. Because *The Denial of
Death* is a most interesting book about this theme, about death, but in an
extremely well-thought-out way.

CHAPTER 10

Manhattan

ISAAC: 'Chapter One. He adored New York City. He idolized it all out of proportion.' No, make that: 'He romanticized it all out of proportion. Now . . . to him no matter what the season was, this was still a town that existed in black-and-white and pulsated to the great tunes of George Gershwin.' Ahhh, now let me start this over. 'Chapter One. He was too romantic about Manhattan as he was about everything else. He thrived on the hustle and bustle of the crowds and the traffic.

'To him, New York meant beautiful women and street-smart guys who seemed to know all the angles.' Nah, no . . . corny, too corny for my taste . . . I mean, let me try and make it more profound. 'Chapter One. He adored New York City. To him, it was a metaphor for the decay of contemporary culture. The same lack of individual integrity to cause so many people to take the easy way out was rapidly turning the town of his dreams in . . .' No, it's gonna be too preachy. I mean, you know . . . let's face it, I wanna sell some books here.

'Chapter One. He adored New York City, although to him, it was a metaphor for the decay of contemporary culture. How hard it was to exist in a society desensitized by drugs, loud music, television, crime, garbage.' Too angry. I don't wanna be angry. 'Chapter One. He was as . . . tough and romantic as the city he loved. Behind his black-rimmed glasses was the coiled sexual power of a jungle cat.' I love this. 'New York was his town. And it always would be.'

(From Manhattan)

STIG BJÖRKMAN: *Why did you choose* Manhattan *to be shot in wide-screen and black-and-white?*
WOODY ALLEN: Because Gordon Willis and I were having dinner one night and we were thinking that it would be fun to work in

black-and-white and it would be fun to work in anamorphic, in real wide-screen. We were talking about how they did all those war pictures with tanks and aeroplanes, and then we thought that it would be very interesting to do an intimate picture like that. I started thinking about it, and then I wrote *Manhattan* and thought, that's the way we should do it. It will give us two things. It will give us a great look at New York City, which is sort of one of the characters in the film. And we will also be able to see what interesting problems and interesting creations you'd come up with shooting a movie like that.

SB: *Your character in the film, Isaac, claims that he cannot function in any other place than New York. Many people think that this applies to you as well. Is this true or is it merely a myth?*
WA: Well, it's partially true. I mean, it depends where the other place is and how long I have to be there. If it's a big city, like Paris, London, Stockholm, a real cosmopolitan place, then I could think of living there for a while. But mostly I like and prefer New York.

SB: *Could you consider making films in some other part of the world besides New York?*
WA: I could consider the idea of going to Europe and make a film. I wouldn't mind that, if the story is right for it.

SB: *The beginning of* Manhattan *is very beautiful and the montage of images definitely expresses a love for the city. This presentation ends with a picture of the neon sign for the restaurant Elaine's. Is that one of your favourite places?*
WA: I've hung out at Elaine's on and off, mostly on, for many years.

SB: *And* Manhattan *was only shot on location? The interiors as well?*
WA: It was all location, yes.

SB: *In the beginning Isaac tells his friend Yale (Michael Murphy), 'You shouldn't ask me for advice. When it comes to relationships with women, I ought to get the August Strindberg award!' You have a couple of characters with similar dilemmas in your films. In the first one,* Take the Money and Run, *for instance, you have the main character, Virgil, say, 'I'm nervous in the company of women. I've a tendency to dribble.' Do you think this is a common dilemma?*
WA: No, not necessarily. I just think that the character that I like to play

19   Mariel Hemingway and Woody Allen in *Manhattan*

suffers in this way. It's one of the areas that I might get some laughs out of. But I don't think it speaks for everybody. I'm sure it speaks for some people. But certainly it speaks for the character that's easiest for me to act in the movie.

SB: *Later on in the film, when Isaac goes shopping with his young girlfriend Tracy (Mariel Hemingway), he says, 'I'm old-fashioned. I don't believe in extramarital relationships. I think people should mate for life, like pigeons or Catholics.' Is this an opinion you share with your character?*

WA: Yes, I think that is the ideal. I definitely think so, though hard to achieve. But that is what everybody tries to achieve, a deep, lasting, permanent relationship with a single other person of the opposite sex. But it's easier said than done. One must be very lucky.

SB: *American morals in particular seem to be very severe and rigid when it comes to the question of fidelity. That's my experience from visiting the States and also from seeing American films. An eventual extramarital affair seems to be totally catastrophic for any relationship. In Europe we might deal with such a situation differently. It needn't always lead to the same catastrophic consequences. Do you think this has to do with the specific American morality?*

WA: Yes, I think in Europe when a man or a woman is having an affair or the husband has a mistress, it's not an unheard-of phenomenon. But here it's very, very frowned upon. So one tries to have a marriage with fidelity in it. And that's it. It's hard to do, but that's what we try.

SB: *In the more bourgeois American settings it also seems that people marry very young, when they're eighteen, nineteen, twenty. And I guess this is a result of the same kind of morals. Because you shouldn't live together unless you're not married.*

WA: Yes, that's the American dream. The American dream is, you grow up and you meet some woman or you meet some man and you fall in love – and you get married. And then you raise children and you're faithful. That's the American dream in terms of relationships. Of course reality does not always allow this to come true.

SB: *There is a scene where Isaac visits his former wife's apartment. He comes to pick up his little son, I think. And Isaac and Jill (Meryl Streep) start a quarrel. This is very beautifully staged, a very long and nicely*

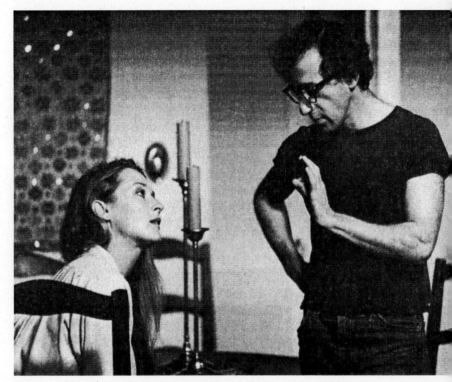

20 Meryl Streep and Woody Allen in *Manhattan*

choreographed scene, where you allow the actors to sometimes leave the frame and disappear from sight. Do you remember how you prepared and staged this scene?

WA: Well, Gordon and I always used to figure out ways of getting the actors off camera and then getting them back again, on and off all the time. And that's what we did with Meryl at the time. I remember the fun of doing that. She's a wonderful actress, and it was fun to work like that. We used that style in many other films.

SB: *Yes, I remember another similarly staged scene between you and Tony Roberts in* A Midsummer Night's Sex Comedy, *where this method is used more for a comic effect. You're backing up some staircase, disappearing from the picture and coming back again.*

WA: Yes, we used to do that all the time. We first started it in *Annie Hall*, in the scene where we're dividing up the books and moving out of the house. Annie and Alvy are talking and arguing, and then I leave the frame to get some books. Then she leaves the frame and there's nobody at all in picture! After this we started fooling around with that kind of staging a lot, in a lot of films. And in *Husbands and Wives* the camera is just fighting for its life to keep the characters in frame.

SB: *When do you decide to stage a scene like this? Is this on the set or do you prepare it beforehand?*

WA: That's strictly on the set.

SB: *You're very fond of using wide shots in* Manhattan. *Take for instance the very beautiful scene at dawn with you and Diane Keaton by the bridge. I think this scene was used for the poster for the film as well.*

WA: Yes, I think wide shots like this give a very special atmospheric quality.

SB: *Talking about composition, I would like to discuss the scenes in the planetarium.*

WA: Part of the planetarium we built. It's three-quarters the real planetarium, but a few little things we made ourselves.

SB: *This sequence in particular is very beautifully and very carefully framed.*

WA: Right, it's very stylish.

SB: *How do you proceed when you decide the framing of a scene? How much do you discuss the framing with the cameraman? And does this differ from cameraman to cameraman?*

WA: It doesn't differ from cameraman to cameraman, but it's all very carefully planned out from that point of view. If the sequence is going to be stylish like that, we're both constantly looking into the camera and going up to the actors and moving them and looking into the camera again and rearranging. It's a very cooperative procedure. It just takes a long time and it's tedious work. But it's the same way whether it's with Sven [Nykvist] or with Carlo [Di Palma] or with Gordon [Willis]. Usually the way I like to work from that point of view is to come in with the cameraman and no actors. We look around and I think, 'What if I have them come in here and we play in this area?' And the cameraman does a general lighting job. Then I bring in the actors and I show them where I want them to stand and how I want them to move. And the cameraman gets a little more specific. And then we shoot.

SB: *When you're acting in a scene yourself, do you have a stand-in so you can check your own positions in the scene?*

WA: Yes, sure.

SB: *An actor who later on has bit parts in some of your films appears here for the first time, Wallace Shawn, who plays the ex-husband of Mary (Diane Keaton). I just knew him from Louis Malle's* My Dinner With André. *How come you chose him for the part?*

WA: I've used him over the years. He's a wonderful, wonderful actor. You know, Mary keeps talking to me all the time about her ex-husband and how sexually potent he was. So I wanted to get someone that was not at all what you would think that this person would look like. Juliet Taylor said, 'I know just the person! Do you know Wally Shawn?' And I said, 'No.' So she brought him in, and the second I saw him I thought, 'Absolutely. He's great.'

SB: *You hadn't seen him in anything before? He's a playwright as well, isn't he?*

WA: Yes, but I hadn't seen him in anything. I don't even know if he had done any plays at that time. But he came in, and he was just perfect. He's just a very natural actor. Later on he was in *Radio Days* and *Shadows and Fog*. I will always use him, when I have a chance.

21 Diane Keaton and Woody Allen in *Manhattan*

SB: *Isaac says at one point, 'I can't compromise. I can't look the other way.' Does your character express feelings close to your own here?*
WA: Well, it's hard to compromise for anybody in life. It's a very unpleasant pill to swallow, the pill of compromise.

SB: *I've heard or I've read that you were very uncertain or very unhappy with* Manhattan . . .
WA: . . . when I had finished it? Yes, I'm never happy with my films when I finish them. Just about always. And in the case of *Manhattan* I was so disappointed that I didn't want to open it. I wanted to ask United Artists not to release it. I wanted to offer them to make one free movie, if they would just throw it away.

SB: *Why were you so unhappy with the film?*
WA: I don't know. I had worked on it for a long time and I was just not happy with it. And this has happened to me on any number of films.

SB: *Are you never content when you've finished a film? Don't you ever have the feeling that 'this time I've made it or almost made it'?*
WA: Only on *The Purple Rose of Cairo*. That's the closest I've come to a feeling of satisfaction. After that film I thought, 'Yes, this time I think I got it right where I wanted to get it.'

SB: *And with* Husbands and Wives?
WA: *Husbands and Wives* was one of the more satisfying movies to me. There are still things that I would have written differently, if I could change it. But I can't go back and do anything about it now. But basically this is one of the most satisfying ones.

SB: *When we talked about* Interiors *you mentioned that that was a film you could consider remaking.*
WA: Yes, I think I could have made that film better.

SB: *In what way? In its content or form?*
WA: Both. I would make it a more fluid picture. I believe the way I chose the photography with Gordon Willis contributed to a feeling of coolness about it, which I could improve on. It would be more fun for the audience. And as I said, I would bring in the Maureen Stapleton character earlier in the plot. I think I was a little too reserved. I've had a funny problem over the years in that the films that I like so much are foreign

films. And they have subtitles. So you read them. When I write my dialogue for certain films, I'm almost writing it in a way you would a subtitle rather than human-speak. It's an odd little problem. So for *Interiors* I think I would have loosened up some of the dialogue. I would make it more colloquial and less literary.

SB: *Do you find the film too static, when you see it again?*
WA: I don't see it again, but I felt it was more static than it should be.

SB: *It's funny what you said about the subtitling. Do you think this may be one of the reasons why your films are more popular in Europe than in the United States? That we do read the film as well and get the dialogue in two versions this way? I mean, we hear and understand the dialogue, because most people speak and understand English, but at the same time we get the written text.*
WA: Well, it's interesting. I know subtitles certainly help some of the foreign film-makers here. It's hard to tell about the acting sometimes when it's in a foreign language.

SB: *Talking about foreign films and film-makers, what do you think of Ettore Scola? He's also a film-maker who puts a lot of emphasis on the dialogue and his films are beautifully staged at the same time.*
WA: I've seen some of his films, and I like them. And dialogue is one of the tools that you work with. It's a very complicated tool. It's much easier to make a picture without dialogue. People used to say to me, 'Comedians today in comedy films, they talk and it's easy. Years ago in silent films they had no sound or anything. It's so much easier.' It's like the difference between checkers and chess. It's much simpler to make a film with no dialogue in it and much simpler to make a black-and-white film. Just see the films of Chaplin and Buster Keaton. So, you'll find over the years, there are very few good talking colour comedies. Most great comedies are silent comedies. The next group of great comedies are talking comedies but black-and-white ones. When you get into the colour era, it is very hard to find comedies that are great.

SB: *Which directors, American or foreign, do you think have been the best in creating good dialogue films?*
WA: There are some directors – and their films are not necessarily great films – who are very good at dialogue. Joseph L. Mankiewicz, for example. The dialogue in a movie like *All About Eve* is wonderful.

Cinematically it's a conventional picture, but the dialogue is full of wit and intelligence. If you think of dialogue in a literary way, *All About Eve* is a good example. On the other hand, if you think of dialogue as a function of making people real, then the kind of banal dialogue in Martin Scorsese's pictures is wonderful. It works in creating real human beings, because that's how these kind of people talk. So it depends what function you're using dialogue for. The dialogue in a Scorsese film is not memor-able for its wit or insight, but it's perfect for what it's supposed to do.

SB: *It's a kind of texture.*
WA: Yes, and a perfect one. The dialogue in *All About Eve* is not really real talk, but it's wonderful in its way. *Unfaithfully Yours* by Preston Sturges has also some wonderful dialogue in it. There's some very good dialogue in Hawks' *The Big Sleep*. And Bergman very often has some very beautiful dialogue. In any number of his films.

SB: *And Jean Renoir?*
WA: Oh yes. *The Rules of the Game* is a great dialogue picture. Prob-ably the best.

SB: *Was* Manhattan *your first collaboration with Susan E. Morse, the editor?*
WA: Yes, I think so. She was Ralph Rosenblum's assistant, so I had worked with her before. But then when Ralph and I stopped working together, she called me up and said that she would like to. And I said, 'Fine.' And since then we've been working together.

SB: *And you're always there during the editing of your films?*
WA: Yes, from the first day I ever made a film. Editing is a part of the making of a film. It's so utterly, utterly crucial that it would be like not being there when I film it. I couldn't do it any other way.

SB: *At the end of* Manhattan *Isaac speaks into a tape-recorder where he talks about all the things that make life worth living and you provide him with a lot of examples: 'Well, first, Groucho Marx … the second movement of the Jupiter Symphony. Louis Armstrong. "Potato Blues". Swedish movies, naturally. L'Education sentimentale by Flaubert. Frank Sinatra. Marlon Brando. The fantastic apples of Cézanne. The crab at Sun Wo's.' Are these choices you could or would give yourself as well?*

22 Isaac (Woody Allen) records 'the things that make life worth living'

WA: I could make a much longer list of course, but they would be on my list. Sure.

SB: *Right now are there other persons or phenomena or pieces of art or something that you would add?*
WA: Sure, I could go on indefinitely and make a very long list of things that I like. The Chinese restaurant that I mentioned in the list is no longer there.

SB: *Do you have other restaurants you would add? Do you go around a lot to different places or do you have one or two places you prefer?*
WA: Both. I go around in general, but I hang out at the same places I've always hung out at. Like Elaine's. But I eat out a lot, so I do go to a lot of different restaurants.

CHAPTER 11

Stardust Memories

SANDY: I don't want to make funny movies any more.
They can't force me to. I . . . you know, I don't feel
funny. I look around the world, and all I see is human
suffering.
MANAGER: Human suffering doesn't sell tickets in
Kansas City.
SANDY: Oh!
MANAGER: They want laughs in Kansas City. They've
been working in the wheat fields all day.
(From *Stardust Memories*)

STIG BJÖRKMAN: Stardust Memories *was a kind of revelation for me
when I saw it again recently. I hadn't seen it for many years, but I was
very impressed and moved by it and I liked it very, very much. It is
definitely a film that has grown with time.*
WOODY ALLEN: That was one of my best films, I thought. It was one
of my most stringently criticized films in the United States. I don't know
in Europe, but here certainly. But it was one of my favourites.

SB: *For what was it criticized? For its style, for the content . . . or both?*
WA: Not the style, but the content. They thought that the lead character
was *me*! Not a fictional character, but me, and that I was expressing
hostility toward my audience. And, of course, that was in no way the
point of the film. It was about a character who is obviously having a sort
of a nervous breakdown and in spite of success has come to a point in his
life where he is having a bad time. But the reaction was like, 'So you think
critics are no good, you think the audience is no good.' But I said, no, it's
not me. I guess, if I'd let Dustin Hoffman or some other actor play the
lead, then it would have been much less criticized. I think. It's only
speculation, of course.

sb: *But isn't that a general risk with your films, that the critics or the audience mistake your film character or your film persona for yourself?*

wa: Yes, it's infantile. I can understand that certain segments of the population would do that. But I would think differently of the more educated critics and the more sophisticated audience. But people used to go up to Clark Gable and pick fights with him and say, 'Listen, you think you're so tough . . .' They confuse the character you play with who you are. People tended to think that Humphrey Bogart was so tough, when in fact he was a very educated man. You know, I've never been the character I've played. And Charlie Chaplin was never the tramp or any of his characters. And Jerry Lewis is not the nutty character he impersonated in his films. There are some similar traits, but it's not me. So here they thought it was me, autobiographical to a T. But I think that *Stardust Memories* will be viewed over the years and there will be much less resistance to it.

sb: *At the beginning of the film a studio executive is saying, commenting on the film director you play, 'What does he have to suffer about? Doesn't the man know he's got the greatest gift that anyone could have? The gift of laughter?' Was this line put into the film as a reaction to the reception of* Interiors *previously? Did you get the kind of reaction after* Interiors, *that you should stick to comedy and not try yourself in other fields?*

wa: I did get that reaction. Many people said, why would you want to do a picture like *Interiors* when you can do this kind of picture? I got that too with *September* and *Another Woman*. They said, if you can do a picture like *Hannah and Her Sisters*, why would you do a picture like *September*? But you can't answer those questions.

sb: *Could you tell me something about the opening sequence in the film, the very steamy dream sequence with the two trains and their passengers. Of course, it does remind one of the opening dream scene in Fellini's* 8½ *to a certain extent.*

wa: If I compare those two sequences, there is a complete difference in content. You see, one is a dream and one is a movie sequence. In the Fellini film it is much more personal, it is a dream. And in that dream a man feels that he is being suffocated, his life is being held down. He is stuck in traffic and would like to get out and fly, and then he is pulled down to earth by his accountant and these mundane people. And that's a dream. Mine was metaphorical in a completely different way. Mine has to do with a sense that one thinks one is on . . . a loser's train bound for a bad life with other losers. And then there are other people on another train going in a completely different direction. And this train is full of people who are having fun. They are beautiful and they are rich, and you're on the one with these grimy looking people. And you want to get off your train and get onto that train. You're fighting but you can't get off the train. And in the end both trains wind up in the same garbage dump. So mine was more philosophically metaphoric, whereas in *8½* it was a personal character trait of the lead character in the movie.

SB: *But still, there is a kind of Felliniesque touch about the film. I gather that Fellini is someone you respect or admire.*

WA: Oh, sure! Absolutely. I love his movies. There is a certain group of film-makers whose films I love. Renoir is one, Kurosawa is one, Bergman of course. And Fellini is right up there with them. He's great.

SB: *Would you say that* Stardust Memories *is a film which discusses reality as opposed to fantasy?*

WA: That's one thing in it, but I think that essentially what I wanted to show, as I do in so many of my films, was man's relationship to his mortality. This character who is seemingly rich and chauffeured around and successful and all that . . . he is in his apartment in the beginning of the movie, and his housekeeper brings in this dead rabbit. And he looks at this dead thing and it reminds him of his own mortality. And then the rest of the film takes place in his mind. All of a sudden he's away at this weekend that reviews his life, and you get to know his character, his life, his girlfriends, his sister, his parents, his predicaments. And then at the end of the film his most devoted fan shoots him. But he doesn't die. And he says – if I recall – that he would trade his Academy Award for just one more minute of life. Again it was more philosophical from my point of view. And that was what I was interested in doing.

SB: *In view of the importance that this film has in your body of work and the importance this film has to you personally, did it take you a longer time to conceive the film?*

WA: It took a long time to shoot it. It took six months to shoot. We were forever shooting. It was a complicated film to do, because it was extremely well orchestrated. And there were reshoots on it. Weather problems. It was just a hard film to do.

SB: *It had many different locations as well.*

WA: Yes. Some of them were built.

sb: *The spa-like building where the film festival was held was a real location, I presume?*

wa: That's a church. We took it over, the outside of it. We built the inside. The interiors were studio.

sb: *Somewhere at the beginning of the film you have your character, Sandy the film director, say, 'I don't want to make funny movies any more. They can't force me to. I don't feel funny. I look around the world, and all I see is human suffering.'*

wa: Right, that was important for the character in the movie. But that was not me. I didn't feel that way personally. I felt that I wanted to make comedies, but occasionally I wanted to make a more serious film. But the audience thought, he doesn't want to make any more comedies. You know, they took everything literally in the film.

sb: *Now and then in the film Sandy gets advice or reprimands from various people about what he should or should not do, what kind of films he should make. From his fans or critics, from the policemen, even from the spacemen who say, 'We enjoy your films, specially the early funny ones . . .'*

wa: Yes, he gets these kind of comments about his early films, but he feels that they are just distractions. Trivia and distractions. Of course, these are comments that I have heard as well, but not to the exaggerated degree as expressed in the film.

sb: *In Sandy's apartment there is a big sitting-room. We come back to this setting a couple of times in the film. The first time we see it, one wall is decorated with a huge photograph of the Song My incident. In a flashback later on in the film we see the same wall, but this time it's covered with a huge photograph of Groucho Marx in the same place as the picture from Vietnam. Could you comment on this choice of pictures and their relation to the main character and his life?*

wa: His apartment is really a state of mind for him. And so depending on what phase of life he's in, you can see it reflected in the mural. So, at the beginning of the picture he's having this enormous obsession with human suffering and guilt, guilt over his wealth and guilt over his position and his success. In the flashback he's in a happier time in his life with Charlotte Rampling; it's Groucho and happy times. Then, I believe, there was a picture of Louis Armstrong, wasn't it?

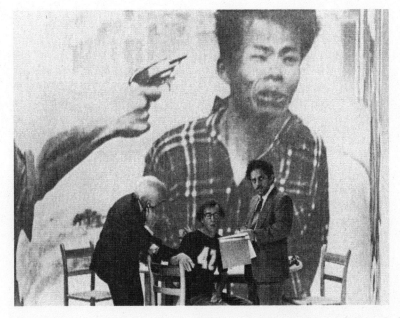

23 'This enormous obsession with human suffering': Woody Allen in
Stardust Memories

SB: *Yes, there was.*

WA: It just reflects a state of mind. (*The telephone rings. Woody goes to answer the phone.*)

SB: *I just heard you answering the phone, and you said 'Woody Allen'. Do you ever use your real name? Or do your friends or relatives use it?*

WA: No! Not even my parents. Because my name was changed so many years ago. It's now . . . forty years ago.

SB: *In seeing* Stardust Memories *it seems that you have a very relaxed attitude towards the medium. Did you feel that at the time when you were doing the picture?*

WA: I felt that I had a command over the technique. I felt that there was a turning point for me, as I said, with *Annie Hall* and the meeting with Gordon Willis. By the time that I made *Stardust Memories*, I felt that the medium was more in my control. And from there on I could use the medium the way I wanted to use it.

SB: *One gets that feeling with* Stardust Memories. *But the realization is bolder here than in* Annie Hall.

WA: Yes, the style of the picture is part of the content as well. But I was much criticized for that picture. It was more than unpopular in the United States. It engendered hostility, enmity.

SB: *Do you think it was because the audience and the critics weren't ready to receive this kind of film from you, or . . .?*

WA: There are two possibilities. Either they're wrong or I'm wrong. That's all I can say. I thought it was an extremely interesting film. The majority of the spectators were quite hostile about it. But I thought that that attitude might change.

SB: *Now, in retrospect, twelve, thirteen years have passed, and one can say that they were wrong.*

WA: I think that people that'll see it and who have seen and liked my other films will see it more relaxed now, and might say, 'It's an interesting film.' But I don't know. It will be curious to see. But till *The Purple Rose of Cairo* that was my favourite film. And everybody said to me, 'Of course it's your favourite film, because nobody liked it. You're protecting your child, even if it's crippled or blind or something.' But I always answered, 'No, I think it's the best work that I have done as a film-maker.' That's how I felt about it. But it's irrelevant. Everything said about it or my other films . . . only time will tell. What is of lasting value will remain, and what is not will not.

SB: *If you hadn't been in the position as you were in as a film-maker, with the economic freedom that your producers guarantee you, the reception of* Stardust Memories *could have been quite a nasty experience. The career of another film-maker might have been quite hurt by this lack of critical and commercial response.*

WA: Yes, because I had two negative reactions in a row. There was *Interiors* and then *Stardust Memories*. But I think what helped me was two things: that I was not in the commercial world and people felt, 'He tries. He tries to extend his limits. He doesn't make a formula film or a safe film. OK, he failed, but let's see what he tries again.' Another possibility, and probably more important, is that I make so many films, that I don't care about individual successes and failures. I made *Interiors* and I made *Stardust Memories*, and before they came out I was working on something else. The film could be a big hit like *Manhattan* or *Hannah*, to me it doesn't matter. I've tried very hard to make my films into a non-event. I just want to work, that's all. Just put the film out for people to see, just keep grinding them out. I hope I'll have a long and healthy life, that I can keep working all the time, and that I can look back in old age and say, 'I made fifty movies and some of them were excellent and some of them were not so good and some were funny . . .' I just don't want to get into that situation that so many of my contemporaries are in, where they make one film every few years and it's a Big Event. That's why I've always admired Bergman. He'd be working quietly on the island and would make a little tiny film and put it out, and then he'd be working on the next one. You know, the work was important. Not the eventual success or failure, the money or the critical reception. What's important is that your work is part of your daily life and you can live decently. You can, as in my case, do the other things I want to do at the same time. I like to play music, I like to see my children, I like to go to restaurants, I like to take walks and watch sports and things. When you're working at the same time, you have a nice, integrated life.

SB: *Many other film-makers have suffered from similar reactions, of misunderstandings or hostility. However, later on their works have been re-evaluated. It has happened to Bergman as well, and quite severely at times. One of his major works and one which he himself values highly,* Sawdust and Tinsel, *got a tremendously insensitive reception in Sweden when it was shown the first time. The critic in the leading Stockholm morning paper, for example, wrote: 'I refuse to perform an ocular inspection of the latest vomit from Mr Bergman.' It was a very harsh and mean reaction. Bergman still remembers this word for word. He must have been very upset at the time, because* Sawdust and Tinsel *was quite an experiment for him.*

WA:　It's amazing. It's a wonderful movie.

SB:　Stardust Memories *is a film that has aged very beautifully; that is, it hasn't aged. The film is like a Chinese box which reveals more and more secrets with every new viewing. Do you think it's a film that needs to be seen a couple of times, and that this is why it was so badly received originally?*

WA:　No, I think the reactions were personal. The audience thought that I was saying in that film that they were fools, that the audience were fools and the critics were fools. They got angry because I *was* that character, Sandy, the film director, and I said that they were stupid for liking my comic films. If I did think that, which I don't, I would be smart enough not to say it in a movie.

SB:　*In the film, one character says to Sandy: 'Comedy is hostility. It's rage. What is it the comedian says when his jokes are going well? "I murdered that audience" . . . "I killed 'em" . . . "They screamed" . . . "I broke 'em up".'*

WA:　Well, that's not my observation. That's a standard observation people have been making for a hundred years. But that's true. There is that element of hostility.

SB:　*Tony Roberts has a part in* Stardust Memories. *In your films from the seventies you have two, one might call them 'buddy actors', supporting characters in whom the main character could confide in. And he was either Tony Roberts or Michael Murphy. Are they personal friends of yours?*

WA:　Yes, though Murph I don't see very much, because he doesn't live in New York. And Tony Roberts, yes, he has always been a friend. I like to work with friends and with people I like, because one spends close time with them.

SB:　*And Charlotte Rampling . . .*

WA:　She's divine! A wonderful actress.

24   Charlotte Rampling in *Stardust Memories*

sb: *There is an interesting scene towards the end of the film, when her character, Dorrie, suffers a nervous breakdown. There you just focus your camera on her face, and her confessions, her thoughts and feelings, directed right into the camera are cut up into short pieces. This method with these split images reminds me somewhat of* Husbands and Wives *with its disrupted character. How did you come to the conclusion of staging and executing the scene like you did?*

wa: I've always admired cubist paintings, and I've thought that it would be interesting if someone was having a nervous breakdown in some way to jump-cut the scene in that way. And this seemed to be the perfect scene for it.

sb: *Was it shot in small segments, so this concept was pre-prepared. Or was it shot in long takes and later cut up in the editing room?*

wa: Both. I shot a few things long and added a few little cosmetics to get that effect. And I thought it was a good scene of hers. She did it beautifully.

sb: *Have you had her in mind for parts in any new movies of yours?*

wa: I have had contact with her, but not with any definite propositions. She is English and you have to cast her just right. She was just right for that part. I mean, she is so beautiful and so sexy and so interesting. She has an interesting neurotic quality. I don't remember now who it was – if it was me – who came up with the idea of using her. But the idea was so good, she was ideal.

sb: *And Marie-Christine Barrault? You had seen her in* Cousin, cousine, *I guess?*

wa: Yes, I thought she would be fun to work with. I liked her very much in *Cousin, cousine.* She had the opposite quality to Charlotte. A very earthy, solid quality. There was nobody in the United States that interested me in that area, that had that quality at the time.

CHAPTER 12

A Midsummer Night's Sex Comedy/Zelig

> ZELIG: It's safe . . . to be like the others.
> EUDORA: Do you want to be safe?
> ZELIG: I want to be liked.
>
> (From *Zelig*)

WOODY ALLEN: I made two pictures at once then, *Zelig* and *A Midsummer Night's Sex Comedy*. I shot them both at the same time.

STIG BJÖRKMAN: *Because* Zelig *took so much more time to complete?*
WA: No, I finished the script of *Zelig*, and while they were budgeting it and doing all the preproduction work, I had nothing to do and I was home and I thought, 'Wouldn't it be fun to do just some little tiny summer picture?' And I wrote the script in two weeks. Just this simple story, like a-day-in-the-country for fun. And I thought, 'Why should I wait? I'll do them both at the same time. What's the difference?' And I did.

SB: *How did you proceed? Were you really working in parallel on the two films?*
WA: Sometimes I went from the one to the other, but I did most of the work on *A Midsummer Night's Sex Comedy* first because of the weather. But *Zelig* overlapped onto it. I mean, I cast them at the same time and I got the locations for them at the same time and they were all ready to go at the same time. I did big chunks of *A Midsummer Night's Sex Comedy* and then I went over to *Zelig* and then back and forth like that. Nobody came to see *A Midsummer Night's Sex Comedy*. One of the critics who likes my work very much said that it was the only trivial picture that I ever made.

SB: *Who was that?*
WA: Richard Schickel from *Time Magazine*. But I wanted it to be light. I

just wanted it to be a small intermezzo with a few laughs. I don't say this was any great picture at all, but in general this atmosphere is something that nobody cares about here in the United States. For me it was fine. I had a great time doing it. I wanted to do for the country what I'd done for New York in *Manhattan*. I wanted to show it in all its beauty.

SB: *Yes, the photography by Gordon Willis is very sumptuous. It has a specific lustre.*
WA: We talked a lot about the colouring. We wanted to film during the most beautiful days in the country that you could think of. We just made it as lovely as we could. And everything was subsumed into that. We made sure that the light was perfect all the time and that the sun was at the exact right place. Finally, by the end of the season we were painting all the leaves green.

SB: *The film can be seen as a kind of comedy of manners. Was this why you wanted to set the film in a historical period?*
WA: Something like that, yes. I just thought, 'Wouldn't it be charming to do some little summer thing from the turn of the century, around that time, 1910 or something, and make it very beautiful? One afternoon with people playing badminton and catching butterflies.' And I thought it was good when I wrote it, and I thought it was good when I made it. But it was not appreciated at all. This one and *September* are my two biggest financial disasters.

SB: *The music by Mendelssohn very much sets the mood for the film. Did this choice of music come before the making of the film or after?*
WA: Before. I knew all the Mendelssohn music and that was the kind of mood I was thinking of. Just light prettiness. But people don't like me in costume. They think that there's a quality about me that's very contemporary, very New York and very urban. So that was one strike against it. And Dustin Hoffman wasn't playing my part. Maybe that would have improved it. But to me it was exactly what I wanted to do. I wanted it to be a bonbon, a little dessert or something.

SB: *You mention Dustin Hoffman and you've mentioned him before. Is he somebody you've considered working with?*
WA: I've always thought, that all the parts that I can play, he can play and probably much better.

SB: *But you've never tried to get him for a part in any of your films?*
WA: No, he's very unavailable. He works for very, very big money, which we don't have. And he's always got some project going.

SB: *Here you work with José Ferrer; he is a kind of rationalist in the film. During his lesson at the start of the film he says, 'Nothing is real but experience.' He reminds me a bit of the characters played by Gunnar Björnstrand in Bergman's films.*
WA: Oh, sure, I can see that. He's completely rational and doesn't believe in ghosts or spirits or anything. And in the end he becomes one.

SB: *This is also the first time that Mia Farrow appears in a film of yours. Did you know her before or did you get to know her during the making of this film?*
WA: I knew her before. I started taking her out during *Stardust Memories*.

SB: *She has since played a variety of different parts in your later films. Which, for you, are her main qualities as an actress?*
WA: She's a good actress. She can play many different roles. She has a very good range. She can play serious roles, she can play comic roles. She's also very photogenic, very beautiful on the screen. She's just a good realistic actress, as opposed to someone like Diane Keaton who is a great comedian, who has a single personality, a very strong single personality. She's always the same, but always great. Like Katharine Hepburn. Mia is different all the time. She's got a wide range for different parts. And no matter how strange and daring it is, she does it well.

SB: *This quality of hers, has that been an inspiration for you when you write your stories? That you might create something totally different for her, and this can be a starting point for a new story?*
WA: Well, the character has never given me the initial spark to start to write a story. The closest I can think of is *Broadway Danny Rose*, but even then I found the character for her to play within the story. But sometimes I've said, 'I've a great story to do, like *Radio Days*. I want to do the old nostalgic radio days, when I was a boy and grew up and radio was so important.' And I think, 'Who can you play in it?' And then I say, 'Why not that kind of thing you like to do, the kind of dumb blonde girl?' And then I develop the character and it changes the story a little bit. To that degree I've written things for her.

25   Woody Allen and Mia Farrow in *A Midsummer Night's Sex Comedy*

SB: *Was the part for Diane Keaton in* Radio Days *created for similar reasons?*

WA: Well, Diane is a very close friend of mine. And she was around and I asked her if she wanted to do anything in the movie, sing a song or something. And she said, 'Sure!'

SB: *Where was* A Midsummer Night's Sex Comedy *shot?*

WA: In a place called Pocantico Hills. About forty minutes from here.

SB: *The house, was it an existing house or constructed for the film?*

WA: It was built. I picked it out of a magazine and said, 'Build this!' The interiors were in the house as well. We built a complete house.

SB: *Does it still exist?*

WA: It was sold to somebody. They, of course, had to do a lot of fixings on it, because when we built it it didn't adhere to the building code. But the company sold it to somebody, and he strengthened it and made it into a house.

SB: *You were working on* Zelig *at the same time. I'd like to ask you about names, how you name your characters. In different ways the names can characterize a person, influence their personality.*

WA: Yes, that's an eccentricity of mine. It's an important thing to me. For the main characters, not for the subsidiary characters. The main characters I always try to name before I begin anything. It's always important to me what I name them. The other characters I name the shortest possible names, so when I type I can go quicker.

SB: *Could you give some example?*

WA: It's how it feels. It's completely emotional. Emotionally some names just feel right and other names feel wrong. But it's very important to me that I have all the names worked out carefully, that I'm happy with the names, before I begin to write the script.

SB: *Do you ponder a long time before you decide a certain name for yourself?*

WA: Sometimes. Sometimes it comes easily, other times nothing feels right and it takes a while. I like my own names to be light. In general, my names are easy to pronounce: Alvy, Ike, Gabe, Sandy. They're light names, they're colloquial.

SB: *So where did the name 'Zelig' come from?*

WA: It just rolled off my tongue as I was writing. I just named the character Leonard Zelig, and it sounded a perfectly fine name. But I never thought of titling the movie *Zelig*. That was a long, long afterthought. We had many other titles for that movie, titles that were actually filmed. *The Cat's Pyjamas* was one, because that's an expression of the 1920s and 1930s. When something is really terrific, that's the cat's pyjamas! And *The Changing Man* was an original one. That's now the title of the film within the film. We even thought of *Identity Crisis and Its Relationship to Personality Disorder.*

SB: *Then you call the principal female character Eudora Fletcher, and I believe that this was the actual name of one of your school-teachers.*

WA: She was the principal of my school, yes. I chose that name, because it's a very good name. I always wanted to use that name. It's a very American name and a very good period name. There are very few Eudoras now. It so happens that that woman was a terrible woman. But she had a wonderful name.

SB: *Can you tell me how* Zelig *was conceived? How did you get the idea for the film?*

WA: Yes, I was sitting here, right at this spot [Woody Allen's working room at home] and I was thinking that I wanted to do a story about a person whose personality changed all the time to fit in everywhere. He wants so badly to be liked that he changes his personality to fit in with every group that he's with. Then I thought it would be very interesting to see the physical changes. He becomes who he is with. Then I thought, it would be very interesting to present him as an international phenomenon and that his story should be told in a very documentary way, as though this was a famous international figure. And that's how it took shape. It was a long and hard film to do, but great fun.

SB: *Yes, I can imagine. But how was the story of Zelig conceived? Did you write the commentary first and then try to find and reconstruct the documentary material necessary for this story? Or did you construct the story for the film little by little, inspired by the documentary material you collected?*

WA: I wrote the whole script first. Then I looked around at millions of feet of documentary and I changed my script with the new discoveries. And this went on for a couple of years. It took a long time to put it together. I had people who'd go and research for me. People from the editing department would find it and we'd look at it, for hours.

SB: *I guess all kinds of trick photography were used to create the style of the separate scenes in the film?*

WA: It wasn't so much of that. We got old lenses from the 1920s, old cameras and old sound equipment. We tried to get all of that kind of stuff that still existed. And we filmed it in exactly the kind of lighting they would have had at the time. We made flicker-mattes, so that our film would have flickering light like the old films. And we put scratches in the negative. We didn't want to overdo it. We just made it as natural as we could possibly make it. There were also a few trick shots, where I was put into old pictures. We didn't do too much of that. Just two or three times in the whole movie. Mostly it was just legitimate photography.

SB: *Was that the most difficult part, when you actually had to move in those old moving images?*

WA: Yes, it was technically difficult. But Gordon Willis is a genius and he was able to see what kind of lighting they had in the original newsreel and match the lighting appropriately in the studio against the blue screen, and then get me in there. But mostly we made our own footage.

SB: *How long did the actual production take? I guess the shooting must have taken a considerable time?*

WA: Not the shooting, the shooting was easy. But the editing and the afterwork was long. You know, sometimes we'd shoot a scene and an actor would be crossing and then the cameraman would say, 'Oh, no, not yet! Come back!' And the actor wouldn't know what was happening and he'd go back. But it looked great on the screen. Because the actor was really caught and confused for a moment. We never warned anybody about anything. And we used amateurs for the speaking roles almost all the time. So you get a very realistic feeling. They don't sound like actors ever. This goes both for those interviewed and for the people who speak on the screen.

SB: *Like Eudora at old age?*

WA: Yes, she's an amateur. She looked just like Mia. An uncanny resemblance.

26   Mia Farrow and Woody Allen in *Zelig*

sb: *The interviews with well-known contemporary intellectuals and media people, like Susan Sontag, Saul Bellow or Bruno Bettelheim – at what stage of the production did they come in?*

wa: As we were going along we needed some interviews. We usually accommodated to their schedule. I was lucky enough to get Saul Bellow, lucky enough to get Susan Sontag.

sb: *How did you come to choose these people?*

wa: They were correct for the film. I wanted it to have the patina of intellectual weight and seriousness. So I asked a number of people, and these people were interested in doing it.

sb: *Were there other people you asked and couldn't get but who you would have liked to have in the film?*

wa: Only Garbo. I wrote her a little letter, but she didn't answer me. I would have had Jack Dempsey, but he was too ill.

sb: *Did you ever meet Garbo?*

wa: No. I saw her once in the street. But I myself never cared that much about Garbo. She was fine, but I wasn't caught up in the mystique. I was maybe a tiny bit too young when I got interested in films. She had peaked before my time.

sb: *But she was the only great figure from the Golden Era of silent films that you wanted to have in* Zelig?

wa: No. I interviewed Lillian Gish, but I didn't use it, because I didn't like the way it came out. She's been around since the birth of cinema. It's amazing. She really spans the whole history of cinema.

sb: *At the beginning of the film you have a thank-you note to Dr Eudora Fletcher and to the photographer Paul Deghuere. This was of course to make the false documentary more convincing?*

wa: Yes.

sb: *The film starts in 1928, the 'jazz age'. Do you think that many people at this time, between the wars, in the beginning of the Nazi era, shared the dilemma of Zelig in wanting to fit in, to be alike?*

wa: I think that's eternal and universal. Many people have their integrity, but many many others lack this quality and they become who they're with. If they're with people who advocate a certain opinion, they agree.

SB: *The scenes with the 'chameleon dance', were they produced now?*

WA: Yes, we made almost everything in the film, except for the obvious old things. And anything connected with the chameleon we made.

SB: *All these scenes have a brilliant texture compared to the real documentary scenes.*

WA: Yes, we were very careful about that stuff. Usually when people make a documentary, they overdo it. We wanted it just realistic enough. Any time we felt that it was not authentic-looking, we didn't use it.

SB: *Did you have any difficulties with the laboratory in creating this? Usually nowadays it can be very problematic whenever you work in black-and-white.*

WA: We have our own lab. Years ago, when *Manhattan* started, we asked them to build a black-and-white one, and they built it just for *Manhattan*. And over the years since then, I've used it about five times. So I have a very good place for black-and-white now.

SB: *You're lucky, because in many other labs the people who used to work with black-and-white films are either retired or dead. There are few people who share their experience.*

WA: Right, it's very hard to get good technicians. For years after we made *Manhattan*, cameramen from all over the world would call Gordon Willis and ask him where he got black-and-white done so well. But there's a little lab here in New York that's doing it.

SB: *The fiction film within the film,* The Changing Man, *was that modelled on any specific film from the period?*

WA: No, just the type of films that you would see in the late 1930s or early 1940s. Gordon and I knew what kind of style we would imitate. We've seen so many of these films in our lifetime.

SB: *There is in your films, not only in Zelig, a touch of eclecticism, of a more or less strong influence from other films or other film-directors. In France some film critic has termed this the 'Zelig syndrome'. Have you heard about it?*

WA: No, but it's interesting. I can understand, I can appreciate it.

SB: *The interview with the old Mrs Fletcher is very funny and ironical. She's constantly giving the kind of answers which the interviewer doesn't want to get to his conventional questions. Was this in some way a comment of yours on the conduct and superior attitude of many TV reporters towards their interview victims?*

WA: Well, she was a funny character, and I thought that that was a funny way to exploit her. But sure, you always count on the interview going the way you want, the conventional way. Here, of course, she was a difficult person.

SB: *Towards the end of the film Saul Bellow says, 'Something in him desired merging into the mass and anonymity – and fascism offered Zelig this opportunity.' Do you see Zelig as a comment on fascism or people under the fascist influence?*

WA: Sure, I think the ultimate result of giving up one's own personality and feeling to be able to blend in for protective reasons, as a chameleon does with its background, is that you're perfect material to be led by fascist persuasive powers. And that's exactly what they counted on.

SB: *Was this an underlying thought when you started to write the script for* Zelig?

WA: Yes, it was one of the main themes of the film. *Zelig* got a very positive response here critically, but the content of the film has not even to this day been evaluated properly in the United States, because everyone was so focused on the technical aspects; that was what they talked about all the time. All the nice things they said about the film were in reference to the technique. To me, the technique was fine. I mean, it was fun to do, and it was a small accomplishment, but it was the content of the film that interested me.

SB: *Do you see similar traits in American politics in recent times or at the time when the film was made?*

WA: Of conformity? Well, I think it's a personal trait in everybody's life. It began in Zelig's life when he said that he read *Moby Dick*. And you often find this with many people. Somebody asks, 'Have you read this or that?' and the other one says, 'Yeah, yes, of course,' even if he hasn't. Because they want to be liked and be part of the group. I wanted to make a comment with the film on the specific danger of abandoning one's own true self, in an effort to be liked, not to make trouble, to fit in, and where that leads one in life in every aspect and where that leads on a political level. It leads to utter conformity and utter submission to the will and requirements and needs of a strong personality.

SB: *Do you think it's difficult for the average man here in the States, with the kind of economic and political and social structure that exists, to express his views freely?*

WA: Here we're very free from a legal point of view. There's an enormous amount of wonderful freedom. The problem is that you get social pressure. For instance, in the 1950s it was perfectly legal for someone to be a communist. But if anyone dared to hint that they were sympathetic with the communists they were totally ostracized. So while we live up to the letter of the law, the spirit of tolerance is not so great here.

SB: Zelig *has music by Dick Hyman. He has also contributed in later films. Who is he, and how have you worked together with him?*

WA: Dick Hyman is a wonderful jazz musician and composer and arranger who lives in New York. He's a brilliant pianist. And whenever I need special things, I contact him. Here I needed special songs written and special arrangements for the chameleon thing and he did that. He composed the music. *Zelig* was a movie where I needed special compositions and special documentary music, and he did that. He's got the same feel that I have. He's basically jazz-oriented. He likes and knows all the kind of songs that I like. When I need the kind of songs that Cole Porter would write or the kind of jazz arrangements that Paul Whiteman or Jelly Roll Morton would do, Dick Hyman knows that code.

SB: *And the lyrics?*

WA: They are his as well. The titles of the songs are mine, but he wrote the songs.

SB: *There is a song in the film called 'Chameleon Days' which is sung by Mae Questel, who later on appears as your mother in* Oedipus Wrecks.

WA: Mae Questel was the voice of Helen Kane, a kind of boo-bopidoo-girl from the 1920s. She was also the voice of Betty Boop, the cartoon. So we used her for this reason.

SB: *Is it from this occasion that you came to choose her for the part of your mother in* New York Stories?

WA: No, not at all! I didn't even see her that time. She just went to the recording studio and recorded it. No, she came in with a lot of other elderly women when we were casting *Oedipus Wrecks*, and she was great.

CHAPTER 13

Broadway Danny Rose

MORTY, A COMEDIAN: I thought this was a funny story. It's terrible!
SANDY, A COMEDIAN: So, what do you want me to do? It's not *my* life.

(From Broadway Danny Rose)

STIG BJÖRKMAN: *At what stage did you decide to use the structure you have in this film, with the men in the bar talking about and commenting on Danny Rose and his artists?*
WOODY ALLEN: Right from the beginning. Years ago, we used to do that all the time when I was a cabaret comedian. Each night we used to go over to one of those delicatessens around Broadway and 7th Avenue and sit for hours and relax after the show and have some food and talk and tell stories. People were very anecdotal.

SB: *One of the men in the delicatessen is apparently your producer, Jack Rollins. Is he one of the leading story-tellers?*
WA: No, he's one of the quiet ones. He adds certain things, he says certain things and he talks. But he was a very famous denizen of those delicatessens. He'd sit there with his acts for hours talking about show-business.

SB: *And you sat with him like this when you worked as a stand-up comedian?*
WA: Yes. And all those people who were in that group in *Broadway Danny Rose*, they are all the real thing. They are all comedians or ex-comedians and they have all done that.

SB: *And they were friends of yours?*
WA: Yes, friends and acquaintances. I knew them all, I've worked with some of them, I've spoken with some of them.

27   Sandy Baron, Will Jordan and Jack Rollins in *Broadway Danny Rose*

SB: *Who is the guy who's the driving force in telling the story about Danny Rose?*
WA: I think it's Sandy Baron. He's a comedian and an actor as well, very talented. He's been in several movies.

SB: *Danny Rose has a kind of motto for his different artists: 'Before you go out on the stage, say the 3 S's: STAR – SMILE – STRONG.'*
WA: I heard a comedian say that many years ago.

SB: *Later, Danny says, 'If it's old-fashioned to like Mr Danny Kaye, Mr Bob Hope or Mr Milton Berle, then I'm old-fashioned!' You've talked about Bob Hope and Danny Kaye. What do you think about Milton Berle?*
WA: If you've seen Milton in person over the years in a nightclub, he can be very, very funny. He has a tendency to be too broad on television. Very broad in his comedy. You know, baggy pants, clownish, lets his teeth fall out. Very, very broad. But if you watch him in a nightclub act, there's something personally very funny about him. He's very gifted and it's not a mystery why he's been a star for 55–60 years in show-business. He was a star when he was younger and he *made* television in the United States.

SB: *You met Milton Berle on some occasion when you were quite young, didn't you? Did he influence you at all?*
WA: No, he was never an influence on me. He was just a sort of giant in American comedy at the birth of the television era.

SB: *Broadway Danny Rose shows a very anonymous New York, a very commonplace New York. How did you find the locations for the film?*
WA: It was quite easy, because we didn't have to seek out particularly beautiful or romantic places. We just took all the authentic places where a character like Danny Rose would be. The restaurants, the streets, and so on.

SB: *The warehouse with the carnival figures looks like a setting for a classical thriller.*
WA: We tried to find a place to do a good chase in, and we thought that, visually, where they have the parade floats would be fun. Then when the idea came to me to use the helium, to change our voice pitch, I thought it was definitely worth doing. That made it a funny scene.

28   Milton Berle and Woody Allen in *Broadway Danny Rose*

SB: *You have Mia Farrow wearing sun glasses all through the film. The only time you get a real look at her is in a very short scene, when we see her in a bathroom mirror.*

WA: That was a very, very brave thing for her to do, because she had to act the whole picture without ever using her eyes, and that's really hard to do. She did it great, but that was also a good character trait for her in the movie.

SB: *When a character trait like this is being decided for a role, is this mainly your idea or can it be the result of suggestions from the actress or actor?*

WA: Usually it's my idea for that kind of a thing. Someone else can suggest it, and then I'll like it. But for Mia's part here, we tested it. We did wardrobe tests. We tested with glasses and without glasses. She looked so great with them. When she took them off, she looked much less impressive. It wasn't as vivid an image on the screen.

SB: *And this fantastic person, Nick Apollo Forte, who plays the entertainer Lou Canova, who is he and how did you find him?*

WA: I looked at a million singers, famous ones and not so famous ones, without finding the right person for the part. We were getting desperate. Then Juliet Taylor went to a record store and bought as many records as she could. And she saw this picture of Nick Apollo Forte on one of the records. And we found him. He was in Connecticut someplace, in a small town, singing in a little joint. And he came to New York, and I tested him. Then I looked at all my tests of everybody, and he was the best one.

SB: *How did you test him? Because I gather he's not an actor?*

WA: No. We did a brief scene and filmed it.

SB: *From the script of* Broadway Danny Rose?

WA: I think so.

SB: *Was he easy to work with, I mean considering he didn't have any acting experience?*

WA: He was easy to work with in one sense. He was friendly and nice. But there were certain times when I had to do fifty takes with him. Because he just couldn't get it. But he was basically very nice.

CHAPTER 14

The Purple Rose of Cairo

'The living ones want their life fiction, and the fiction ones want their life real.'

(From *The Purple Rose of Cairo*)

STIG BJÖRKMAN: *Of course you have seen* Sherlock Jr *by Buster Keaton. Was this film in any way an inspiration for* The Purple Rose of Cairo?

WOODY ALLEN: Let me explain this: it was in no remote way an inspiration. I had seen *Sherlock Jr* years ago. I think I've already told you this: I think Buster Keaton made very, very brilliant films, but he's not my favourite. This thing about entering the screen was a much later after-thought. I wrote a story based on only this: that a woman's dream man comes off the screen and she's in love with him, and then the real actor appears and she's forced to choose between reality and fantasy. And of course one can't choose fantasy, because that can lead to madness, so one has to choose reality. And when you choose reality, you get hurt. As simple as that. All the rest was just stuff that came up as I was writing. I saw the Buster Keaton film maybe 25 years ago. It had nothing to do with my story. The whole thrust of the idea is different. Her entering the screen was an afterthought really. Originally, it was just that the Tom Baxter character was going to be in her life.

SB: *Did this film take a longer time to write than the others?*
WA: No. I wrote half the film and I couldn't figure out where to go. So I put the script away and started to write something else and then came back to it. I got the idea that the thing that made it work as a film was to have the real actor enter the story. And that gave me the whole development.

SB: *I guess you enjoyed making* The Purple Rose of Cairo, *the film within the film.*

WA: Yes, I did. It was like one of those films I saw as a kid, what I called 'champagne comedies' – those comedies from the 1930s and 1940s with all those romantic people who wore tuxedos and went to big nightclubs and lived in penthouses and drank champagne all the time.

SB: *Of course, it's not by chance that you made it this kind of period film?*
WA: Right. It helped to abstract it more. Because if it happened today, it wouldn't be nearly as charming.

SB: *Stephanie Farrow, who plays Mia's sister in the film, is she an actress as well, or did you choose her because she also happens to be Mia's sister in real life?*
WA: She had been standing in for Mia a lot. She wasn't serious about being an actress, but she had a little of the family talent.

SB: *The Swedish writer and one time Nobel Prize winner, Harry Martinson, who also at times wrote about films, on one occasion designated the movie houses as 'temples for the cowards of life'. What would you say to such a description?*
WA: I would say that that's a very, very accurate description. It's only a definition, but that is one function for sure. And in my case, for sure. Certainly, I agree with him completely that one of the pleasures of going into a movie house is to avoid the harsh realities of life.

SB: *Was it like that to some extent when you were growing up?*
WA: Totally. I lived in Brooklyn, and on these hot, hazy summer days when it was humid and you couldn't move and nobody had anything to do, there were thousands of movie houses around, and you could walk in for 25 cents. Suddenly it was cool and air-conditioned and dark, and there was candy and popcorn. You could sit down and there would be two features. And you would see pirates and you would be on the sea. And then you would be in a penthouse in Manhattan with beautiful people. The next day you'd go to another movie house, and you'd be in a battle with the Nazis and in the second feature you'd be together with the Marx Brothers. It was just a total, total joy! The greatest kind of tranquillizer and embalmment you could think of.

SB: *Do you think that the morning or afternoon films on TV nowadays can function in the same way?*

29   Karen Ackers, Jeff Daniels, Mia Farrow, John Wood and
Zoe Caldwell in *The Purple Rose of Cairo*

30   Mia Farrow with her sister Stephanie in *The Purple Rose of Cairo*

WA: To some degree. It's a different experience, because it lacks ritual. It was fun to go into a large, dark place with huge chandeliers. That had a certain quality to it. It really blocked out the outside world. In your home your telephone rings while you're watching television. And it's light in the house. It's not the same, but it's OK. There are times when I'm home and I have nothing to do or I'm depressed or God knows what. And I start to look at TV and there's a film on that's interesting. Probably something I've already seen, but I stop . . . and I watch.

SB: *It's like your film hero, Tom Baxter, says, 'In my world the people are consistent. You can rely on them.' It's a very consistent world we're watching.*
WA: Right.

SB: *How did you come to choose Van Johnson? He's the only name actor in the film within the film.*
WA: Right, I wasn't looking for names. I was just trying to find appropriate people to play those kinds of roles. Then somebody suggested him, and he seemed just fine. He hadn't acted in films for some time then.

SB: *I find that in many ways* The Purple Rose of Cairo *is a story about innocence.*
WA: Well, Cecilia's life is completely innocent. And the character who comes off the screen, Tom Baxter, is totally innocent. And also the girls at the brothel are moved by his purity. But innocence is fiction. We can't live that kind of innocence.

SB: *This is the first time you worked with Dianne Wiest. She plays the good whore, Emma, in the brothel. How did you choose her and for which reasons did she later become a member of your 'actors' group'?*
WA: She came into my office, my cutting room, one day along with other actresses, and the second I met her, she lit up the room! The minute she walked in there was something terrifically special about her. And I knew I had to use her.

SB: *And what do you see as her special qualities as an actress?*
WA: She's one of the greatest actresses in America, I think. I'm not just saying that as generalization or a nice thing. She's just as great an actress as we have. In any form, comedy, tragedy. She's a truly great actress.

SB: *I agree. She radiates a very personal and human warmth in all the parts she plays, big or small.*

WA: In anything. She's just brilliant. She hasn't wanted to work much in the last few years, because she's adopted two children and she's been spending most of her time with them. But they don't come any better than her.

SB: *Have you seen her on stage?*

WA: Yes, she's great on stage as well. She's just a natural.

SB: *One very nice and nostalgic sequence in the film is the night on the town sequence . . .*

WA: Yes, that's right out of the movies of my childhood. Very typical. You know, Gordon Willis, who photographed the film, and I, we grew up with these kind of films. It's like mother's milk to us, so we didn't have to go looking for special films to do this sequence. We could sit down in two seconds and make something like that.

CHAPTER 15

Hannah and Her Sisters

'We all had a terrific time.'
(Caption from *Hannah and Her Sisters*)

'The only absolute knowledge attainable by man is that life is meaningless.' Tolstoy.
(Caption from *Hannah and Her Sisters*)

STIG BJÖRKMAN: Hannah and Her Sisters *was photographed by Carlo Di Palma, and this was your first film together. Was your collaboration very different from the one you've had with Gordon Willis?*
WOODY ALLEN: Gordon was doing another film when I was going to make *Hannah*. And his film was running much too long and we had to begin, we couldn't wait. So, I needed to get somebody else. And Carlo had always been one of my favourite people, as I told you before. He was available and he came to the United States. And we talked a lot. The collaboration is only different in one respect. They're both wonderful cameramen. Gordon has a greater technical mastery, Carlo has more of a European style, movement and mobility. Gordon would have been great for John Ford, with his beautiful pictures in a very American style. The only difference was, that when I started working with Gordon, I knew very little; Gordon was a genius and he educated me. So I was always a little bit in awe of him. When I was with Carlo I was much more mature and knew what I wanted. And I had developed a style. With Gordon I was learning. It's like when you leave your parents' house; now you're grown up and you go out and do your own thing. So with Carlo I knew what I wanted, and by that time I'd really started to make films in a more, what you would call, European style. So he just fit in perfectly for me.

SB: *Do you look in the camera as much with him as with Gordon Willis?*
WA: Yes, that I have to do, because I don't know how else to do it. I always look into the camera.

SB: *Why did you choose to use the chapter captions?*
WA: I've always wanted to use that. I experimented and tried them one day in this film. And they made the film so interesting-looking that I thought, that's what I'll do.

SB: *It reminds me a bit of classical English novels, like Fielding or Dickens.*
WA: Right. That's what I aimed at.

SB: *Then each chapter in a way is dedicated to one of the main characters.*
WA: Yes, more or less. This was not contrived. This emerged, it evolved during the making of the film.

SB: *The start of the film, with the Thanksgiving dinner, has a very improvised feeling and quality. Was it your intention to create an atmosphere of familiarity for us in the audience?*
WA: Yes, but it isn't improvised, it's written. But in the direction of it, I wanted to give that impression that we're just at home with the family. Then they're good actresses. They understand how to give it that quality.

SB: *How long did it take you to stage such a scene? I'm thinking about the whole dinner sequence.*
WA: I don't remember. A few days. Maybe three days, four days, something like that.

SB: *I thought it might have taken you longer, considering all the characters in the scene.*
WA: Yeah, I hate to direct many characters. It's such a bore. Some people love it. I can't stand to direct multitudes. It's just much more complicated. There are many people you have to account for. And everybody's got to be acting and acting properly. It's a lot of work. I'm just lazy.

SB: *This is the first film where you're creating a collective portrait of a group of people. You can't point out one main character in the story.*
WA: Right, it's an ensemble. I like those novels, I like those books, like *Anna Karenina*, where you get a little bit of somebody's story and a little bit of somebody else's and then somebody else's and then back to the first person and back to the second . . . I like that format of ensemble, and I wanted to experiment with it. And I've done it a few times since then.

31   Mia Farrow, Barbara Hershey and Dianne Wiest in *Hannah and Her Sisters*

32   Lloyd Nolan and Maureen O'Sullivan in *Hannah and Her Sisters*

SB: Hannah *is a very urban story, but it has a Chekhovian feeling about it . . . Not only because there are three sisters in it.*
WA: I certainly love Chekhov. No question about that. He's one of my favourites, of course. I'm crazy about Chekhov. I never knew anybody that wasn't! People may not like Tolstoy. There are some people I know that don't like Dostoyevsky, don't like Proust or Kafka or Joyce or T. S. Eliot. But I've never met anybody that didn't adore Chekhov.

SB: *There is a quotation from Tolstoy in the film, which is also used as a caption for a chapter: 'The only absolute knowledge attainable by man is that life is meaningless.' Was this in any way a kind of point of departure for the film? Do you think* Hannah *confirms or disputes this quote?*
WA: It was not a point of departure for *Hannah*, but it's certainly what my story was about, what my thread was about. I think, if I'd had a little more nerve on that film, it would have confirmed it somewhat more. But I copped out a little on the film, I backed out a little at the end.

SB: *In what way, do you think?*
WA: I tied it together at the end a little bit too neatly. I should have been a little less happy at the end than I was.

SB: *You mean, you should have left the characters more open in their different destinies?*
WA: Yes, I should have opened it up more, not resolved so much. It's a habit from my growing up and from American films – trying to find a satisfying resolution. It may not be happy, but it's satisfying in some way. But as I've gone on I've started to resolve the films less.

SB: *Your character in the film, Mickey, is a hypochondriac. Is that one of your personal traits as well or just something you presented your character with?*
WA: No, I'm an alarmist, not a hypochondriac. I don't think I'm sick all the time. But when I do get sick, I always think it's fatal. I get alarmed quickly.

SB: *Julie Kavner plays Mickey's assistant in the film. How did you find her? She's also been incorporated in your group of actors.*
WA: I had seen her on television years ago, and I thought she was so funny. Then I lost track of her completely. Then somebody suggested her.

And I said, 'Yes, Julie Kavner, she'll be great. I've always thought she's wonderful.' And then I used her – and she is wonderful.

SB: *Sam Waterston is also somebody who regularly shows up in your films.*
WA: Yes, I like him. He's a regular man. He's not a gunfighter or a machismo figure. He's a man.

SB: *He plays an architect in the film and in a scene he's showing his favourite buildings in New York to Dianne Wiest and Carrie Fisher. Are they your favourite buildings as well?*
WA: Some of them I like very much, yeah. I'm very aware of the architecture in New York and I'm very angry at the new buildings that are built with no regard to the context they're in.

Radio Days

STIG BJÖRKMAN: *How close is the story in* Radio Days *to your own childhood?*
WOODY ALLEN: Some things are very close and some things are not. But a lot of it is based on an exaggerated view of my childhood. I mean, I did live in a family with many people present in the house: grandparents and aunts and uncles. And a certain period of my childhood I did live in a house right by the water. In Long Beach. But I didn't want to travel all the way to Long Beach to shoot the film. Yes, many of the things you see in the film did happen. My relationship to the school teachers was like that. My relationship to radio was like that. The same with the Hebrew school. And we used to go out to the beach and look for German aircraft and German boats. And I did have an aunt who was forever getting into the wrong relationships and unable to get married. She never did get married. And we did have those neighbours who were communists. Much of all that was true. I was taken to New York to the Automat and to radio programmes. My cousin lived with me. We did have a telephone line where we listened in on the neighbours. All these things occurred.

SB: *Was* Radio Days *a story you'd been planning to make for a long time?*
WA: It originated from an idea that I wanted to pick out a group of songs that were meaningful to me, and each one of those songs suggested a memory. Then this idea started to evolve: how important radio was to me when I was growing up and how important and glamorous it seemed to everyone.

SB: *Did you then pick out the songs before you wrote the script for the film?*
WA: Yes, I did. Many of them.

33 Woody Allen's alter ego: Seth Green in *Radio Days*

SB: *Did you discuss this part of the job with Dick Hyman, the composer, as well?*
WA: No, not that part. The only thing I needed from Dick was a couple of arrangements of the songs. And I wanted him to create the music for the pretend commercials and things like that. But basically the songs were songs that I chose from my childhood. Songs that were significant for me.

SB: *One song is used as a kind of theme song and that's 'September Song'. And you always use it in connection with scenes from the seaside.*
WA: Right. Because that was a major song. Many people consider that the best American popular song ever written. And it may well be.

SB: *Did you choose it because of its lyrics or because of the melodic qualities?*
WA: Everything. It was a very dominating song when I was younger. One heard it interpreted by everybody all the time.

SB: *Did you choose to be the narrator of the film, because the story of* Radio Days *was very close to yourself and the memories of your childhood?*
WA: Yes, I felt that I should be the one who talks about it.

SB: *This offered you a great liberty when writing the script as well.*
WA: Yes, enormously.

SB: *It's a very elaborate script, considering all the elements in it: the family, the school, the radio events, the radio personalities . . .*
WA: A film like *Radio Days* presents a particular type of problem. When you don't have a 'What happens next?' story, when you're working with anecdotal material, the trick, I feel, is that you have to sustain each thing on its own brilliance, on its own rhythm, on its own style. So you really have to work very, very hard to make a movie like that, because you have to know that the anecdotes that you're relating to the audience an hour, an hour and a half into the film are not going to bore them. That they're still going to find them fresh and funny. It's a difficult kind of film to do, a non-plot, a non-conventional plot film.

SB: *Did you write it in a different way, compared with your other scripts? Like first finding the anecdotes before creating the pattern and structure for the film?*

WA: No, I wrote it mostly the way it is. But I did switch a few things around. For instance, the opening sequence with the two robbers robbing the house, that was originally located later in the movie. But I thought to myself, it's so arresting as a first image on the screen, these flashlights sweeping around the room, that I brought the scene forward a bit.

SB: *Was that a choice you made during the editing of* Radio Days?
WA: Yes. I always feel, that with a film, you're writing it every moment. You write it in the script, you rewrite it and change it when you cast, you rewrite it and change it when you see locations, and so on. My classic example of this was in *Annie Hall*, when I made my father a taxi-cab driver living in the Flatbush section in Brooklyn. And driving around looking for other locations, we saw the house under the roller-coaster. And, instantly, I changed the location for the film. So I change the script when I'm casting, when I'm looking for locations, or sometimes just because I come up with something completely new. Or sometimes because the producer tells me that we can't afford to make a certain scene the way I want it. And I change the script while we're working on the set, and I change it in editing the film. I have no problem with that at all. I'm happy to take a scene which was supposed to be scene number 20 and stick it first. Film is a constantly evolving thing.

SB: *Did your father work as a cab driver? In* Radio Days, *as well, the father of the main character is revealed as having this profession.*
WA: Yes, he did.

SB: *How did you find the boy, Seth Green, who plays the main character, your alter ego, in the film? Did you test a lot of child actors or non-actors?*
WA: Juliet Taylor is very, very conversant with everything that's going on in terms of actors, on Broadway, on film, in radio, on television. She usually suggests a pretty good list of names for each part, some I know and some I don't know. Seth was among the child actors she suggested, and when he came in, he clearly was a natural actor.

SB: *Did you do any tests with him then?*
WA: No. I rarely test people in front of the camera. You could tell right away. He was good enough without testing. He was a very brilliant kid, very smart.

s B: *Do you find it harder, more difficult to work with kids, with child
actors, as compared to 'real' actors?*
WA: Yes, in a way, because it's harder to find good ones.

s B: *But do you work in any different way with these younger actors?
Do you use another kind of method?*
WA: No. I just try my usual group of tricks to get them to do what I
want them to do. No, I've had the good fortune of working with good
kids. I have had the experience of working with a young person who has
not given me what I've wanted, so a wonderful role that I had written for
a young person was greatly reduced; when you see it on the screen, it's
only half of what it could have been. I don't want to say what film or
what part this was. I hate to insult that young person, but it has happened to me.

s B: *Apart from* Radio Days *your interest is, quite naturally, centred on
the adult roles. There are children in some of your films, but they are
usually kept out of the way from the general story line. Like in* Hannah
and Her Sisters, Alice *or* Husbands and Wives. *Is this out of practical
reasons or just that you find it unnecessary to introduce them into the
story?*
WA: Well, I show them when you need them. But since they don't figure
in the unfolding of the story, I don't dwell on them. They are there. You
know that, for instance, Alice has children. You see them. You see them
getting tucked into bed, you see them in the kindergarten school. But they
don't advance the story in *Alice* in any way.

s B: *The mixture of well-known and very little-known actors in* Radio
Days *provides the acting with a feeling of spontaneity and vividness.
How did you choose the actors for this film?*
WA: I think of *Radio Days* basically as a cartoon. And I picked out the
actors for their cartoon quality. If you look at my uncle Abe, my mother,
my schoolteacher, my grandparents, they were supposed to be cartoon
exaggerations of what my real-life people were like.

s B: *Did it take a long time to find the right actors for the parts?*
WA: Yes. Whenever we do what I call cartoon casting, like here or in
Stardust Memories, it takes a long time. Sometimes you get great faces,
but the people can't act very well. But they look great and you want to
use them very much. So it takes much longer to cast this kind of

character. For a film like *Husbands and Wives*, I go to Juliet Taylor and I give her the script and say, 'It's going to be Mia and myself and I'd love Judy Davis or Dianne Wiest to do the other female part.' There the casting takes no time at all really. Except if there's an odd part in it, like the girl Sydney Pollack was sleeping with. It took us some time to find the right girl for that part. But that kind of casting is a cinch. What's tough is the cartoon casting.

sb: *I wasn't aware originally that Lysette Anthony, who played that part, was English.*
wa: Oh yes, she had a very British accent.

sb: *Is it more difficult or different to direct this mixture of amateurs and lesser-known and well-known actors, like in* Radio Days, *than when you only work with professional actors in the parts?*
wa: No, sometimes the amateurs or the people who have never acted before are better than the professionals. I've had many professionals who have spent their whole life acting in small parts, and they're not very good, not very convincing. When you get a natural who's an amateur, he's better the minute he speaks.

sb: *Could you give an example of any of these natural talents?*
wa: Yes, someone like Nick Apollo Forte in *Broadway Danny Rose*, the singer. He had never acted before in his life, he was just a nightclub singer. But he was better than every actor that I tested for that role. He was just instantly better. Screen acting is a different thing than stage acting. So if you have a natural personality, if you sound natural, that's all you need.

sb: *But you don't have to direct them in any different way?*
wa: No, usually they're fine. Directing them means mainly keeping them from doing too much. That's usually 90 per cent of direction. It's to calm people down.

sb: *The original script of* Radio Days, *did it contain more material than what is shown in the actual film?*
wa: Yes, there was more. Some scenes I couldn't shoot, some scenes I did shoot and didn't use. But there were more diverse elements, some more radio. I did a brief history of radio with the very first radios and the first antennae. But I couldn't sustain that much, because I felt there was just too much material.

SB: *I saw in the still photo material some scenes with Sally at a station kissing goodbye to different guys in military service. I guess that was an episode from her 'career' saga which was cut out of the film.*
WA: Yes, that's true. I didn't use that. But this happens to me a lot on movies, where I shoot material and don't use it, because later I find out that I don't need it. It's hard to envision that when you're putting it together. Again, without a plot it's very hard to sustain a movie. For instance, one of my favourite movies is *Amarcord* which has this plotless structure as well.

SB: *Yes,* Radio Days *has a kind of Felliniesque flavour to it. Was he an inspiration for that movie in any way?*
WA: No, not really. The inspiration was that I wanted to make a memory for each important song from my childhood. It was the way it happened. And when I started to write the memories of the songs, I got inspiration for other scenes and sequences which could strengthen and support these memories. If I had done *Radio Days* faithfully, I would have done about 25 different songs and described what comes into my mind when I hear them.

SB: *Could you give an example of how one specific song led to a situation or scene in the film?*
WA: Well, I would think back to those songs I heard when I was young, the Carmen Miranda song, for instance. And I remembered how my cousin used to dance to that music all the time and pantomime to it and put on a fancy hat. So, in a way, I reconstructed this, or rather my feeling for this. You know, those songs did have memories for me. They were real songs with real memories. And I don't know if I attached the exact, correct memory to the song. But they were real memories of mine, and some of them were quite accurate.

SB: *There is quite a lot of Glenn Miller music in* Radio Days.
WA: Sure. Glenn Miller was one of the giants of my childhood.

SB: *One very touching episode is when you play 'In the Mood' and we see Aunt Bea coming home with the young man, the homosexual.*
WA: The scene in the kitchen? I think, it's Tommy Dorsey and 'Getting Sentimental Over You', which was a very big song in my childhood. And that was a memory from my childhood. My aunt had been going out with a man for a while, thinking he was so gentle and sweet and nice – which he was – but he was also gay.

34 Aunt Bea introduces her young man: Robert Joy and Dianne Wiest in *Radio Days*

SB: *In the first scene, where we see her with one of her beaus, she goes roller-skating, and later on she and her boyfriend are caught in the fog and they hear Orson Welles' famous version of* The War of the Worlds *over the radio in the car. How did you get the idea for this scene?*

WA: I was a little too young for it, but my parents told me about the Orson Welles broadcast. And I wanted to do something about this incident. So I invented this anecdote, but it seemed to me that this might have happened. And I wanted to set it in an atmosphere which was frightening. You couldn't see too much around you. Also that helps in a studio. Like in *Shadows and Fog*. Fog in a studio helps on exteriors.

SB: *The man who plays another one of Bea's boyfriends, the man who takes her and little Joe to Radio Music Hall, is apparently one of your crew members, a sound engineer. How come you chose him for the part?*

WA: Yes, he's still working with me, Jimmy Sabat. I remember I went to lunch with Tom Reilly, my assistant director, and I told him I had difficulty in finding a funny-looking guy to take Dianne Wiest to Radio City Music Hall. So he said, 'Why don't you take Jimmy Sabat?' And I thought it was a brilliant suggestion. And I asked Jimmy, and he said, 'Yes, sure!'

SB: *That's a beautiful sequence.*

WA: Yes, it's lovely. Radio City Music Hall is so beautiful.

SB: *I think your comment there is, 'It was like entering Heaven. I'd never seen anything so beautiful.' I guess this scene has a direct connection with some childhood memory of yours?*

WA: Yes, sure.

SB: *When you created the character of Sally, was that because you wanted to create a part specially for Mia Farrow?*

WA: Yes, we didn't have that character in the beginning. And we did some tests, or rather some scenes, the first day of shooting with her, where we tried a number of different voices and things. And then, when I saw which one was funny, we started to develop that character for her.

SB: *There's a brief scene of Sally when she's in acting class. She sits in the back of the room, by a window, and outside the window there's a neon sign. I guess that was arranged by you.*

WA: Yes, we put that sign up ourselves. In those days you saw a lot of

35   Tony Roberts and Dianne Wiest in *Radio Days*

that. Rather than just looking at a flat window, it was nicer. And it gave a stronger period feeling.

SB: *Radio Days is partly shot in studio and partly on location. Which are the advantages of working in a studio, do you think? And which are the disadvantages?*
WA: It's much more pleasant to work in studio. You have much more control. It's quiet. You don't have to travel any place. You have a dressing-room. You establish permanent quarters. The only drawback is that it's expensive. And the second drawback is, if you're doing a certain type of film, the studio has no authentic, real quality to it.

SB: *But isn't one of the advantages that you can create exactly the kind of world you want and need for the film?*
WA: Yes, you have control in every way. It's wonderful.

SB: *Doesn't it also provide another kind of intimacy when working with the crew and the actors?*
WA: There's an intimacy with the crew anyhow. No, I would say no to that. And not concerning the actors either. It's really convenient, wonderful for control obviously. And for a certain kind of movie ... perfect.

SB: *We haven't talked very much about your family, but I know you have a sister. Has she been an important person in your life?*
WA: Yes, we're very close. She's eight years younger than me. She's always been a wonderful person, and I've been friendly to her to this day.

SB: *You end* Radio Days *in a more tragic way with the incident with the little girl who's got caught in the well.*
WA: Right, that actually happened. It was a famous thing in the United States. Families were brought closer together, huddled around the radio, listening to the fate of this poor little girl that died. But *Radio Days* doesn't end with this episode. It ends on an up-beat.

SB: *That's true, but this incident is told towards the end of the film. What were your ideas behind including this in the film?*
WA: It was done for a number of purposes. To show my relationship to my parents. And to show something which was a typical radio situation. You not only heard funny things and trivial things and sports and quiz

shows on the radio. It also brought you tragic events. That was a part of everybody's life as well. I was a teenager when I heard this specific news feature.

SB: Radio Days *ends with a New Year's Eve party, celebrating the coming of 1944. And there you have Diane Keaton at the nightclub singing 'You'd Be So Nice to Come Home To' by Cole Porter.*

WA: Yes, that was an important song from my childhood as well. It was an important song during the war. And I wanted to make sure, since Diane was making one little appearance in the picture, that the song was potent.

CHAPTER 17

September

STIG BJÖRKMAN: September *can be characterized as a 'Kammerspiel', a chamber play. What initially caught your interest in giving the film this form? Was it the story itself that caused it to become this tight and consistent chamber play or was it that you were interested in trying to construct this kind of strict theatrical structure for a film?*
WOODY ALLEN: I used to go up to Mia's country house. And I've always thought it was a terrific location for a movie. I tried to think of an idea that could take place up there. But by the time I had the idea finished and written, the summer was over; they were all coming back and we couldn't use the place because it was the winter. So I thought, why don't we do the whole thing indoors in a fake location, in a studio set? Which we did.

SB: *And does the set resemble Mia Farrow's country house as well?*
WA: A little bit. Not nearly as much, because her place in the country is bigger and more open. But to some extent. I mean, Santo Loquasto, the production designer, went up there and looked. I'd always wanted to make a play, a movie, about a very flamboyant mother who had been involved with a gangster and who killed him, but the daughter took the blame for it. So this story just formed.

SB: *The dramatic basis for the film, the murder story, was it inspired by the famous Lana Turner–Cheryl Crane incident many years ago?*
WA: I wasn't inspired by it, I was aware of it. No, because that happened many, many, many years ago. Maybe the slightest bit, but not much. Again, I was manufacturing a plot. The origin of it was more to find something that would work at that house in the country.

SB: *How come you used the title* September *for the film?*
WA: We had a hard time thinking of a title. And then we felt *September* seemed to say the right thing, because it was taking place at the beginning

of September, and September is sort of the time of life of the people. It just seemed to fit in.

SB: *But somewhere towards the end of the film one of the characters says, 'Soon it's the end of August'. So I thought your idea for the title was that it implies the future as well.*

WA: No, no, they are moving into it. It was just coming into September, but not in a positive way of the future. They are entering, not the winter of their lives, but the fall of their lives.

SB: *Just like in 'September Song' which you have sometimes used in your films.*

WA: Yeah, it has the same sad elements in it. But *September* was an enormous disaster here. It was not well received and nobody came to see it.

SB: *It's strange, because I think it's one of your best films. I talked to Carlo Di Palma the other day, and he said that for him September was the best picture he had made together with you.*

WA: He did beautiful, beautiful work on it.

SB: *I know that the production of September was rather special. Could you tell me the story about the two versions of the film? As I understand it, you made a complete first version of the film, with other actors in some of the parts, and you weren't satisfied with this version. Then you made a second version, the one which was later shown in the movie theatres.*

WA: Yes, that's true. I completed a first version, edited it and everything. You know, I always do re-shooting on my movies. Sometimes a little bit of re-shooting. On *Husbands and Wives* I had two days of re-shooting. Other times I've done a month of re-shooting, five weeks of re-shooting, an enormous amount of re-shooting sometimes. In *September*, when I'd finished it and put it together, I felt I needed to do a lot of re-shooting.

SB: *For what reasons?*

WA: You know, Mia's mother, Maureen O'Sullivan, played the part of the mother in the film. And I wasn't happy with her performance. And Charles Durning, who's a wonderful actor, played the part of the neighbour. But I felt that I had miscast him, that I would have done better to put Denholm Elliot in that role. So I said to myself, 'Well, as long as I'm going to do four weeks of re-shooting, why not re-shoot the whole thing and do it right?' The set was right there, I didn't have to go to twenty-five locations, the actors were minimal, it was a chamber piece. And I thought, 'Why not do it right? I will cast different actors. I will get another actress for the mother's role. I'll switch Denholm Elliot over, and so on.' I had always had a problem with the young male lead. The first person I hired was Christopher Walken, who I think is a truly great actor. But he just wasn't right for the part. I can't explain this exactly, correctly. He was a little too sexy, a little too – not macho, but manly in a sexy way. Then I hired Sam Shepard. I like him very much, but Sam Shepard is not that interested in acting. He was only acting to supplement his money so he could write his plays. So he wasn't that interested. But I liked him. He was a good person. But when we re-shot the picture, I felt that I couldn't ask him to do the whole picture again, because he just wouldn't want to.

SB: *I see, so you started the film with Christopher Walken and then you had Sam Shepard in the part. They were both in the first version?*
WA: Yes, they were both in the first version. And then in the second version I asked Sam Waterston to play the part. And Sam was really more correct for it. Sam was not available when I first made the picture. He was doing some kind of television mini-series or something.

SB: *But you had him in mind originally for the part?*
WA: More that kind of person, yes. I mean, it didn't have to be Sam, but Sam was a perfectly correct actor for the part.

SB: *Did you re-shoot the second version in exactly the same way as the first one?*
WA: Yes, but I corrected those mistakes that I could see from looking at the first draft. And I was satisfied with it, the second version, when it was finished. I didn't think it would be a popular film. I knew it was not common fare. But I got some support on the picture. Richard Schickel in *Time Magazine* was very positive. I don't know about Europe, but here in America it's not their cup of tea. It's not the kind of thing they're interested in, good or bad. Comparable – or, I don't mean comparable, because his is a much greater film – was the Russian *Uncle Vanya* by Andrej Konchalovsky. It's the best *Uncle Vanya* I've ever seen. I don't think you can get a more perfect rendering of the play. Sergej Bondarchuk plays the doctor. It's so perfectly done. It opened here and *nobody*

went to see it! And I mean nobody! Diane Keaton and I saw it and we were the only two people in the theatre. It just ran for one week or so. I knew that *September* was in that genre, but was never going to be as good as that. Because to begin with *Uncle Vanya* is an immortal piece of writing and Konchalovsky did a beautiful job on it. So I thought to myself, 'If *Uncle Vanya* is here in that genre, my film will be here. (*Woody indicates with a hand the two different levels of quality and appreciation which he grants the two films.*) And nobody will come and see it!'

SB: September *has very strong Chekhovian traits as well.*
WA: It's in that genre, yes. It tries to evoke a similar atmosphere. But there are a number of films that I've made where I knew before I made them that they would not be popular here. I thought they might be critically popular, possibly, but would never catch the interest of a wider audience. One was *Stardust Memories*, *September* was another. And then *Shadows and Fog*. I knew that these three films were not what anybody cares to see here. *September* ran at the Paris Theatre for some months. It had a small following. And out of town ... It did OK in a few college towns, a few big cities, but very few! In most places in the United States it wasn't even shown.

SB: *So what has happened to the first version of the film? Have you kept it?*
WA: I haven't, no. It's gone.

SB: *There are some connections between* September *and* Interiors, *I think. Both films have similar openings, for instance. They both open with pictures of empty rooms, though your camerawork in the two films is very different. In* Interiors *the opening pictures have the quality of still life photography, in* September *the camera is moving, searching into the house.*
WA: When I shot *Interiors* I was working with Gordon Willis, and we always used to argue – or rather discuss – the framing and the compositions. Gordon used to tell me the way he imagined the cinematography would be. He would always tell me, 'No, we should do it this way. Believe me, trust me. It will look better if we do it this way.' And I would sometimes protest, but he would correct me and ask me to trust him and his opinions. And I did, I deferred to him on a number of decisions. But then when I stopped working with him, I went into a different direction completely. So now all my films have very long sequences. It's easier for

me to work that way. It's harder for me to work with shorter
sequences. It's something I never was really comfortable with.

SB: *I think the first couple of images in the film, where the camera
slowly investigates the house while we're listening to the conversation in
France between Dianne Wiest and Denholm Elliott in the distance, are
very beautiful. And they also set the mood and the pace for the film.*
WA: The mood, yes, but also the house. Just like in *Interiors*, the
house is a character. The house was the initial inspiration for the script,
so it was important; I wanted you to see it, just like I wanted you to see
the house in *Interiors*. In *Interiors*, the main figure, the mother, was
also an interior decorator so there the house had a further significance.
But in *September* there is also some question about selling the house. So
the house was an important character for me.

SB: *So how did you proceed when you constructed the house together
with the production designer, Santo Loquasto? What kind of discussions did you have with him before he designed it?*
WA: It was very important, since the whole movie took place in the
house, to provide the house with a lot of perspectives that were interesting. I wanted to be able to see deep all the time, that the rooms were
not too flat off and separated from each other. And I wanted a warm
colour for the house. That was important for me. It should be warm
and homey. But the key thing was that I wanted Santo to provide me
with sufficient angles, so that you wouldn't get bored with the house, or
claustrophobic. At first we tried to light it so you could see out through
the windows. We had backdrops. But I didn't like that look so much, so
we changed it.

SB: *And the backdrops aren't necessary either. I'm thinking, for
instance, about the scene after Dianne Wiest has called her husband.
She goes to the front door, hesitates on the threshold and we sense that
someone is standing outside on the porch. And there is Sam Waterston
waiting for her. That scene works beautifully without us having to see
the exterior.*
WA: Yes. We had bushes and trees brought into the studio, but we just
didn't need it. And it didn't look good either, when we first tried it.

SB: *You worked more on the sound instead; that helps to heighten the
atmosphere throughout.*

WA: Yes, but that was not too difficult. But, yes, we put in crickets and wind . . .

SB: *. . . and frogs and birds.*
WA: Yeah.

SB: *When I mention the resemblances between* September *and* Interiors, *I also thought about some resemblances between the characters. Lane (Mia Farrow) in* September *has some character traits in common with Joey (Mary Beth Hurt) in* Interiors. *They are both speculating over the possibility of taking up photography, they are both thinking over the possibility of having a child.*
WA: Right. To me the most tragic, the most sad quality is if a person has profound feelings about life, about existence and religion and love and the more deep aspects of life, and that person is not gifted enough to be able to express it. To me that's a terrible feeling. I mean, if someone suffers and that person is a poet, he or she can at least get it out through the poetry. But there are intelligent and sensitive people who suffer and they have no talent whatsoever – and they are aware of this lack of talent themselves – and can't express these feelings. This is very, very sad.

SB: *Do you see children as a kind of surrogate for them? Because both these characters express the desire either to realize themselves in some kind of art form or to have a child.*
WA: Having a child is a compensation for people. It sometimes gives total meaning to a man's or a woman's life, or partial meaning or enough meaning, so that the other pains of their life are bearable. In, for instance, *A Streetcar Named Desire* the fact that Stella is going to have a baby is so painful to Blanche, because having a child is such a positive thing in life and it does help to some, or even a great, extent to overcome all one's sufferings.

SB: *One film that comes to mind in relation to* September *is Bergman's* Autumn Sonata. *What do you think about it?*
WA: It's not one of my favourite films of Bergman's. I like all his films so much that, on his level, a film like *Autumn Sonata* is better than everybody else's movie. But it's not one of his best films, in my opinion.

SB: *Not in his opinion either.*
WA: No, I don't think it is. But there are things in it, like that moment at

the piano between Ingrid Bergman and Liv Ullmann, which is really a tremendous scene. Full of feeling and full of impact on the screen. Otherwise, I love his chamber films a lot.

SB: *Bergman and I discussed the film recently, and he said that he made* Autumn Sonata *completely wrong. He originally had a more poetic concept for the film, in the line of* Persona. *But he abandoned this idea and made it into a more realistic account, which he now regrets. He wanted to build the film in the same structure as a sonata, with the changing moods of that kind of a musical piece. But he didn't stick to the idea and therefore he looks back at the film with a more critical view now. But to me there seemed to be a few striking resemblances between* September *and* Autumn Sonata. *There are the two mother figures, two very flamboyant and outgoing characters with a certain* grandezza. *They are both artists, one an actress, the other a concert pianist. And then there are the two daughters who are incapable of handling their lives.*
WA: That's interesting; I had always felt a little similarity between *Autumn Sonata* and *Interiors*, because they came out at the same time. Even to the point where Ingrid Bergman came in wearing that red dress. Both films were mother-daughter stories. And there was the cold, artistic mother.

SB: *But the mother in your film is different. True, she is very egotistical, but she also expresses more warmth and understanding towards the daughter.*
WA: No, she's not cold, she's just selfish.

SB: *How did you come to choose Elaine Stritch for the part? I think she's excellent in it.*
WA: Me too, she's great in it. First I picked Mia's mother because Mia used to tell me that her mother was like that. That she was funny and flamboyant. And I knew her mother, and I did think that she was sort of like that. But when she acted it, she wasn't strong enough. So when I got to recasting the film I wanted somebody who could really embody those qualities. And I looked at some television things which Elaine Stritch had done, and I decided myself for her.

SB: *She has made very few films in recent years. I can't recall having seen her in anything since* Providence *by Alain Resnais, where she was also very impressive.*

36 Elaine Stritch in *September*

WA: Right. She did a lot of stage work and some television work. But she's great and I'd love to use her again.

SB: *We've talked a bit about the structure of the film. I would like to take out one more typical scene from the film and discuss it. There is one between Dianne Wiest and Denholm Elliott by the pool table, a very long and very beautifully choreographed scene. Do you remember how this scene was prepared and staged?*

WA: Well, the problem always was – and is in many of the films – how to keep it interesting without falling back on the conventional way of putting the scenes together. (*Woody snaps with his fingers to illustrate the rhythm of very conventional editing and cross-cutting.*) In a more realistic film, when you're doing the camera choreography, people can't just walk as naturally as they do in real life. They have to move at a certain pace and show up at the right time in front of the camera. And it requires a certain amount of staging so that the statement is made both by what the actors are doing and by the camera. So they are not working at cross-purposes; the actors acting in a poetic fashion and the camera too rapid or insensitive. It's trying to stay with the mood. What we usually do is that we just meet and I slowly, painstakingly choreograph it and we – the cameraman and I – take a long time doing it. But when we shoot it, we shoot the whole scene, so it's worth it. We don't have to get back and make coverage or close-ups or anything like that. And one of the tricks is to try and get the actors to walk naturally but get into different positions, in medium shot, in close-up and in longer shot at different times, so that you don't have to cut to a close-up. The person will instead give you a close-up by the way they are going. It's just tedious work. In this scene, we sat around the pool table, Dianne and Denholm Elliott and me, and I moved them around and I moved the camera around. And then you make a mistake and you correct that and new problems arise. But gradually you get it all together.

SB: *How long does a scene like that take you to do?*

WA: The choreography, the plotting out of the scene takes a couple of hours. Then, the actual shooting of it is no problem, because the actors are so good. I mean, Denholm Elliott and Dianne Wiest are brilliant and very professional.

SB: *When you planned the structure for* September, *was your idea that the form in some way would express the content of the film as well?*

WA: Yes, I always try to get the form to reflect the content of the film. You know, when you write a short story or a novel, the very first sentence takes a long time to get. But then, from that first sentence, everything spins out. The second sentence reflects the first sentence, in rhythm and in other ways. And it's the same thing in a film. In *September*, when the camera slowly moves towards the people in the first scene, you're committing yourself to a certain rhythm, to a certain style. And if later on you do something wrong, you immediately know you're wrong, because it's just not consistent with the way you've gone.

SB: *Right. You can see the same thing in* Interiors *with the kind of 'still life' opening shots or in* Husbands and Wives *with the reckless camera looking up from the TV set and then trying to catch up with the persons moving around in the apartment.*
WA: Yes, there is already a nervous feeling in that attack. You commit yourself to it and then everything has to follow or you will feel bad about the handling of the scenes, you will know that you're making a mistake.

SB: *In* September *you have the camera discreetly moving towards the characters, and you have the characters discreetly moving towards each other. Discreetly, because everybody loves the wrong person, which is also very Chekhovian.*
WA: True, it's unavoidably Chekhovian, because what we have here is a group of middle-aged people in a country house with unfulfilled dreams and unfulfilled passions and sad futures.

SB: *One thing I like about* September, *and something you seldom see on film, is the love expressed between older people. In films – and especially in American films – love after, say, forty is almost obscene, or at least it's something you shouldn't talk about and definitely not show. But the scenes in* September *between Elaine Stritch and Jack Warden are both very tender and light-hearted. As well as very outspoken. She very openly declares that they are having sex together and that they are enjoying it. The same goes for other elderly couples in some of your films, like E. G. Marshall and Maureen Stapleton in* Interiors *or Maureen O'Sullivan and Lloyd Nolan in* Hannah and Her Sisters.
WA: Yes, and in *Another Woman*. That's some of the criticism I got for that film, not from the press but from cinema-goers. They thought that those characters were too old to have those problems. But I don't see it that way, because I know people who have these kind of problems at that

age. I wanted the mother in *September* to be a character who is shallow and selfish, egotistical. But even at her age, she dresses and thinks of herself as beautiful and feminine and sexy. And the annoying thing to her daughter is that she attracts men of substance. Her 'boyfriend' is not a gangster or a gambler or another actor. Lane, the daughter, thinks 'God, why doesn't he see through her? He's an intelligent and cultivated man, he's a physicist. He should know better, when he sees my mother, that she's shallow and vain and obsessed with her physical appearance and her own persona.' But even men of substance are attracted to her.

SB: *You have also provided her with some nice lines so that she herself can express this. At the end of the film, for instance, you have her say, 'It's hell getting older, especially when you feel twenty-one inside!' Or, 'Something is missing, and you realize that it is your future.'*
WA: Right. The sadness of it.

SB: *In* Interiors *Joey had this very cold and rigid mother who in some way was the cause behind her life being unhappy or difficult. Now, Lane's mother provides her daughter with both encouragement and at least some care and interest, but Lane is the same unhappy and unfulfilled person. So, is there a cure for parents?*
WA: Yes, Lane's mother has wrecked her over the years. Lane loved her father, and her mother couldn't care less about that. Lane had a miserable childhood. Then having to pretend to have killed somebody in an accident just to get her mother off the hook was also quite a heavy burden. And her mother had no problem allowing her to do that. So her mother has not been very nice really. But she doesn't know better. She's shallow. So, these mothers, they are talented and beautiful but they have a wrecking effect on their daughters. The daughters lose on every front. The mothers get good men, they get attention and yet they are still cruel and cold and without generosity.

SB: *But still you have some sympathy for the mother in* September?
WA: Yes, I have, because she's unaware of all this. She doesn't act maliciously. She just does what she does, because she doesn't know better. And of course Elaine Stritch's acting helps, because she's a witty woman.

SB: *I guess you have a fondness for embarrassing situations in films like this. I'm thinking about the scene when Dianne Wiest and Sam Waterston are revealed secretly kissing in the larder.*

WA: Yes, it's an old dramatic device, but very effective. And this was an embarrassing situation when Lane is showing the prospective buyers through the house. This was a terrible way to learn, or rather confirm the truth. This is standard stuff for drama.

SB: *Dianne Wiest had now become a member of your 'group of actors'.* *When you wrote the script for* September, *did you write the part she played with her in mind?*
WA: She's one of our greatest actresses, so I probably did have her in mind. I can't remember, but I probably had. I always gave Mia first choice. But I also give top choice to Dianne Wiest and of course to Diane Keaton. They can call me up any time and say, 'I want to be in your next movie!' and I would always change something so they could be in it. They're both so great.

SB: *Has it ever happened that they or some other actors have said, 'I'd like to be in your next film,' and you haven't had a character suitable for them, so you've changed something in the script to fit them in?*
WA: Usually they've told me in advance. They haven't told me that late. I would love to do a movie with Dianne Wiest and Diane Keaton and Judy Davis. With the three of them. And I think that Judy would like to join as well. In that case I would use the three most exciting actresses there are for the moment. And it would be so great!

SB: *So, do you think that a story might evolve just from this idea?*
WA: Yes, I think it's very possible that I could think of something that way.

SB: *I read an interview with Judy Davis in* Cahiers du Cinéma, *where she said that her part in* Husbands and Wives *was her best and most important part in an American film.*
WA: Well, she is incredible. She was great from the second I saw her. But this has nothing to do with me or my film. Whatever you put her in, *Barton Fink* or an Australian film, Judy Davis is great. And the same goes for Dianne Wiest. If she's in some little light film like *Parenthood* or whatever, she dignifies it. Or Diane Keaton. She can be in a commercial film like *Baby Boom*, but she outshines the material. And of course they make the directors look good. When you have weapons like that.

SB: *Howard, the neighbour, played by Denholm Elliott, is one of these unhappy characters whose love (towards Lane) will never get fulfilled. Towards the end of the film Lane asks him, 'How will you get home?' And he answers, 'The same way as always. Thinking about you.' In the first version of the film you had Charles Durning in the part, then you switched to Elliott. What are his main merits as an actor, according to you?*

WA: Durning was great, I must say. I thought he was wonderful. But I thought that I had miscast him. I didn't think he was right for the part, but he did a tremendous job on it. And, you know, I had Denholm Elliott as the physicist, the lover of the mother. But as soon as I started to see him act, I thought to myself, 'Oh no, I made a mistake. It would be much better, if he was the neighbour and I get someone else for the physicist.' I've always wanted to work with Denholm Elliott. I think he was a great actor. I already wanted to use him as the father in *Interiors*. But I didn't want a British father. And his agent said that he could do an American accent perfectly. Then, the only way to reach Denholm Elliott was to call a bar in Ibiza at a certain time of day and they would call him to the phone. So I called there. This was years and years ago. I called the bar and asked to talk to Denholm Elliott. And they went and fetched him. We talked, and he sounded very British. So I asked him over the phone, if he could do an American accent. And he said, 'Yes.' And I asked him, if I in any way could hear it to see if it was OK. And he said, 'I could do the nursery rhyme "Hickory Dickory Dock, the Mouse Ran Up the Clock" for you.' So I was on the phone, the phone right here, and I said, 'OK.' And there he was, in Ibiza in a bar, saying, 'Hickory ... Dickory ... Dock ...', trying to sound like an American. 'The Mouse ... Ran Up ... the Clock'. And he sounded totally British to me. So I said, 'Well, let me think about this.' And I did not hire him, because he just sounded too British. But I always felt that some day I would make it up to him. And I got this chance. It was wonderful. He was a very fine actor. Tremendous.

SB: *The scenes when the lights go out are very suggestive and beautiful.*
WA: Yes, yes. Carlo really outdid himself there. I think he did a great job.

SB: *Was it just natural light? I mean, the light from the candles?*
WA: There was just a tiny bit of help. Very little.

SB: *In this scene there is a rainstorm, which becomes very important for the story and the situation between the people in the story. You have used*

37　Mia Farrow and Denholm Elliott in *September*

rain in very significant situations in many of your films. Do you like rain and rainy weather yourself?
WA: I love rain!

SB: *Rain is an important element in quite a few films of yours.*
WA: Sometimes when we survey the location they say to me, 'Look, we can make rain here, but it's going to take us all morning to cover the whole scene with the rain machines, and you're just saying a few words here . . . So is it worth it?' And they talk me out of it. In the beginning of *Radio Days* I show where I grew up, by the ocean and the beach. And it's the dreariest day. The ocean is crashing against the beach. And I'm saying – as the narrator – and I'm saying it quite innocently, 'It was so beautiful where I grew up.' And the audience laughs. But I was serious. To me it's beautiful. Therefore, I'm always filming exteriors when it's dreary out. If you look at all my films over the years, you'll find it's never sunny, it's always grey. You would think that it rained in New York like in London. That it's always grey and bleak in New York. I love the idea of rain. I just think it's so beautiful. Of course, it's a pain in the neck to do these rainy scenes, it's a nuisance. But I want this rainy atmosphere in my pictures. It rains in *Hannah*, in *Radio Days*, in *Crimes and Misdemeanours* and in *Manhattan Murder Mystery*. It just looks so beautiful. And I named the girl Rain, in *Husbands and Wives*, because that's a beautiful name.

SB: *Do you know anybody with that name?*
WA: I only knew of one Rain in my lifetime. There was a singer in New York, many years ago, thirty years ago, with the name Rain.

SB: *And in* Alice *you have a couple of very important rain scenes. For instance, the scene in the jazz musician's apartment, when he and Alice make love for the first time. There the rain is really pouring down on them, on the glass roof above them.*
WA: Yes. You know, I would love to do a movie where every single time the lovers are together, it's raining. When they meet, when they go out together, when they make love, no matter what. Whenever they're together, it's raining.

SB: *Do you think that rain has some kind of specific psychological effect on people in general?*

38 'I want this rainy atmosphere in my pictures': Woody Allen in
Crimes and Misdemeanours

39 'I'm always filming exteriors when it's dreary out': Woody Allen
with Carlo Di Palma on *Alice*

WA: Oh, yes! When I get up in the morning and I look out the window, if it's like this, I'm OK. (*Outside the panoramic windows of Woody's living room at the moment it's cloudy and grey.*) The more dreary the better. If it's really grey and raining, it's fine. If it's bright and sunny, I have trouble dealing with the day, personally. It's the exact opposite of what you're supposed to feel.

SB: *Do you have trouble in working, in writing for example, if it's too bright a day?*
WA: I don't have trouble writing, but I have trouble being happy. If I'm writing, I'm writing. But if I could control the weather, I would like to have five or six dreary days a week and one sunny day. Maybe two, but preferably one, I think. Just to break it up. So, in movies for me, it's only romantic when it's raining. The mood is so important.

SB: *Could it also be that rain also gives you a sensation of haste. Usually people move much quicker in rainy weather and maybe have to take quicker decisions because of the rain.*
WA: I don't know. I always think it gives me a feeling of intimacy. People are confined to their households. They seek shelter. They succour inside their houses. They run from the outside to the inside to protect themselves. They go inward and move inward. Also that feeling gets associated with the ocean for me, the water of the ocean. So, the ocean is meaningful to me. And I've done ocean scenes in a number of pictures, like in *Annie Hall* or *Interiors* or *Crimes and Misdemeanours*. It's the dreary moods I'm seeking there. I never photograph the ocean in beautiful sunshine. The only thing I would do where the sun and the ocean is involved, I will photograph the ocean when the sun is *really* drooping, so you just get a red smear on the sky. I think also that rain forces people together. In *September* when it rains, suddenly the people have to stay inside the house, they have to be together, and it becomes more intimate. It gives an atmosphere for more intimate things to happen, whether it's falling in love or in other ways sharing a togetherness. It effects their mood in some way. In the same way, I guess, if you're in a bedroom with a woman to make love and all the bright lights are on, that's one atmosphere. But if you turn it *way down*, and it's very soft lighting, the atmosphere becomes much more romantic and gentler. The same thing with the sunshine. If you take the sunshine away, it becomes more moody, more confessional. You tend to want to confess more and express your deeper feelings more.

SB: *So, in that respect rain helped Alice. Maybe she wouldn't ever have made love to Joe, if it hadn't rained.*

WA: Right, there were two moments in *Alice*. When she meets him, it's pouring with rain. When they go to school, they have all their umbrellas, and there's something lovely about that. And then, when she's in bed with him, the rain is just flooding down the windows. It's an important thing for me. And as I said – I know how cumbersome it will be – but I'd love to do a movie, where there are two characters that are together, and it always rains when they're together.

SB: *So then I guess you like* Singin' in the Rain?

WA: I love *Singin' in the Rain*!! It's a wonderful film. I also love the beginning of *Rashomon*, when there's that terrible rainstorm. They all sit there and take shelter . . .

SB: *. . . and start to tell the story.*

WA: And I love the rain that happens in *La Dolce Vita*. You know, it suddenly starts to rain when they're witnessing the miracle. It's very poetic.

CHAPTER 18

Another Woman

MARION: Fifty. I didn't think anything turning thirty. Everybody
said I would. Then they said I'd be crushed turning forty. But they
were wrong. I didn't give it a second thought. Then they said I'd be
traumatized when I hit fifty. They were right. I'll tell you the truth. I
haven't recovered my balance since turning fifty.
HOPE: Fifty's not so old.
MARION: I know it isn't, but . . . You suddenly look up and see
where you are.

(From *Another Woman*)

STIG BJÖRKMAN: Another Woman *is your first film with Sven Nykvist
as cinematographer. Which are his foremost qualities to your mind?*
WOODY ALLEN: I think Sven is one of the few great cameramen in the
world, and what's great about him is that he has feeling for his work. You
can always try and analyze what makes a cameraman great. One person
lights like Carlo Di Palma, which is quite light. Another one is quite dark,
like Gordon Willis. They all have their own philosophies about what to do.
One likes to move the camera a lot, one likes not moving the camera too
much. But, in the end, all that counts is feeling. And Sven gets feeling into
his work. I mean, his work together with Bergman is extraordinary.
Persona is a beautiful piece of art, very poetical also when it comes to the
cinematography. *Cries and Whispers* is beautiful, *Fanny and Alexander* is
beautiful. They are all wonderful, but those three are particularly exciting.

SB: *What specifically in his cinematography do you like?*
WA: Well, the aesthetics of his photography. Like with any cameraman
you can break it down and talk about lighting and composition and
movement of the camera. But it isn't really that anyhow. It's something
you can't really define. Many cameramen make good compositions and
light well, but finally there are some indefinable elements. It's like saying,
'Why is Charlie Chaplin funny and another comedian not so funny?' Sven

40 Woody Allen and Sven Nykvist working on *Crimes and Misdemeanours*

just has that inner gift. Sven would probably be able to take a photograph of something, and it would just look good. The same with Carlo. It's some intangible effectiveness that some people have. And Sven has that.

SB: *Sven was, of course, one important collaborator in* Another Woman. *Another one, and maybe more important, was Gena Rowlands. To me she and the story is almost synonymous. It's hard to think the film with anybody else but her. Did you write the script with her in mind?*

WA: I didn't write it with her in mind, but she was my first choice for the part. Originally I had asked her to play the mother in *September*, but she didn't think that she could do that part. She didn't think she had that flamboyant quality. Then she was worried that, because she turned that part down, I would never offer her anything in the future. Actors sometimes think that directors get mad at them, if they don't want to be in their movies. But this, of course, is silly. So for *Another Woman* I asked her, and she wanted to play the part. She is also one of our great actresses. She has a huge talent and she's completely professional.

SB: *What was the origin of this story?*

WA: That's an interesting one. Many years before I wrote the story of *Another Woman*, I started to think about a comedy where I would be in an apartment and through the heating vent would hear what was going on in the apartment below me. And what I heard was a psychiatrist treating patients. He starts to treat a woman and she talks about her most intimate secrets. And I look out the window, because I hear her talking, and I see that she's beautiful. So I run downstairs and I contrive to meet her. I know exactly what she dreams of in a man and what she wants, and I make myself that person. I thought about that idea for a while. I had it and I kept it. Then one day I said to myself, 'Wouldn't it be interesting to use this idea in a dramatic movie? With a woman overhearing a conversation in a neighbouring apartment. But what kind of a woman would that be?' And I thought, 'What if it's a woman who is strong intellectually but blocked out in her feelings? And she comes to realize that her husband is having an affair, that her brother doesn't really like her, that her friends don't really like her.' She would be a philosophy teacher but she has kept everything personal in her life totally blocked out. And finally she reaches a point in her life, where she can no longer block out things in this way. They literally start to come through the walls, the sounds of her inner turbulence start to come through the walls to speak to her. So that's how it started.

SB: *But you never wrote anything on your original idea, the comedy idea?*
WA: No.

SB: *Do you ever get ideas for stories by eavesdropping on people or by studying people and starting to concoct stories about them?*
WA: No, they come either by a complete accident, by a complete, spontaneous accident, or I just sit down and start to imagine a story. I am going to do this Tuesday. I'm going to sit down in a room, this time with a collaborator, just for fun. Mostly I write by myself, but once in a while I like to collaborate. It breaks up the monotony. I'm going to sit down in a room, probably this room, and start to say, 'What's a good idea?' And then go right from scratch and invent an idea.

SB: *And then, what might happen? Does a character sometimes enter the room, enter your mind? Or is it mostly a situation which forms the basis for an idea?*
WA: It can be anything. For instance, when I wrote *Broadway Danny Rose*, it was a character that I knew Mia wanted to play. And that helped me to find the story. In *Radio Days* it was those songs I wanted to use in some way. In *Another Woman* it was those sounds coming through the wall. It's always different.

SB: *As far as you remember have there been other characters besides Tina Vitale in* Broadway Danny Rose *who in a similar way have entered your imagination and requested your attention and then called for more importance and more definite contours?*
WA: Sure, someone like Zelig. *Zelig* was strictly a character thing. I've often made this observation, that there are certain people who change their personalities, their tastes and likes, depending on who they're with. If you're having a conversation with them, on the simplest level, you can say, 'I saw that movie and I hated it. What do you think?' they would say, 'No, it wasn't very interesting.' An hour later they're with someone else, and that person is saying, 'I really liked that movie. It was so funny.' And they will say, 'Yes, I had some reservations, but it was really a funny film!' They shift to accommodate. This can happen on a simple level, but when it occurs on a more important level, it becomes very complex and dangerous. There was a character that started the whole story and the film.

SB: *At the beginning of the film, Marion (Gena Rowlands) says, 'If anybody would ask me to re-evaluate my life at fifty, I would probably*

*maintain that I've managed to fulfil myself, both privately and profes-
sionally. I wouldn't go further. It's not that I'm afraid to reveal darker
sides of myself. But I've always felt that one should let things be as they are,
if they work.' You yourself were about the same age as Marion when you
made the film. Did you feel the need to re-evaluate your life at that stage as
well?*

WA: I've never re-evaluated my life! I've always kept my nose to the
grindstone. All I do is work, and my philosophy has always been that if I
just keep working, just focus on my work, everything else will fall into
place. It's irrelevant whether I make a lot of money or don't, or whether the
films are successful or not. All that is total nonsense and superfluous and
superficial. If you just look at the work and try and keep working and
striving and setting ambitious goals for yourself, the rest is unimportant.
You find that, if you just do that, everything else falls into place. That's
why I had so much trouble making *Manhattan Murder Mystery*,
because I found that it wasn't ambitious enough for me. It was purely an
indulgence, a kind of a pleasure.

SB: *Did you feel guilty then?*
WA: Oh, yes. I put the film off for twelve years.

SB: *But guilty in what way? Guilty towards yourself or guilty towards
the audience or the critics?*
WA: Both. I felt guilty towards myself that I should be wasting almost a
year on something that's pleasurable to me but not significant. Now I don't
say that my work is usually significant, but it tries to be significant. It fails
maybe, but it tries. At least I want to try. I don't mind if I strike out and it
doesn't work. That's different. If I feel I did the best I could on a movie, I
aimed as high as I could, I tried, and failed, that's OK. But if I feel I didn't
aim as high as I could, then there's no redemption, even if the movie succeeds.

SB: *But you aimed at making a very entertaining movie.*
WA: Yes, an escapist movie. And I think it does work on that level. But
it's not what I should be doing. It was like a vacation from film-making.

SB: *Of course, when seeing* Another Woman, *a film like Bergman's*
Wild Strawberries *comes to mind. Bergman's film is also an exploration
into an isolated and considerably more frozen human being. Have you
ever seen a link between these two films?*
WA: I haven't, but I can when you mention it. *Wild Strawberries* is such

a great movie, such a wonderful, wonderful movie, so I haven't really . . .

SB: *We talk about 'road movies', and* Wild Strawberries *is in a way Bergman's version of a road movie.* Another Woman *could also be defined as a kind of a road movie, a journey into the mind and into the soul in the same manner as* Wild Strawberries.

WA: That's interesting . . . Yes, it certainly is a journey into the mind. Without question, I mean, that's what I wanted the film to be.

SB: *The film has this free structure as well. You allow yourself and the film to take whatever direction you feel it should take. You use Marion's memories, her dreams, her previous experiences to carry her through the story. Was any of this invented along the way or when you started to edit the film?*

WA: No, it had to go in that direction, because the film had a very tight plot. But it was not a very successful film. People thought it was a very cold picture.

SB: *Could that be because the character has a certain coldness?*

WA: Probably. But it's probably more my fault.

SB: *But this phenomenon is quite interesting. When you have a central character like this who also happens to be a cold or even negative personality, the audience tends to react towards this character. They want to be able to identify with the main character, especially when that character – like Marion here – is a very strong and leading one. Everything in the film revolves around her. And when this figure isn't a positive person, the audience has difficulties in following her through the events, the identification process is hurt.*

WA: Yes, I think that is certainly true. By making the characters cerebral, like I did here and in *Interiors* and in *September*, they might be harder to sympathize with. In *Crimes and Misdemeanours* or *Husbands and Wives*, where the characters are even more violent, we are more willing to follow them along the story, because they are warmer.

SB: *One of my favourite Hitchcock films is* Vertigo, *which at the time of its release wasn't very popular with the audience. And I think that one of the reasons for this was that the part James Stewart played was not a very positive character. To a very large extent, Hitchcock played on the identification between the main characters and the audience.*

WA: That's interesting, because usually the audience loves his films and its heroes.

SB: *True, but the James Stewart character here is an obsessed person, and obsessed in a fairly sickly way. Nobody wants to become this obsessed policeman he impersonates. So* Vertigo *was one of Hitchcock's few commercial failures at the time of its release.*
WA: That's interesting, because now people love it.

SB: *And what about you?*
WA: *Vertigo* is all right. It's not my favourite Hitchcock by far. I much, much prefer *Shadow of a Doubt* and *Notorious* and *Strangers on a Train*. But I do not agree with Truffaut that these films are meaningful or say something of substance. I think they are just delightfully entertaining. One hundred per cent successful in what the director wanted to do.

SB: *I noticed a similar reaction towards my film,* Behind the Shutters, *where the central character isn't one you'd want to sympathize with, but yet he's an identification figure.*
WA: Yes, but Erland Josephson is a warm actor though. And I see Gena as a warm actor as well. *Another Woman* is a kind of film which just isn't popular here. I've had much more success with all my more dramatic films in Europe. I don't know why, but maybe the average person in Europe is brought up to have a greater interest in that kind of literature and film.

SB: *Yes, I find it so. Most Americans are not very well read. The average American doesn't seem to be very interested even in contemporary American literature. And yet you have so many interesting writers, like Raymond Carver, Paul Auster, Richard Ford, Tobias Wolff, Ann Beattie and others.*
WA: Yes, but they don't have big followings. I read a certain amount of contemporary fiction, though I don't read a lot. And you could compare it with the classical films. I've talked to college kids who've never seen *Citizen Kane*. Or early Bergman films. *The Seventh Seal, Wild Strawberries* and *Persona* they don't know at all. And they haven't even heard the titles of films like *Through a Glass Darkly* or *Winter Light*. And the same goes for pictures by Fellini or Truffaut or Godard. There's a very very influential school of film criticism in the United States that's populist. And I think that's not good. There's a number of critics, intellectual critics, who are extremely sceptical and critical of, let's say, the fine European works and of fine works in general, but gush tremendously

over populist junk films. I won't mention names, but there are a number of film-directors around who make very popular films, and they're delightful films. But to extol them the way they do and to find meaning in them is not right. I know one film critic who was very, very severe on Bergman. Not always negative, but Bergman really had to live up to a standard. The same with Fellini. Whereas some very junky American film-makers just were worshipped beyond belief.

SB: *You said that you hadn't felt any need of re-evaluating your life, the way Marion does in* Another Woman. *Has it always been like that for you.*

WA: Yes. I knew this when I was in my late teens, that there were always going to be distractions as well. And I felt that anything that distracted from the work and minimized your effort on it was a self-deception that was going to be detrimental. So to avoid getting caught up with a lot of writing rituals and time-wasting, you've got to get there and just work. Art in general, and show-business, is full to the brim of people who talk, talk, talk, talk. And when you hear them talk, theoretically they're brilliant and they're right and this and that, but in the end it's just a question of 'Who can sit down and do it?' That's what counts. All the rest doesn't mean a thing.

SB: *Marion in* Another Woman *wanders through reality, memories and dreams. I'd like to hear your comments on the dream sequences in the film which are very imaginative and expressive.*

WA: I felt that once you're inside the character's mind anything was permissible. So once we've established in the early part of the picture that this voice was coming through the wall and that this was not going to be a realistic picture, then I felt I was free to do anything I wanted. I felt that the key was that Mia always was the one that led the Gena Rowlands character to some revelation. Mia was in some way an incarnation of her own inner self.

SB: *Yes, you very often establish direct links between the two characters. There is, for instance, one point where Hope (Mia Farrow) says to her psychiatrist, 'I have moments when I question myself, if I've made the right choices in life.' And then there's a direct cut to Gena Rowlands and Gene Hackman. There's a conversation at a party between them with very strong dialogue and acting.*

WA: Yes, because Marion did not make the right choices in her life. She made safe choices and cold choices, but never the right ones.

SB: *Do you think she made speculative choices as well?*

WA: No, I think she made safe choices, but non-speculative ones. Speculative would have been choices where she didn't really know where she was going. But she made safe choices. I mean, Ian Holm was a safe choice: a doctor, an established man, a safe, cold person like herself. But Gene Hackman is not. He's a warm, rough, sexy person. But Hope led her to these encounters with the other people and to an encounter with herself. Marion would think she saw Hope on the street and she would follow her and meet someone from her past. The Mia character is always leading her to where she can find out things.

SB: *Do you remember how you constructed the dream sequences, where you got the elements for her dreams from, the scenes in the theatre, the interrogation, the altercation with the first husband about having a baby?*

WA: No, I can't say that I recall exactly. It was just whatever inspiration I had at the time for that. I knew, for example, that some of the dreams should take place in the theatre. Her friend was also an actress. I wanted to give this information out in a very theatrical way. I thought it was an aesthetically pleasing way of doing it rather than doing it just as a straight natural memory.

SB: *When Marion is in her work apartment, there are a couple of very sudden close-ups of Gena Rowlands listening by the ventilation net. You're usually very sparse with close-ups in your films. What's your opinion about close-ups and about how and when they should be used?*

WA: In a dramatic film I can see myself using them more. In the more comic films, in films that aren't so heavy, I like to use them very sparingly, because I don't think they're much fun. It's different in a dramatic film, because they create a certain heaviness. They're so massive. But it's great for certain effects. But in a film of movement, a film like *Annie Hall* or *The Purple Rose of Cairo* or *Husbands and Wives*, any of them, there's no real need for them. There's almost an artificial quality about them. I mean, Bergman uses them in a theatrical way. And, of course, it's brilliant, because he's developed a language that can convey inner psychological states to audiences. I said this when I reviewed his book, *Laterna Magica*, that when the area of concern shifted from the external world to the internal world, Bergman developed a grammar, a vocabulary, to express these inner conflicts very brilliantly. And part of his grammar was the use of the close-up in a way that it really hadn't been used before. Very close and very long, long, long static close-ups. But the effect is not at all static. The effect is quite exciting, because it's infused with his special genius. So that's part of his technique. I feel less at ease with the close-up than he does. I feel that you become suddenly aware of being in a movie. I've used them in poetically dramatic situations. But very, very rarely. It's funny, Bergman once said in an interview at some point that he felt the use of music in films as barbaric. That was the word he used. But I don't. I feel the use of music in films is a very, very important part of the tools that you're working with. Just like light and sound. But the enormous use of the close-up can be barbaric, I feel. Not in his hands. In his hands it's genius. But in other people's hands, for the most part – and mine as well, because I'm not as skilled – it's very hard to handle. For directors who don't know anything, the close-up seems to be an easy way out. But it really doesn't work that way, they just think it works that way. They think a close-up is very emotional. It's like a writer who has his characters commit suicide or talk in foul language in an effort to be dramatic or powerful. Or to show a lot of blood in an effort to be strong. It's heavy-handed. I don't think I have any close-ups in *Manhattan Murder Mystery*. I don't think there were any in *Husbands and Wives* or *Hannah and Her Sisters* either. Michael Caine, I know, warned Gena Rowlands after he did *Hannah and Her Sisters* that I never do any close-ups. Then she was surprised, when I did do a couple of close-ups of her in *Another Woman*. She has such a good and expressive face as well.

SB: *But here they work very well, with the character of the movie, with her character and what you want to say through her.*
WA: I think if I do them, you'd think they'll work, because I wouldn't take a chance with one unless I was so sure that it would work. I use them so sparingly. When I first started I didn't, because I didn't know anything about directing at all, and I made the same mistakes any inexperienced director makes.

SB: *Some very stunning scenes in* Another Woman *are the meetings between Gena Rowlands and Sandy Dennis, between Marion and Claire, the actress who was once Marion's best friend when they grew up.*
WA: Well, Sandy Dennis is a great stylist as an actress. She is one of those people who is capable of doing great things. Sometimes she did and sometimes she didn't, but she was capable of it. And here her character was acting out Marion's life.

SB: *And to some extent reveals it for her. Like in the meeting in the bar, where Marion is concentrating all her interest on Claire's husband or lover and totally neglects her female friend, and Claire suddenly bursts out, 'If any of us should be an actress, it's you, not me!'*

WA: Right.

SB: *You have a very mixed and very exciting and excellent cast in this film as well, with actors like Gena Rowlands and Mia Farrow, Gene Hackman, Sandy Dennis and John Houseman, but also lesser known but fine actors like Harris Yulin whom I've mainly seen in action or adventure films in tough guy parts.*

WA: I first met him when I did *Interiors*. He was in the original cast of *Interiors*. He was one of the men married to one of the sisters. I don't remember which part now. And in rehearsal he felt uncomfortable and he said he wanted to quit. And I said, 'Sure, if you feel uncomfortable'. And he quit and I replaced him. But I've always wanted to work with him, so years later I called him and asked him. And he was happy to come in and do this. He is a wonderful type and a fine actor.

SB: *You have this legend in American theatre and film – the producer of Orson Welles' Mercury Theatre and Citizen Kane – playing Marion's father, John Houseman. This must have been his last role.*

WA: Yes, he was wonderful, very friendly and nice to work with. It's strange, but there are a number of actors who've died shortly after they've been in a film of mine. Houseman was one, Lloyd Nolan, the father in *Hannah*, was another.

SB: *When Marion is visiting her father's house, she finds her mother's favourite poetry book, which is a book by Rilke. She quotes a few lines from the poem 'The Panther': 'Because here is no place where you can't be seen. You have to change your life.' You've quoted Rilke at other occasions in other films. Is he one of your favourite poets?*

WA: I like Rilke very much, yes. He's a poet whose ideas I like.

SB: *In what way?*

WA: Because he was interested in some of the same existential things. He was a philosophical poet, and I like that. He is not my favourite poet, but he is among those I like best. My number one favourite poet would be Yeats. He still astonishes me. And of course T. S. Eliot because of what he writes about and how he writes it. And I love Emily Dickinson. She was the first poet that I ever really enjoyed.

41 Woody Allen directing Gena Rowlands and Gene Hackman on
Another Woman

SB: *Did you read her when you were young then?*

WA: Yes, and she was the first one I really understood and loved. And then e. e. cummings you have to like, because he's so witty. And William Carlos Williams. And Rilke, of course, is one of them, but Rilke I only get to read in translation. But Yeats is number one for me. It's hard to think, after Shakespeare and Milton, who wrote better English than Yeats. He's right up there, with them.

SB: *In one of the dream sequences you use music by Erik Satie. Do you like him?*

WA: Yes. Again, he's not my favourite composer, but I do like him. And I use a pretty piece of music, one of his 'Gymnopedies'. Because it fits. I listen to his music sometimes, but not often. I have many great favourites other than Satie in the classical world. Naturally I like those composers who most people like: Mozart, Beethoven. But I like Mahler very much and Sibelius still more. I love Sibelius. Outside of the old masters I would say that Mahler and Sibelius are my favourites. And I like Stravinsky very much too.

SB: *There's a painting with a certain importance in the film as well, a painting called 'Hope' by Gustav Klimt. How come you chose that painting for the film? Was it by chance or is he an artist you appreciate?*

WA: It just looked right, it just had the right feel for the movie. It turned out to be a coincidence later, that the name of the painting was 'Hope', because the character that Mia played was named Hope. You never hear it in the movie, but you can read it in the credits. But the painting just felt right. Since Gena played a professor in German philosophy, I was trying to find someone fitting as an artist.

SB: *And the painting has a visual connection with the Mia Farrow character as well, as the woman on the painting is pregnant.*

WA: Yes, that's right.

CHAPTER 19

New York Stories

STIG BJÖRKMAN: *Your episode in* New York Stories, Oedipus Wrecks, *is pure comedy. This short farce was made directly after* Another Woman. *Was this a conscious choice of yours to jump into something lighter after a more dramatic film, to interrupt the drama with a more purely comical distraction?*

WOODY ALLEN: Usually after working on something for a long period of time you just want to go on to something else, to something completely different. So that does happen.

SB: *I've heard or read somewhere that the original idea for* New York Stories *was yours.*

WA: Only to a certain extent. I did mention it to my producer, Robert Greenhut, and he thought it would be a good idea to get three people to direct one episode each. And originally he suggested that I and Martin Scorsese – whom he had worked with once – and Steven Spielberg should be in the project. And he got the three of us together, and we agreed to do it. We all thought it was a nice idea. And then Spielberg couldn't do it, so they got Francis Coppola instead. It was an easy project, because I had a funny idea. You know, no problem.

SB: *How come Francis Coppola was brought in. He isn't a New Yorker. Wasn't that the idea from the beginning, that the directors should be from New York?*

WA: No. In fact that the project was called *New York Stories* wasn't my idea or any of our ideas. That was just the working title for the company, Disney. And then they liked that title, and they used it. I didn't think that was a good title for it myself, because I felt it was limiting. But it was as good as any.

SB: *Well, Coppola doesn't limit his episode to New York either. He brings his story over to Athens in the end.*

WA: To tell you the truth I never saw the picture. As I never go and see my own films after they're finished, I was deprived of seeing the episodes by Scorsese and Coppola. I've seen all their other pictures, and I think they are both great film directors. But these ones I didn't see, because I didn't want to see mine.

SB: *Now you can always see theirs on video and run through your own episode.*
WA: Yes, easily, because mine is at the end.

SB: *The names of the characters you and Mia Farrow play are Sheldon and Lisa, and apparently those were the names of two characters in an episode in* Everything You Wanted to Know About Sex . . . *which was eliminated from the film. I don't know if this episode was shot or not.*
WA: Oh yes . . . that's right! It was shot. It was an episode with Louise Lasser, my former wife, and me. It was the two of us on a huge spider's web. She played the black widow spider and I played the male spider. We had sex, and then she killed me in some way, devoured me. It was a very good idea, but I couldn't bring it off, so I cut it out of the film.

SB: *Do you remember why you kept those two names, Sheldon and Lisa, for the characters in* Oedipus Wrecks?
WA: No, but when I type, I usually try and type short names for everybody, because I don't want to type too much.

SB: Oedipus Wrecks *seems to some extent to be a homage to your childhood interest in magic.*
WA: There's an American film critic, Diane Jacobs, who's one of our brighter critics. She just published a book on Preston Sturges. She wrote a book once about me, . . . *but we need the eggs*, relating so many of my works to magic. She felt there was magic in this one, in *Oedipus Wrecks* and *Another Woman* and in *Zelig* and in my play, *The Floating Light Bulb*, which was about a magician. And of course *The Purple Rose of Cairo*. She pointed out that magic and magical things appear constantly in my films. In *Alice* the main character meets this Chinese magician doctor. There's magic in so many of them. She made this thesis, and she was right. She was able to point out the theme of magic over and over and over again. Of course it appears very directly in *Oedipus Wrecks*.

SB: *And this was a favourite hobby of yours when you were a child?*

wa: Yes. I practised and studied it and I performed for my family and friends.

sb: *Were you good at it?*
wa: Yes, I can still do it. I've practised it many, many hours, many days, many years. And I can still do all kinds of card manipulations and tricks with coins and similar things.

sb: *In some behind-the-camera photos on several films I've seen you and Mia Farrow playing chess together, between takes. Are you interested in chess as well?*
wa: Well, I can play. I'm not very good, I'm quite a poor chess player. But I love the game, and I love to watch it. I don't get to play enough, so I lose the visualization. There was a time years ago, eight, ten years ago, when I was playing a lot more chess and I was much better then. Now I haven't played in some years, and I've forgotten so quickly and so much. But I do love the game.

sb: *You have very many mother figures in your previous films. Was Oedipus Wrecks an attempt to settle the account with this mother figure once and for all in comical terms?*
wa: The truth of the matter is that I was sitting in this room one day, and I was listening to a Sydney Bechet record, and I was looking out into the sky, and I thought to myself, 'Gee, I miss him so much. It would be so dramatic and so fantastic, if I could see a huge figure of him playing up there. That big brown face he had with his soprano saxophone.' His music was so beautiful, and I could almost visualize him out there playing. That image stuck with me. And I thought, 'Wouldn't it be funny, if it was my mother, and she would be such a nag . . .' But how would I get her up there. Then I got the idea of taking her to a magic show. She disappears and then appears in the sky. In my original story, everybody in New York was bothered by her. First they just thought it was cute, but then they realized what I've been up against for all those years, when they had to take it. But it went better in this direction, just bothering me and my girlfriend, and then going to an occult person and then falling in love with the occult person.

sb: *The introduction of a 'goy', a non-Jewish person, into a Jewish family, is that a severe offence against Jewish family rules?*
wa: It was mandatory that you marry a Jewish girl. It has loosened up

over the years. But it's one of the many unattractive things about all religions, the sheer stupidity of insisting that your child not marry out of the religion. I just think that's atrocious. And the Jewish religion is at least as guilty of it as every other religion.

SB: *So when you were young and you started dating, your family expected you to date a Jewish girl?*

WA: Yes, but for me it wasn't a problem for two reasons. I didn't care about what they thought, it never meant a thing for me one way or the other. But by chance I grew up in such a Jewish neighbourhood that everybody around was Jewish. So you just met with Jewish girls. But it wouldn't have bothered me for a second if I had fallen in love with a gentile girl or a black girl or a Chinese girl. All of these religious do's and don'ts ranged for me from the laughable to the offensive.

SB: *Projecting the mother figure in the sky, did it cause you any trouble?*

WA: Ah, did it! Not so much for Sven Nykvist maybe. But we got an expert in to tell us how the mechanics should be done. And we did it. It was fun, and Sven shot it correctly, but it was a long time getting it to work up there. You know, to get the proper way of tapering her off. That was a big nuisance. Whenever I have to do any kind of special effect, it's always a problem, because I can't afford it. When I had Mia and Alec Baldwin flying in *Alice* and the mother in the sky here and the little spirit at the end of *A Midsummer Night's Sex Comedy*, there's a problem. Usually when people who're good at them do these things, people like Steven Spielberg or George Lucas, they have enough money and they make tests. They spend more money on tests getting it right than I spend on half of my picture. And then they get it beautifully. I don't have money to really do it properly, so I always do the bargain-basement version of it. When we did this flying scene with Mia and Alec Baldwin in *Alice*, if we'd had the money to bring in the very best stuff and the best computerized cameras, then we could have done like in *Superman*, just done it perfectly. But it was such an ordeal for us and it takes forever! And I wind up cutting three or four shots out, shots that took you a day to make.

SB: *Do you find it boring as well having to deal with this very technical and time-consuming process?*

WA: I find it very boring! Now, I will say, that if I was working with

Gordon Willis, it might have gone a little smoother, only because in addition to being an artist he's a technical wizard. But maybe not, because Gordon shot *A Midsummer Night's Sex Comedy*. Whenever you have to rely on an outside laboratory to help you, it's very, very tough.

SB: *But the effects work very well in* Alice.

WA: But you only saw the end of everything. After agonizing work, we did finally have to get a camera with a computer. The whole process was very, very difficult.

SB: *Were there other scenes in* Alice *you wanted to have in the film which you had to cut out for technical reasons?*

WA: Yes, there were. For instance, when we made the scene with the German submarine in *Radio Days* the U-boat was only about one yard in length. And it was so much work to get it done, it was so hard. Finally, in the end, the only way I could go back and re-shoot it, the only way that I could make it look right, was to put a binocular matte around it. I didn't want a binocular matte. I just wanted the boy to look – and see the boat. But I had to go back and shoot the boy again and give him a pair of binoculars. In this way I managed to cover a multitude of sins. I hate special effects!

SB: *I'd like to talk about the two little ladies in the film, Mae Questel and Jesse Keosian, as Sheldon's mother and aunt. Mae Questel, I know, was the 'Betty Boop girl' and she also happened to sing one of the songs in* Zelig, *but how did you come across these two for the parts?*

WA: Well, Juliet Taylor tried almost every Jewish old lady in town. She went to old ladies' homes, she went to acting groups. And finally, after I had seen about thirty actresses, Mae Questel came in as part of a routine thing and (*Woody snaps his fingers*) the second I saw her, the second she read, she was right on the nose. She couldn't be better. She even looks like my mother. And Jesse Keosian, that's another story. Many years ago, when I was in high school, when I was fourteen, fifteen years old, she was my biology teacher! She was a little, tiny lady, and we used to make jokes about her. You couldn't see her behind the biology desk. She was a little, tiny biology teacher. I had her for one term, and I never said a word to her in class. Then I graduated and I never saw her again . . . for thirty-five years. Then one day Juliet Taylor said to me, 'A wonderful little woman came into my office, after my scouting at the older persons' retirement homes, and I think she's the greatest looking little woman. And she says

42   Mae Questel and Woody Allen in *Oedipus Wrecks*

she knows you from school. She says she was your biology teacher.' So I said, 'Mrs Keosian?' And she got the part. Everybody on the set called her Jesse, but I still could only call her Mrs Keosian, because I only knew her that way.

SB: *Had she had any acting experience?*
WA: No, none at all.

SB: *So how did she come to visit Juliet Taylor?*
WA: Well, Jesse Keosian is a very bright woman and very cultivated. She spends all her time going to art galleries and concerts and things. She's retired and she read this notice in the retirement village that they were looking for older women for some small parts in a movie. And she showed up just for her own interest. Since then she's done another movie and several commercials.

SB: *And how did she treat you when you worked together? Were you still the young schoolboy for her?*
WA: No, she was just as amazingly bright as always. She had never acted in her life, but she would often pose questions like, 'Would this character do it this way or wouldn't she more likely be doing it this way?' A completely lucid analysis. She was just wonderful.

CHAPTER 20

Crimes and Misdemeanours

JUDAH'S FATHER: The eyes of God are constantly watching us.
(From *Crimes and Misdemeanours*)

STIG BJÖRKMAN: *I understand you wrote the script for* Crimes and
Misdemeanours *during a trip to Europe. Is that true?*
WOODY ALLEN: Right, but always remember what I said the other
day, the real hard work is the pre-work. Once the pre-work is done, the
rest is easy. I can do the writing just anywhere. I can check into a hotel
and on their stationery write some pages, and then as we move on to the
next town I grab more stationery and write. And this was exactly the way
I wrote this script. But all the hard work had been done before.

SB: Crimes and Misdemeanours *is, I think, a very rich film in many
aspects. In some respects it recalls the literature of the Romantic era,
which strived to break down the prevalent order that existed between
different genres.* Crimes and Misdemeanours *expresses similar aims. It's
drama, comedy, comedy of manners, all at the same time.*
WA: Yes, there are certain movies of mine that I call 'novels on film',
and *Crimes and Misdemeanours* is one of them, wherein a number of
characters are being dissected and a number of stories are going on at the
same time. Some of these stories can be more humorous, while some
other stories can be more philosophical. The trick is then to keep all the
stories up in the air at the same time, so that you can follow them all and
get involved in them all without getting bored.

SB: *Is this something you like and look for in literature as well?*
WA: Yes, certainly when you read a Tolstoy novel, for instance. That's
an extreme example of it. But it's wonderful the way some novels are
constructed and executed.

SB: *Someone has defined Romantic literature as a mixture of chaos and eros, which also in a way characterizes your film.*

WA: Yes, I can see that, 'chaos and eros' . . . I do think that in *Hannah and Her Sisters* and *Crimes and Misdemeanours* there is this combination. But these are the standard devices of the dramatist as well. Chaos is either exciting or amusing and eros is fascinating. So, sure, the combination is great. If you have pure chaos, you'll have farce, I guess. And if you have pure eros, I don't know what you would have. But the combination is, I think, an apt one.

SB: *Crimes and Misdemeanours could be defined as an existential film as well, as it takes up some of these universal existential themes about our position in life and in the world.*

WA: Right, that's the only interesting theme to me. Contemporary philosophy is hardly interesting from a dramatist's point of view. There was an era in which existential themes emerged with Kirkegaard and Dostoyevsky and those themes were the natural material of the dramatist. So all those existential pieces of literature and drama are wonderful and fun. But dramatizing linguistic philosophy, for instance, is not as much fun.

SB: *When you made the portrait of the philosopher in the film, Louis Levy, did you model him on any known person?*

WA: Interestingly, people have spoken to me about Primo Levi, because even the name is similar. But he was not an inspiration for me, oddly enough. I had long ago thought of doing an existential murder mystery in which a college professor commits suicide and I then go about proving that given his philosophy, there's no way he could have ever committed suicide. That could not have been a choice he could have made given the content of his intellectual life. And so I prove that it's a murder. That's what got me interested in doing something about a person whose life defied any sense that he might want to commit suicide.

SB: *When I saw the film the first time, I got a feeling that this part of the film was a documentary, that this Louis Levy existed as a real person.*

WA: Well, he is a real person in a way. The man acting him is a psychoanalyst.

SB: *The other day you mentioned a book to me which has meant a lot to you,* The Denial of Death *by Ernest Becker. This subject or discussion seems to be of great interest and importance for you.*
WA: Oh, yes.

SB: *Especially in* Crimes and Misdemeanours, *death is the prevailing theme of the film.*
WA: Yes, death and one's position in the universe. And certain moral issues.

SB: *You've dwelled on this subject before as well. It's the theme of one very short play of yours,* Death Knocks *and in the one-act play* Death, *which also was the basis for* Shadows and Fog.
WA: Yes, it's a key theme. Bergman made the definitive work on the subject with *The Seventh Seal.* And I've always wished that I could come up with the correct metaphor that would be able to express my observations and feelings on it. But I've never come up with a metaphor as good as his. I don't think you can. I just think he got the definitive, dramatic one for it. The closest I've come so far is *Shadows and Fog,* but it's not as good a metaphor as his. Bergman's is right on the nose. It's great.

SB: *But do you need a metaphor? Here, in* Crimes and Misdemeanours *you deal with the subject in a very serious way without the need for any metaphor.*
WA: Right, this is a realistic story; but, you know, I'd love to get a poetic take on it somehow. I'd love to be able to transmit it through poetry rather than through prose. On the screen one does poetry or one does prose. Usually you can tell the difference, clearly. *Persona* and *The Seventh Seal* are poetry, whereas a John Huston film is usually prose, of a wonderful kind. But once in a while you get a film that looks like prose but it turns out to be poetry, like *The Bicycle Thief.* It seems so realistic, but it passes beyond that. I don't think that's true of Jean Renoir's films. I don't think that *The Grand Illusion* or *Rules of the Game* are poetic. I think they're realistic and fabulous. They are great, great prose, just as Huston's movies are great prose. But Bergman works with poetry so frequently, I have to think . . . which of his films are not poetic. If there are any that are not.

SB: Scenes from a Marriage, *for instance.*
WA: Yes, that's a thought. And a number of those early ones. His early

films were just like good Hollywood movies. His early comedies and romances, they looked like the standard kind of movies that would have been done in Hollywood. But the best of them!

SB: *Yes, his early films could be defined as prose, but then it's hard to find films that are predominantly prose after that.*

WA: Yes, after the one he made with Harriet Andersson.

SB: *Yes,* Summer with Monika *is prose, but the one he made the year after,* Sawdust and Tinsel, *is already poetry.*

WA: Even *Summer with Monika* starts to get a little poetic. Certainly with his beginning and ending of the picture. It's not realistic. It moves on to a slightly different level. And then you get on to the works of poetry of his.

SB: *So, you think you want to try and deal with death again in a poetical way?*

WA: I was trying with *Shadows and Fog*, but . . . Yes, I would like to. Because, first off, the so-called — it's become such a tiresome phrase — existential subjects to me are still the only subjects worth dealing with. Any time one deals with other subjects one is not aiming for the highest goal. One can be aiming at some very interesting things, but it's not the deepest thing for me. I don't think that one can aim more deeply than at the so-called existential themes, the spiritual themes. That's probably why I'd consider the Russian novelists as greater than other novelists. Even though Flaubert, for example, is a much more skilled writer than, I think, either Dostoyevsky or Tolstoy — he was surely more skilled than Dostoyevsky, as a technician — his work can never be as great, for me, personally, as the other two. Very often people avoid making value judgements, but I think the opposite. I think it's very important to make them; it's almost an obligation. One can say, 'I appreciate Flaubert more than Kafka or Stendahl more than Tolstoy.' But I don't. I myself don't. I just feel that you must — if you're operating at the maximum of your capabilities — aim at very, very high material. And that to me would be the spiritual, existential realm. It's great when it's done realistically, and it's great when it's done poetically. But poetically is more intriguing for me. Take, for instance, a movie like *In Cold Blood*. It's full of natural, existential material. This little town which suddenly finds these brutal killings. Everybody's lives change. It's done realistically, and it's a fascinating story. It was fascinating in the novel and it was pretty fascinating on the screen as well. But I just appreciate it more, when it's done poetically. To me, *The Trial* would be great fun to be able to do, because you're able to deal with some very substantial and profound feelings and intuitions and ideas and deal with them in a very poetic way. It's very seductive.

SB: *I mentioned romantic literature in connection to* Crimes and Misdemeanours. *In Wordsworth's play* The Borderers *he creates what one could define as the first existentialist, a man who through his deeds creates not only his autonomy and unique self but also his own scale of values. In this respect Judah in your film resembles him.*

WA: Absolutely. He has a set of values and they are his values. And we live in a world where there's nobody to punish you, if you don't punish yourself. Judah is someone who does what's expedient for him when he has to. And he gets away with it! And leads a wonderful life after, presumably. If he doesn't choose to punish himself then he's gotten away with it.

It's just like the conversation around the dinner table at Judah's parental home, when they're talking about the Nazis. We happened to have won the war. But if we didn't win the war, then history would have been created differently.

SB: *Why did you name the central character Judah?*

WA: Because I thought it was biblical, and I thought it had wisdom to it. It suggested weight and wisdom. It made him more of a patriarchal figure in the story, and I wanted that.

SB: *In* Crimes and Misdemeanours *we see the Jewish background in a more explicit way than in most of your other films.*

WA: Well, Judah's problem and its relation to religious teachings and religious belief is significant, and the only religion that I feel I can write about with any kind of accuracy is the Jewish religion. I have no feel for the details of Christianity.

SB: *One thing which struck me in the film is the conversation between Judah and the rabbi, when Judah discusses the eventual murder of Dolores. Why doesn't the rabbi react more strongly against these thoughts?*

WA: You mean in the scene in the study, during the lightning storm?

SB: *Yes.*

WA: Because the rabbi doesn't really exist there. It's just in Judah's mind. He's just utilizing the rabbi to have this mental dialogue.

SB: *One central theme in the film is about seeing and sight. Not only does the rabbi go blind, we see Dolores get completely blinded through the killing. In the scene when Judah goes to her flat and finds her dead, you have a very intense close-up on her face, and he closes her eyes. Eyes and sight are shown or discussed throughout the film. Was this an important subject for you in the film?*

WA: Well, eyes were a metaphor in the story. Judah was an eye doctor who heals people on the one hand, but is willing to kill on the other. And he doesn't see well himself. I mean, his vision is fine, but his emotional vision, his moral vision is not good. The rabbi is blind to other things, to the realities of life. On the other hand, he can triumph over it because he has spiritual substance. *Crimes and Misdemeanours* is about people who don't see. They don't see themselves as others see them. They don't see the right and wrong of situations. And that was a strong metaphor in the movie.

SB: *Yes. And then we have your character in the film, Cliff, the documentary film-maker, who sees the world through the lens of his camera. And the same goes for his brother-in-law, Lester, even if we never do see him at work behind his camera.*

WA: Right. And Lester has no idea of how I, how Cliff sees him at the end of the picture. He imagines that I see him differently throughout. He's being seen through my camera throughout.

SB: *Well, this is being commented on all through the movie. Shortly after the murder scene, for instance, there's a flashback with Judah and Delores, where she says to him, 'My mother always told me that the eyes are the windows of the soul. What do you think?' And he answers, that he doesn't believe that.*

WA: Right.

SB: *When you have such a strong and recurrent theme in a story, how aware are you about it when you write the script? Have you consciously planted it there, or did it just present itself to you while writing?*

WA: It's instinctive. I don't take special notes on that, for instance. You feel, when writing the script, when it should surface again. When one feels it's correct for it to surface, you let it happen.

SB: *But when you started to write the script, did you know that this would be one of the main themes of the story?*

WA: I knew I was going to use eyes. Definitely. When I started to write the film, I made Judah an eye doctor. And before that I thought of the eye metaphor. That was the first instinct for it. Then, when he's accepting his award at the beginning of the film and I was writing the speech for him, it occurred to me then that it was a decent metaphor to be mined there. And so I tried my best to do it.

SB: *For the part of Judah you chose Martin Landau, and I think he's excellent. Although he's a very fine actor, he has not been considered a leading actor, according to Hollywood standards. He has had big and important supporting roles though, important character roles, one shortly before* Crimes and Misdemeanours *in Francis Coppola's* Tucker. *Why did you choose Martin Landau for the part?*

WA: I had nobody for the film. It's very hard to find these actors who exist in the British theatre but not in America. I just couldn't find anybody good for the part of Judah. But I found Martin Landau very good in *Tucker*. Coppola sort of dug him up out of obscurity, and Francis, who's a fine director, came up with a wonderful performance together with Martin Landau. Martin is a talented actor, and Francis had the foresight to see that. So Francis really put him back on the map in a big way. I didn't do any pioneering work there at all. I just saw him in Francis' movie, and I liked him, I was impressed. Juliet Taylor recommended him. Then Juliet Taylor and I flew him into town, with the prospect that he should play the brother, the Jerry Orbach part. We let him read the script, and he accepted the part. Then we thought we might test him for the other part, while he was in New York. We hadn't found anybody for it yet. So we asked Martin to read this other part. And he was more than delighted and said he'd love to do that part, 'It's really got dimensions.' He read it, and he was completely natural. It's an interesting thing. Of all the actors I've ever worked with, he gives expression to my dialogue exactly as I hear it. His colloquialisms, his idiom, his inflection is exactly correct. So of all the people who've ever read my lines, he (*Woody snaps his fingers*) makes them correct every time. He never misunderstands what a line should sound like. I've worked with some pretty terrific actors, but he just makes it sound the way I wrote it. One of the reasons for this must be that Martin Landau came from my neighbourhood in Brooklyn, right near where I lived, only a few blocks away. So he grew up the way I did, surrounded by people who speak like that.

He just understood instinctively. It's baked into him, the nuance. So it was easy to work with him.

SB: *And Angelica Houston? With Manhattan Murder Mystery, you've worked with her twice, but in* Crimes and Misdemeanours *she had her first acting part with you.*

WA: I wanted to get a big and impressive woman who's interesting. Of course Angelica is one of our great actresses, but I didn't think she would want to do this part. Because it's too small a part and the character gets murdered. But she said she would. And of course she was great and she made that part a hundred times more interesting than anybody else could have done. She also looks so right for the part, the minute you see her, with her hair up, when she's coming back with her groceries. Her attitude, her anger, her size. She just had enough craziness and anger. It couldn't have been better.

SB: *Some of the best scenes in the film, I think, are between these two, Martin Landau and Angelica Huston, in her – Dolores' – apartment. They are very skilfully staged as well. The apartment is very small and you have to economize their movements to a great extent. Was this a real location? And do you remember how these scenes were prepared and staged?*

WA: Yes, it is a real apartment.

Over the years, because I'm doing these long master shots, I've found out just through experience how to do these scenes so that they're effective and what to worry about and what not to worry about. The trick is to keep the action moving in the right way. To keep the camera and the actors moving and to make sure that the actor – or the actors – are seen the correct way at the right time. There's many times when the actor or actors don't have to be seen, and you don't have to worry about it. You have to know that. You have to sense when it doesn't really matter if the camera is on that person. For their biggest lines, their most effective lines, sometimes you don't need the camera on them for these lines, and it will be just as effective or more effective in this way. You have to make sure that the choreography is such that they cross in and out of closer shots and wider shots at the right times. Usually it takes a while to stage these scenes. But that's how I shoot. I go in there in the morning and don't let the actors in. I work out the situation myself, Carlo and I, and we decide the staging of the scene. Then he does a general lighting. Then I bring the actors in, and I show them where I want them to walk. I never work with actors who question this. Of course we make *certain* adjustments. Certain things are guessed incorrectly. But then finally, after a long period of time, we have the shot. And then we do it, and we suck up a lot of pages at once. So you don't really lose any time at all with this procedure. There were times with Sven or Carlo or Gordon Willis when we would work and work and work all day long and not shoot anything at all until five o'clock in the afternoon. An entire day was spent with planning. And then at five o'clock we'd shoot for ten minutes and we would have seven pages of dialogue in the can. And that would be it, a very respectable day's work from a production point of view.

SB: *Do you like to set up scenes in very restricted areas like this one? I saw you work with Angelica Huston in a similar very, very small flat. In fact, it was impossible to stay there as an onlooker, because it was so small. Is it a kind of challenge for you to work in these restricted locations?*
WA: No, but I like the apartment to smell authentic. That's important to me. So if the characters would have a small apartment, I get them a small apartment. I get them the apartment I think that they would have. Carlo complains, but I can't help it. Once in a while when I pick a location and Carlo comes and says, 'No, I can't possibly shoot here. It'll just be terrible,' then I don't use it. Then we try to find another small apartment, maybe one with a terrace where he can put his lights. But generally, all of them, Gordon and Sven and Carlo, are very good at shooting in small spaces.

SB: *A very arresting sequence in the film is the scenes after the murder of Dolores. There you have a couple of shots which are totally concentrated on Judah, with him alone in the bathroom of his home, one slightly decomposed picture of him studying his face in the bathroom mirror, among other things. Do you remember the ideas you had for this montage sequence?*
WA: My feeling was that once his brother calls and tells him that the deed is done, Judah crosses an irrevocable threshold in his life from which he can never return. At first it starts to dawn on him. He meets it with a mixture of relief and terror as well. And when he sits there with the group of people, he's like in a different world. They're all talking about mundane things, and he's realizing that he has to get back to the flat of his mistress. He instantly starts to feel anxiety and fear. When he's

in the flat, he's able to get possession of himself, sufficiently. But what's interesting to me there is what goes through his mind at the time. What I'm interested in is just his mind.

SB: *Yes, here you allow yourself time and you allow Judah time together with us to go through this experience, to share his state of mind. Like most of your films,* Crimes and Misdemeanours *is told in quite a fast pace, but here you allow yourself and Judah a pause in the narrative.*

WA: Right, because it's too meaningful a moment. It's very important that we stop the forward flow of the narrative and look in there for a while. His internal conflict is so important at the time, because the deed that he's just been responsible for is so immense.

SB: *We talked about close-ups in connection to* Another Woman *and the Gena Rowlands character in that film. This is how you're presenting Martin Landau in this film as well.*

WA: Right, because so much of Martin's conflict, just like Gena's conflict, is inside the character. And the best you can do with the camera in these situations is to get close and see if you can get a clue there. You can never really get inside.

SB: *Do you remember how you came to stage the scene when Judah finds Dolores dead on the floor? It's very eloquently staged. You start with a close-up on his face, the camera moves down to his shoes and we follow him over the floor, to a close-up on her face, and then he apparently sits down, because the camera goes back to him for a new close-up on his face.*

WA: I remember that very well. I wanted the flow going in that scene because I felt that that moment of the movie had to be a poetic moment. It had to be a reflective moment. So everything was done legato to keep the mood from breaking, to keep the bubble from breaking. I tried to get him into a trance and keep in that. So the camera, moving like that, doesn't break the rhythm, doesn't snap off the rhythm with an awakening cut. It lulls you further and further into his state of mind.

SB: *How did you choose the music for the murder scene? You have a quartet by Schubert there.*

WA: Yes, it's the same as when I chose the music for *Manhattan.* I've loved that piece of music for many years. And long before I wrote the story for *Crimes and Misdemeanours* I thought, 'What a wonderful piece

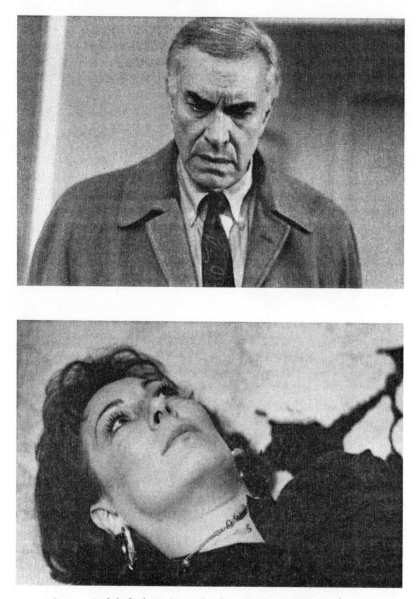

43 & 44   Judah finds Dolores dead on the floor: Martin Landau and
Anjelica Huston in *Crimes and Misdemeanours*

of music, gripped with tension and gripped with portent.' So when I thought of music for that spot, this Schubert quartet came back to me and it was an instantly correct feeling for me. Then I went back into the script and changed one of the pieces of dialogue to include Schubert in it, so there was a relationship.

SB: *The music reaches a very dramatic peak, when Dolores opens the front door to get into her house.*
WA: Right, the strings are riddled with anxiety. That's a beautiful piece of music!

SB: *One recurrent theme in the film is also the question of money. For instance, there's the threat of blackmail from Dolores, the discussion of money to be paid to the hired killer. And the fact that your character, Cliff, is very poor and that his brother-in-law and rival, Lester, is very rich. And so on. What's your own attitude towards money? Are you generous or do you have difficulty in parting with money?*
WA: I've never thought about money. I'm very generous and I never think about it. I only think about my work. If you ask me, would I like to be very, very wealthy, the answer is that I would. I'd love to be extremely wealthy, but I would never do anything to obtain wealth. I mean, I would never make a movie or write a script to do that. If somebody comes along and asks me to act in a movie and offers me a lot of money and it's a silly movie, I will act in it. I don't care about that. But in my own work, I'll never do anything for money. One of the ideas of the picture was that I wanted to make an ironic comment on success as exemplified by money, fame and the material rewards of life. It isn't enough to have a good heart and to aim high. Society pays off on success. The fact that Lester is a fool doesn't matter. He's successful. And because he's successful, they want him at universities to lecture, they want to give him awards. And a woman like Halley (Mia Farrow) winds up liking him. Then, when it comes to Cliff, it's irrelevant to people that your intentions are good. In real life, when I finish a movie, I can pound on people's chests and say, 'But look, my intentions were so good!' They don't care. They pay off on winners. And winners mean fame, money, material success.

SB: *At the start we see Lester completely through the eyes of Cliff; we see him as the clown he also is, an upstart and a careerist. But later on you try to modify our view of him, to show other sides of him. For instance, in a scene at a dinner-table Cliff starts to quote a poem by Emily Dickinson which Lester can complete for him.*

WA: Yes, because he's not stupid. These Lesters of the world who you meet now and then, they're not stupid troglodytes who have won a lottery or something. They're educated and intelligent, but their values are shallow. They take themselves very seriously. The sad part of the film is that everyone takes Lester seriously. But he's not a bad guy.

SB: *The poem by Emily Dickinson which they're quoting is about death as well. I guess that's not by chance?*

WA: It's 'Because he could not stop for death, he kindly stopped for me', isn't it? Sure, that's a wonderful poem. I used that poem in *September* as well, but I cut it out. The Sam Waterston character quoted it. That is to say, Sam never quoted it. Christopher Walken quoted it. It was in the first version, before Sam was doing the part.

SB: *You use excerpts of films in* Crimes and Misdemeanours *in a more commentary way than usual compared to your other films. For instance, you show a scene from Hitchcock's* Mr and Mrs Smith, *with Carole Lombard and Robert Montgomery, where they quarrel and she says to him that she's given him the best years of her life. This follows immediately after a quarrel between Martin Landau and Angelica Huston. And later on you have an excerpt from* Murder, He Says.

WA: Yes, there are direct connections, because one of the themes of the picture is the difference between reality and fantasy. There's a real life and film life and a fantasy life. Film being synonymous with fantasy. In real life high ambitions don't mean anything, only success does. People commit murders, and they get away with them. They're not punished. Good people go blind. But there's also a fantasy life that people live by and escape into all the time, and it juxtaposes against the reality of real life. Betty Hutton can be singing about 'Murder, He Says' on the screen, but in the end it's real murder. There's a definite difference between our fantasy life and our real life, unfortunately.

SB: *And in the end you do discuss this. You make the connection in the scene between yourself and Martin Landau, when you meet at the wedding. He tells you about someone who's planned the perfect murder, and you ask him, 'A movie plot?' And he says it's not a movie plot but something which happened to a friend of his. You conclude the discussion you've made visual throughout the film through the film clips.*

45   'A movie plot?' Judah (Martin Landau) recounts his 'perfect murder' to Cliff (Woody Allen)

WA: Right, because the truth of the matter is that I tend to think of it as a fantasy world, but in truth it's the real world. My character can only talk about it in terms of movies. Such things don't happen in real life. But they do.

SB: *Your character, Cliff, and his niece are mostly seen visiting the Bleeker Street Cinema, which doesn't exist any more, a pity. Was this cinema a favourite of yours?*
WA: Yes, it was, for two reasons. First of all for a cinematic reason. It was visually a wonderful-looking theatre. It had a real good look to it. Secondly, their programmes over the years had been wonderful; I consistently used to attend the Bleeker Street Cinema, because it was one of the places in town where you could always see . . . Antonioni, Truffaut or Orson Welles or other film-makers like them.

SB: *Cliff points out in the film that he feels a certain responsibility for his niece and that he has promised her father when he was ill that he would provide her with the best education possible. So for you that's the movies in the afternoon?*
WA: Yes, for me education doesn't necessarily mean the academic curriculum. There are other things to learn. And one of those things is cultural education, film education. Also good fishing, good baseball.

SB: *Cliff also gives the advice to his niece, that she shouldn't listen to what her school teachers say but she should see what they look like.*
WA: Sure, because they talk, talk, talk, talk, and when you see them – the ones I had in school – they were mean-looking, sorry, sad and bitter. You looked at them and you knew what their lives were like and you knew what their values were, and you imbibed more from that socratically than you did intellectually.

SB: *One thing which is being discussed throughout the film as well is the relationship of love between the sexes. At some point you show a piece of interview with the philosopher in the film, Louis Levy, to Halley (Mia Farrow). And there he says, 'What we are aiming at when we fall in love is a very strange paradox. And the paradox consists of the fact that when we fall in love, we are seeking to refind all or some of the people to whom we were attracted when we were children, and then we have to attempt to return to the past and at the same time to undo the past.' Is this your belief as well?*

WA: Yes, I think that's true. We spend our whole life trying to do that. We try to go back and rectify our problems.

SB: *An important character in the film is, of course, the rabbi, Ben. He says at one point, 'I can't go on living, if I didn't feel with all my heart a moral structure with real meaning and forgiveness and some kind of higher power.'*

WA: Yes, my own feeling about Ben is that, on the one hand, he's blind even before he goes blind. He's blind because he doesn't see the real world. But he's blessed and lucky because he has the single most important lucky attribute anyone could have, the best gift anyone could have. He has genuine religious faith. It's not artificial. He genuinely believes what he's saying. And so even in the face of the worst adversity, he is OK. He goes blind. He still loves everybody and loves the world and loves life and loves his daughter. Judah's father has faith. And Ben also has faith. They have faith in God, real faith, and it takes them through all kinds of adversity. The worst kind of adversity can be surmounted with faith. But as the author, *I* think that Ben is blind even before he's blind, because he doesn't see what's real in the world. But he's lucky, because he has his naïvety.

SB: *All this really comes through Sam Waterston's performance as well.*

WA: Yes, because he's basically a sweet actor.

SB: *Is this why you wanted to end the film on him, on Ben dancing with his daughter at the wedding?*

WA: Yes, because I thought that he's one of the people that triumphs in the film. Cliff loses out. Lester remains a pompous fool. Judah gets away with murder. And doctor Levy commits suicide. Life is really quite hard for everybody, they're really having a tough time of it. But Ben triumphs over it because I think the only thing, or the best thing, that gives you a chance to triumph in life is religious faith. It surpasses even earthly love between a man and a woman. Because even if that's very sustaining and wonderful, there comes a time when one of them dies. Then all you have is your spiritual content. So unless you have a strong spiritual feeling, spiritual faith, it's tough to get through life. Ben is the only one that gets through it, even if he doesn't really understand the reality of life. One can argue that he understands it more deeply than the others. I don't think he does myself. I think he understands it

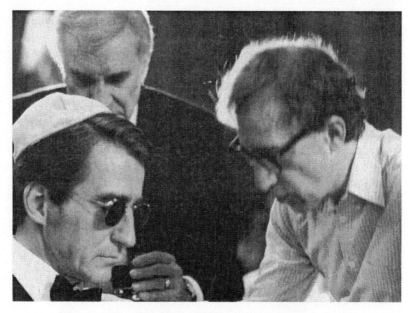

46 Woody Allen directing Sam Waterston and Martin Landau on
Crimes and Misdemeanours

less, and that's why I wanted to make him blind. I feel that his faith is blind. It will work, but it requires closing your eyes to reality.

SB: *What about your own religious faith? Is it like that of the average person?*

WA: Worse! I think that at best the universe is indifferent. At best! Hannah Arendt spoke of the banality of evil. The universe is banal as well. And because it's banal, it's evil. It isn't diabolically evil. It's evil in its banality. Its indifference is evil. If you walk down the street and you see homeless people, starving, and you're indifferent to them, you're in a way being evil. Indifference to me equals evil.

SB: *You have Louis Levy say as well that the 'Universe is a pretty cold place. We invest it with our feelings.'*

WA: Right, so we create a fake world for ourselves, and we exist within that fake world. On a lesser level you see it in sports. They create a world of football, for example. You get lost in that world and you care about meaningless things. Who scores the most points, etc. People get caught up in it, and others make lots of money with it. People by the thousands watch it, thinking it's very important who wins. But, in fact, if you step back for a second, it's utterly unimportant who wins. It means nothing. In the same way we create for ourselves a world that, in fact, means nothing at all, when you step back. It's meaningless. But it's important that we create some sense of meaning, because no perceptible meaning exists for anybody.

SB: *You mentioned the homeless, and when you walk around in New York the streets are filled with a shockingly high number of poor people. It's almost like visiting a Third World country. Do you think that the United States and the Americans have become more indifferent when it comes to social politics and humanistic values?*

WA: I don't know if America is more indifferent than anywhere else. No, it never works as a national attribute. There are many Americans who are indifferent, and there are many who are very, very responsible and torn by the plights of the people of Somalia or the homeless people. America, on balance, has been a generous country over the years in many ways. They've done some very insensitive things too, without any question. Some pretty awful things. But in the end all those things seem to balance out. Every country, every national power group does some good things and some bad things. I don't think one is worse than the other though. Unless you're talking about fascism which is an illness, not a political movement.

SB: *Do you think that by the end of your film, by the end of the story of* Crimes and Misdemeanours, *Judah has managed to solve his moral dilemma?*

WA: Solved it? No! It's not a big moral dilemma for him at all. As soon as his brother suggests the murder of Dolores, his first reaction is the stereotypical reaction dictated by his social milieu, but even minutes later, before his brother leaves, he's already thinking, 'Well, you know, maybe I should give this idea some thought.' And all his thinking after that becomes rationalizations to permit him to carry on with the plan. Judah's never really in too much of a quandary. Any quandary he has, he's going to rationalize it away to do what he wants. And he does it, and gets away with it. He has a couple of tense moments after, a couple of bad moments, but that's all. He leaves the party with his beautiful wife. His daughter is going to get married soon. Everything is fine for him. So, if he doesn't choose to punish himself, nobody else will. Evil is only punished if you get caught. He's a terrible person, but he himself is fine.

SB: *Where do you place* Crimes and Misdemeanours *among your other films?*

WA: I think it's one of my better films. I think it's one of the more successful ones, because I felt it had some substance to chew on and it portrayed the philosophical and intellectual interest that I had in this subject matter in a reasonably entertaining way. I thought there were some laughs in it and some tense moments. So, in general, I felt more positive about it.

CHAPTER 21

Alice

DR YANG: Freedom is a frightening thought.

(From *Alice*)

STIG BJÖRKMAN: *I guess it's not by chance that you've named your heroine and titled your film* Alice?
WOODY ALLEN: It is, in a certain sense. It did not have to do with *Alice in Wonderland*. Alice is a quintessential kind of rich WASPy name. It's not a Jewish name, it's not an Italian name, an ethnic name. I wanted to make Alice Tate a clean, blond, rich person. I could just as easily at the time have thought of another name, Leslie Tate or something, and then I would have called the movie *Leslie*.

SB: *The main characters in* Alice, *the Tates and their friends, are they a kind of people you know very well? Because* Alice, *of course, is a satire on this kind of upper-class person and their milieu.*
WA: I live in that kind of milieu. I live in a penthouse on Fifth Avenue. I live on the upper East Side of New York, which is very chic. When I used to pick up my children or deliver my children to school, I'd go there on a cold winter morning, and the other mothers would be bringing their kids to school, and there'd be fifteen mothers there in huge mink coats and sable coats. They live a very protected life and they have homes in Connecticut or the Hamptons and they live in designer apartments on Park Avenue and Fifth Avenue. And they spend their days shopping and having lunches, and every now and then one of them will get into some kind of project with artists or writers or politicians. But it's quite superficial. I don't dislike those people. I don't think they're bad people. They have a certain kind of lifestyle, and I think it's amusing. But I think they would be better off if they spent their time focused on better things. Which some of them do. There are many, many socialites, who spend a huge amount of time with charity-raising. No, I don't dislike them. I think they're funny. They're rich. And they do some nice things and some shallow things.

SB: *But you wanted in some way to awaken Alice?*

WA: Yes. I thought it would be a funny story to concentrate on a woman like Alice. Because all these women are always involved with acupuncture and nutrition and massage and cosmetics and face-lifts and things like that. So I thought it would be a funny story that she goes to an acupuncturist, but he's really a magician. And he turns her life around completely. Because what's bothering her is nothing physical. There's nothing physically wrong with her. It's all emotional.

SB: *And you want to awaken her through her dreams and her journeys into fantasy?*

WA: Yeah, I want her to see her life differently. To embark on a different kind of a life.

SB: *Many American films in recent years have shown an increasing interest in supernatural phenomena, like ghosts, people who get the chance to live their lives over again, people who revive their youths and so on.*

WA: Well, nobody is really religious any more, and people are running around craving some kind of spiritual life. They attach it to psycho-analysis, they attach it to acupuncture, to nutrition, to health food. People need some kind of inner life, something to believe in. There are many things that serve that purpose. And so it's gotten into films.

SB: *But there is also a revival of a certain kind of genre film, a genre which was very popular during the Second World War, in the late thirties and early forties, films like* I Married a Witch *or* Heaven Can Wait *and so on. Now, during the later part of the eighties, this kind of film appears again. Do you see any connection between the political and social situation during these two eras?*

WA: Only that they are two escapist eras. At the earlier period people wanted to escape from the terribleness of the war and in this period it's the empty spiritual life people have. I wasn't interested in that when I made *Alice*. I was interested only in one specific woman and in turning her life around. *Alice* is the comedy version of *Another Woman*. Through magic, in *Another Woman*, Marion, the main character, hears voices through the wall, and these voices provoke her to change her life. And in this story it's a comic approach. The same kind of woman comes to re-examine her life, in a different way, but still with a similar purpose.

47   Mia Farrow and Keye Luke in *Alice*

SB: *Do you think this part in any way was a challenge for Mia Farrow?*
WA: No, she liked the role and did it well. She was great! She looks the part. We couldn't have gotten a better casting visually. Alice was a good thing for her.

SB: *And William Hurt, how did he come into the picture?*
WA: I wanted a perfect kind of blond WASPy banker husband. I never thought William Hurt would do it. I thought he might read the script and say, 'It's too unlikeable a character and too small a part. There's nothing to do with it.' But no, he did it, and he was great. He was fun to work with, and he did a great job.

SB: *I think so too. There's one great scene between the two of them, in the bedroom, where Alice asks her husband, if he's ever been unfaithful. He denies it, but feels obliged to ask her the same question. Which he does with a little ironic and smug smile, which is very revealing of his character.*
WA: Yes, he's an actor who's watchful of these kind of subtleties.

SB: *Alice is about freedom, about one woman's liberation. But as the Chinese doctor says, 'Freedom is a frightening thought.'*
WA: This is an old axiom of existential thinkers. There's no question that, when you're free, it's terrifying.

SB: *I was thinking about this line in comparison to Gabe's attitude in* Husbands and Wives, *when he asserts to his wife the opinion that 'change is death'.*
WA: Yes, change is death. That's an opinion of mine. I'm against change. Because change equals ageing, change equals the progression of time, the destruction of the old order. Now, you can say that somebody in a certain station in life wants nothing more than change, because they want the destruction of the old order. But ultimately, to me, change is not your friend. It's like nature. Change is your temporary friend sometimes. People who live in poverty and misery, of course, long for change. And when they get change, change is their friend for that period of time. But change beyond that is not going to be their friend. Change is a fair-weather friend, a short-term friend.

SB: *But in the case of Alice change must mean life, don't you think?*
WA: Yes, in a short-term way change with a small 'c' is OK for her. But

change with a big 'C', change itself, she's not going to be happy as the years go by as change happens. Her children are going to grow up and leave her and go out in the world. She's going to get older. She's not going to be happy with change. If she could have her wishes granted like an ode on a Grecian urn, she would like to freeze herself in time and stay that way. She would like to stay just where she is at a certain age.

SB: *But where would that be? I gather she doesn't want to stay in time the way she is at the beginning of the film?*
WA: No, but eventually she'd settle for anything. That's right, she doesn't want to stay there. She wants to change. And now that she's changed, she will lead, I think, a more fulfilling life. But that life will change. And when that life changes, at some point she's going to be faced with a very, very bleak end and she's going to say, 'Look, I will take anything now. I will be happy to go back to my husband (William Hurt). I will be happy to do anything you want. This final change I don't like.'

SB: *The change in Alice after her first cup of herb tea at Doctor Yang is very entertaining, when she starts to seduce the Joe Mantegna character at the kindergarten.*
WA: Yes, Mia did this scene great.

SB: *How did you come to choose Joe Mantegna for the part as the lover? Had you seen him in any of David Mamet's plays or films?*
WA: Yes, I saw him in *Glengarry Glen Ross* on the stage. And I saw him in Mamet's first movie, which I liked very much, *House of Games*. And I liked him very much.

SB: *I just saw Mamet's* Oleanna *yesterday and I think he's one of the best American playwrights of the moment. I like him as film director as well. Have you seen much of him yourself?*
WA: I haven't seen everything he's done, but I enjoy him. I like his work, and I love his movies. *House of Games* was absolutely wonderful. I enjoyed his movie with Don Ameche, *Things Change*, and I liked the film version of *Glengarry Glen Ross*. In general, I just find him a big plus.

SB: *He writes in a completely different manner compared to you. His dialogue seems almost to be a row of one-liners, even when they're put together into long speeches. There is a short sentence, pause, another short sentence, pause, and so on.*

WA: Right, his writing is musical. It's a very poetic writing. He gets many, many effects with the rhythm of his speech.

SB: *We've already talked some about the technique behind the dream sequences, in connection to* New York Stories. *So I'd like to talk about the music in these scenes. The music when Alice's former boyfriend, Eddie, appears, for instance. It's very beautiful. Isn't it 'Alice Blue Gown'?*

WA: No, it's 'I Remember You' with strings. It's so pretty, it's a very, very beautiful piece of music. The most romantic music is when Eddie appears, definitely. 'Alice Blue Gown' is very beautiful too, it's a waltz. That's being played when Alice is thinking back to her sister (Blythe Danner). That's very nostalgic.

48   Alec Baldwin and Mia Farrow in *Alice*

CHAPTER 22

Shadows and Fog

THE CLOWN: We're not like other people. We are artists. With great talent comes responsibility.

(From *Shadows and Fog*)

STIG BJÖRKMAN: *As usual with a new film of yours,* Shadows and Fog *offers quite an unexpected experience.*
WOODY ALLEN: It is unexpected, yes. But the film was fun to do. I enjoyed working on it very much.

SB: *When and how did you get the idea for the film?*
WA: Years ago I had written a little one-act play with a similar theme. And over the years I've said to myself that it would make an interesting film, but it would have to be done in black-and-white. And I thought, where can I do it? I have to go to Europe to do it. Then it occurred to me that I could do it all in a film studio. And then the idea started to take greater active shape.

SB: *What was the name of this play?*
WA: The name of it was *Death.* I had written three one-act plays called *Sex, God* and *Death.*

SB: *Has it been performed as well?*
WA: Yes, it has been performed. But I've never seen it.

SB: *And what does this play have in common with* Shadows and Fog?
WA: The basic theme of being awakened in the middle of the night and being sent out into the street and having to be part of this group which is keeping the street safe or searching for a killer and then becoming more deeply enmeshed in it as the night progresses. That was there in the play, that theme.

SB: *The story of the film – or rather your character in the film, Klein-mann – reminded me of the German novel* Kleiner Mann, was nun? *by Hans Fallada. It is a depiction of the average German in German society during that specific time.*

WA: Well, I don't know this novel; I just felt that it was a good metaphor to be awakened in the middle of the night and sent into the street to have to confront these dramatic events. And I felt that if I could get the movie going in a way that was meaningful to people – entertaining and engrossing and amusing and frightening – that there were many ramifications that could be drawn from it. Some psychological, some philosophical, some social. Because that's always the case with a metaphorical idea.

SB: *What I also like about the film is your mixture of tragedy and comedy.*

WA: This is what I've been fooling with for a while now, the attempt to try and make comedies that have a serious or tragic dimension to them. And this is not so easy for me.

SB: *Why do you think so?*

WA: Why it's not so easy? Because it's very hard to strike a balance in a story so that it's amusing and also . . . tragic or pathetic. It calls for a lot of skill to do that; one tries and one is afraid of failing and then sometimes one gets lucky and accomplishes it.

SB: *I think you've managed to accomplish this in the film, because there is a sense of uneasiness about it from the start and we're very uncertain about where the story will lead us. It takes quite a while – long into the second reel of the film – before we're able to see the pattern behind the events of the film. You've also constructed a similar pattern in the shooting, the execution of each individual scene. And this, I believe, was planned before you started to shoot the film.*

WA: Yes, we thought that the content of each scene would dictate its own form. The thing that tied it all together was that there was the shadows and fog going on throughout the night all the time. And then there was the occasional respite in the brothel. An occasional warm respite indoors.

SB: *Take for instance the scene with Kate Nelligan – who is playing Kleinmann's fiancée. We just see her in the distance up in a window. The whole scene is shot in one long circular take, starting on her in the window and going down to you and the Mia Farrow character in the street.*

WA: Yes, she's meant to be just a vague figure representing Kleinmann's innocuous clerk's bourgeois life; his attempt to get married to a woman who doesn't really love him and will love him only if he gets the promotion at work. She's just a superior voice to him up there in the dark.

SB: *But very many scenes are constructed in the same way. They are very solid, as if cast in one piece, with no cuts at all.*

WA: I usually don't cut much anyhow. If you go back to *Alice* or *Crimes and Misdemeanours* I've done less and less and less cutting. And there is very little cutting in, say, the last half dozen films of mine. It's very hard for me to bring myself to cut. I don't know what it is, but when I'm shooting it's very difficult to think in terms of cuts. Now maybe some idea for a movie will occur to me where cuts are absolutely necessary to the idea. But generally speaking, it's not my body rhythm.

SB: *Is there any specific reason behind this attitude towards cuts? Moral, for instance? I'm thinking about the actors who can feel more safe within their work when you apply this method.*

WA: Yes, I think it's good for the actors because they don't have to do it over and over. From a different angle and over again from a third angle.

SB: *Yes, and it gives them a feeling of security, because they know that what they perform during a specific scene is what will come up on the screen later on.*

WA: Right. They are not at the mercy of having their performances altered in the editing. But one thing they complain about is having to learn all the lines. That part they don't like. But they do like the fact that once they shoot the scene, it's over. It can be seven to ten pages of script, but then it's over. When actors are hired for my movies, they're always told that they're going to have to come back for re-shoots. That's how I work. I re-shoot once, twice, three times, five times, the whole picture. And they all say OK. That's on the minus side. But on the plus side, they're told that they never have to come back to do any post-synchronization work at all.

SB: *Are there considerations or ideas like these which have convinced you to construct your scenes in this way? Or are there other reasons, technical reasons for instance, behind your choice of these more intricate and complicated takes as well?*

WA: Emotionally it feels that way to me. I see no reason to cut. There's no necessity. Except once in a great while in a film, I feel that that point cannot be made in any other way except by a cut. But, otherwise, it's rare that I feel that I have to resort to cuts.

SB: *Shadows and Fog reminds me a lot of a silent film-maker I like very much, F. W. Murnau.*

WA: Well, yes, Murnau was a master. With the idea of this particular story one almost automatically tends to think back to German expressionism, because the idea of doing it in a contemporary atmosphere is not right. It requires some kind of European village as a setting. It's not an American idea. It doesn't have the rhythm and the tempo of an American idea. It would never happen in America that way. It could happen in America, but then it would happen very differently. So when I think of shadows and fog and menacing figures and being out in the night, I tend to think back to those German masters who worked so frequently with that kind of atmosphere. And who made their films in a studio.

SB: *But the atmosphere in the film calls forth more of Murnau's films than those of Fritz Lang with which some critics have compared it.*

WA: Yes, it has maybe a more poetic approach. Fritz Lang is a harder hit. Murnau had a more legato approach.

SB: *Yes, sometimes his* Sunrise *comes to mind.*

WA: *Sunrise*, yes. It's overwhelming.

SB: *Shadows and Fog is very atmospheric with a very suggestive style and construction. It's constructed in a row of quite long and premeditated takes. When you execute these more complicated scenes, to what extent do you discuss them with Carlo Di Palma? Do you listen a lot to his ideas or do you have very fixed, preconceived ideas about the shooting of the individual scene yourself?*

WA: We discuss all that beforehand. We discuss in some detail what the effect has got to be, depending on what scene it is. Let's say in *Shadows and Fog* a scene on the circus grounds. We discuss clearly that we're going to have hot lights coming from underneath things, unrealistically, and that we're not going to care, and that we won't see a face here but a silhouette there, etc. It's pretty well worked out as what it's going to be.

SB: *There is also a lot of very strong backlight in* Shadows and Fog.
WA: Yes, because when you backlight the fog, you get a very unrealistic but poetic look at it.

SB: *Was this your idea or Carlo Di Palma's?*
WA: Before the shooting of the film we did one half day of tests. We went on the set and tried many different lightings. We tried natural lighting, we tried different film, we tried backlighting, we tried very, very low lighting in certain areas. When we saw the results of the tests, we came to the conclusion that the film would be served best by being shot non-realistically with very dramatic backlight.

SB: *Yes, there is one very dramatic scene where you're being chased and running by a long fence . . .*
WA: Yes, we could have lit that realistically, but it's much more fun to do it dramatically. And since we were working on a set and nothing is real, we felt the licence to light like that.

SB: *Were there no real locations in the film?*
WA: No, everything was constructed. We were never on the street, always in the studio. The scenic designer, Sandro Loquasto, is quite brilliant. And, of course, it helped tremendously that the film was in black-and-white – and in fog. When the set was finished we had no idea if after a week of shooting we would have used up the whole set and think, 'Oh, God, we need ten sets like this! We can't do this picture.' But we found that by judiciously moving around things and switching things we were able to do the whole thing on a single set.

SB: *Is it a big studio, this Kaufmann Astoria you used for the film?*
WA: Yes, it's a good-size studio.

SB: *I'd like to talk about the actors. To me it seems that you must have a certain curiosity about actors. Very often you work with actors completely new to you. In* Shadows and Fog, *for instance, there are John Malkovich and Jodie Foster, Kathy Bates and Lily Tomlin, Kate Nelligan and John Cusack. Is this an expression of a desire of yours to sometimes work with completely new creative talents and temperaments?*

49 Michael Kirby in *Shadows and Fog*

WA: No, it's not conscious. We just think, 'Who would be best for the part?' And when we've decided who will be best, that's the person we try and get. We're unmindful of their stature in the business. It doesn't matter to me if they're completely unknown or very famous. Only if they are the best person for the part. Once in a while someone will call me up, like Jodie Foster, and say, 'I'd love to do something in one of your movies.' And then I looked through the script and I said, 'Well, the only thing I have and that she could possibly do, is work in the brothel.' And I called her and told her that it would only be three or four days, and she said, 'Perfect, because that's all I want to do.' So sometimes people will call up and want to work, and other times we'll just cast as to who will be the best person for the part with no regards for anything else.

SB: *The scenes in the brothel are very amusing. I especially like the scene at the table, where you film the whole scene in one long take with a revolving camera totally disregarding whether the characters who are talking are in picture or not.*
WA: Yes, because it doesn't matter. The important thing is the conversation and the ambience that you should feel when you step inside the brothel. That it's up and energetic and people are talking and eating, as a contrast to the street which should be cold and dark and menacing.

SB: *You have told me some about your work with the actors. But, I wonder, don't you ever meet them before the production? Like seeing them for lunch or dinner and discuss the part with them?*
WA: No, I never do that, because I'm just not social that way.

SB: *But you could meet them here, in your office, or . . .*
WA: No, I try to avoid that. If they're considered for a regular part, I give them the whole script to read. And then maybe they'll call me up and say, 'I liked the script and I would like to play the part,' and I say, 'Great!' Then maybe they have a question or two, but very often not. So I say, 'See you on the set.' And they come to the first day of shooting with no rehearsal whatsoever. And on the set that morning I go into the scene. Then, after they've done it once or twice, I start to work with them a little bit. But I like the first virginal attempts to be their ideas without inhibition or guidance from me.

SB: *So when you rehearse for the camera, the actors are not supposed to act out their scenes or say all their lines in the right mood and with the right expression?*

WA: Right, I tell them not to do very much when we're rehearsing for the camera. And I try to keep them fairly free, so they don't have to be overly precise. I don't like them to rehearse. I set the shot up before they even come to the set. While they're still in their dressing rooms Carlo and I and the stand-ins plan the shot for them. And when the actors come to the set I just tell them, 'Come here and go over there and then you walk over here and take the drink and then you go over there.' And this is all they do, this is the only rehearsal we have. The first time you hear the dialogue is when we shoot the scene. And sometimes that take is the best ever.

SB: *But if an actor feels uncomfortable doing a certain thing, what do you do?*

WA: Oh, I never make them do it. I always say to the actors, 'Don't ever feel that the script I'm giving you is absolute. If something makes you feel uncomfortable, just change it! Just feel free.'

SB: *But when you make pure comedy, where the lines are very important, then, I guess, you can't allow the actors to change too much.*

WA: Right, but then they tend not to. When you hire a comic actor, he can usually see where the joke is. And they tend to protect it. I'm usually in the comedies and I do most of the jokes. It's a little different with comedy, because there the actors tend to stick to the script more themselves.

SB: *The character you play in* Shadows and Fog *has very much in common with the characters you play in your more contemporary films. Kleinmann is living in a fictional 1920 or so world, but he is sharing quite a few traits with some of your other screen personalities.*

WA: Right, I don't think that I can act anything else really. I don't think that I'm an actor. I think I'm a comedian of a certain type, so that's what I would be doing.

SB: *But you have acted other kinds of parts for other directors, like* The Front *by Martin Ritt.*

WA: Yes, but that wasn't too far from what I do.

SB: *In the beginning of the film the clown (John Malkovich) says, 'We're not like other people. We're artists. With great talent comes responsibility.' Do you agree with that?*

WA: I do think that some of that is vanity, that the artist considers himself not like other people, and in a secret way he considers himself in a way superior to other people. I don't agree that the artist is superior; I'm not a believer in the specialness of the artist. I don't think that to have a talent is an achievement. I think it's a gift from God, sort of. I do think that if you're lucky to have a talent, that with that comes a certain responsibility. Just in the same sense as if you were born rich.

SB: *There is another line in the film where you say, 'The night is a free feeling.' Is that a kind of key line for the film for you?*
WA: Yes, that's a part of the metaphor of the film, that once you get out in the night, there is a sense that civilization is gone. All the stores are closed, everything is dark and it's a different feeling. You start to realize that the city is just a superimposed man-made convention and that the real thing that you're living on is a planet. It's a wild thing in nature. And all the civilization that protects you and enables you to lie to yourself about life is all man-made and superimposed.

SB: *The city and the decor of the film can also be seen as a projection of the inner chaos and imprisonment of the main character. Take, for instance, the scene where Kleinmann and Irmie confront his boss. All three are literally cornered in the very narrow dead-end part of an alley. The decoration also becomes a description of the situation.*
WA: Right, for the emotional state. I've always thought this to be very important in films, the setting, the environmental atmosphere, going back as far as *Stardust Memories*. In fact, in that film every time I was in my apartment in New York, I changed the wallpaper. The apartment was only supposed to be representational of the condition of my mind. That's an important aspect for me: the outside world really being just a function of one's own inner state.

SB: *In* Shadows and Fog *this idea is very obvious, and of course you are able to complete this idea as the whole setting for the film is constructed in a studio. But how does the concept for the setting, the construction of this idea of an inner architecture develop? How does your work together with the production designer, Sandro Loquasto, proceed?*
WA: We sat down and talked about each scene and what we wanted to do with each of them. Then he made some drawings and some models. If it was a much less studio production, if it was just locations, then

we'd talk and go to locations and discuss them. But *Shadows and Fog* required much more planning.

SB: *Did Carlo Di Palma join you at this point of pre-production as well?*

WA: Yes, Carlo was there from the second meeting on. And he would always say, 'Don't do that, because I can put lights on that,' or similar things . . .

SB: *Your films usually start as 'Untitled Projects'. Have you ever decided the title for a film before the shooting?*

WA: Yes, once in a while. For instance, *Hannah and Her Sisters* was a title that I had right from the first day, from the minute I started shooting. Usually not, though. Not for any other reason than that I can't think of a title. Then when I see the film, I try and think of a title. And very often ask other people. I mean my editor, my cameraman, my costume designer . . . We sit around and somebody suggests a title, and we say 'No, that sounds terrible, that's too dramatic, that's too frivolous.' And eventually we get one. This is usually when the film has been cut and we can see it.

SB: *Your choice of music is as always very important, very precise. How did you come to choose the music for this film?*

WA: Here in *Shadows and Fog* I didn't know what I was going to do for music. I looked at some classical music, but that was too ponderous. I looked at some Edvard Grieg at one point, and I couldn't get what I wanted. Then, after the film was finished, I played a piece of Kurt Weill and it seemed very good. And I played another and another, and then it took shape and we did the whole picture with it. It just seemed to fit in perfectly.

SB: *I hadn't heard these recordings of his music before. The orchestration is very atmospheric.*

WA: Right, because we used period material. We found lots of recordings. We sent our guy out, and he brought back everything he could find.

CHAPTER 23

Husbands and Wives

'I'm writing with film'

STIG BJÖRKMAN: Husbands and Wives *is in many respects quite a daring project. I like it precisely for its boldness, for its directness and for its raw and rough surface. How was the style for this film conceived? At what stage did you decide to make the film the way it was made?*

WOODY ALLEN: I've always been thinking that so much time is wasted and so much is devoted to the prettiness of films and the delicacy and the precision. And I said to myself, why not just start to make some films where only the content is important. Pick up the camera, forget about the dolly, just hand-hold the thing and get what you can. And then, don't worry about colour correcting it, don't worry about mixing it so much, don't worry about all this precision stuff and just see what happens. When you feel like cutting, just cut. Don't worry about that it's going to jump or anything. Just do what you want, forget about anything but the content of the film. And that's what I did.

SB: *But do you think that one has to reach this stage of one's career, with the experience you yourself have obtained after a little more than twenty feature films, to be able to work in this way? To dare to work in this way, to neglect all the accepted 'rules' of film-making? To attain the assurance that this way of film-making is not only possible but also functional?*

WA: Yes, I think you need a certain amount of confidence. Confidence that comes with experience enables you to do many things that you wouldn't have done in early films. You do tend to become bolder, because as the years go by you feel more in control of what you're doing. When I first made films anyhow – and I know this is true about a number of other people – you tend to, as we've already discussed, do a lot of coverage and protect yourself in many ways. And then, as time goes on, you get more and more knowledgeable and experienced and you drop all that and you let your instincts operate more freely and you don't worry so much about the niceties.

SB: *When you discussed this new style with your photographer Carlo Di Palma before the shooting of the film, what were his reactions?*
WA: He was interested, because he always likes it when there's something exciting and provocative photographically.

SB: *Was his work in some ways easier on this film? Did he spend as much time as usual on lighting for the scenes, for example? Or was he less careful when it came to lighting of the scenes?*
WA: Yes, it was easier, because he would light a whole general area. And then I said to the actors, go where you want, just walk wherever you want. Walk into darkness, walk into light, just play the scene as you feel it. You don't have to do it the same way the second take, just do whatever interests you. And I told the camera operator, get what you can get! If you miss it, go back and get it. If you miss it again, go back again. Find your way yourself. And we did no rehearsals with the camera or anything. We would come in, he'd pick up the camera and we would do the scene and he would do the best he could. And I was wondering after this film, if it's worth it to try and make films in the old regular way. Because this way it goes very quick, and all that counts is the end result. So I may try and make a few films in that style. Because it's fast and inexpensive and it does the job.

SB: *Was this a quicker shoot as well? Compared to your previous films?*
WA: Quicker, yes. And it's the first time in years – *in years, decades* – that I came in under budget. It was both cheaper and faster.

SB: *Did you have a lot of re-shoots on this film?*
WA: Three days. Usually I re-shoot weeks and weeks and weeks. You know, sometimes a month of re-shoots. I was always a famous re-shooter. Here I had three days only.

SB: *How did you come to think of this style for the film? In a way it's congenial with the theme and the story of the film.* Husbands and Wives *is about disrupted relationships and disrupted lives so in a way the style also . . .*
WA: . . . complements the story. But I think you could say that about a lot of stories. The style would work for a lot of stories. After the fact it

looks like it's perfect for this story. But it's also perfect for many films that I've done.

SB: *Which of your films, do you think?*
WA: I could have done *Shadows and Fog* like that, if I'd wanted to. I could have done *Alice* like that. Any number of them. Right down the line. Because what the audience comes away with emotionally, spiritually, is the content of the film. The characters, the substance of the film. The form of the film is just a simple, functional thing. It can differ in style, like baroque or gothic architecture. The only important thing is that the audience is moved or amused or made to think or something. And you can do it this way.

SB: *Did the script for* Husbands and Wives *leave more space for improvisation, or did the actors follow a script similar to those you've written for your previous films?*
WA: No, there was a script, and they basically followed the script.

SB: *The film has also the character of an investigation into the lives of the characters. I guess this was present in the script as well?*
WA: Yes, I was thinking that these people were living their lives and the camera is there and can just do whatever it wants; when I need the people to say what they feel about things, they just talk about them. I just felt there was nothing I couldn't do, that I wanted to do. I didn't have to make any concessions to any formalities.

SB: *And who in your mind is this investigator, the interviewer in the film?*
WA: I never thought of it. Just the audience. It's a convenient way of letting the characters explain themselves.

SB: *These confessions or confidences given by the characters, were they all in the script? They are not ideas expressed by the actors in any way?*
WA: No, the whole film is written. I mean, the actors add words here and there to make the dialogue colloquial. That's all. It's all written.

SB: Husbands and Wives *is, in many ways, a more violent account of relationships than your previous films. Not least in the acting and, particularly, in the case of Judy Davis and Sydney Pollack.*
WA: Yes, it's more volatile and explosive.

sb: *One of the more dramatic scenes in the film is Sally's telephone conversation with her husband in the home of the opera lover. It's embarrassing and astonishing, tragic and at the same time dense with a very black humour. It's handled with great bravura by Judy Davis.*

wa: Sure, I know that kind of situation, because I've been in it myself . . . as a person calling having something on his mind. And Judy Davis is probably the best movie actress in the world today.

sb: *The actor who plays her lover, Liam Neeson, was a new acquaintance to me.*

wa: He's an Irish actor. He's been in a number of movies. He was in one with Diane Keaton, *The Good Mother*. He combines this mixture of masculinity and intelligence. He is a superb actor and is a 'real person'. There is never a trace of fraudulence about him at all. He is authentic, in every gesture and in every word.

sb: *Why did you choose Sydney Pollack for the part of the husband?*

wa: I was trying to think of who would be good for that part, of men that looked that age, and his name came up when we were discussing casting, Juliet Taylor and I. And he came to see me, and he was very nice about it. He read for the part. And I said to myself, God, I hope he is going to be able to read this, because I will be so embarrassed if he doesn't read it well and I will have to not engage him. And he read it, and I could see from the first reading that he was very natural and good. He was great!

sb: *I've never come to think about it in the same way, when I've seen you act in your own films before – maybe it's due to the unseen interviewer in the film – but somehow I was more aware of your double role as director and actor in* Husbands and Wives *than in your previous films. Could you tell me something about your feelings when you are 'directing' yourself in your films? Are there any kind of problems for you in that process?*

wa: No, there's nothing to it. It's a misnomer. I mean, I don't direct myself. I wrote the script. I know what I want from me and I just do it. I don't ever have to direct myself.

sb: *So then it's just an inner feeling for you? You know when you have to make another take, you know when your own performance is right?*

wa: Yes, it's an inner feeling. If it feels good, it almost always is good.

50   Judy Davis in *Husbands and Wives*

It's very rare that I'm fooled on that. It's usually the other way around. It doesn't feel so good when you do it sometimes, but it's better than you thought later. That does happen.

SB: *There is a scene in the film between you and the young girl, Rain, played by Juliette Lewis, where you are walking in Central Park discussing Russian writers. You talk about Tolstoy and Turgenev, and then you make a vivid description of Dostoyevsky, of him being 'a full meal, with vitamins and wheatgerm added'. Now and then you come back to Dostoyevsky in your films, and some of your films have a certain 'Dostoyevskian', novelistic flavour and quality, like* Husbands and Wives, Manhattan, Hannah and Her Sisters *or* Crimes and Misdemeanours. *These films seem to have a certain link.*

WA: Well, I think that among the films you name, *Manhattan* is not quite in the same category as the others, because it's more romanticized. *Manhattan* has one foot in nostalgia and romance, in a certain way. But *Crimes and Misdemeanours* and *Hannah* and this film are darker. They are definitely darker. I also like this novelistic idea, in general. That always provokes me. I love the idea of working in a novelistic manner on the screen. I always feel I'm writing with film. It's something about the novelistic approach that I like. And even though I stray from it now and then, in a movie like *Alice* or something, I always seem to come back to it. I like real people and real situations and human life unfolding. You can do in the novel what you do in the film and vice versa. The two media, physically, are very close together. Not like the stage. That's a different thing entirely.

SB: *When you write the script for a film like* Husbands and Wives *or* Crimes and Misdemeanours *or* Hannah, *do you in some way make up a general pattern for the characters or do their dramas develop along with their interchanging relationships and so on?*

WA: It's very instinctive with me. I think about it for a while and get a general idea of where it can go. I just like to think for a while and make sure that I'm not going to start writing with all my energy and then stop after ten pages. When I realize that there is room for development, then my first draft is exploratory. I write it and see where I'm going and often I don't know where I'll be going and I make it up at the time. And finally when it's over, I make a few corrections, and give it right to my producer and have him start budgeting it and get the production going.

SB: *In the scene in the taxi between you and Juliette Lewis the girl,
Rain, is making comments on Gabe's novel. She abandons her previous
overt and spontaneous appreciation of the book and displays a more and
more critical view of it. Do you find this to be a common habit among
critics or judges of art or even friends? They can start from a very positive
attitude and then gradually withdraw from their original point of view.*
WA: Yes, people's feelings about things change, and they are not
always so candid with you. It has happened to me in my life where
someone who had loved a film of mine is confronted by other people
who don't love it so much, then they lose confidence in their own
judgement and start to feel more critical about it.

SB: *In the scene in the taxi you have chosen to concentrate your image
on Juliette Lewis and use jump-cuts instead of conventional cross-
cutting to the other character – yourself. Were parts of the dialogue cut
out in this way?*
WA: Yes, there were things cut out. That was the most difficult scene
in the movie to do. The lens made us look ugly when we were both in
the same shot in the taxi. And the shot from the side looked better than
the shot taken flat on. So I looked terrible, the lens was disfiguring my
nose. Then I tried doing singles, I tried everything, but we couldn't
make it work. So then I thought, she looks pretty. Why don't I just
leave the camera on her? I thought, OK, you can hear me, so, you
know . . . And now it looks more interesting.

SB: *Yes, I think so too. Definitely. In a way we are put in your
position and we are experiencing her in the same way as the character
you play.*
WA: Juliette Lewis is a wonderful actress.

SB: *Is she an actress with whom you would like to collaborate again?
Like you've mentioned earlier about Diane Keaton, Dianne Wiest and
Judy Davis.*
WA: I sure would. Sure. She is great.

SB: *You use this jump-cut technique throughout the film. Even to the
extent of leaving very, very brief glimpses of the actors and then immediately cutting forward into the next situation. In the beginning of* Husbands and Wives, *for example, we see a very brief scene with Mia Farrow
in the apartment. The shot is maybe just a few seconds long, and then*

51   Juliette Lewis and Woody Allen in *Husbands and Wives*

you cut to a conversation scene where she has moved just slightly from the position she was in before. Was this done with the intention of keeping the same feeling for the scenes throughout the film?

WA: Yes, to make it more disturbing. It's what we were talking about the other day, more dissonant, like the difference between Stravinsky and Prokofiev. I wanted it to be more dissonant because the internal, emotional and mental states of the characters are dissonant. I wanted the audience to feel that there was a jagged, nervous feeling. An unsettled and neurotic feeling.

SB: *Do you think this would have been possible without us having seen and experienced Godard and his early films?*

WA: A film-maker like Godard invented so many wonderful, cinematic devices. It's very hard to say whether it just would have been something that came over me one day, or that he's part of the rich treasure of wonderful film-makers that have contributed to the vocabulary of film. You know, very often you do something and it's stimulating and exciting, but it's coming from your heritage of film literature or film semantics. I can only speak for myself on this, but sometimes I will do something in a film that you just couldn't relate to anybody else ever having done. And sometimes it's in the tradition of the vocabulary that other film-makers have given us. So I don't really know. But I do very much love Godard's contribution to cinema.

SB: *Yes, so do I. I mean, Godard in his way just went out and made his movies and undauntedly proposed that from this day, from this film, this way of making films is also possible, is now permitted.*

WA: Right. He is probably the original guy who made just the content count and who just did what he wanted, put anything in what he wanted. So I do think he is and was a fine contributor.

SB: *When seeing* Husbands and Wives *there is, in fact, a film of Bergman's that came to my mind. The only thing these two films have in common is this investigative attitude and the attack on the audience. It's one of my favourite German films,* From the Life of the Marionettes. *It has, as well, this quality of being a deep investigation into the lives of unknown people.*

WA: Yes, it's a very interesting film. I haven't seen it in a while. I saw it when it first came out. It hasn't played much here. It was not a commercial success at all. I ought to see it again. It's a wonderful movie.

SB: *The marital dilemmas and the marital problems that the two couples in the film expose and unveil are dilemmas shared by many people today. There is a great amount of possible recognition in your story about Judy and Gabe and Sally and Jack.*

WA: Yes, those dilemmas are common. I've observed them around me all the time.

SB: *There is another small but funny link between* Hannah and Her Sisters *and* Husbands and Wives: *the relationship between the Dianne Wiest and Carrie Fisher characters and their mutual romantic object, the architect played by Sam Waterston, and that between the Mia Farrow and Judy Davis characters to the editor played by Liam Neeson.*

WA: Yes, I see that as a not uncommon thing that people do. Somebody likes a member of the opposite sex and they fix that person up with their friend. But I don't know what they hope to gain by it.

SB: *It could be a check-up. In* Husbands and Wives *Judy gets her friend Sally to check up whether this guy Michael really is the kind of romantic possibility she herself imagines him to be.*

WA: Or else she really wants to do it for herself, but doesn't have the nerve. So she sublimates and does it for her friend.

SB: *Do you think the secretive way that Gabe and Judy behave towards each other is common in many marriages? I am thinking about their hiding away their works. She doesn't want to show him her poetry. He gives his novel to another woman to read.*

WA: I think that happens. There are private parts or there are private things that carry some shame with them or some aggression or some guilt that one doesn't share with one's closest person. And that always is a problem, that always becomes a problem. It grows.

SB: *Why did you want to show us parts of Gabe's novel visually and act it out in actual scenes? Why didn't you just let him read the parts for us?*

WA: I wanted you to know some of his observations very clearly on certain aspects of relations between men and women. And I thought that this was a way of doing it, rather than just have him reading it. It would be interesting for the audience. It would be amusing for them, a little interlude, just to clarify certain feelings Gabe had about human relations.

SB: *When you started to work on the editing of* Husbands and Wives, *had you talked about and discussed beforehand this new technique, this new style with your editor, Susan Morse?*

WA: Yes, I wrote it into the script. I explained in the description that we would just cut where we would want to, we'd just jump and wouldn't pay attention to anything.

SB: *And did she find it exciting and enjoyable to work in this unorthodox way?*

WA: Yes, she loved it. We both had fun. Everybody – from a physical point of view, from a technical point of view – had more fun on this movie than anything else. The actors loved it. They didn't have to block, they didn't have to think about where they went. They could do what they wanted. It was very good that way. For everybody.

CHAPTER 24

Manhattan Murder Mystery

LARRY: I take back everything I said about life imitating art.
(From *Manhattan Murder Mystery*)

STIG BJÖRKMAN: Manhattan Murder Mystery *is a murder story* . . .
WOODY ALLEN: Yes, and it was just a lark for me. A vacation. I've
had the idea of making a murder mystery for a long time. In fact,
Annie Hall was originally a murder mystery. But during the various
rewrites of the script this element was abandoned. I'm very fond of
these kind of stories and their genre conventions. But this was the
first time that I explored it in an entire story.

SB: *Does the story in* Manhattan Murder Mystery *relate much to
your original ideas from the time of* Annie Hall, *plot-wise and intrigue-
wise?*
WA: Yes, and I feel it was an unambitious undertaking. I feel it's a
trivial picture, but fun for me. It's sort of like giving myself a little
personal reward. Just an indulgence. It's something that I've always
wanted to do. I just felt I had done – I don't know, twenty-two,
twenty-three pictures – and I just wanted to take part of a year and
do this little thing for fun. Like a little dessert or something. Not a
real meal. And I'm glad I did it, because it was a pleasurable experience
to do it.

SB: *Would you see it as a pastiche on this specific genre?*
WA: No, it's a plain, simple idea for a murder mystery that I had
and which I wrote together with Marshall Brickman. And I wanted
to do a little comedy as well. I didn't want to make it a serious
murder picture. I think it's nice, light entertainment.

SB: *But are you interested in this genre – the detective story, the
murder mystery – in literature and in film?*

WA: There are two types of murder stories, I feel. The type where the murder is utilized as a springboard or a metaphor for a deeper story – like *Macbeth*, *Crime and Punishment* – where the murder is only a vehicle upon which the author is able to explore very deep and philosophical ideas. And then there is the simply enjoyable, trivial, purely light murder, that can either be serious or comic, but does not strive towards being anything deeper or greater. Of course, everyone likes the first kind, because these are great and important works, wherein the author's ideas about the world and about people are expressed through a killing or a murder. Closer to that – and obviously not on that same level – would be something like *Crimes and Misdemeanours*, where the murder is used for a moral discussion. In *Manhattan Murder Mystery* it isn't. Here it is used strictly for entertainment values. It's shallow and entertaining. Now, I don't mean to be hypercritical of pure entertainment. That's fine. That has its place. Take Balanchine's *Nutcracker Suite*, for instance. That's light entertainment exclusively, but wonderful. And there's a very important and significant place for this kind of things. But I don't want to have any illusions about the movie. You know, many times people watch Alfred Hitchcock movies and they read many things into them. I'm not of that school. I think Hitchcock himself never intended anything significant, and indeed his movies are not significant. They are delightful, but completely insignificant. And that's the direction I wanted this film to be in. I wanted it to be just light entertainment.

SB: *Do you read any detective stories?*
WA: There are no good ones. The only good murder mystery that I've ever read in my life was *A Kiss Before Dying* by Ira Levin. They made it into two movies, neither one of which is very good. But the book is superb. I haven't really read very much more that I've really enjoyed. That one seems to be the best. The movie of *Double Indemnity* I think is fabulous. I think that's a tremendous American classic. *In Cold Blood*, the Truman Capote novel, his journalistic account, was also very, very fascinating and compelling. As a general rule I love detective and murder movies, but there are again very few good ones. *The Maltese Falcon* is wonderful. *Double Indemnity* is the top. You just don't get anything better than that. I also liked the Costa-Gavras' film *The Sleeping-Car Murder*. It was a good one. And a couple of the Alfred Hitchcock films of course. There are a couple of them that I think are quite wonderful.

SB: *When we met prior to the shooting of* Manhattan Murder Mystery, *you ordered two films to see in your projection room,* Chinatown *and* The Big Heat. *Was this as a kind of inspiration or preparation for yourself before the shooting or just out of pure interest?*

WA: I had seen both of them before, and – by the way – I couldn't get *The Big Heat*, they couldn't find a print of it. But *Chinatown* I did see. It's an interesting piece of work, a very interesting script and of course Roman Polanski is a wonderful director and Jack Nicholson is a genius of an actor.

SB: *But you've never been a fan of those classical writers of detective stories like Raymond Chandler or Dashiell Hammett or James M. Cain?*

WA: No. I mean, they can all write and they are all good writers. But I don't like to read them. No, I can't think of any of those writers that I like to read. But I've always had what we call here a 'junk tooth' for *The Thin Man* and those kinds of things. I don't think that *The Thin Man* is a very good picture myself, but I have a good tolerance for that kind of junk. There's also a Bob Hope movie called *The Great Lover* with Roland Young and Rhonda Fleming, which is a very broad comedy, but also a murder mystery. And it's wonderful. It's just a weakness of mine.

SB: *In the new film there's a big part for Diane Keaton again. How was the experience of working with her again?*

WA: Diane is equal to the greatest screen comediennes we've ever had. I think she's the top of the line. The two best female comedians would be Diane Keaton and Judy Holliday. It's always fun to work with Diane. She's a good friend of mine, and she brings out the best in everybody. She has the kind of personality that lights up the whole project. She's such a positive personality.

SB: *Do you think that her part in* Manhattan Murder Mystery *gave her more opportunities to show her talents as a comedian than her parts in your previous films?*

WA: No, because originally I wrote the part for Mia, and I had written it more to what Mia likes to do. Mia likes to do funny things, but she's not as broad a comedian as Diane is. So Diane made this part funnier than I wrote it.

SB: *But you didn't change the part so it would suit her and her personality more?*

WA: No, I couldn't do that. In a regular script I would have done that upon hiring Diane Keaton. But I couldn't because it's a murder mystery, and it's very tightly plotted, so it's very hard to make big changes.

52   Diane Keaton and Woody Allen in *Manhattan Murder Mystery*

SB: *What struck me when I saw you working on the locations was the lightness which characterized the whole working situation. This was amazing considering all that has happened to you in your personal life between August '92 and now, January '93. Isn't it hard for you to separate your work situation with your personal situation?*

WA: Well, it's funny, all the time I've known you and we've had our discussions this has been going on. But no, they're separate events. I thought it was important in this time of stress to work, that it was healthy for me to work and healthy for me to focus on my work. And I'm a good worker, a disciplined worker.

SB: *In a scene backstage at a theatre, where Diane Keaton is kept captured as a hostage, your character upon saving her says, 'I take back everything I said about life imitating art.' It seems to be something of a key line.*

WA: Yes, it was a key line. Earlier in the movie Diane's character was pointing out to me how life imitates art. And I was saying to her that life unfortunately imitates life. It doesn't imitate art. And this is an argument that we've always had. But the end of the picture shows that life does imitate art.

SB: *This recalls a line in* Husbands and Wives, *where the young girl, Rain, says, 'Life doesn't imitate art, it imitates cheap television.'*

WA: Yes, that's right. That's true too.

SB: *You have been working with mostly the same close collaborators over a long, long time. Kay Chapin, the script-girl, for instance, has worked with you since* Annie Hall. *And most of the others in key positions have been your collaborators for at least ten to fifteen years, people like the production designer, Santo Loquasto, the editor, Susan E. Morse, the producer, Robert Greenhut, Thomas Reilly, or the costume designer, Jeffrey Kurland. Could you tell me how they came to work with you and why you've wanted to carry on working with them and they with you?*

WA: The concept of having the same group seems to me – as to anybody – clearly an important thing. It would be twice as much work to have to break somebody new in on each picture. All these people came to me strictly by chance. Jimmy Sabat, the sound engineer, was already on *Bananas* with me, Kay Chapin joined me when I did *Annie Hall*, and Jeff Kurland came over as Santo Loquasto's assistant for a while. And there's been no reason to replace anybody. Whenever anyone works in the group, if they do a good job, I automatically go to them for the next picture. The same goes for Sandy Morse, who's worked for me for years. We worked first on *Manhattan* together, and I don't see any reason why our co-operation shouldn't go on. I've become friendly with a few of them – of course I wouldn't continue to work with them if I didn't like them personally. But basically it's a work relationship. We were thinking about this the other day! In the course of my films, over the years, people have given birth and have died and gotten married and gotten divorced. It's amazing the amount of life that's been lived in the time we've been making these films.

SB: *Some people in the crew must have become sort of extra family members in some respect, I guess?*

WA: In a certain way, yeah. You spend so much intense, close time with them when you're making a film. It's not only that you see them every single day from early morning till late at night in a most intense way, month after month after month. If you work in an office or something similar, you see your colleagues, but it's much less critical every second.

SB: *Do you find that you, in your capacity as director and in that sense also a works manager, become a kind of paternal figure for the group, on a psychological level? And if so, is that a tough thing to handle?*

WA: I think the position is an ambivalent one. I think on the one hand it's paternal in a sense, and on the other hand I think they consider me totally incapable of tying my shoelaces unless they help me. And both are right. I mean, once when my father was ill in Florida, I flew down there to be with my parents. And when I came back, the crew was just amazed that I'd flown down by myself. 'You mean you went to the airport by yourself?' And I said, 'Yes, I've flown all over the world by myself.' But they couldn't believe it. It was such an amazing thing for them. They see me as an 'idiot savant' who can make movies, but is completely incompetent in every other area.

SB: *Somebody has pointed out that the job of a professional film-maker is one of the toughest jobs on the whole, because a film-maker has to make so many more decisions of different kinds during one day. They say that the average important decisions for an ordinary working person a day would be between five and ten. But for a film-maker it amounts to many, many more.*

WA: There's no question about that. It was also illustrated in the Truffaut movie *Day for Night*. Everybody has questions for you to answer, the actors, the set constructors, the costume people and the cameraman. It's endless, endless decisions.

SB: *So do you find the process of film-making tiring, exhausting?*
WA: No, that's what it is. You don't think of it. You don't think, 'Oh, God! Decisions, decisions!' That's what it is to make a film. You don't isolate it in thinking in that way.

SB: *Do you feel relief when the shooting is over and the editing is well on its way? Or do you feel sad, when you leave the set and the actors and the members of the crew on the last day?*
WA: No, but there's always a little moment of separation, because you work with all these people so closely for months and then (*Woody snaps his fingers*) you don't see them again for a long time.

SB: *But then you know that you will see most of them again in about six months, when you start your new film.*
WA: Yeah.

SB: *How much time does Carlo di Palma spend in New York? When your new manuscript is finished, will he then immediately come to New York and start to discuss the new film with you?*
WA: He may do any number of things. Usually, he just goes on vacation and relaxes. Once in a while, every few years, he may do another film.

SB: *You told me earlier that on Tuesday you will start to work on your new script. How do you proceed? Do you sit every day between certain hours, like office hours, and work?*
WA: Yeah. I get up early, because I naturally get up early. And I come down here and have breakfast. Then usually I work by myself. Once in a while it's a collaboration, but usually not. And I go into the backroom or this room (*Woody's living-room*) and I start to think. I walk up and down and I walk up and down the outside terrace. I take a walk around the block. I go upstairs and take a shower. I come back down and think. And I think and think. Then just by the sweat of the brow, eventually something comes. People who can't do that – which is most people – they can't understand an act of imagination. So every film I make, they feel is an autobiography of mine. Many people just can't comprehend that –

53   Woody Allen in *Manhattan Murder Mystery*

and I don't say this critically, it's just that they don't understand. They always think that my stories and ideas are based on reality. Therefore I have to explain to them, that *Annie Hall* wasn't, that *Manhattan* wasn't and *Husbands and Wives* wasn't. When I finished the script for *Husbands and Wives* it was strictly an act of imagination. I finished the script long before anything happened that you read in the newspapers. It had nothing to do with that. And I gave the script to Mia, and I said to her, 'Which person do you want to play? Do you want to play Judy or do you want to play Sally?' And she said, 'I don't know. I'll think about it.' And, finally, she picked the one she wanted to do. But she could as easily have picked the other. I usually give her her choice in the script of which character she wants to play. There was nothing autobiographical in the script at all. I didn't know anything about the Sydney Pollack character or the Judy Davis character. I was making them up as I went along. I don't know a young woman like Juliette Lewis, I hadn't met a young woman like her character. I mean, young women I've known, but not that character. As a matter of fact I don't know if one like her exists. I had a hard time casting that role, because that kind of character may not even exist in real life. She was imagined. And my personal relationship with Mia had nothing to do with that. There's no similarity. These things are just imagined in this room or on this terrace. They're just dreamed up. People thought that *Annie Hall* and *Manhattan* were autobiographical, but in fact both those scripts I wrote with Marshall Brickman, and he had lots of input on them. So whose autobiographies are they? His or mine? It's just so silly.

SB: *When you start to write your new script, will you then work regular hours, every day, like any other office work?*
WA: Yes, I work every day. And even when you're not thinking about it, when you get it going, your unconscious is cooking, once you've turned it on. But sometimes I'll say to myself, 'OK, I'm exhausted, I'm going to give it a rest for a while.' I'll go and play my clarinet upstairs or something. But even when I'm playing my clarinet or seeing a movie or something, even though I'm not consciously thinking of it, the unconscious is percolating.

SB: *But do you write evenings and nights as well, or do you keep to your 'writing hours'?*
WA: When I'm writing, it's easy. When I get up the day when I'm going to start the actual writing, I can celebrate. Because that's the day when

everything is over. The day I put the pen to paper, it's all over. Because all the agonizing work is done before that. And to write it down is pure pleasure. And I write it fast. I will be as fast as I can write, because I've done the work already. Once in a while I'll get hung up on some special thing, but very rarely. And I can write in any place, under any conditions. I've written in hotel rooms, I've written sitting on a sidewalk. I've got scenes written on the back of envelopes. I don't need all that nonsense I've seen certain purported writers do. They have to have nice white paper and sharpened pencils. I don't have any of that, I don't care about any of that. I can write something in longhand and then type the next few pages and write the next thing on the back of a laundry bill. The script can look like anything at all. It doesn't mean anything to me. But once I'm writing, then the pleasure sets in. Writing is a complete pleasure for me. I love it. It's a sensual, pleasurable, intellectual activity that's fun. Thinking of it, planning it, plotting it, is agony. That's hard.

SB: *This agony, do you experience it the same way every time, for every project?*
WA: Mostly it's the same, but every now and then there'll be an idea that will come along that I just can't get a handle on. And so after a period of time I put it away and maybe come back to it two years later or something. I do a different film. So in that sense the thinking process has taken a very long time, but most of it takes not that long.

SB: *What would you say then, a couple of weeks or more?*
WA: Yes. Now I'm going to collaborate with a writer on the next script, and I will probably spend the first week or two in what I will normally call 'free-form uninhibited talking'. And we talk about just anything. Should we do a movie about cannibals? Should we do a movie about air planes? Just no inhibitions at all. A black-and-white movie, a silent movie? I don't know, just anything. And then something will turn up that will be a little bit more interesting, that kind of sticks in your imagination. You come back to it a couple of times, because it had a nice feel to it. And then we start developing it.

SB: *You will work with a co-writer this time. Is he somebody new to you?*
WA: His name is Doug McGrath and he's a writer. I've seen some of his small works and I've liked them. They're amusing. I've read some prose work he's done. And I've seen him. He's a performer. And in the social conversations we've had, he's been quite witty and on the ball. I just

thought that I've written so many scripts by myself that it would be fun to try a new collaboration. I mean, if he called me and said, 'Look, I've got to go to Europe for something. I can't do this,' I'll just begin by myself. But I thought it might be pleasurable just to see if the mix gives us something off-beat or different. I've collaborated with Mickey Rose. We grew up together. He was my school friend and we've been friends a lifetime. I'm still a friend of his, but he lives in California. I don't see much of him nowadays but we speak on the phone. I did *Take the Money and Run* and *Bananas* with him. And I've collaborated on several pictures with Marshall Brickman who lives right across the park, in that building with the two tall towers. (*Woody points out the building.*) And we've been friends since our nightclub days, when I was in my midtwenties. Every now and then I like to collaborate with him, because he's a good writer and very funny, and we have a good time together. It's a pleasurable experience. We walk the streets together, we have dinner together, we talk together. And now it's another fellow that I've met that I've had some pleasurable social evenings with. He's just finished the adaptation of *Born Yesterday* for Disney. Now he was happy and thrilled to do that job, but I do not think it's a good idea to remake this film, because I think *Born Yesterday* is the best American comedy ever written for the stage and the movie version with Judy Holliday was a first-rate film comedy as well.

SB: *I liked Judy Holliday a lot and I think Melanie Griffith is a nice comedian as well.*

WA: Oh sure. No, she's fine, she's great! But it just happens that there are a couple of pictures – I would say *Gone with the Wind* is one, *A Streetcar Named Desire* is one and *Born Yesterday* is one – that you cannot disassociate from the original actors. Through some miracle you cannot get anybody more perfect and better played than Judy Holliday and Broderick Crawford in *Born Yesterday*. As you can search the world over and have all the great actors of the world play Stanley Kowalski, but it will never ever be Marlon Brando playing it. Because Marlon was that Polish character totally. Anthony Quinn has played him at some point, and he's a truly great actor and he played the part great, but it was still different from Brando's interpretation. And you can never get a Scarlett and a Rhett Butler like Vivien Leigh and Clark Gable. You could remake the film with an actor much greater than Clark Gable – I don't think that Clark Gable was a great actor – but it would never be the same. And *Born Yesterday* is one of those projects that I feel should not have been remade. I don't say that the original film was great directing, because it's a play on film. But it didn't matter. It's such a wonderful comic play. And the electricity, the chemistry between those three characters – Judy Holliday, Broderick Crawford and William Holden – is great.

SB: *You said you sometimes write with pencil and sometimes on a typewriter. You haven't changed to word processors or computers?*
WA: No, I don't know if I ever will. I still work on the same little portable typewriter that I got when I was sixteen. I bought it then for forty dollars; it was a German typewriter, an Olympia portable. And it looks the way the Germans built those kind of things. It looks like a tank. And I said to the man when I bought it, that forty dollars was a lot of money for me, 'Will it last?' And he said, 'I promise you, this typewriter will be around long after we're all gone.' And he was right. I've used it since I was sixteen and this is forty years ago. And every single thing I type, I type on it. It's a wonderful piece of machinery. I've seen word processors, but I don't think I'll ever switch over to one.

SB: *Then when you've finished a script, do you let it be for a period of time and then you do a rewrite, or how do you proceed?*
WA: I rewrite instantly. As soon as I've finished the story I type it up, because it's in such a clumsy condition. I type up a clearer version, and quickly go over that version with a pencil. This just takes me a couple of days. I make all the rewrites quickly. I clean it up once again and give it to the typing service. And my deals have always been such that I'm in production instantly. I never have to waste one minute looking for the money or anything. So, as soon as I pull it out of the typewriter, (*Woody snaps his fingers*) we go, 'Now!' Then I give the script to Bobby Green-hut, the producer, and he, of course, can call me later on and say, 'This film will cost twenty million dollars to make and we only have twelve, thirteen.' But I'm mindful about that. I never miss the mark by that much. But he might say, 'We have to get it down somewhat. We have to take a half million dollars out of it someplace. Can you live without this? Is it possible that instead of doing ten rain scenes, you can do five?' And then certain compromises have to be made.

SB: *But you just do one rewrite of the script, while clean-writing it?*
WA: Yes, that's it. And then I never look at the script again.

SB: *And you never show it to other people besides the producer, Robert*

Greenhut? To get other opinions of it?

WA: (*A very long pause.*) No, I usually showed it to Mia or Diane Keaton or if I knew the other star in it. But no, I've gotten more and more self-reliant over the years. When I first was making films, I used to have many screenings. And I would sneak into the back of the cinema and listen to the reactions and make my changes and cuts according to that. Then I had less screenings. I had like maybe two big screenings. Then I started to screen the films in my screening-room. And now that's pretty much all I do. When I've finished a film, I screen it five, six times in my screening-room. I invite my sister and some friends. And when it's over I say to them, 'Is there anything you want to tell me about this? Anything you don't understand or anything I should know?' And they might say that they liked it or didn't like it, or that there might be some scenes which were unclear or misunderstood. And then I take that into consideration. But basically, when I show a film to them, I'm 99 per cent finished.

SB: *Your production situation is quite unique for any film-maker. You have a total freedom to write the films you want, to make the films you want – and at least one film a year. There is but one small limit, which is an economic one. Do you think that, in some way, you limit your fantasy, limit your ideas to the expense? That there are projects you've put aside for this reason?*

WA: Perhaps to some degree. For instance, I've always wanted to make a jazz movie. And I think I could do a good one. But the concept that I have for it would be very, very expensive. So I've just tabled it and put it back in my mind. It would just cost too much money. It would be a film that would start quite early and go from early New Orleans through Chicago and New York and Paris. You know, it's a big deal. Costumes, recreation of things. It could be wonderful, but I can't do it for less than a lot of money.

SB: *Is this something you've written as a script already?*

WA: No, it's nothing I've written. I wouldn't spend the time writing it because of that, because I would have to raise an immense amount of money to do it. Maybe some day I'll see the opportunity to get that money, and then I might do it.

SB: *Which is the most satisfying part of the film work do you think?*

WA: It's getting the idea for a film. As the process goes on with making a film, from casting to shooting to editing, it gets worse and worse for me, because I get further and further away from the idealized perfection of the first idea. When a film is finished, I look at it and I'm disappointed and I dislike it very much, and I think that one year ago, I was sitting in my bedroom and I had this idea for a film that was so beautiful and everything was just great. And then, little by little I wounded it, in writing, in casting, in shooting, in editing, in mixing it, I want to get rid of it. I don't want to see it again. The wonderful part is getting the idea. When you start off with a film, you have such grandiose plans and such high goals and aspirations. And by the time you edit it, you just hope that you can fit it together some way so you can make it breathe. Just breathe. Making a film is a big struggle. But the fact that there's struggle helps me. I'd rather struggle with films than struggle with other things.

CHAPTER 25

Interlude

STIG BJÖRKMAN: *Our conversations for the first edition of this book took place during one of the most crucial periods in your life – your break-up with Mia Farrow, and the whole aftermath of that affair. I remember that the news of the break-up was published on a Thursday morning, and we had set up for a meeting for the next day. That Thursday, your then-assistant Lauren Gibson called me to say that the meeting was off – which I had already suspected. But then later that same day she called back to ask if I could see you on Saturday, and at your home rather than your office as was usual. And on Saturday morning we continued, and you seemed to be almost unperturbed by the whole affair. At the time I was very struck by the way in which you seemed able to so completely separate your professional life from your private life.*

WOODY ALLEN: Yes, the one thing has nothing to do with the other. One was a legal matter that I dumped into the hands of lawyers, because I'm not competent to handle that sort of thing. Of course, they called me now and then to ask me certain questions, but I was free to work. So it was not something that bothered me enough to prevent me from going on with my work. During all the time this affair was being commented on in the newspapers, I was very productive. I finished a few films, I wrote a one-act play for off-Broadway, I did a television production, I played with my jazz band every Monday night.

SB: *But all the writings and all the speculations concerning you and your relationship to Mia Farrow must have affected you in some way?*

WA: I never read anything that's being written about me. I found out many years ago – many, *many* years ago – that the best way to work is not to read about yourself or watch yourself on television. I lead a very ostrich-like existence all the time. I never read the reviews of my movies. I don't read the articles about me. Of course, if you ask me to proof-read your book, I'll do that. But during all this period I just kept on working. I never saw myself on television or in the newspapers, because none of that stuff had any meaning to me. You know, when I first started in movies, I was written about all the time. Some people liked my work and other people didn't. It never meant anything to me. It never added up to anything. If all the people liked my work, it didn't mean that the work was good – and it certainly didn't mean that audiences came to see it. If nobody liked it, it didn't mean that the work was bad – although it usually did mean that audiences would not see it. So I gave up on reading about myself many years ago – thirty years or more.

SB: *Well, if you were unaffected by all of the public comments on the affair as far as they concerned your private life, did they in any way influence your professional life?*

WA: No, I made my films exactly as I've always made them. I made *Manhattan Murder Mystery* in the streets of New York, and right after that I made *Bullets Over Broadway* here in New York . . . To me it was a non-issue. It didn't affect any of us in any way whatsoever. Now, there might have been talks in film companies and distribution companies – about my bankability or reliability – that I'm not aware of. This is possible – people saying, 'My God, what are we going to do?' But nobody did anything. Nobody ever called me to say, 'We don't want to do this movie, and maybe we should wait a little while to make your next film.' Nothing of that sort. And nobody ever asked me in the street any questions about what had happened. It was a press fiesta, but of no consequence in my actual life. The fact that I couldn't get custody of my children was of grave concern, but it could only be solved in court.

SB: *In the first edition of the book, we discussed your films chronologically. And strangely enough on that Saturday morning, when we took up our discussions again, the first film we were due to consider was* A Midsummer Night's Sex Comedy, *your first film with Mia Farrow. And you talked about her as an actress and commented on her talents and abilities in exactly the same way as you had talked about other actors you had worked with previously. I found that quite admirable.*

WA: She's a good actress, and in my opinion she's actually underrated by Hollywood. And I attribute this to the fact that she grew up in Hollywood, with a famous Hollywood actress as her mother and a Hollywood director father. So I always felt she didn't get her just acclaim as an actress. I never had any problems with her as an actress. Our problems were purely personal. Professionally, she was easy to work with. She was creative. She had a good range, she could do broad comedy as well as very serious parts. As a performer I have only good things to say about her. I always thought she was neglected in terms of her approbation. And I think this might have been a result of her background and her early fame – not as an actress but as a public figure, as the child of Hollywood 'royalty' and, of course, as the very young wife of Frank Sinatra. There was a kind of public perception of her belonging to a certain Hollywood play-scene, somewhat frivolous and not really serious. Maybe she was too pretty as well. They didn't take her seriously – in the same way that Tuesday Weld had to earn her status. Tuesday Weld is another very fine actress who at first didn't get the recognition she deserved. But there are people that suffer for the silliest reasons. It's possible that Tuesday Weld's name evoked a less serious connotation to people. Which is ridiculous. We have a wonderful actor in America named Rip Torn. He's always been marvellous, in films and on stage. But it's an infelicitous name. He had to struggle against his name. He had to prove all the time that he was not one of those Hollywood people with one of those silly Hollywood names. Eventually he has been taken very seriously by virtue of his sheer talent. Because his talent demanded it. But he had a hard time because people got stuck on his name, without understanding that he was a fabulous actor and a very versatile one. The oddest thing can change the public's perception.

SB: *You were planning the shooting of* Manhattan Murder Mystery *at that time, and I understand that you wrote the script with Mia Farrow in mind as your leading lady.*
WA: Yes, she was going to be in the film, but then everything collapsed. So I called Diane Keaton and asked her if she would take over the part. And she said, 'Sure.'

SB: *Rumours have it that Mia Farrow nevertheless persisted in wanting to play the part . . .*
WA: No, that was just legal posturing at the time, because we were in court. She was of course happy not playing the part under the circumstances. I mean, it was hard to imagine us working together at that moment. But I could have worked with her on that movie. And years after, when I was casting *Mighty Aphrodite*, I was sitting in this room with Juliet Taylor, my casting director, we were discussing the Helena Bonham-Carter part, and I said, 'What about Mia? She would be perfect!' And everybody in the room said, 'No, you hire her and we leave! How could you possibly come up with an idea like this? It's so crazy! You two having

been through these terrible legal procedures!' And I said, 'Yes, but she would be good for the part and she would probably want the job. I will direct her, and she will be professional. We will both go home to our respective homes after work, we don't have to go out for dinner afterward, we will just work together.' But nobody would hear of it. But I could have made *Manhattan Murder Mystery* with her, although it was not such a great idea from a legal point of view – it would have undermined my legal position. At the same time her lawyers wanted to maintain the posture that she wanted to play the part, to maintain her legal position concerning the contract and the money involved in this contract. Her claim on the part was of course not very serious at the time.

SB: *Do you think that Mia Farrow would have accepted the part in* Mighty Aphrodite *if it had been offered to her? It's a hypothetical question, of course.*

WA: I don't know. I have a different attitude than many people about these things. I've offered parts to people in my lifetime that were outspokenly against me. And it didn't matter to me. I felt, 'That person is the right person for this part.' I don't care about their politics or religion or their feelings towards me. I think that's irrelevant. If they can do the job, that's fine. I don't hold any grudges against anybody as long as they can do the job. Whether Mia would share that attitude, I don't know. She might. She has a personal, dramatic streak in her, and she might have felt, 'Yes, why not? Why shouldn't I do this? I can act it. It's a legitimate job. It pays money. I'll say "Good morning" and I'll do my work and I'll say "Good night". And that's it!' But she could as well think, 'Is he crazy?! I wouldn't go near him with a ten-foot pole!' But if Juliet Taylor at that meeting had said, 'Hey, that's beautiful casting,' I would have had them call Mia right away.

SB: *You say you have worked with some actors who have had a more critical attitude towards you. Has this caused you any trouble, or forced you to work with them in a different way to how you direct actors with whom you are more familiar?*

WA: No. I'm in a certain sense so distant when I'm directing anyhow. You know, I'm very polite to everybody – and not familiar. One actor who was being interviewed about working with me said, 'He never spoke to me. He only said "Good morning. Did you get your coffee?" And that's the last thing I heard him say!' And that's true. That's what I would do with anybody. I greet them, when I see them in the morning. And then we

54 Allen takes a phone call during the shooting of *Bullets Over Broadway*

work together. And when the work is over I say 'Good night'. And that's it. I generally don't go to lunch or to dinner with the actors. If they have any questions I answer them, or if they want anything special I tell them.

SB: *I've visited the sets of two of your films,* Manhattan Murder Mystery *and* Bullets Over Broadway. *And it struck me that you have very little contact with the actors between takes.* On Bullets Over Broadway, *I specifically remember when you were filming a scene in the gangster boss's apartment with John Cusack, Jack Warden, Jennifer Tilly and Joe Viterelli. It was a scene with very lively dialogue, loaded with arguments. But between takes you just went away, leaving the actors to themselves, and sat in another corner of the room, either alone or with the script girl, Kay Chapin. Then, just before the next take, you would confront the actors with some further instructions, mostly consisting of suggestions to give the dialogue a faster pace and rhythm. And then there was another take, and when that was over, you went away again.*

WA: Right, I rarely have anything to say to the actors, unless there is some little correction to make. Most of the actors and actresses I work with are terrific, and they do their work beautifully. I don't want to bother them every two seconds. If there is a problem, if they're going too slowly, if they're being too emotional, then I have to say it. But I don't have to do that too much, I don't have to interfere very often, because the instincts of the quality of actors I use are usually good.

SB: *Take Bergman then, by comparison. You have probably seen photos of him when he has been filming. Very often in these photographs you see him sitting in a sofa, like the one you are sitting in now, with an actress or an actor by his side, holding his arm around them.*

WA: I know him to be very touching and warm.

SB: *Apparently he has that need of comforting the actor – always this very intimate approach.*

WA: I know from people who have seen him work that he will take an actor around by the side and be very warm personally. And that's a wonderful trait, and I am sure the actors respond to it. I mean, they must, because the performances he gets from them are wonderful. It makes them feel good, and more creative.

SB: *Maybe it makes him feel more like a father figure.*

WA: Yes, he feels some real affection for the actors, and real empathy.

CHAPTER 26

Bullets Over Broadway, Mighty Aphrodite, and TV and theatre work

DAVID: I'm an artist and I won't change a word in my play!
(From Bullets Over Broadway)

STIG BJÖRKMAN: *In the previous edition of this book, we talked about the project you were going to start after* Manhattan Murder Mystery, *and you said that you were going to collaborate with Douglas McGrath. You didn't yet have a story in mind, but it appeared that you didn't want to write on your own. Why do you decide to write with someone else? And why did you choose McGrath?*

WOODY ALLEN: He is a personal friend of mine, in the same sense that Marshall Brickman is a personal friend of mine. And every so often, every sixth or seventh picture, I just get lonely writing myself. I mean, after doing it year after year after year, you know, and then getting prepared for the experience again, I think, 'Why not give myself a little reward and call one of my friends who I like to spend time with, and collaborate with him?' Then it becomes a much more pleasant process. We sit in a room together, we take walks, we go to dinner, we talk about the project, and it's less lonely. So every once in a while I treat myself to that little reward, and this was one of those times.

SB: *Besides* Bullets Over Broadway, *were there other possible projects that you discussed?*

WA: I presented Doug with a list of ideas, wanting to see which of them he might respond to. And *Bullets Over Broadway* was one that he liked very much. On my list it was one of my lesser favourites, but I went forward with it on his enthusiasm to a large degree. I myself would have picked a different idea, but Doug said, 'No, no, you have dealt with these other kinds of ideas before. This is very different and as an audience member I would like to see this film.' So I started working with him, we started our conversations, and then the story emerged.

SB: *But why was* Bullets Over Broadway *a less interesting project for you at that time?*

WA: Because I thought that the idea of a gangster boss who wanted to put his girlfriend in a show was not too original. What I thought *was* original was that the helping hand of the boss, the young gangster, turned out to be a more gifted writer than the playwright of my story. When the idea emerged that the gangster becomes so possessive over his script that he kills the girl, then I knew there was something there, and I went ahead. Because then I felt the story really had something to say. It said that you couldn't really tell who the artist was, and that the relationship between the playwright and the gangster was based on a mutual passion, a passion for the art. That's what really sold me.

SB: *You mentioned that you had four or five other projects that you suggested to McGrath. Did you later on turn any of your other ideas into screenplays?*

WA: Yes, *Small Time Crooks* and *Curse of the Jade Scorpion* were both on the list; they were both ideas that we thought were funny and should be done.

SB: *Chazz Palminteri, who plays the young gangster Cheech, is a writer himself. Were you familiar with his work at all?*

WA: No, his first movie hadn't come out at that time, and I had never heard of him. Juliet Taylor just said, 'I want you to meet Chazz Palminteri, because he might be very good for this part.' I said, 'Fine,' and then he walked in that door. The second I saw him, I said to myself, 'That's what I was thinking of when I wrote the part.' You couldn't get better casting.

SB: *The very first line of the film comes from the playwright David Shane, who tells his agent that he refuses to change one line in his play. Then, little by little, he has to give in, to the gangster, to the producer, the stars, et cetera. Do you ever receive comments on your screenplays from people involved in the making of your picture? Do they in any way try to influence your work?*

WA: Yes, from nobody and everybody. Nobody sees the script. I don't give it to anybody to read and give me an opinion on it or anything. I finish the script and we go into production with it. I write the script I want to, and nobody ever tries to influence me beforehand – not my producer nor my casting director or cameraman or anybody. But on the set, when I am filming the movie, everybody tells me how to do it – the script girl, the assistant director, the focus-puller. Everyone contributes with their comments. 'That joke is not funny, you should do this joke instead.' Or, 'That doesn't look real!' I mean, everybody has opinions. And I listen to all of them, and sometimes they are right and sometimes not. But nobody ever comes around in a serious way with suggestions of changes in the script. People feel I've made enough movies to know what I am doing.

SB: *I think the relationship between David and Cheech is the most important aspect of the film, because it constantly develops in a very positive way, from initial suspicion and rivalry into a sense of companionship and respect.*

WA: Sure, that was the nucleus of the story – the development of Cheech taking over the play, first with a small amount of suggestions, and then taking over the writing. Then starting to refer to it as 'our play', and then 'my play', and in the end being willing to kill for it.

SB: *John Cusack, who plays David, is playing a character very similar to characters you've played yourself in earlier films.*

WA: I could have played it if I was younger. It's a kind of part I can play, but Cusack is a much better choice. He is a fabulous actor and completely believable as an intellectual. I've worked with him a few times and I would use him again in a minute. Whenever you see a movie with John Cusack, whether the movie is good or bad, he is always good. He has that special quality.

SB: *One of the characters in the film, the Marxist Sheldon Flender, says at one point, 'An artist creates his own moral universe.' How far are you willing to go to defend your ideas in a confrontation with producers or financiers?*

WA: When I was very young I had to defend my ideas very strongly. On some occasions it was hopeless. I mean, I couldn't. I was just a hired hand, but I didn't like that, of course. When I did my first movie, *What's New, Pussycat?*, I defended and defended and defended, but I lost, because I had no muscle. My defence was of no use or consequence.

55   Allen directs Dianne Wiest and John Cusack in *Bullets Over Broadway*

SB: *All the characters in* Bullets Over Broadway *seem to have dreams and ambitions. David wants to be recognized as an artist and to be successful. Helen Sinclair, the actress, wants to make a comeback. But smaller and more surprising dreams are also revealed, as when Cheech confesses his dream to David at the billiard hall. ('I always wanted to dance. Have you ever seen George Raft dance?') So dreams seem to connect almost all the characters in the film.*

WA: Well, of course, characters that have ambitions are good characters to write about, because it makes a film active.

SB: Bullets Over Broadway *is set in the late twenties. Do you enjoy making this kind of period film?*

WA: Yes. Nobody else enjoys it, because it's expensive. But I enjoy it, because in New York the three great decades were the twenties, the thirties and the forties. There was great music and great automobiles and great nightclubs, and theatres and clothing styles and gangsters and soldiers and sailors. It was just a great, colourful time. Everything was very glamorous. Everyone smoked cigarettes and dressed for dinner and went out to nightclubs. It was really highly sophisticated. So I like to set some of my films in those years, because it's fun.

SB: *But there was also another side to it. The thirties were marked by the Depression, which you show in* The Purple Rose of Cairo.

WA: Yes, the thirties were marked in that sense, but in the twenties everyone was living high and in the forties, even when the war started, people were still living high. But during the Depression years, people were out of work, they had no money, and the country was having a hard time. And so people looked for glamour and escape. They loved to see movies and hear stories and see plays about those people on Broadway who lived in luxurious penthouses in New York. In fact, the New York theatre scene in the thirties was just tremendous. I mean, there must have been a hundred plays a night that you could go to. All over New York City, one theatre after another. And all the important playwrights, like O'Neill and Thornton Wilder and Clifford Odets and so on.

SB: *Would you have liked to live in that era as an adult?*

WA: No, because they didn't have penicillin and a lot of other things that I have come to depend on. But I do like making films about that era, and I do wish that New York was a more formal and elegant place now. Like when I watch Katharine Hepburn and Spencer Tracy as the two lawyers in

Adam's Rib coming home for dinner in their own apartment and Tracy goes upstairs and puts on a tuxedo. You know, when I was a boy and there was an opening night on Broadway, you knew it was so much fun to go, because you would see the limousines pull up and there would be all these people from the New York theatre, all wearing tuxedos. There would be a party afterwards. I mean it was really an event. It had a celebratory feeling, a special quality to it. But not any more. Now it's just very casual. Now a show opens and they have some silly little party at a yuppie restaurant somewhere, and everyone is in their jeans and T-shirts and it has no real lustre. Even though the superficiality of dressing up is meaningless, it's too bad that the glamour no longer exists.

SB: *That is also a feeling that you convey in* Radio Days.

WA: I am one of the least formal people. But nevertheless, I think it would be nice if people dressed for dinner, and if the theatre didn't start at 7.30. The theatre used to be at 8.40, so you would have a little bite of dinner and then see the show, and then you got out about 11.15 at night and you went to a supper club, and there might be some kind of a show, or just supper. And then you would go home and it was great. Then what happened was that the city got so riddled with crime and drugs, and people were afraid to go out. And everybody started to move out of New York, so the theatre-going public lived in Connecticut or Long Island or in the suburbs. And they don't want to finish at 11.15 and take the train. They want to go home earlier because they have a big trip. So the whole schedule became much earlier and much less glamorous.

SB: *You usually don't film in a studio – you prefer to find actual settings. So I guess making a period picture means more problems, maybe not for you, but for your collaborators?*

WA: Santo Loquasto, the production designer, has to solve them. And he knows that we don't have a big budget. We can't afford to construct night clubs and theatres and apartments. So he goes out and he finds settings that are in the right direction, either a little bit or to a great degree, and he supplements them. You know, a few lights here and a little something there, and all of a sudden it looks just fine. New York is full of surprises. I mean, I've made thirty movies or more and I'm still surprised when I go location-hunting at the amount of unusual places there are for every need. When I shot *Sweet and Lowdown*, it took place in Chicago and New York and California and on the road across the country. And I usually shot within thirty blocks of my house.

56   Wiest and Cusack in *Bullets Over Broadway*

s b: *Have there been settings – not only for your period films – that have inspired particular scenes in your films?*

w a: Yes, sometimes I see something that gives me an idea. I remember once when I was working with Doug McGrath, and he showed me a building that had a brewery in the basement where they used to make liquor. You could still see the big barrels. And I thought I should write a scene someday for that. Very often I see a beautiful street in New York and then, at home writing my script, I put the people on that street, because that setting has to some extent influenced me and inspired me.

s b: *So, then you make a note of the street or the block you've visited?*

w a: I make a note and a description for Santo to check it out.

s b: *Do you save these settings in your memory for future projects if they are not suitable for the film you're working on?*

w a: Oh, yes. Sometimes Santo comes up with suggestions: 'I saw a great building today. We don't need it right now, but you should pass by when you take a walk next week and take a look at it. It might be suitable for the scene in *Bullets Over Broadway*, when we are to enter into Valenti's apartment. It's a hotel on Broadway, the Edison Hotel, the first floor of the hotel. We can add a few lamps.' So I thought, 'Why not?' And the setting was very pretty. It looked great. Things like that happen all the time. We did not build anything for *Bullets Over Broadway*. Everything was found, and occasionally supplemented. We put a wall up here and a fake cover window there, and so on.

s b: *Dianne Wiest's performance in* Bullets *is something of a tour de force.*

w a: She is a great actress.

s b: *Did you create the role with Dianne Wiest in mind, or was she engaged for the part at a later stage?*

w a: She is a friend, and while I was working on the script she contacted me and said, 'I really want to be in your next movie. I'm not doing anything for the moment. I'm not on any shows. I'm not going to be in California.' So I said, 'Fine, it's great for me.' Later on, when I gave her the script and suggested the part to her, she said, 'I can't do this. This is not for me.' But I said, 'Yes, you can,' and it took me a couple of talks to convince her. When we started shooting I acted the part for her at the rehearsals. Which is something I almost never do with the actors. But I had to come flouncing down the stairs and act a few sentences for her to give her the level that I wanted. When she got it, that was it and she was great.

SB: *I agree, but of course this part is quite different from what we have seen her doing before.*

WA: Right. Dianne is a very versatile actress. She can do anything. Now, I know Dianne personally, and I know her capacity as an actress. Another director might have cast a different actress, someone who's more of a diva or with a seemingly tougher surface. But there are so many actors and actresses out there who are capable of wonderful things but they just never get a shot at it, because producers and directors don't always recognize their talents in full.

SB: *Typecasting is sometimes a problem in American films – not least for many actors who can't escape the kind of parts in which they're always cast.*

WA: That's right, because American films are mythological. A producer would give a part to someone like John Wayne, because John Wayne would do the things you've always seen him do. Wayne was a mythological hero and you saw him over and over again in the same kind of movie. He worked on maybe a hundred films, but people were never tired of hearing him say the same things and doing the same things for the hundredth time. That's what American films generally are – re-enactments of myths. We have these movie stars with their mythological status. You can liken them to the Greek gods. There's Bette Davis doing her thing. Or Humphrey Bogart doing his thing, or Clark Gable. They could all be living up there, always ready to re-enact a myth. An actor like Dustin Hoffman is not a mythological hero. He is simply a great actor. It's rare to find such an actor who can do all of these different roles, and do them beautifully. There is usually much more money and popular adulation to be found in being a mythological hero.

SB: *It might also be that these kinds of mythological actors don't dare to abandon their positions, and risk their status and their popularity.*

WA: It's a combination of both. Some are willing to try something else and can't get people to trust them to do it. And others are nervous about trying something else because they've hit the jackpot. They might say they want to deviate, but they don't.

Mighty Aphrodite

> THE GREEK CHORUS: Of all human weaknesses obsession is
> the most dangerous.
>
> (From *Mighty Aphrodite*)

> THE CLOWN: I know exactly what I think about this, but I can
> never find words to put it in. Maybe if I get a little drunk I could
> dance it for you.
>
> (From *Shadows and Fog*)

SB: *Another mythological actor in American cinema is Marilyn Monroe.*
Did she represent anything for you at the time when you were growing up
and starting to go to the movies?

WA: I was a little bit young when she burst on the scene, and she was so
overwhelmingly sexual for some magical reason. She had that indefinable
quality that some people just have, just such a powerful sexuality. As an
actress I feel she was untested. There were a couple of occasions where she
seemed quite good and promising, but not enough to really be conclusive.
I mean, I am not one of those people that went crazy over her acting. I saw
her play comedy and I felt there was very good potential there. Maybe
more than potential. She realized some very good moments. But obviously
her personal problems really militated against her ever coming to flourish
as an actress. If she had been more of a stable individual, it's possible that
over the years and with hard work – which she apparently was willing to
do – she could have exploited and developed her talent to its maximum.
But we never got that out of her. We got just flashes of very good things,
but not enough to really know how good she could have been. In a couple
of movies, though, I liked her very much.

SB: *Movies such as . . .?*

WA: The wonderful William Inge play *Bus Stop*. She was terrific in that.
And she was appropriately funny in Billy Wilder's *Some Like It Hot*.

SB: *Of course, she was really stuck in the studio system of the fifties. She*
was on monthly payments and didn't make very much money, until late in
life she became independent and could choose her own parts.

WA: It was hard for me to see beyond the sexuality. Because if you are
casting and one of the people that you are considering is Marilyn Monroe,
it's a very tough decision. Especially in a contemporary film. I mean, if

you can hide that overwhelming sexuality in a period piece, that's one thing, but realistically she is not exactly the girl next door. She was so devastatingly beautiful, so it wouldn't have been easy to cast her and accept her in a role in which her sexuality was not a factor. I guess if you're convinced that she could carry the acting part of it, you could have torn down that aspect of her and written a demanding role for her and given her at least a fair chance to play it. She might have been able to. If her own insecurity didn't hurt her. She had such a troubled background, she was so sexy to men, she was an unproven actress who was trying to prove herself in a system that really doesn't give you much leeway. I mean, someone comes along like that, and the reason that she becomes an overnight sensation is just because of her looks and men become overwhelmed by her. It's tough.

SB: *As you say, though, she really tried. She went to New York for a year and studied with Lee Strasberg. She had ambitions.*

WA: Her heart was in the right place. It was just that she was emotionally a mess and she never had an opportunity to really show us what she could do. A more stable person, in her position, might have fared better. Because there have been people, actors or actresses, that we have come to know as one thing, and then because they were ambitious and hardworking and talented and stable enough, they have been able to show us that they had a lot more to them. Take Clint Eastwood, for example. You've been thinking, 'Oh God, he is just handsome and a cowboy actor,' but he is much more than that. He has been able to show us that he could do far more.

SB: *I digressed a little about Marilyn as we are going to talk about* Mighty Aphrodite. *If Marilyn Monroe had lived now, do you think she could have taken the part Mira Sorvino played in the film?*

WA: Absolutely, if she had been young enough. Yes, no question about it. To think of her as a prostitute with that overwhelming beauty and sexuality – she certainly would have been a rich prostitute. I mean, she would have been top of the line. But she could have done that part, because she would have had the wide-eyed, naïve sense of humour to do it. That much she did prove, even in her short career. But I was very lucky to get Mira, I must say. I found it hard to find someone to play that part.

SB: *How did you find her? It was her first big film role, wasn't it?*

57   Allen and Mira Sorvino in *Mighty Aphrodite*

WA: Yes, it was her first major role. I looked at many women for that part – Americans, then Europeans as well – but I couldn't find anyone. And suddenly her name came up. Juliet Taylor knew her as a good actress. We had met her before for something, she had been here to read for a part in another film, a part that she wasn't right for. But we could tell from her reading that she was a good actress. Then we happened to be in London at the Dorchester Hotel, and we asked her to come in and read. And Mira is one of those actresses that really gets into the part in real life. So she dressed tarty and came to the hotel. I'm surprised they let her up. But she came into the room and she looked great. She looked exactly right for the part. She had the right clothes on, she carried herself right, she had all the body language. Then she read the part, and she read beautifully.

SB: *Did she read in that incredibly squeaky voice she went on to use in the film?*
WA: I can't remember. But that voice was her own invention completely, and she developed it by herself before the shooting. I mean, I didn't tell her or suggest to her to use that voice. She characterized the part as she saw fit and, as usual, my job, I felt, was only to stop her if I felt she was making a terrible mistake. It seemed to sound quite good. She's very bright and a very serious and talented actress, so I tried not to mess up with her. She had a number of needs, she didn't want to be photographed from this side or that way, and I was happy to give in to all of them, because it made her happy. I didn't care if it was really a nuisance. She was worth it, and funny in her needs – her silly health-food candy bars. Very endearing. Sometimes, just before we were going to do a scene together, while we were waiting for the extras or the camera to get ready, like twenty or thirty seconds before action is called, she would start talking to me as her character and with dialogue that she would make up that theoretically preceded the scene. I would look at her like she was nuts and say, 'What?' And she would be talking as the character, delineating the problem. That's how she works, and the results speak for themselves.

SB: *So you were just standing there thinking, 'These are not my lines?'*
WA: I was thinking to myself, 'Oh God, I hope she doesn't expect me to answer in character.' I was just embarrassed. But she was very good about it. She would do it perfectly to my dumb face, as I stared back at her. And, you know, she also played Marilyn Monroe on television. So yes, Marilyn could have played this part. I enjoyed working with Mira, and she made a big contribution to the movie.

SB: *Yesterday you mentioned that the moment you saw Chazz Palminteri coming into this room, you thought, 'There is my character!' When you have these readings and test actors for a part, do they mostly read passages from the script you are going to film?*
WA: Yes.

SB: *Do you ever video the actors as well?*
WA: No, they come here and I hide in a corner. Then Juliet Taylor asks them to read, while I watch. The only thing I want to get is just some sense of what they sound like in the character. I know they are not going to present a finished performance, or even a good performance. I just want to see if their instinct is to be real. That's very important. Many actors and actresses come into this room and we sit and talk, like you and I are doing now. Then I present them the character, and suddenly they go into their acting mode and start sounding in a way that no human being talks. So I want to say to them, 'Just read the lines the way you were talking to me, like a human being talks.' If they miss that, then I generally don't hire them, because I feel their instinct is going to be false. I know at once when the person sounds real and decent. That's all I need to know. I do very short readings, I mean a page, just to get a little suggestion.

SB: *Are they prepared beforehand or do they get this page from you during the session?*
WA: They get it here. If they look like what I want, I ask them if they would read a page and they almost always say, 'Of course.' Then we give them the page and we say, 'Look this over in the other room and let us know when you want to come back in here and read.' They look it over for two minutes, five minutes, or maybe ten. Some actors or actresses quite superfluously try to memorize it. That's completely unnecessary and it screws them up sometimes. We don't need it so perfect, we just want to get a little taste of them, but they don't know this. They are poor creatures who are looking for a job and they want it so badly, and I am trying to be as kind as possible to them, because I know that I could never do what they are doing. It's a nightmare to go through that, to come into a room full of strangers who say, 'Read this.' They want the job, and you know it's an awful thing. So I try and hire them without reading as much as possible. But sometimes they have to read.

SB: *You say you met Mira Sorvino in London, and I know you went over there to publicize* Manhattan Murder Mystery. *This, I think, was something new to you, because you seldom go abroad to talk about your pictures. Was this a new necessity because of the new production company?*

WA: No, no. It's a much baser motive than that. People are always asking me to go to Europe to make a tour of the countries, and this is something that I've always resisted, because I don't like to travel and live in hotels, and I don't like to fly. But Soon-Yi likes it and I want her to have a nice time. So I go to Paris for a few days, for instance, or to London for a few days, or to Italy and Spain, and she enjoys that very much. She has a nice time and sees the city, and I do interviews. So I do it for her, really. Because Soon-Yi enjoys every now and then going to Europe and touring the countries. Otherwise I would probably be saying, 'Could you send the journalist to New York, or could I do it over the phone?' Because I don't like to disrupt my life. I play at the Café Carlyle every Monday night, and I don't like to disrupt my jazz band.

SB: *But I understand that after this trip to London you went to Ireland to see your son?*

WA: That must have been seven years ago. He was in Ireland, and I was going to Europe on a tour and we detoured to Ireland. I like Ireland very much, I find it very beautiful. Like all my travelling, I like those places for a couple of days. It's hard for me to get used to spending a long period of time in any of those places. I could spend a long period of time in Paris, because Paris is just like New York. It's full of all the things that I am used to – noise, traffic, restaurants, art galleries, shops, theatres, sports . . . I also love Venice very much, but it would be difficult for me to spend a long period of time there, because it's such a different city. But it's a relaxing city, and I do love it. Whenever I go to Europe I always make sure to stop in Venice for at least a couple of days, because it's a very wonderful place.

SB: *For* Mighty Aphrodite *you went to Sicily, to Syracuse, to film at the amphitheatre there. Had you visited it before?*

WA: Many years ago, when *Bananas* came out, I was sent to Europe to promote the film, and one of the places I was sent to was the Taormina Film Festival. I've always remembered it as an incredibly beautiful spot. When we planned the shooting of *Mighty Aphrodite* Santo Loquasto went over to Europe to look at possible places for the shooting, and one of the places he came back with was Taormina. So I decided on Taormina, because it's such a beautiful place. It's Italy, and I love Italy.

s b: *How did you come up with the idea of the Greek chorus that opens the film and punctuates the action at various intervals later on?*

wa: I've always wanted to use a Greek chorus and the techniques of the Greek theatre in a contemporary piece. I had thought of other pieces for it earlier on. But when this idea came to me, a story of an adopted child, of two children with unknown parents – my character being the father of a child which its mother is unaware about, and she being the mother of my child which I had not been aware of – I felt, 'My God, it's got a kind of Grecian irony to it.' Then I thought, 'This film is the one to do as a Greek fable.' So I put it together and hired a choreographer, and she choreographed the chorus for me. This was Graciela Daniele, who had done the musical numbers for *Bullets Over Broadway* – and later on for *Everyone Says 'I Love You'* – and it was a very pleasant experience.

s b: *Destiny is a very common ingredient in the Greek dramas, and it's also very important to the moral of this comedy.*

wa: Destiny, or Fate, is beyond you. You think you control your life, you think that you are pulling the strings, but that's not what's happening. That's happening to some small degree. But to a very large degree, and a much more important degree than your control, Fate is controlling it. In the film, I think I am taking charge of her life and running it, and I think I am investigating after the truth, but in the end I wound up having completely lost control over things. She has had my child, and I don't realize it. None of us is in control of our destinies, really. We like to brag that we are, but we're not – not even close.

s b: *Music is always very important in your films, and you choose your music most meticulously. In* Mighty Aphrodite *you start with a non-American composition, a Greek song, 'Neominoria'. Did you listen to a lot of music before you made this choice? And why did you pick this one?*

wa: It just sounded right. It had the right feel for the movie, the right ambience. The story starts in Greece, and then we have a quick switch to a New York restaurant – a restaurant which is one block from here, on Lexington Avenue – where I put in a Rodgers and Hart number, 'Manhattan'. But in the beginning I wanted to set a Greek atmosphere and I wanted to show the amphitheatre and the chorus marching up to its position, and I didn't want the cinema audience to know what was going on, to know what to expect.

58   The Greek chorus of *Mighty Aphrodite*

sb: *From the prologue with the Greek chorus, you cut directly to the scene in the restaurant and the line uttered by Helena Bonham-Carter: 'Lenny, I want a child!' Of course, this is what the whole film is about. The child, the adopted child, is the centre of the story. And this opening line is delivered immediately and on the spot.*

wa: I like that. I had a similar start in *Bullets Over Broadway* too. John Cusack's first line is: 'I am an artist.' And *Hollywood Ending* has a very similar, direct start. Because I want to get right into it and go, particularly if it's a comic film. Get into it and go right from there.

sb: *I like this directness, because in so many films the characters have to be introduced, we have to know their names and where they live, and sometimes the director or the writer wants us to know their profession before the story has a chance to start . . .*

wa: Their jobs, their names, all that comes out in due time. But what's important for the audience to focus on is the goal and the ambition of the movie.

sb: *A bit later, there is a scene where your character is on the phone with his wife and we hear him say, 'The answer is no!', and we are very well aware of what question has been posed. Then you cut and we see your character with this small child in his arms. Here you show the same kind of directness and efficiency in your editing.*

wa: These things happen in life, too, where you are completely insistent upon one course of action, but where destiny or luck will interfere. If you look at a film like *Hannah and Her Sisters*, for example, there is a scene where Michael Caine is saying to himself, 'Don't do anything now, wait until Monday, there will be a better time. Don't kiss her now, just relax and do it on Monday, it will be perfect.' And then the woman he adores walks in and he grabs her instantly. Because we, ourselves, are always one thing, but our emotions are a whole different thing than our minds.

sb: *Apart from* Radio Days – *and, later on,* Deconstructing Harry – Mighty Aphrodite *is one of the few films of yours where a small child has one of the major parts. Kids do appear in some of the other films, but usually they are pushed away into the background.*

wa: That's right, they are not significant players.

sb: *We just hear them in the children's room, or there's a nanny taking*

care of them. But in each of the three films aforementioned, a child is a very important figure, and he has also some acting space.
WA: Right.

SB: *I guess the idea or the inspiration for the story must have come from the fact that you have an adopted child too?*
WA: No, I got the idea years ago from watching Mia adopt children. And she would adopt many children, as we all know. And I would think to myself, 'Who is the mother of that child? Who is the father of that child?' Then different ideas, comedies about adoption, started to occur to me, because it was so much a part of her life. And I thought to myself, 'So she adopts a child and the child is so wonderful, so charming and so spectacular, and of course there must have been a mother and a father to this child. Who is the mother? Who is the father?' I thought that would be a funny idea to deal with. But when I decided years later to realize this idea into *Mighty Aphrodite*, the story wasn't inspired by me getting involved with adoption. It was rather seeing Mia being so involved in it.

SB: *Do you find it more troublesome to direct child actors, or do you just have to direct them in another way?*
WA: Yes, and it's very hard for me to describe. There are directors who do incredibly good work with child actors. I am not one of them. I have always had trouble getting performances out of child actors. I find it very difficult. It's just a very tough thing for me. I had trouble in *Radio Days*. The kids in that film were in no way bad actors. On the contrary. But to get the nuanced performances I wanted was very, very difficult, and I wound up throwing out a lot of good material that deserved to be in the movie. But the child actors couldn't bring it off. The same thing has happened to me in a number of movies that I have done – even in films where children were playing only small parts. I have had to cut some wonderfully funny scenes, because the children couldn't do them. I tried re-shooting them, I tried every conceivable thing to get the children to play it the right way. But I couldn't manage. Yet, there are directors who get performances out of children that are as good as the best adult actors. I don't know how they do it. I have never been able to.

SB: *Do you try to trick them into acting the way you want?*
WA: I try everything I can. I try to speak to them on their own terms. I try to let them improvise. I try to give them guidance. I try to give them examples and I show them what to do. I do everything that any

commonsense person would – the same things that I would do for an actor who's not getting it. You just try every imaginable thing. So finally I cut the material down to the few lines that they can manage.

SB: *Sometimes you might exchange actors in your films, and get another actor for the part. But it must be more difficult to exchange a child actor?*
WA: It's tough for the child actor, but I have done it even with child actors. Take for instance a classroom scene in any of my pictures – *Annie Hall* or *Radio Days* – where I've hired a couple of child actors. If, after trying every conceivable device in the world, I can't get them to do what they're supposed to do, I will pick somebody else. It could be somebody hired as an extra, but somebody who can do it much better.

SB: *How do you choose the child actors? Do you have them read, or do you just sit down and talk to them?*
WA: They come in here and they usually have some acting experience. Then I ask them to read, and generally these child actors have memorized everything with their parents. They have memorized every emotion, so when they want to say, 'Oh my gosh!', I hear them deliver the line in a most over-explicit way: 'OH my *gosh*!!!' So I try to get them to sound more natural. It's tough, and I rarely succeed.

SB: *I guess Juliet Taylor must have a list of professional child actors?*
WA: Yes, sure, and we usually use professional child actors. Of course, at their age there is not a huge difference between a professional child actor and a non-professional one. It's not like a professional actor who's been acting for twenty years or something. The child might have done one or two things. Once in a while we get a good one, but even the good ones have a tough time with the comedy lines.

SB: *I can imagine that. Most children don't understand irony. They can't handle that.*
WA: They don't get the humour of it, which I understand, because the humour is in the inflection of the voice. They can imitate me, but it never really comes from within them. You don't get the sense that the kid is really nailing the line because he or she understands it. They are just doing it the way I am telling them to do it, and it has a hollow ring to it.

SB: *One of the great merits of the film, I think, is your presentation of the everyday married life of the couple in the early part of the film. It has an intimate and immediate character which I think is a very important ground for the comedy.*

WA: It wasn't too difficult to do. I mean, Helena is a terrific actress, and it was very easy to develop this relationship and the idea of having a child. There was this little conflict, a little apprehension. And Helena was playing the part with an American accent. I never know how these British actors manage this, but not only can she do that but she does the acting great.

SB: *You have a certain flair for English actors and actresses, don't you?*
WA: They have a wonderful tradition. And they can play the parts of ordinary people. Most American actors go for glamour and beauty. They can play cowboys or gangsters or handsome young men. It's hard to find just an ordinary man that you would see in an office. When you see a Swedish film with, for instance, Erland Josephson – you know he is like a regular man. He could be a lawyer or an accountant. He is not a man with a gun, not a tough guy, nor very glamorous. He is a man that could play my father or your father, and we don't have that kind of actor here. We've never valued that, because our films are myths, so we always need the hero, the gunfighter, the larger-than-life person. But England has these kinds of actors who are believable as regular men. Actors like Albert Finney or Michael Caine or Ian Holm or Anthony Hopkins. So I very often have got to resort to English people, you know. Tracey Ullman is another – a great comedienne, truly great, and with no noticeable difficulty she plays these American parts with a perfect American accent. I don't know how she does it.

SB: *It's very refreshing to see Helena Bonham-Carter walk away from those James Ivory films and into this depiction of daily American life.*
WA: Some of her best work is in *Fight Club*. She is great in that film, just wonderful. There she really shows what a range she has – full of surprises.

SB: *Since we are discussing actors who can play average, ordinary men, I think you found one in your next film,* Everyone Says 'I Love You' – *Edward Norton. That was one of his first parts, but he is an actor with that special quality.*
WA: He has been trying to resist playing the heroic roles, and because of it he is not quite the commercial star as is his co-star in *Fight Club*, Brad

Pitt. But he is truly one of our finest actors and I admire the direction he has gone in. He has been taking the artistic route. I never heard of him before he walked into this room and read the part, and I was just stunned. I thought, 'This kid is absolutely great', and I hired him immediately. I didn't even ask if he could sing or not. I couldn't care less, I just wanted him. I was going to let him sing even if he sang as bad as I sing. But he could sing. And talk about acting range!

SB: *If we go back to* Mighty Aphrodite *and the ambience that you create at the beginning of the film – on the wall in the married couple's apartment there hangs a very beautiful and somewhat solemn painting. It shows a room in half-shadow with a large sunlit window, and in the room we see only two wooden chairs and a bit of a table. This interior is quite a contrast to the elegant home of the couple. Do you often select props such as paintings for your films?*

WA: Sometimes; it depends. There are times when Santo Loquasto just knows what to put on the wall, and there are times when he will say to me, 'What do you think these characters would hang on their walls?' He will say, for instance, 'I assume these characters would hang prints of Matisse on their wall,' and I will say, 'Yes, you're right,' or I say, 'Just photographs.' For *The Curse of the Jade Scorpion* Santo suggested that we should decorate the walls of an office with moose heads and antlers. The character's hobby might be hunting. I never thought of that but I thought it was a wonderful idea, and he decorated it that way, but we didn't make a big thing out of it. So it depends, but there are times when he just decorates the room, because it goes without saying what should be in it – an expensive and very sombre print by, say, Franz Kline. Or just a poster. He works from character.

SB: *What is your own interest in art? Do you go to exhibitions? Do you have any favourite artists?*

WA: Sure, I have many favourite artists. In contemporary art I have always liked minimalist artists. I very much liked Cy Twombly and Richard Serra. And going back a little bit, I like the same artists that everyone likes – Mark Rothko, of course, and Jackson Pollock. Then, as you go further back, you wind up again liking very much the same artists everyone likes. But the most joyous and wonderful arena of painting is represented by the three schools I like best. I like the German expressionists very much. And I like what we call the 'ash-can painters'. These were American painters of the twentieth century who painted average scenes, like the subway, backyards, and prosaic settings. Of course, like everybody else I am crazy about the French impressionists, because to me they represent the highest point of sheer unadulterated joy. I really like them all, but of those painters I am particularly fond of Pissarro, because his paintings of Paris are so evocative to me, and I just wish he would have been around to paint New York that way. It's exactly as I think of Paris at its most wonderful: grey and rainy, and the boulevards with the horses and carriages. So there are many painters that I'm crazy about, and many of them contemporary. I get a big kick out of Jim Dine and Ed Rusha, the witty painters, the painters that are amusing. If I could own anything, I'd probably like to own a Pissarro, a metropolitan scene of Paris. But I wouldn't turn down a Cézanne or a Bonnard.

s b: *You don't buy art? You are not a collector?*

w a: I have a few little things in my house. I have a very pretty Nolde, a watercolour, and I have a very lovely ink drawing by Oskar Kokoschka. I have some prints that are very pretty. I have a very pretty Elsworth Kelly print and a nice Rauschenberg print and an Ed Rusha print. But, you know, it would be too expensive for me to collect in a way that would be satisfying to me. If I opened that bottle and the genie got out, I wouldn't like that. I could easily go broke filling my house with paintings, and I don't want to.

s b: *Talking about decoration and art, we can quickly move over to the apartment of Judy or Lucy or whatever her name happens to be – the Mira Sorvino character. Because that is also a kind of art collection that she has in her apartment.*

w a: Yes, of course that was exaggerated. My guess is that in real life someone like that would probably bend over to be conservative, but it wouldn't be as funny. Santo found all that stuff and showed it around, and we all looked at it and agreed that it would make the most sudden impact. The other joke is more subtle – that she is basically conservative, or that she has photographs of John F. Kennedy, or Madonna. We thought that the best impact would be that she just has a kind of mindless sleazy taste, and that would be funniest.

s b: *From what we see of her, we might just write her off as another dumb blonde. But the way Mira Sorvino plays this character, she becomes the pillar of the film. I guess this was also your idea, when you invented the character?*

WA: Yes. She is a poor thing, but in the end she can be reformed. If somebody takes a little time with her. It's not my character who reforms her. I try and try and try and she still remains kind of a dumb piece of sexy merchandise. The change is out of the Greek theatre – *deus ex machina*. It is the only way that you can save a person like that. You really need a force to come out of heaven and save her, and that's what did happen to her. That's in keeping with the theme of the movie: that fate is out of your hands. It's pure luck. I mean, she is driving along and suddenly a helicopter lands next to her, because the pilot is having engine trouble. It's a typical *deus ex machina* ploy. She falls in love with the pilot, and it changes her life. My character tries and tries to give her lessons, but none of that means anything in the end. If you are going to be saved, most of the time it's from luck.

SB: *In a way she also becomes a comment on the bourgeois family that you introduce in the film. They are smart and ironical and they turn this irony towards each other as a weapon. Judy doesn't understand when ironical comments are directed towards her. She just drops them.*

WA: Right, and at the end she will live a very bourgeois life with the person who she is married to, and the bourgeois life will be better than the life she was living. It's not the best kind of life, but it's better than the one she had, for sure. Incidentally, I am not as critical of the bourgeois life as many of my friends are. Because I feel that there is something about the middle class, as Tolstoy felt, that keeps everything going. They are the ones that keep the world turning and like all classes there are people within that who are good and bad. There are bourgeois families that are quite nice and that lead very decent lives, and also others that are greedy and empty. But I'm a big fan of the middle class. I don't have a big tolerance of the artistic temperament. I feel the artistic temperament is unearned privilege based on good fortune. I don't have an unrealistically high opinion of the lower classes either, because I feel they are quite often full of prejudice and ignorance. The middle class tries. They don't have the talent necessary to rise too high and they don't have the business genius, but they are often sweet. The ones who are most critical of them all the time are the artists. They criticize from a position of unearned superiority. They are born with a gift and they have contempt for those who just carry out the daily work. But that is nonsense. Or else they condescendingly try to save the world with their art.

SB: *And what about the upper class here in America?*

WA: Well, we haven't been a pronouncedly class-ridden society, because the US is a democracy with a very large middle class. The upper classes in America, they vary. And they often have become unfair targets of resentment, because they are the upper classes. They are no worse than the middle class or the lower classes. They have their percentage of people who are very benevolent and decent citizens, and also scoundrels who have become the upper class through terrible dealing. But there is sort of an automatic resentment against them, simply because they have a great deal of wealth, and that's not right. If you recall when the *Titanic* was sinking, the wealthy people behaved very well. They were very organized, they were very decent, they were brave. They acquitted themselves admirably. In the end there is no comforting generalization that one can make about any class or any occupation. There are very nice people in all classes, very nice film directors, very nice policemen, very nice dentists. The exceptional are rare in any area. And of course there are many bad ones. But in the end there is no helpful observation or comfortable observation to be made about any of this. The banality is true: there are good and bad in every department.

SB: *Obsession is also an effective ingredient when constructing comedies. And Lenny, your character in* Mighty Aphrodite, *is an extremely obsessed character. 'Of all human weaknesses, obsession is the most dangerous,' is the warning from the Greek chorus leader to him.*
WA: Yes, obsession is dangerous, but a real staple of comedy. The comedian is always obsessive. He is obsessively in love with the girl, or obsessively frightened, or obsessive about his project, and that makes him funny. The obsession becomes such an exaggeration of what would be natural that it becomes funny. You see this even in Chekhov, who is not hilarious, but is humorous. It's the humour of obsession in *Uncle Vanya*. The characters become so obsessed that they become comic. They suffer, but we laugh, because their obsession to us seems so exaggerated. In Sweden you probably didn't see the Jackie Gleason television show *The Honeymooners*. Gleason is dead now, but every week he would confront us with his character's major obsessions. He had tremendous ideas, grandiose schemes to become rich, to change his life. All these obsessions were hilarious, and of course his wife was a much more grounded character. She would say, 'This is crazy. You are going to wreck the whole family.' But he would just go on with his obsessions.

SB: *Obsession is a major trait in many of the figures in your previous films.*

WA: Sure, sure. In *Bullets Over Broadway* the playwright is obsessed with his artistic self-image, and the gangster playwright becomes so obsessed with the play to the point of killing the girl. Once you get the characters to believably exaggerate to that dimension, the comedy comes very quickly. Because it's funny to watch these characters and you understand them. You just know, 'I would never do that but I understand exactly what he feels in carrying this to an extreme.'

SB: *You play a sports journalist in* Mighty Aphrodite. *I know you like to watch sports, and baseball in particular. Which is your favourite team? The New York Mets, or the Yankees?*

WA: It differs from season to season. Right now I prefer the Yankees. The Mets are so boring. They are having a terrible year, so it's not much fun to watch them. The Yankees are much more fun to watch.

TV, theatre and other activities

SB: *During this period you were very, very productive. You directed your own play* Don't Drink the Water *for television, you appeared in Neil Simon's* The Sunshine Boys *on TV, and you wrote the play 'Central Park West'. How come that you engaged yourself in so many activities at this time?*

WA: I just think the opportunities came up. By sheer accident I was asked if I would do *The Sunshine Boys* with Peter Falk, and I was asked if I would like to direct *Don't Drink the Water* for television. I am always trying to write something for the theatre whenever I have spare time, and if something turns out good, I generally try to put it on. I felt that 'Central Park West' was a decent one-act play, and it was fun writing it. I have just the same productivity now. I have finished two movies that have not come out yet, and I have written two one-act plays and one full-length play. And in a few days I will be starting on another play. So I am always writing. I don't know who will produce the plays I write. If there is a one-acter, I wait until someone asks me, if they might be doing an evening of one-acters. I am very cautious about my full-length plays. If I think I have an idea that's special, then I will proceed with it. It would be very easy for me to write one of those commercial comic plays, but I'd like to try to write something more interesting, which is hard for me. But if a play turns out well, I would want to produce it.

SB: *So what do you do with these plays once they are finished? Do you present them to an agent?*

WA: If I want to produce it, then I get it in the works, I take it to producers and start to move it ahead. If I am ambivalent about it, I just leave it in the drawer. In the case of a one-act play, usually what happens is that someone will call and say, 'We need a one-act play. We have two others.' If I accumulate enough one-act plays, I might do an evening of just my one-act plays. But then a one-act play is a very light kind of entertainment, usually. I guess what I am saying is that mine are. So I am more interested in a full-length play.

SB: *'Central Park West' was your contribution to a project called* Death Defying Acts, *which also featured works by David Mamet and Elaine May. Were you in any way involved in the production?*

WA: I was standing in the wings while it was being directed, and I had to make many, many corrections. If I had to do it all over, I would direct it myself. I prefer to have someone else direct my plays. I've never directed in the theatre. But I would like to do it, if the circumstances were correct.

SB: *You said 'corrections'. Were these changes in the dialogue?*

WA: Yes, and also constantly explaining to the director what I meant. The direction that he was going in was not correct for the material. I wanted it staged differently. There were spots that were faster, and other spots slower. I didn't feel in comfortable hands with the play.

SB: *Were you happy with the result in the end?*

WA: The evening was a success. The end for me personally was fine. I mean it worked, but it took a lot of hovering and badgering to see it got on right. I have rewritten it since it opened, and I've improved it. There were a couple of spots that, even when it opened, I felt I could write better. So maybe some day I'll do it. I will write one or two more one-acters and put them together into an evening of one-acters or something.

SB: *You weren't involved in the first version of* Don't Drink the Water, *were you? And you haven't acted in it previously?*

WA: I was much, much too young at that time. I just wrote the play. It was my first experience in the theatre, and the play was successful, but the experience was awful.

SB: *Did you ever see the first film version of your play? With Jackie Gleason in the same part as you play in your version?*
WA: Yes, I did. The film was a disaster, an embarrassment. Though Gleason – in *The Honeymooners*, the TV series – was a genius.

SB: *Did you have to rework the play when you directed it for TV?*
WA: Yes, but not very much. I did a little rewriting to spruce it up a little bit. I do think this is the best production of *Don't Drink the Water*. I was able to supervise it and I could at least get what I thought the thing should be. It was made for very little money.

SB: *I guess the narrator who comments on the action now and then is an addition?*
WA: No, no. The priest has the function of the narrator in the original film.

SB: *You worked with most of your ordinary technical team on* Don't Drink the Water: *Carlo Di Palma and Santo Loquasto and others. Were they difficult to get? I guess it's not very common for TV plays that you bring your own crew and people?*
WA: Well, we set it all up. I had my own group, and they were willing to work for practically no money. *I* was working for practically no money. We did it for fun.

SB: *How long did it take to shoot?*
WA: Only about two weeks. But of course I shot most of it in big master shots, which helped.

SB: *And you enjoyed the experience?*
WA: Sure. We shot it in the Ukrainian Embassy, which is three blocks from where I live. I got up in the morning and walked over there, and we were indoors and it was very controlled. And I loved working with Julie Kavner, who plays my wife in the film.

SB: *The story of this American family, Walter and Marion Hollander from New Jersey on a tourist trip behind the Iron Curtain, who are forced to seek refuge at the American Embassy, is an ingenious base for a farce.*

59   Allen with Julie Kavner and Michael J. Fox in *Don't Drink the Water*

They succeed in completely taking over the embassy and making a mess of everything.

WA: This was an idea I had thirty years ago or something, when those kinds of things were common. There was a priest, for instance, who was stuck in an embassy in Hungary, or one of those Iron Curtain countries, and he couldn't get out. And I thought, If my parents went to Europe and got stuck in that way, what a nightmare it would be for everybody involved. So I wrote this play, and it was a silly little play. But it was successful.

SB: *Your TV version doesn't feel dated at all, even though the events are supposed to take place in the sixties, during the Cold War and the Kruschev era.*

WA: I took a lot of pains to set it in its right period. In the first minutes you are made aware of the fact that we are going back in time to an era where the relations between the two countries, the US and the Soviet Union, were terrible. It's in the same sense as if you make a picture now about blacklisting. It's important to make it clear for the audience.

SB: *One of the driving forces of the farce is the continuing quarrels between the Hollander couple. Very often these quarrels take place in front of other people, like the young son of the ambassador. Do you find it more effective to have these kinds of exchanges where there is an audience at hand?*

WA: Sure, the impact is stronger, no question. I wrote *Don't Drink the Water* when I was quite young and very much under the influence of George S. Kaufman and Moss Hart. They wrote those kinds of plays, although they were much better at it.

SB: *You have a very diverse and entertaining cast in* Don't Drink the Water. *Dom DeLuise, who plays the priest, seems to have more or less disappeared from the film scene.*

WA: You see him on television now and then. He is hilariously funny, just as funny as could be. There were times while I was filming that I had to suppress laughter, because I just found him so funny.

SB: *Michael J. Fox contributes with some very comical intrusions as the ambassador's son. You seldom see him in parts like this.*

WA: I was lucky to get him. He thought it would be amusing to do the part.

s b: *Whatever happened to* The Sunshine Boys? *The play has hardly been seen on TV.*

wa: I have no idea. They called me and asked if I wanted to make a very significant amount of money for just two weeks' work in New York – much more than I make on my movies. It was this Neil Simon play, and it was to be with Peter Falk, who is a wonderful actor. So I said, 'Sure, I would love to do that. I mean, everything about it sounds good.' I went in and did it. What happened in the end I don't know. I never saw it.

s b: *You have also appeared in a couple of other films that were not 'your own':* Antz *and* Picking up the Pieces. *What are your decisions based upon when you choose to be in those films?*

wa: Antz *was a favour to Jeffrey Katzenberg.* Picking up the Pieces *was a lucrative offer.*

s b: Picking up the Pieces *deals a lot with death, a subject you've dealt with in a lot of your work. The most interesting scene in the film, I find, is when your character, Tex, the butcher, is visited in the prison by his deceased wife, played by Sharon Stone. And she talks about this 'extra' that is waiting for us on the other side . . .*

wa: Uh-huh.

s b: *But overall the film was quite disappointing. Was the original script more promising?*

wa: I believe if the movie had been made in Spanish or Italian, it might have had a prayer. In English it was an uphill battle for some very nice and talented people.

CHAPTER 27

Everyone Says 'I Love You', Wild Man Blues, Deconstructing Harry

Everyone Says 'I Love You'

STIG BJÖRKMAN: *What has been your relationship to the musical?*
WOODY ALLEN: I've always wanted to do some musicals – not just one, but a few. But I didn't want to get bogged down in a conventional way, so I thought I would do a musical where everybody would sing, whether they can sing or not, and dance, whether they could dance or not. The important thing was not the technique, because what I wanted was an untrained quality to the voices. So I wrote this script, and I had a very nice time doing the film. I think I would like to do another musical, maybe this time one that has music written especially for the movie. For *Everyone Says 'I Love You'* I was using songs I know.

SB: *Were any of the lyrics rewritten or are they the same as in the original songs?*
WA: In each case I picked a song that would be appropriate to move the story ahead. This was not difficult. There are thousands of wonderful songs out there, and I know a lot of them. I just made my pick, and it was fun to do.

SB: *You have of course seen most of the classical musicals, the MGM musicals and so forth?*
WA: I think I've seen just about all of them.

SB: *Which ones are your favourites?*
WA: The best musical in my opinion is *Singin' in the Rain* – that's number one. *Meet Me in St Louis* is a wonderful musical too. *Gigi* is a lovely musical, very sophisticated. The movie version of *My Fair Lady* was a good musical. So was *The Band Wagon*. *On the Town* was also full of ideas and very inspiring. Then you come to musicals like *An American in Paris* and *Guys and Dolls*, which are good but not great. *The Music*

Man is great on stage, but the movie of the musical is not. Then there are the black-and-white musicals that are just charming little relics of an era, with wonderful musical numbers. Mainly because of Fred Astaire. But the movies are nothing. If you see a movie like *Gigi* or *Singin' in the Rain*, then you're in for something special.

SB: *What specific qualities do you like in these musicals?*
WA: All of the ones I have mentioned have good books, and that's an important thing for me. And the musical numbers and the lyrics are wonderful, whether they are original, as in *My Fair Lady* or *Gigi*, or classical songs like in *Singin' in the Rain*. The choreography works from start to finish. They're exciting and they move you and you are involved in the story. And it's funny when it's supposed to be funny and charming when it's supposed to be charming. You are in very good hands all the time. *Meet Me in St Louis* is sort of unique, because it's almost like American folk art in a way. It's of a certain era and it depicts a certain part of America. And basically it's just singing. Quite unique and great, and based on a great book. *Guys and Dolls* has a great book too and great songs. It's a good movie musical but not a great one, because the director just didn't have the touch of Vincente Minnelli or George Cukor.

SB: *Do you go and see musicals on Broadway?*
WA: I don't see any now.

SB: *But you did before?*
WA: Yes, sure. I didn't mention *West Side Story*, which has got incredible music and lyrics, but I don't like the book so much. I never really loved *Romeo and Juliet*. It's one of my less favourite plays of Shakespeare. There is also some wonderful music and lyrics in *Gypsy*.

SB: *What do you think about more modern musicals with a more experimental choreography, such as those by Bob Fosse?*
WA: I love Bob Fosse's work. I think he was great. He was a wonderful director and a wonderful choreographer. I don't like modern musicals though. *Cabaret* is a wonderful movie, but it doesn't have the quality that I look for in a musical. It's a little bit too serious, but still a great picture. A wonderful musical by any standard was *Oliver*. That was beautifully directed and some of the music is very beautiful. Carol Reed is one of my favourite directors. I admire musicals like *Cabaret* and *Oliver* or *Fiddler*

on the Roof, because they are examples of wonderful work by everybody involved. But they don't grab my heart as much as the other ones. This is purely personal taste, because the next man on the street could say, 'Those are just the ones I like, and I don't like those that you like.' I like a musical that has a slightly frivolous quality to it, and those don't. They don't have to be funny. For example, I don't find *Gigi* funny. It's just sort of wonderful. The evocation of the atmosphere, the sophistication of the lyrics, the beauty of the melodies are more to my liking.

SB: *Have you seen Jacques Demy's musicals,* The Umbrellas of Cherbourg *and* The Young Girls of Rochefort?
WA: Yes, they represent a completely different kind of musical, and I did like them. But what I like most is just the old-fashioned American musical, which we don't see in the theatre any more, because the style of music has changed. And with the change in the style of music, that's been the end of the kind of musical that I liked.

SB: *When you wrote the screenplay for* Everyone Says 'I Love You', *did you write the script first and then checked what kind of melodies and lyrics you would insert?*
WA: I would stop my writing and think, 'I would like a song here. Which song do I like here?' and if I couldn't think of one off the top of my head, I took my book and I looked through it to find some old song that I liked, and then I put it in.

SB: *When you say 'my book', do you have a listing of music?*
WA: Usually the music companies send you books with all their songs, or just the most important songs of each year. So I look through these books. I may start at 1920 or so and look through until about 1955, and then I generally stop. But there are hundreds of songs.

SB: *And did you get the rights for all the numbers you wanted to have, or did you have to make any changes?*
WA: No, we got the rights to all the songs. That was not too difficult. You can get the rights to virtually anything, if you pay. The only person that ever used to give a hard time was Irving Berlin, but you can get his songs too, if you pay.

SB: *Didn't you have the idea of introducing music in the same way in* Annie Hall?

60 Allen and Julia Roberts in *Everybody Says 'I Love You'*

WA: Yes, I brought up this idea a couple of times, years ago in the seventies when I was collaborating with Marshall Brickman on films like *Annie Hall* and *Manhattan*: 'Why don't we make a movie where people are talking and then suddenly burst out into song? We just sing the song, and it moves the story ahead. But without any big production numbers. We tell the story in dialogue and occasional songs.' He thought it might be a possibility, but we never got too serious about it.

SB: *In these classical Hollywood musicals by Vincente Minnelli or Kelly-Donen or George Cukor, the camera has a role in the choreography that is just as active as that of the dancers. But in the musical numbers of* Everyone Says 'I Love You', *there is very little camera choreography. Was it your intention from the start to be very simple?*

WA: When I watch a ballet or any kind of dance on film or television, it drives me crazy when they cut. I like the perspective from a proscenium, as if I was sitting in the audience watching the dance number on the stage. I don't like to get my experience split into pieces. Suddenly the camera cuts and I'm right next to the dancer, looking across the stage, and then they cut to the dancer's feet. I don't like that. I like to watch the dancers dance. I don't want to see the feet, the faces in close-up. I want to see the whole person, the way I saw Fred Astaire or Charlie Chaplin. So I vowed, when I did this musical, that I would just set up the camera and let the people dance – the way Charlie Chaplin did his work, or Buster Keaton – and not try to be the star with camerawork. It would just ruin the enjoyment for people. So I did very, very moderate camerawork on the musical numbers, deliberately, all the time. Consequently I shot them very quickly. People would say to me, 'It's going to take you days to shoot each number.' But it didn't. It took me a couple of hours. I set it up, I shot it, and that was the end of it. I wouldn't change the camera positions much. Once in a while I had to, but when I changed it, I did it in a very simple way. I just cut from one side of the set to another.

SB: *As in the scene in the jewellery shop, or the musical number at the hospital, where you just shoot from two different angles?*

WA: Right. There were certain times when the cut was completely unobtrusive, but I never wanted to do any cutting for effect. I don't like cutting for effect anyhow. I find that to be a little slick. I like to cut when you have to cut, but not just for the sake of cutting. This probably comes from me being a comedy director essentially. All that montage doesn't help your comedy. If you look at the great comedies, Lubitsch, Chaplin or

Keaton, there is a great simplicity in style. And you need that simplicity, because every little cut, every angle change, every little extra thing always takes its toll on the joke. Everything has to be sacrificed for the joke. But when you've done a couple of those comedies, you start to think, 'Oh I want to direct a little bit, I want to feel the camera and enjoy myself the way Martin Scorsese does.' But if you direct a comedy like that, you're just making trouble for yourself. I mean, if you do get your laughs you are lucky, and it's in spite of any kind of bravura directing.

SB: *I agree. In Chaplin, Keaton, the Marx Brothers, or even in Jerry Lewis's films such as* The Bellboy *or* The Errand Boy, *the most efficient comic scenes are those that are shot in totals. The moment you start to cut into close-ups, you spoil the joke.*
WA: Right, the rhythm breaks and then it breaks attention. It's tough on the director who would like to enjoy the potential of the medium. Someone like Bergman, who is the master of the close-up, can just focus on the eyes and create images so full of feeling. But if you do that in comedy, you are dead.

SB: *The film ends with a very beautiful musical number featuring yourself and Goldie Hawn. How did you stage that?*
WA: I wanted to take advantage of the beauty of Paris, and that river bank by the Seine is one of the prettiest spots in the city. Then Carlo di Palma had five thousand lights across the river and around the church and just everywhere you could imagine. Again it was not a very complicated musical number. It took us only two or three hours to shoot, and we did it with wires.

SB: *So there are no special effects involved in that scene?*
WA: No. We did about seven or eight takes, and that was it. I can't remember if there was any cut, but there might have been one when Goldie runs and jumps. We used two cameras all the time and tried to keep it as simple as possible.

SB: *How did you get the idea for the scene?*
WA: I wanted the numbers in the movie to express ideas – like the dead man, the ghost that was dancing, or people singing in the streets of New York, or the mannequins in the windows. So I needed another kind of idea for the last number with Goldie and me. I thought it would be great if I could just throw her up and she would float in the air. We couldn't figure

out how to do that until finally we realized that the best way would be with wires. If I did that scene again today, it might be done with special effects. It's possible. But I don't get along with special effects. Not because I don't like them; I think that when they help you to tell a story, they are great. But most people use them as an end in themselves, and that I can't see, because they bore me. I generally don't get involved with them too much, because they are expensive, I can't afford them. And most of them are done out in California, so we have to fly somebody in to look at the film and then we talk and then they fly back. Six weeks later they show us something that's not right, and we send it back to them; and then it drones on for months and costs us a fortune. So I would prefer not to use them. It's just like the people that feel obliged to make these *tour de force* steadicam shots. The steadicam as I was taught – and I agree with the person who told me – is a tool to help you tell the story. It's not an end in itself. But it's very often used by directors as an end, wanting to show off for the audience and show the duration of a shot or how complex a shot they can invent. Although nobody cares. They only care if that shot is important for the story. Otherwise it doesn't mean anything.

s b: *There has been a kind of ongoing competition between directors as to who can make the longest steadicam shot. Both Scorsese and Brian De Palma have run endurance races with the steadicam.*
w a: Marty's very elaborate, long camera march in *Goodfellas* was a well-integrated shot, I thought. But once he had done it, everybody else wanted to do it. There was also a very good and functional steadicam shot in the beginning of *Boogie Nights*, by Paul Thomas Anderson. That was a nice one.

s b: *Did it cause you more work to shoot the musical scenes in the streets of New York and Paris and Venice?*
w a: No, there was no big problem. We shot mostly in New York. We went to Venice for a week and to Paris for another week. And as you know, these are two places I like to go to, so it was very simple. It was not a difficult picture to do. It was mainly great fun.

s b: *I understand that the original script contained much more material, and that early cuts of the film ran much longer. Also I have seen some-where the names of a couple of actors who were to appear in the film, but whose characters were later cut out.*

WA: That's right. Liv Tyler played the girlfriend of Alan Alda's son, and she was fine in that part, but I had to cut a certain amount of things way down, because the film did run at least half an hour too long.

SB: *Were there musical numbers you had to cut as well?*
WA: Yes, there were two. One with Tracey Ullman – she played Alan Alda's first wife, and she had a song, but I had to cut it. It was a pity, because she was great. And there was a wonderful number with Alan Alda and Goldie Hawn that I really didn't want to lose, but I had to.

SB: *Where in the film would it have appeared?*
WA: When they were waiting for the future in-laws to come over to the house for dinner, they sang together. Then there was a memory that the grandfather had of how he met his wife in the twenties, a sort of speakeasy song with some dancing. And that had to be cut too.

SB: *When you make these kinds of cuts, which you have had to do in other films too, is it with regret, or do you have a feeling of rationality, that this is what's best for the movie?*
WA: When I actually make the cut, to me it's like removing a tumour. I mean, I find it a mercy-killing. It's just great, it's such a pleasure. In the long run, when I look back now and at this much distance, I might think it's a shame I couldn't get that particular piece in. But when you are actually face to face with the film, and you want to move along, you take it out and suddenly it's like taking a weight off your back. It's just amazing.

SB: *But I think very many directors have difficulty in this.*
WA: To lose something? I don't know why. I mean, I would think that they would be sitting there looking at their film thinking, 'My God, this is moving like a turtle.' Then it's one of the great privileges to be able to say, 'Throw that away!' And no one will know the difference, and the picture will move twice as fast.

SB: *Now we have all these 'Director's Cuts' instead – old but not forgotten scenes being put back into films such as* Blade Runner *or* Apocalypse Now *or* The Exorcist, *just to name a few.*
WA: I've never had that problem, because I have the film that I want to have when I put it out. And I don't save anything for the DVDs. Once I've thrown away a scene, it's gone.

SB: *You have a fantastic company of actors in the film. Did any of them have anything to say about the singing requirements? Were any of them hesitant or afraid of doing it?*

WA: Yes, Drew Barrymore was, and I had to get someone else to actually sing for her. She was the only one. Everyone else said, 'I can't sing, but if you want me to, I will.' But Drew said, 'I can't sing and I don't want to sing. I just can't do it.'

SB: *Did she ever try?*

WA: No, I didn't want to make life miserable for her, so we got a friend of my wife's to sing for her.

SB: *How did you like singing in the film yourself?*

WA: It was hard, because I can't sing.

SB: *And do you like to dance? Do you ever do it socially?*

WA: I never dance. I feel awkward. But I'm an actor and the part required it.

SB: *Nevertheless, I guess that the whole experience of making* Everyone Says 'I Love You' *was a pleasant one?*

WA: Yes, it was very easy to make. It was shot right in my neighbourhood, where I live. It was not a difficult movie.

Wild Man Blues

SB: Wild Man Blues *is a documentary by Barbara Kopple about your tour in Europe with the jazz orchestra you play with. At the start of the film you say, 'In New York I can live my life, going from where I make films to the theatre, to movies, to Madison Square Garden. I never have the sense that I have to go away over the weekend.' So, why did you undertake this concert tour?*

WA: It's a very good question. I was talking to the banjo player in the band about a tour, just in a very, very superficial way. We mentioned it to see if there would be any interest in it. I couldn't imagine there would be any interest at all, and suddenly we found that in these concert halls and opera houses all over Europe, they would sell out every ticket. So we started to think, 'It might be fun to do it. We'll play in Barcelona and London, in Paris and Vienna.' Then Jean Doumanian said, 'Why don't we make a movie out of it?'

SB: *So it was your and Eddy Davis's idea from the start? There wasn't originally a request from anybody in Europe?*
WA: No, it was just something we loosely talked about.

SB: *In the beginning of the film you talk about your life in New York. What is an ordinary day like for you here, when you're not working?*
WA: Well, usually I am writing. I get up in the morning and exercise, and then I have breakfast. I play with the children a little bit, and then I go into my room and I start to write. I come out at lunch time and I have lunch with my wife and the children. Then in the afternoon, if the writing is going well, I usually go back and write some more. Then I practise my clarinet. I take a walk with my wife, play with the children. That's pretty much what I do. Then we might go out with friends for dinner, or I stay home for dinner. Usually we go out for dinner. And then we come back home, watch the end of the baseball game or something and go to sleep. It's very, very uneventful.

SB: *Would you say also very disciplined?*
WA: I don't feel disciplined. The only thing that I feel is discipline is practising the clarinet and doing those exercises. Those things require discipline. But writing doesn't require any discipline for me.

SB: *So you practise on the clarinet every day? For how long at a time?*
WA: If I'm not playing anything special, I practise for forty-five minutes or so, just to keep up a general sense of confidence. If I am going on a concert tour or something like that, then I practise longer – an hour or an hour and a half every day in the few weeks before I go.

SB: *I'm not a musician. Is this practice for the actual music, or is it mainly for the technique and the breathing and so forth?*
WA: Yes, for the physical. It's for my lip and my fingers. Breathing I can't do. I never learned to breathe properly, so it's basically for the lip and my fingers.

SB: *So, an ordinary day when you're working and one where you're not would be actually quite similar. The only thing that differs between them is that when you are not working, you are writing?*
WA: Right. Otherwise, I'm being picked up in the morning and I go filming. I get up early before I go shooting. I do my exercise. Then I always take half an hour or forty-five minutes during the day when I practise the

clarinet. When the day is over, I come home and have dinner with the family and with friends. By then I am tired, and I usually go to bed early and watch half an hour of baseball or basketball or something like that. Then I'm gone.

sb: *Can you tell me a little about how the whole thing with the jazz orchestra started? How did you come to meet Eddy Davis and play with him?*

wa: I have been playing jazz with a band for thirty or thirty-five years. I met Eddy in Chicago. We both were sitting in with a band, and then we met again in New York about ten years later. And he said, 'Do you remember that we played in Chicago together?' I said, 'Yes, I do.' Then we started to play in New York together, and then the first band that I was with for so many years dissolved when Michael's Pub changed hands. Now Eddy has this band that I play with at the Café Carlyle.

sb: *What does music give you? – both the music you play yourself and the music you listen to.*

wa: I am a big jazz fan, and I like all kinds of jazz. I like classical music and opera too. But New Orleans jazz, that's my favourite. For some inexplicable reason it just rang a bell with me years ago, and I love it. I know a lot about it, and I like to play it. It's fortunately a simple music to play – not to play well, but it's simple to play.

sb: *You say somewhere in the film that you had doubts as to whether a European audience would appreciate the New Orleans jazz music, because it's such an American thing.*

wa: It has always surprised me that jazz music in general – contemporary jazz, modern jazz – has seemed to be more appreciated in Europe and Japan and South America than in the United States, where it was actually born. It may just be that something that's imported always has a slightly better cachet to it. But in America jazz has always had a tough time, and particularly New Orleans jazz. Very few people are interested in that.

sb: *Did you use to go to The Blue Note and other jazz clubs when you were younger?*

wa: Yes, when I grew up I always went to hear jazz. Always! A week couldn't go by without me going someplace to listen to jazz. Then, as I got older, you couldn't hear New Orleans jazz any more. That faded away.

But I went to listen to all the modern players – Thelonius Monk and John Coltrane and Miles Davis, all those people. And I went to The Blue Note and The Half Note and The Five Spot and all those places in town that played jazz and I heard everybody play over the years. But I have remained most faithful to the music of Jelly Roll Morton and King Oliver and W. C. Handy.

SB: *Do you have any favourites among the modern jazz players?*

WA: Yes, I love the same ones as everybody else. I love Thelonius Monk. Of course I liked people such as Charlie Parker, John Coltrane, Ornette Coleman. They were all wonderful. But my number one favourite has always been Bud Powell. I've always felt that if I could have anybody's talent in the world other than mine, I would like to have had his. He was just supreme. He had it all for me as a musician.

SB: *What is it specifically that you love in Bud Powell's music and his playing?*

WA: I like him for the same reason that I like Bergman, for the same reason that I like Martha Graham. Bud Powell is a tragedian, and everything he plays is full of feeling, full of genius. His rhythm is unbelievable. His technique is superb. His feeling is so highly emotional. But everything is infused with a kind of dark view of life. So he can be playing a song like 'Over the Rainbow', that Judy Garland song from *The Wizard of Oz*, and it's full of neurotic starts and stops and dark shadings. And this is Bud Powell and his personality. He is an artist whom I feel in contact with, in the same sense as when I see Ingmar Bergman's films or Martha Graham's work. You feel the profundity of their gift, of their mentality, of their talent. Bud has that, whereas a wonderful piano player like Thelonius Monk or Errol Garner is very light. Errol Garner's art is like a dessert, and it's wonderful. Thelonius Monk, who was a tremendous genius, also was full of humour and lightness. But not Bud. Bud is dark. Everything he plays is serious and dark, and yet it's full of passion and blues and an enormous swing and drive and turbulence and craziness. He was just a major, major talent.

SB: *This streak of tragedy, was it also there when you saw him playing?*

WA: I never saw him playing. I saw Monk play a number of times, but I never saw Bud play. When he was in Paris, I was in New York. And when I went to Paris, he was in New York. He was not in good mental health, but someone who was to rehabilitate him and who was also a piano player told me that every time Bud would just touch the piano and play a few chords, there was a totally different feeling. It was suddenly like you were in a cathedral.

SB: *Which record or which songs by him do you like best and would you recommend?*
WA: *The Amazing Bud Powell* on Blue Note, Volumes 1 and 2.

SB: *Do you still listen to jazz records at home?*
WA: Yes, I still listen to these legendary jazz players, like the Modern Jazz Quartet. But most of my listening is still either classical or New Orleans, when I have spare time to listen. I am still mostly listening to Sidney Bechet and Louis Armstrong.

SB: *Did you find it difficult to have this camera crew of documentary film-makers around you all the time during the European tour?*
WA: No, because Barbara Kopple is brilliant at what she does. After two minutes she fades, and she was never intrusive in the whole two or three weeks that we were there.

SB: *Had you seen any of her previous documentaries before you became the centre of this one?*
WA: I had seen a few – *Harlan County USA*, of course, and her film on Muhammad Ali and a few other things she had done. She is one of our best documentary film-makers, and I really think that in *Wild Man Blues* she took a very unexciting tour and made it kind of amusing or interesting to people. It's strictly a tribute to her. And she didn't fake anything. It's just her own instincts.

SB: *One of the best and funniest parts of the film is your visit to Venice. There you didn't have only the camera team to contend with, but all the Italian paparazzi too, which is a very special phenomenon in Italy.*
WA: Throughout Italy we had them after us. I am much better with that than I was. Years ago, I used to shy away, but I found over the years that if I give them their pictures, then they are usually very nice about it, and they take their pictures and go.

SB: *It's funny, because there Barbara Kopple uses Nino Rota's music, and it's just like a Fellini film when we see you and Soon-Yi with the Mayor of Venice.*

WA: Right, outside the theatre where we were going to play.

SB: *This was Il Teatro di Fenice – a very beautiful opera house.*

WA: Yes, it was incredibly beautiful, and then it just burned to the ground. When I took a tour of it, I was shocked. It was just gone. They have been trying to restore the theatre, and I have tried to be helpful, as one of many people who have. We had a benefit performance for the restoration. I don't think they have restored it yet, though. There was some political infighting there. Not everybody wanted it restored.

SB: *In Venice you say about the crowd of people that they don't go to see your movies, but they still love to throw their cameras at you.*

WA: I always find that to be true. If you were to go out with me into the New York streets, you would get the impression that my movies were selling out in the movie theatres and that everybody was rushing out to see my films, but it is not true. If I took a walk from my house and walked down Park Avenue, after one block somebody would stop me, and after another two blocks someone else would, or someone might yell from a car. And you think, 'My God, they all seem to love me!' But they don't come to see my films.

SB: *Does it bother you very much to be recognized all the time here in New York?*

WA: I don't love it, but it doesn't make me angry or anything. People are very nice. I mean, they generally just say, 'You are great,' or, 'I love your films.' Nobody ever says anything bad. If someone doesn't like you, they usually just ignore you. People who do speak to you are generally well-wishers. And I've learned to say, 'Thank you.' When I was younger, before I was known, one of the great pleasures I used to have was writing in the street. I used to go out for long walks around the city and think, plot my plays, plot my movies, plot my ideas. I can't do that any more.

SB: *Now you don't dare to sit down . . .*

WA: No, I can't do that. But even when I'm walking, I can't get the concentration. People talk to me. Sometimes, if I am really unlucky, I will be walking and someone will be walking in the same direction and come up right next to me and say, 'Oh, hi, you are just the best film-maker I know, and you are wonderful.' And they walk along next to me, and they want to be nice, and I don't want to be rude. They don't know how to say, 'I like your movies,' and then move on.

s b: *So you don't walk between your office and your home very often?*

wa: I will walk, but only with someone. I walk if Soon-Yi is with me or some friend of mine. I would love to be able to walk home and plot out the second act for my new play or plot out the script I'm working on. But I can't, because I will be recognized too many times. If, for instance, Madonna walked that distance from here, she would never make it. There would be ten thousand people who would bother her. I might have only eight or ten people. But it's still a distraction.

s b: *In Venice you were presented with a Life Achievement Award. What do awards mean to you or represent for you?*

wa: I know the Venice Film Festival was sincere about it, because I didn't have to show up to get it. I have this policy that I never accept any award the bestowing of which is contingent upon my presence. There are many people that call and want to give me awards. But I have to be there, so I never accept them. Here, I felt they were sincere. They wanted to give me an award and I said, 'Look, I can't come,' and they said, 'That's OK, we'll still give it to you.' But I always think in those situations that I am undeserving and that off the top of my head I could think of a dozen people that should get the award sooner than I should. But some of it is an expression of affection, more than accomplishment. Over the years I have done a lot of movies, and some people have liked them and they want to make some gesture of affection. But still I always feel that it's a joke that I should get an award.

s b: *We talked at some point about the Academy Awards, and you took José Ferrer and Marlon Brando as examples. They were both nominated as Best Actor in 1951 for* Cyrano de Bergerac *and* A Streetcar Named Desire. *And Ferrer got the award.*

wa: I was just an adolescent at that time, but I could see something was wrong. Because I went to all the movies. And Marlon Brando had delivered a portrayal that changed the history of acting in the world. But as I got older, and now when I am much older, I can see what goes on to get those awards. All the backbiting and campaigning and money spent. It's not a sign of merit, it's a sign of a good press department for a picture.

s b: *You have been keeping many of your prizes and awards at your parents' place. Were they impressed by them and by your career?*

wa: Yes, but not overwhelmed. They were very sane.

61   Allen and Soon-Yi in Venice

s b: *How has your relationship with your parents been over the years?*
w a: Very good. They're dead now. Dad at 100, Mother at 95.

s b: *At the end of* Wild Man Blues *you say, 'I like to make films like the films I saw when I was growing up.'*
w a: Yes, Sydney Pollack once said that to me when we were working on *Husbands and Wives*, and I felt the same way. Steven Spielberg once said the same thing. Even Bergman has often referred to Victor Sjöström. You just like to make the films that you once liked to see. It's a natural thing.

Deconstructing Harry

LUCY: How could you write that book, huh? Are you so selfish?
You're so self-engrossed you don't give a shit who you destroy.
You told our whole story! All the details. You gave me away to
my sister. Marvin's left me. He's gone.
HARRY: It was loosely based on us.
LUCY: Don't bullshit me, motherfucker! Who do you think
you're talking to? One of those retarded talk-show hosts?
I lived through all of this. I know how loosely based it is.
(From *Deconstructing Harry*)

s b: *You just mentioned Victor Sjöström and Ingmar Bergman, and when seeing* Deconstructing Harry, Wild Strawberries *comes into mind. They are two different stories all right, but there is a kind of kinship between the two films.*
w a: I think you could say that fairly, although when I made the film, I didn't think of that. The only reason that I made *Deconstructing Harry* is that I wanted to make a movie where you showed a writer and you also showed what he wrote, and from looking at what he wrote you could tell about his character. That was the only thing I had in mind when I wrote the story. It was not an autobiographical movie. It was just the idea to be able to do a half-dozen little short stories, and see them reflected in the character.

s b: *You named your character 'Harry Block', and he is a writer who suffers from writer's block, so the name is a kind of characterization.*
w a: Yes, it's true.

SB: *But then the main character played by Victor Sjöström in* Wild Strawberries *is named 'Isak Borg', 'Isak' referring to ice and 'Borg' meaning 'castle' in Swedish. And he could be characterized as a frozen soul in an isolated castle, unable to show real feelings. So there is a coincidence that these two characters have been given names that fit their characters.*

WA: That's true, Harry Block is a character with writer's block.

SB: Deconstructing Harry *is one of your richest films, I think – rich in ideas, and in the execution of those ideas. It's very energetic and fast-paced, but it also dissipates those energies, not least in its sudden jumps from fact to fiction, real life to fantasy. And this is also mirrored in the form of the film by its erratic editing. How did the idea of the split cutting at the start of the film arise?*

WA: Just as I said – I thought it would be a funny idea to do a story about a writer who you learned about through a series of stories in the film. Then I had to give him a life, which I was making up to fit the ideas for the different stories I had. Because I had the ideas for these stories before I wrote the movie. So I constructed it almost backwards from the stories. I made his character one that would enable me to get to those stories.

SB: *How did you get the idea of the very rapid cutting at the start of the film, when Judy Davis is leaving the car?*

WA: I have done that before, in *Husbands and Wives*. Sometimes, if I am dealing with a very neurotic character, I like to cut neurotically. I like the cuts to be atonal or asymmetrical and not balanced. So I just cut when I want to cut, and keep it moving very fast, and jump when I want to jump. Because I feel, since I am dealing with those kinds of people, that kind of rhythm is completely acceptable. I knew in advance while I was shooting that sequence that I would be jump-cutting it, so I had no problem. It enabled me great freedom in shooting it, because I knew I didn't have to put myself in a position to make the cuts match anything. When I wanted to cut, I would cut, and move it in that nervous way throughout.

SB: *I noticed in the titles that you had changed some of your old associates. Jeffrey Kurland, the costume designer, for example, wasn't any longer in the team.*

WA: He moved out to California. He has two children, and he and his wife decided that the time had come for them to move into a house. He lives out there, and he works there. I still speak to him, and I saw him when I was down in California this past weekend.

SB: *The film starts with your first fictional character, Ken, who is Harry's alter ego in the film, played by Richard Benjamin. This put me in mind of the film of Philip Roth's* Portnoy's Complaint, *in which Benjamin played the lead. Roth is also an author who deals with Jewish tradition in his novels. They are also, supposedly, quite autobiographical, and have strong sexual implications. Are these little connections a mere coincidence?*

WA: The choice of Richard Benjamin was something that just happened. He is an actor who I have known for many years, a very talented one, and I thought that he would be hilarious playing that part, and indeed he was. It's hard for me to talk about Philip Roth. I think he is a dazzling writer, a brilliant, brilliant writer, a genius. Thinking of his insights and his work, I can't mention mine in the same breath. I don't have the same Jewish preoccupation as he does. His insights are far deeper and far richer. I am a comedian, and doing comedy for a live audience I use the Jewish preoccupation for a fast amusing score. He is much more profound on those issues, like Saul Bellow. For me it's like a comic using a buzzword to score quick laughs.

SB: *You just said that nothing in the film is autobiographical. I know you have always denied this charge when the question has arisen in regard to other films of yours. But some of the material must have some connection with you?*

WA: What has connection with me is only some of the sentiments. There are preoccupations of mine. The characters in the film are Jewish rather than Catholic or Protestant. I know some people might still think the character is me, because he's a writer. But that I don't care about any more. I mean, I've denied it, and people don't want to believe it. And that's fine with me. I mean, I am not a writer who's ever had writer's block. I don't sit at home and drink alcohol. I don't have women visiting my house. I don't have all these turbulent marriages. I just don't have the same life my character in the film has had. I would not be a person who would be driving someplace in order to be honoured. I would not have the imagination or courage to kidnap my son and take him with me. It's just not me.

SB: *Judy Davis seems to be your favourite temperamental actress. You very often use her in the kind of role she plays here.*

WA: Well, she is one of my favourite actresses. She is hilarious and she can do that brilliantly. She can do anything brilliantly. But it's hard to find people that can do that thing that she does brilliantly. She is one of my favourite neurotics.

SB: *You and Santo Loquasto always find settings for your films that one feels are really 'lived in'. In that early scene here, the quarrel between you and Judy Davis in your apartment, you seem very familiar and at ease with the setting. For instance, we see you go behind a pillar and grab a bottle of whisky. It's not a big thing, but it gives the audience the feeling that this man really lives in this apartment – he knows there is a bottle of whisky there. When you are acting in a film of yours and being introduced to a setting, do you go around the place to get acquainted with it before acting in it?*

WA: Yes; while we are setting up the shots, I usually walk around in the setting to drink in the atmosphere. Here, you just know right away what it is – it's a very typical kind of apartment. I have lived in a number of apartments that are like that one, and I've been to many others like it. That's what New York living is; that's how people live.

SB: *The other actors – do they get acquainted with the settings the same way?*

WA: That I leave to them. They are free to walk on the set and look around and get the feel of it if they want to. Or if they don't, they don't have to. I mean, I don't care as long as they deliver. When they come on the set, I've already worked the shot out. So I say to them, 'Come in, walk over here, put your pocket book down, go over there and throw those books off the table.' And if they have a problem with it, they tell me. And if they don't, it's fine.

SB: *In that scene you continue this very abrupt editing. We see you stand by this pillar, having your glass of whisky, and then you cut to Judy Davis in exactly the same position. This is something which, say, ten, twenty years ago would have been totally forbidden and against all conventional editing rules.*

WA: I did the same thing in *Husbands and Wives* too. Because you can do it. If it's natural for the scene and for the character, it's just fine.

SB: *Over the years you have come to deal with the technique of film-making more and more. Can you see a development, not only in style but also in attitude, when it comes to your technique – the way you set up the shots, the way you edit?*

WA: I still feel the same way: that content dictates form. Because I am a writer, the only important thing for me is to tell the story effectively. What plagues me all the time, as I am usually dealing with comedies, is that I can't really exercise the fun of cinema as much as I like to, but I have to be austere and very simple. And I wish I could do more. That's why I like it when a picture like *Deconstructing Harry* comes along. It's a comedy, but it has a serious component to it, and that frees me. I don't have to do everything just for the laughs. It frees me to function the way I want. And yet, whenever I was doing anything comic in the film, I couldn't do that kind of cutting, because it would ruin it. I can do it in the filming of my character's real life. But if I did that kind of cutting in the story with Robin Williams, or in the story with my parents, or the story with me as a young boy, it would ruin the comedy. It enhances the dramatic part, but it ruins the comedy.

SB: *Some of these memories or the stories that Harry is writing – like the first one, when death comes to Mendel Birnbaum – remind me of some of your early short stories that were published in* Getting Even *and* Side Effects.
WA: Right, that's what these are – little short stories that could also be written as little prose things. That's what I wanted. I wanted Harry to be a writer of short stories, of prose.

SB: *For the short story 'The Actor', how did you get the idea of having Robin Williams be out of focus all the time?*
WA: I have wanted to do that for a long time, and I felt this was an opportunity to do it. It was really that simple. So many times I have been on the set and heard the camera people yelling, 'It's out of focus!' So it occurred to me, many years ago: what if the actor was out of focus? What if the camera was just fine, but the actor was not? There is a man who is losing his focus in life.

SB: *In the role of your first wife you cast Kirstie Alley, and I have never seen her as good as she is in this film.*
WA: Yes, she was wonderful. I was lucky to get her. I had seen her on television, and she is a very funny girl, and a very talented actress. She had a funny thing to do, and she did it well. I wanted the people in Harry's fiction to be more idealized, more glamorous. So Demi Moore, who plays the writer's first wife in his short stories, is a more glamorous actress than Kirstie Alley. I wanted her to be the writer's idea of

the person, who in real life gets a more realistic personification by Kirstie Alley.

s b: *Like Richard Benjamin as Harry's fictional counterpart.*
wa: Yes, another more idealized character.

s b: *Demi Moore's character says at some point, 'There is a value in tradition, and there is not only meaning in Judaism but true beauty.' Jewish tradition is commented upon in different ways all through the film, also in the scenes with Harry's sister and brother-in-law. What is your own attitude to Judaism and Jewish tradition?*
wa: I was raised in a Jewish family, but I am not a religious person. I have no interest in any of the religions at all, including Judaism. I find all the religions silly and unsatisfying and not very honest. I am not a big believer that there's a difference between Jewish people and non-Jewish people. If you are on a desert island with two babies of different religions, I don't think you can tell them apart. These are man-made clubs and I'm not a joiner. But I can see tradition as a light thing, as something that's enjoyable, like a tradition in the theatre or in sports or certain things that are not dogmatic, but pleasantly traditional. Not like enforced traditions, dogmatic traditions.

s b: *As Harry says in the scene with his sister, 'Tradition is the illusion of permanence.'*
wa: Right.

s b: *Earlier we spoke briefly about Philip Roth. Do you have other favourite writers, American or otherwise, who you read and whose careers you follow?*
wa: In my generation I would say that Saul Bellow is the most important writer. Philip Roth is also a very important writer. And there are writers in the past that I like very much, Flaubert and Kafka and so on. But I would say Bellow and Roth are my two contemporary favourites. Of course, like everybody else, I like Salinger, but his output has been small.

s b: *What is it in Bellow and in Roth that you appreciate?*
wa: They are both brilliant writers, and they are both very funny. The voice of the author always comes through in their work. They are two dazzlingly perceptive, highly intelligent and extremely funny writers.

62   Allen and Judy Davis in *Deconstructing Harry*

SB: *Do you have time to read novels, when you are working as much as you do?*

WA: I read non-fiction mostly. But I do read a certain amount of fiction. And yes, I have time to read. Not as much time as I would like to, but I do have time.

SB: *In one brief scene in* Deconstructing Harry, *you wear a T-shirt with a huge hole in it. Was that by any chance your own choice for your character?*

WA: Sure, because whenever I am in a film myself I like to wear my own clothes. It makes me comfortable. There I thought that when you see what he wears when the prostitute comes over to his house, it's a clue to his personality.

SB: *He doesn't care very much. The prostitute, Cookie, is one of very few black characters who have an important part in a film of yours. How come there are so few black characters in your movies?*

WA: They are no less in my films than in anybody else's. People always mention this, but if you go down a list of other directors – I don't want to mention names – you will find the same thing. People make films about what they know. I know the way my family sounded. I know the way the people in my neighbourhood sounded. I know what goes on with the people that I deal with every day, and that's what I write about. It's something I don't give any thought to whatsoever. I cast as I see the character. If the character that I am casting is supposed to be black, I would cast a black. People have asked me, for instance in a picture like *Hannah and Her Sisters*, why I would cast the maid as black. But, you know, ninety per cent of the maids in that type of family are black maids. Some people have mentioned this to me over the years, and for anyone who is not a fan of mine, or doesn't like my pictures, it's used to imply that I have a bad view of black people or that I have a disregard for them. But this is in no way so. It's just something that would never occur to me. When I am casting I don't think of social benevolence or equal opportunity. I cast who I think is right for a part. And once this genie was out of the bottle and someone mentioned it, it was taken up about my films all the time. I would decline to mention all these other directors, but the identical thing could be said of all of them. But it's never mentioned about them, and I don't want to mention it about them. But people are forever asking me about why I don't have more blacks in my films. And the only answer I ever give them is, 'I cast who I think is correct for the part.' If

I cast a black just to have ethnic diversity, then I must also cast Hispanics and Chinese and Japanese and Koreans. The whole notion is anti-art, and silly.

SB: *It's true as you say that some critics do hold things like this against you. Do you ever read what is being written about your films?*

WA: I don't read any reviews. You have to factor in all kinds of views and idiosyncrasies. There are writers and critics that are very much disposed to one positively, and other writers that are neutral, and others that are very much against one. So if I show my film to a critic who is against me, no matter how good the film is, he will find fault with it. If I show my worst film to critics who have loved me over the years, they find nice things to say. Then there are people that have no positive or negative feelings and judge the films on their merits, because they have no special great feeling about me or no special bad feeling. But I don't read the critics. Not out of disdain but not to become confused by their conflicting ideas.

SB: *But are you aware of certain critics and what they might think?*

WA: I am aware of certain things that have been said over the years. I don't read them in criticism, but they are on the lips of people. I am aware that some people think that I don't use enough blacks in films. I am aware that some people think that I am too narcissistic in films. Just in conversation with people this comes back to me. There have been about thirty books written about me and with the exception of proof-reading yours and proof-reading the book by Eric Lax, I've never ever read any of the others. And I haven't looked at a review of a picture of mine or an article about me in twenty-five years now. There was a time when I read them all. When my first pictures came out, I used to go to United Artists, and they had stacks of reviews. I would read them all, and most of them were good. But after a while I thought, 'This is crazy. I'm reading one review from Kansas, and an opposite review from Detroit . . .' And I found it's better not to. I learned one thing at an early age. If you just keep your nose to the grindstone, if you just try to do good work and don't get distracted from this work by either pain or pleasure or reviews or temptations, everything takes care of itself. Because over the years you accumulate work, and if you have anything to say that is meaningful to people, it's there. And hopefully there are always some people that you are communicating with. And you can never think about money. There have been many times over the years that I have given my whole salary back to the film company for five or ten extra days of shooting. I have at times worked the whole year for virtually no money. I have found that if you don't think about it and you just work, even the money comes. So the best thing to do is just work and not get distracted. Divorce yourself from the world and just work. I've always had an ostrich mentality. It's got its drawbacks, but it also has its compensations. And the compensations are good, particularly if you are a writer. I like being alone. I like to work by myself. I like not to participate. Let's say someone else does a film, and enjoys the process of making the film. Then the film comes out and there's an opening night and a party. The director gets pleasure from reading the reviews and he goes to the Academy Awards and he gets recognition and enjoys it. The director and his collaborators genuinely have an enjoyment for this, they are not shallow people. I miss that enjoyment in life. I don't get that climax out of it. I finish something and get to work on something else, and I couldn't care less. I get the pleasure of being able to be productive and work and be untouched by criticism, positive or negative. But I don't get the pleasure of the human dimension that goes along with being a film-maker. Something can be said for both things. I mean, there is something nice about being part of the human race and enjoying these interactions. But I never go to dinner with the people in my movies. I never speak to them much and I never socialize much, and I am fine that way. Other people on the picture, working with Helen Hunt or Charlize Theron or Sean Penn, they like to take them to dinner and become friends and socialize, and so on. But not me. I am not judging one above the other. My way of social intercourse is certainly not better than theirs. It's just a personal taste. If there was a fund set up for me, where I could just make a movie every year, and no matter what the outcome was, there would always be the next year's fund and the next year's . . . My guess is, I would make movies as I make them – the same movies I'm making – and I would never care for a second if anyone came to see them. The truth is I don't spend too much time over that now because it's out of my hands. Unless I'm willing to change my films – which I'm not. They give patients in a mental institution baskets to make or finger-paints, and this work helps general health. That's also why I make films. I found out years ago that the rewards from films are always disappointing and not fulfilling. It's the actual making of the film that's got to be the fun. I am happy when I have finished a film and when I show it in this room to a couple of close friends of mine. The fun is in making it, in inventing and fabricating it and then to look at it and see if I have achieved my goal. Politically, I have over the years had to make some kind of pretence of caring that people come to see it. But the truth of the matter is, I don't. I would not be publicizing my films if it wasn't out of strict responsibility to the people who put the money up. They would be heartbroken if I just made the film and said, 'Goodbye.' So I do a certain amount of things – not a lot but a certain amount – to try and help them.

SB: *As a gesture of loyalty?*

WA: Yes, exactly. Because they have been nice to me and I want to be nice to them. But I don't really care. Tomorrow *The Curse of the Jade Scorpion* opens. To me that is ancient history. I couldn't care less. I've already finished another movie, and I am working way beyond that. But when I first started, I remember that Marshall Brickman and I, on the night *Sleeper* opened, drove in a car in New York to look at the lines around the block by the cinema. And we were both proud and amazed: 'My God, look at that! It's ten o'clock on a Saturday night and the line goes around the corner. How amazing!' Then we started to think, 'So, now what?' We still had to go and eat some place and then go home and take a shower and get into bed. Your life doesn't change by a film opening. I should say it doesn't change in an existential way, which is where you wish it could.

SB: *But, of course you are in a very lucky position. You have finished another film, you have written a play, and you are planning new things. But then there are those film-makers who have made one film and they don't have another film in their contract. So for them the reception of the film and being there at the opening and providing publicity for the movie becomes very important.*

WA: At the beginning I had that too. I mean, you have to earn your way past that. If my first or second or third film had been failures, I am sure that would have been the end of me.

SB: *Your position seems anyway to be a very sane one.*

WA: It keeps me sane, yes ... I remember once when I was in Boston with my play *Play It Again, Sam*. We rehearsed and rehearsed and we had our opening night. The audience seemed to like the play. Everybody was happy, and the whole ensemble went out to party. I went right up to my hotel room and started writing something for the *New Yorker* magazine. The play was old news to me by then. I just wanted to get it up on its feet and running. Because the fun for me is in the doing of the thing. I had this conversation with Bergman once, because we both had the exact same experience. Your film opens and somebody from the production company calls after the first show and says, 'Well, the first show is sold out, and we are predicting ninety million dollars.' But after two days their predictions are that we are going to have to leave the theatre in a couple of days, because not enough people are coming. So the film companies are always saying to me, 'Where will you be during the weekend?' Because most films open on a Friday. 'Could we have your home number? We'll keep you posted about the grosses?' But I couldn't care less about the grosses. I don't want to get a phone call every couple of hours. And they have this pseudo-science, where they will call you up and say, 'You know *Small Time Crooks* did two million dollars, and this is July and it's a weekend and the other pictures did four million dollars, and on the same date another picture did this or that.' And they factor all these things together and the net result in the end for me is always a disappointing gross. All this talk and speculation, and then we are sitting here, in this room, saying, 'The picture opened. Most of the reviews were wonderful. The audience is laughing and laughing. The theatre owner says that all this is terrific. But nobody comes to see the film.'

SB: *Was* Deconstructing Harry *a title you gave the film at an early stage?*
WA: Yes, it was the only title, and I had that quite early on.

SB: *The language in* Deconstructing Harry, *and later in* Celebrity *as well, is somewhat bolder and more vulgar than in previous films of yours. Do you think that this is a necessity because of a general change in social attitude and language now, or was it just something specific for these films?*
WA: No, it was just because of those particular films. If you go past *Celebrity* to *Small Time Crooks* or *The Curse of the Jade Scorpion* or *Hollywood Ending*, there is absolutely none of that. It just depends on the content of the film. The content of *Mighty Aphrodite* and of *Deconstructing Harry* and *Celebrity* required that. It may have been that I was writing in that mode at the time because it interested me, but it was not indicated in the next three films.

SB: *But do you think that everyday language in general has changed in this direction?*
WA: If anything, it has changed for the better. I am one hundred per cent in favour of just total open use of any language. To me the connotation of 'dirty' or 'vulgar' language doesn't mean anything. There are people

who use language well and people who don't. There's an interesting documentary film that two black brothers made called *American Pimp*, in which they interview a lot of black pimps. And the language is so beautiful. It's street language, but it's so beautifully articulated and beautifully spoken. It's just a thing of great beauty, which you couldn't have had because of stupid censorship problems years ago. Now you can have it. On the other hand, you see all these comedians on television walking around the stage, and they are just relentlessly what you would call dirty or vulgar. It becomes in their hands like a naughty child trying to be funny, using forbidden language. And it's brainless. But the use of any language, any words, in the right hands can be beautiful. In my lifetime the possibilities have only increased. They did not decrease, and I think that's a good thing.

SB: *Of course the rap and hip-hop scenes have had their influence on our attitudes on language; daily language has become bolder and more imaginative.*

WA: And creative, yes. And that's good, when it's good. Much of popular music, contemporary popular music – and not just contemporary but popular music over the last thirty years or so – is mistaken for poetry, when in fact it's not. It's just junk. People who don't know any better think it's pure poetry. But it's not, it's just bad use of language. That's not peculiar to this generation. When I was growing up, there was an element of popular music that was quite terrible. It's just like we imagine this 'golden age' of cinema in the United States. But if you look back to the thirties and forties, most of the films that came out were terrible. They were like bad television, factory-made garbage, stupid and undistinguished. Every now and then, because of some hard-fighting director or some series of fortunate circumstances, a good picture emerged. But given the thousands that were made, it was a very rare thing. I don't find that to be a golden age of cinema. My guess is that the actors that we've had after the 'golden age', like Brando and De Niro and Hoffman and Nicholson and Pacino, are quite a bit better than the actors of days gone by. And directors like Martin Scorsese and Francis Coppola and Robert Altman are every bit as good as William Wyler and George Stevens and John Ford. And sometimes better. The thirties and forties are a very romanticized age, and I like that. There will never again be that kind of relationship between movie stars and the public as during that time. And we will never again have mythological characters like those that Clark Gable and Humphrey Bogart played. But an actor like Cary

Grant, who had a great personality, is not as good as some actors of today, like Brad Pitt or Edward Norton or Leonardo DiCaprio. Actors like Cary Grant or Humphrey Bogart were wonderful personalities to watch, but they were certainly not better than what we have today.

SB: *Returning to* Deconstructing Harry – *some more critical voices, especially those of women, have sensed a certain misogyny in Harry, in his attitude towards the female characters. Have you been aware of this at all?*

WA: I am not aware of it, but I wouldn't say that he is misogynistic. I would say he is a neurotic character who has the same problem with men that he has with women. And the men in the picture are depicted just as ludicrously as the women. But if I am wrong and he is misogynistic, I would say, 'So what?' I mean, this is a fictional character, and misogyny may be one of the characteristics of Harry Block. Maybe he has trouble with women or is angry towards women or doesn't like them down deep, but so what? To me that's interesting. But I wouldn't have thought he was misogynistic, because he seems to have no more or less trouble with the opposite sex than most men have with women or women with men.

SB: *What's so nice with the film is the total freedom that characterizes your storytelling. I think, for example, of the scene where Harry is confronted with his own fictional character. How did you come up with the idea that the fictional figures actually could meet the real figures?*

WA: That has always been in my psychic repertoire for some reason. This mixture of fictional characters and real characters appeared in *Purple Rose of Cairo* and also in my short story, 'The Kugelmass Episode'. For some reason I have found this interplay interesting, so it crops up in my work now and then. I found it particularly interesting for a creative personality like Harry.

SB: *Where did you film Hell and how did you create it?*

WA: I told Santo Loquasto that I wanted a Hell as it appears in the visions of Bellini or Giotto or one of those artists who illustrated *The Divine Comedy*. But Santo and the producer came back to me and asked if I couldn't think of another concept of Hell, a more modern concept, because my idea was expensive. But no, I wanted the classic Hell with fire and pits of sulphur and people chained to the walls. So Santo created it. We went out to an armoury in New Jersey, and he built as best he could.

s b: *Was it a fun sequence to do? Did it take a long time?*

wa: It took a long time to build it and to get it right, but it didn't take long to shoot it. Nothing really ever takes me long to shoot, because I am not so meticulous and obsessive. If I was Stanley Kubrick it could have taken me two months to shoot it, but it took me a couple of days only, because I am not compulsive about that. If the effect works for the humour, then I'm fine. I don't have to go beyond that, whereas Kubrick or Visconti work with such an eye for detail. I think part of what they offer in their personalities is the building up of these details, and you are overwhelmed by them, in a positive way. But I have the lighter touch. I want to see Hell and then get to the humour and go from there.

s b: *The ending of the film, where Harry is being confronted with all his fictional characters, is very beautiful. Harry says, 'I love all of you, really. You have given me some of the happiest moments of my life and you have even saved my life at times. You actually taught me things and I am completely grateful.' Is it really like this? Do you think that art can function as a life-saver in some way?*

wa: Yes, I think it can be a life-saver. As a social phenomenon I find it useless. Its value is that it entertains. I find that the artist doesn't compare to the revolutionary – the artist does not function as a mover of social change in a significant way. I mean, the artist might make a very light contribution, but you wouldn't miss it if it wasn't there. But the revolutionary, the guy who sets himself on fire or takes up arms, contributes more in that respect.

s b: *Harry was an atheist. Are you?*

wa: I'm agnostic. But I think that it's possible for an honest person to have some kind of inexplicable moment, where he feels that the universe is about something or that there is something more to existence, and so have a genuine religious experience, untainted by priests or rabbis or clergy-men. That I have respect for. And this can happen with art. I can get a feeling from a piece of music or a book or a film that is so meaningful to me that it gets me through a bad period or a tragic period. Or some-one can say, 'I had a terrible childhood, and if it wasn't for the poetry of Emily Dickinson, I never would have got through.' There I think art does have a tangible contribution to make. As I said before, basket-weaving, fabricating art, is a life-saving thing. It's work; it helps you. But in a general social sense, I don't think it means much. All the plays and films about race relations, and blacks and whites coming together and all that, don't do as much as one small group of black people who say, 'We are not going to take this any more. We are going to boycott your store, or blow up your store.' And then they get something done.

SB: *The film ends in a very positive key, as Harry starts to write: 'Notes for a novel. Opening possibility: Rifkin leads a fragmented, disjointed existence. He had long ago come to this conclusion – all people know the same truth. Our life consists of how we choose to distort it. Only his writing was calm, his writing which had, in more ways than one, saved his life.' You can compare this to the ending of* Manhattan, *where your character is thinking about the possibilities and the joys of life. The artist is going on with his work . . .*

WA: This is much more serious than *Manhattan. Manhattan* is, not just tinged, but *riddled* with romance. This is not. This is much bleaker, and you can tell because one of the things Harry says at the end is that everybody knows the same truth: 'Our life consists of how we choose to distort it.' And that's a very pessimistic thing to say. We all know the same reality, we all know the same truth. Each person puts a different spin on it and rationalizes his own spin. Everybody distorts the reality in some way to try and live with it, because the reality that we all know is not a very pretty one. This is a thought that never would have been expressed in *Manhattan.*

SB: *Do you feel that* Deconstructing Harry *has more significance for you, more importance than other films from this later period of your film-making?*

WA: Not any more than *Husbands and Wives.* There are a number of types of films that I like to do. It falls into the type of film that is comic, but with a little seriousness to the comedy. But I also enjoyed doing the musical and *Manhattan Murder Mystery* and *Small Time Crooks.* There is a large spectrum of films that I enjoy doing. Sometimes I get stuck on one kind for a few years. But *Deconstructing Harry* falls into the category of more serious comedies for me.

CHAPTER 28

Celebrity, Sweet and Lowdown, Small Time Crooks, The Curse of the Jade Scorpion, Hollywood Ending

Celebrity

> LEE: I just hit forty. I don't want to look up at fifty and realize I measured out my fucking life with a coffee spoon.
>
> (From *Celebrity*)

STIG BJÖRKMAN: *Celebrity is the only film of yours where I have read the script before the film went into production, as I translated it into Swedish for Sven Nykvist. What struck me after seeing the finished film was how close it was to the original script, because sometimes during our conversations you have said that you give the actors quite some freedom in their handling of the dialogue. But* Celebrity *is very faithful to the dialogue as written. Also one could have imagined from the script that some of the scenes could have come in a different order, yet the film is respectful throughout to the structure and the continuity of the script. Is it always the case that the finished film is very close to your original script?*

WOODY ALLEN: No, sometimes they are not. *Celebrity* was closer. One of the reasons for this might have been that Kenneth Branagh played the main part and not me. If I had played it, I would have been more reckless with my own material. He was more respectful of it. People mostly don't realize that I am very conservative in terms of structure. They think there is a looseness to most of my films. When I was first making films, people would think, 'Oh, *Take the Money and Run* and *Bananas* – they are such crazy films! This Allen might become a much better director if he only learns structure.' They didn't realize that those are very structured films. I remember that Herbert Ross, when he was directing *Play it Again, Sam*, wanted to put some things in, and I said, 'Sure.' Then he called me and said, 'I had to take those things out again, because I didn't realize how structured the story was.' So when you imagined those scenes could have come in a different order, you would find that they wouldn't be as good in a different order. The films that seem anecdotal or episodic are not. There is a real structure there.

SB: *But there are two exceptions in* Celebrity. *One of them is not very important. It's when Robin (Judy Davis) is going to get her advice and training in advanced sex. In your script there were a couple of scenes regarding this, and not just one hooker, but I think three or four. Robin went first to one and then to another, then there was a scene with a group of women.*

WA: It was just too long, too much with all these scenes. But I did shoot all of them.

SB: *But the other missing scene was a very important one, I thought. It was located towards the end when Lee, your character, is invited to the home of Martin Morse, one of his former schoolmates, whom we have met in the school reunion scene. Morse wants to talk with Lee about 'the human heart'. He is very bitter. He says that he and his wife are 'two teachers who teach humanism and who are depressed over the growing loss of humanity'. He expresses his despair over a culture that has become more and more cheap, flashy and evil. Morse and his wife have formed a suicide pact. She has shot herself three hours ago and is lying dead in their apartment. Now he doesn't dare or want to fulfil their pact. The question he poses to Lee is: what shall he do?*

WA: I did shoot that scene, I just couldn't get it right. But that is a scene that I do plan on doing at some point, either in another film, or as part of a stage thing, or somehow. I am not going to throw that away, because I think that it is a good scene.

SB: *It is. It's terrible, but so filled with emotions, and it really gets you upset.*

WA: The movie stopped for it. It was also a very long scene. It just stopped the flow, so I removed it. But it's a good premise.

SB: *Yes, and I thought that this scene could have worked as a kind of moral corrective to what you had been illustrating elsewhere throughout the movie.*

WA: Yes, when I wrote the script, I felt the scene would be good there. But then when I was projecting *Celebrity* here, I felt that the film was moving and moving and moving, and then it just stopped when this scene appeared. It was too long, and I couldn't handle it.

SB: *Why did you decide to shoot* Celebrity *in black and white?*
WA: Every now and then I like to shoot a film in black and white, because I like black-and-white photography. I find it pretty. When I am shooting around the streets of New York, they look good in black and white. I just felt I hadn't made a black-and-white in so many years, and I wanted to. I just felt that it would look nice.

SB: *It wasn't because you wanted to give the film a more documentary character or look?*
WA: No, it was an aesthetic rather than an intellectual choice.

SB: *Of course, another film that very easily comes to mind when watching* Celebrity *is Fellini's* La Dolce Vita.
WA: I should be so lucky.

SB: *But you can see the comparison? The main character is a journalist and he goes through similar events with women he meets and women he tries to seduce. Also your missing suicide scene brings to mind the scene in* La Dolce Vita *with the intellectual writer (Alain Cuny) who does commit suicide after having discussed the meaninglessness of existence.*
WA: I wasn't really thinking of Fellini's film when I made mine. Maybe one of the differences would be that I am primarily a comic film-maker. So, even though Fellini has got a wonderful comic sense, *La Dolce Vita* is quite a serious film. And he can stop for those kinds of scenes and you don't mind. But I set a quicker pace. If I had set a slower pace, I might have been able to do a scene like that. But I started at a certain pace, and the film moves along and I can't stop it.

SB: *But then Fellini's film is also a comment on life in certain parts of big towns in Europe – and not only in Italy – at that period, the late fifties and early sixties. Isn't that what* Celebrity *wants to depict as well, to give a kind of similar view of New York in the late nineties?*
WA: My main motive in making the film was an awareness of the phenomenon of the celebrity, in New York and the United States in general. It seemed to me that everybody was a celebrity. Every doctor, every priest – everyone was a celebrity. The chefs were celebrities – and so were the prostitutes. We live in a culture filled with celebrities and

privileged people. So I wanted to make a film that showed the various celebrities and how this woman, Robin, goes from being a lacklustre housewife and schoolteacher to becoming a celebrity herself. That was really my only thought on the film: to picture for people the culture of celebrity. I had no tremendous insight into it, only to record that it was a phenomenon that permeated my culture at that point, that everybody had such a reverence for celebrity and that it meant so much. This was what I was trying to do. To what degree I succeeded I don't know, but I tried.

s b: *Clearly contemporary society celebrates this kind of easy celebrity – as in all of these documentary soap operas, where those taking part become overnight celebrities without having manifested anything worth celebrating. Which could be seen as an illustration of Andy Warhol's famous lines about everybody's fifteen minutes of fame . . .*

wa: In *Celebrity* there is a scene where the mother of Joe Mantegna is talking about some hostages, and she says, 'What did they do? They got captured? Why are they celebrities?' They went out and got captured and that's a bad thing, and then suddenly they are naming schools after them? I think Andy Warhol's line about fifteen minutes of celebrity is one of those lines that sounds great, but it's not really so. The truth of the matter is that while there are many celebrities, and more and more, in actuality there are two hundred million Americans and just a very, very, very, very small amount of them are going to be celebrities. Not everyone. That's why it's such a coveted, rare, idealized, revered status. But celebrity profile is so high it seems the culture is celebrity-inundated.

s b: *At the beginning of the film you have a scene between the two main characters, the husband and wife Lee and Robin, quarrelling in a car. He has told her he wants a divorce and she is shocked and infuriated. In your script you suggest that in the scene following this, they either disappear into Central Park or to the harbour or into an alley in Tribeca or to the meat market. How do you make your final choice?*

wa: This is the advantage of being both the writer and the director of a film. When you have to handle somebody else's script, the scriptwriter has been very specific about those things. I don't. I just make a note for myself and then I sit here with Santo and discuss where this specific scene might take place. Have we done too many scenes in Central Park? And Santo – or somebody else – might say, 'I know a great spot that you've never used, down in Tribeca,' or, 'Maybe they could be watching the fireworks in

Harlem.' I just give a general feel. And when I don't do it, even the places I name specifically, I am just naming; but they change ten times.

SB: *But I guess you go scouting with the cinematographer as well?*
WA: Of course. But Santo and I decide on locations before the cinema-photographer. Then we show them to him, and he tells us whether he likes them or not. If he finds he cannot do a good job on a certain setting, then we eliminate it.

SB: *The story of the different paths of Lee and Robin after their divorce is a very ironical one. For Lee, who is a careerist, the path goes steadily downwards, and for the insecure and unstable Robin it's quite the opposite. But at their final meeting at the opening night for the film-within-the-film at the end of* Celebrity, *there is a kind of reconciliation. So the film ends on a very positive note.*
WA: Right. Their first meeting after the divorce is also at a film-screening, and Robin is frightened and panicky. Now they meet a year later or something, and there is a complete difference in her behaviour. She is no longer tense or frightened. She is happily married and she has become somewhat of a celebrity and she is very poised meeting him. She doesn't duck under the table or hide, like she did at the previous occasion. I wanted to show that – show her development, which had been a confident one.

SB: *The class reunion is a very funny sequence. Have you ever attended any of your old class reunions?*
WA: No, I'm sure it would be very depressing.

SB: *It seems that Lee's main concern in going to the class reunion is to show off his own importance and success, and to obtain some kind of recognition from his former classmates.*
WA: That's often people's motivation in that situation. You like to go, you like to compare where you are in life – in your professional life and in your emotional life. If you have had some accomplishments, you have to flaunt them a little bit. I don't think people go to these things when they feel that they haven't accomplished anything. They generally go with a positive feeling.

SB: *Maybe hoping that they might be a little bit more successful than the others?*

WA: Yes, exactly. For a comparison.

SB: *How did you come to choose Kenneth Branagh for the main role?*
WA: I was too old to play the part. So I needed a younger, talented actor who also could be funny, and there are not many of them around. But Kenneth definitely is one. My only worry was if he could do the part with an American accent. And of course he could, so I used him.

SB: *I can admire him as an actor, but he belongs to a kind of British acting tradition which presents magnificent results on stage but which is more difficult to digest in films. Laurence Olivier is, of course, the foremost representative of this tradition. Their portrayals are always impeccable, but I mostly have a feeling when seeing them that there is a shadow-figure standing next to the actor, saying, 'Look, am I not playing this part well?'*
WA: Sometimes I can get that feeling as well. But I don't get it with Kenneth, or with actors like Albert Finney or Ian Holm. I got it sometimes with Olivier, and at times with actors from a former generation like Gielgud or Richardson or Olivier, because they come from a generation where part of the pleasure was to show the audience what a prodigious technique they all had. But I don't find this to be the case with Kenneth at all. Kenneth is more of a regular guy, a street person, a bar person. Certainly lacking the gunfighter appeal of someone like Jack Nicholson or Robert De Niro, but he is the kind of actor that I always look for, who is believable as a real person, not a cowboy or a hero. He is completely convincing, and in this case with an exceptional sense of humour. I have always been a big fan of his, and I think he – like Finney and some of those other actors – has escaped that formal thing you are talking about that does permeate some of the older English actors.

SB: *Alec Guinness is another British actor from a former generation who acted in a row of brilliant comedies at an early stage of his career. Do you feel any relationship to him?*
WA: I thought he was a brilliant actor, and I thought that he had some of that obvious technique too. He wasn't quite the average man. He was never greater than in *Tunes of Glory*, playing this Scottish army person. That can be compared with anybody's great performance. I found him a great, great actor, no question about it. Comic and serious. He was the like of Olivier or Gielgud.

63   Leonardo DiCaprio and Kenneth Branagh in *Celebrity*

sᴮ: *Whose idea was it that Kenneth Branagh should act and talk the way you usually do in your films? Was that his idea or yours?*

wᴀ: This is more his interpretation of the part. There were times when we talked about it, and I said, 'You certainly run the risk of people saying that you're doing me.' But that didn't seem to bother him. That was the way he saw the role, and that was how he wanted to interpret it. And that's fine. I mean, I would not argue with an actor of his stature, if that's the way he is most comfortable acting the part. And it never bothered me. It wouldn't have bothered me as long as he played it believably. I've felt that has been a criticism made by people who didn't like the picture and who didn't understand *why* they didn't like the picture. They were searching for a reason why they didn't like it. And they thought that I should have played the part, instead of Kenneth trying to play me. But I would always answer that Kenneth is doing me better than I ever could have done me.

sᴮ: *The first female character that we meet in the film is the film star Nicole, played by Melanie Griffith, a favourite of mine since her first film performance in* Night Moves. *Was she your first choice for that part?*

wᴀ: She certainly was in the list of people whom Juliet Taylor said would be great. Juliet mentioned her name right along with a couple of other people. I can't recall if we jumped on it instantly, but I believe we probably did, because she is perfect for that part. And I was thrilled that she agreed to do it.

sᴮ: *Had you ever considered her before? I had often thought that she might sometime appear in a film of yours.*

wᴀ: I did. I think I considered her for *Mighty Aphrodite*, but I didn't think she was quite right for that part. But she is wonderful. She can do comedy and she is a very believable actress. I liked her in Mike Nichols' *Working Girl* very much, and in *Night Moves*. I've always thought she was a very strong actress. Very beautiful, very sexy and very gifted.

sᴮ: *The young rock musician is played by Leonardo DiCaprio, and he played this part before the* Titanic *hysteria started. Had you seen him in any film previously?*

wᴀ: Yes, I saw him in *Marvin's Room* with Diane Keaton and Meryl Streep. I thought he was just wonderful there. I cast him in no way for name value, because he was no special name when I cast him. I cast him because I thought he was right for the part. And I think he is a genuine master actor. I don't think he is just an attractive young thing who is hot right now but will then cool off. If he is serious about his work, he will just go on being great.

SB: *Modern life sometimes risks making film-making a little bit less expressive and cinematic. I am thinking of the scene when Famke Janssen, who plays the new lady friend of the main character, throws his manuscript in the river. Nowadays writers don't have manuscripts, just files saved on disks. And almost everybody has a cellular telephone. Do you think that modern life in this way makes some part of movie-making duller?*

WA: It will lead you to its own set of images. But I am a writer who writes exclusively on a typewriter, so I made Kenneth a typewriter-writer. But certainly in real life it would have been a computer disk in there or something.

SB: *Or she would have just had to throw the whole computer into the street.*

WA: She would have had to do something radical to ruin it, yes.

SB: *This was Sven Nykvist's last film as cinematographer for you. Could you comment on your co-operations with him, not only on* Celebrity, *but also on your previous films together?*

WA: There is no doubt – everyone knows – that Sven is one of the all-time great cinematographers, and I have been very lucky. I have worked with some really great cameramen, like Gordon Willis and Carlo Di Palma and Sven. My collaboration with Sven has not been any different from my collaboration with any other cameraman. He reads the script, and if there are any questions, we go over them. But usually, again like with the actors, it's common sense. We know what to do. Usually I set up the shot, then the cameraman sees what I have set up. If he detects a problem or something that he hates about it personally, he might suggest some changes. Or he will say, 'Great, I like that shot,' and then he lights it. We have always had a conversation before the shooting starts about the lighting on the picture, how the colour tone and lighting should be. Then we look at dailies, here in this room, together. Above all, we check the lighting, and we discuss that. And we make our corrections. That's usually during the first week of the shooting. And then it plays out.

SB: *Did you pick Sven for* Celebrity *because the film was in black and white, and Sven is such a master when it comes to black-and-white photography?*

WA: No. He is truly one of the great black-and-white photographers. But I had worked with Carlo Di Palma for a number of years, and Carlo didn't want to come in from Rome every single year. He wanted a couple of years of vacation, of taking it easier. I am sure I will work with him again, but he wanted a few years of not coming to New York. So I had to find a different cameraman, and as I had worked with Sven before and he was available and it was a black-and-white picture, I contacted him. If it had been a colour picture, I still probably would have called Sven, because we have gotten along very well.

Sweet and Lowdown

> THE GIRL: I've never met anyone that keeps his feelings so locked up.
> EMMET: My feelings come out in my music.
> THE GIRL: Yeah, well, maybe if you let your feelings out in real life, then your music would be even better.
>
> (From *Sweet and Lowdown*)

SB: *When we finished the first edition of this book you mentioned some projects you had and that you hoped to realize at some time. One was a big project you thought might be too expensive to make called 'The Jazz Baby'. Did anything from that project lead to* Sweet and Lowdown?

WA: Yes, *Sweet and Lowdown* is a rewrite of 'The Jazz Baby', a film where I was going to play the lead.

SB: *Playing the clarinet?*

WA: No, I was going to take guitar lessons. But I rewrote the script and made it a vehicle for Sean Penn and Samantha Morton.

SB: *Did you have Sean Penn in mind when you rewrote the script?*

WA: No, I didn't. I rewrote it, and then Juliet Taylor and I talked about people who might be right for the part. Johnny Depp's name came up, but he was working at the time. Then she mentioned Sean. And, of course,

Sean would be sensational, but I had always heard that he was difficult to work with, and I don't really like that in a person. But there is no question that he is a brilliant, brilliant actor. So then I made some telephone calls to some people, to a few directors. 'How is it to work with Sean?' And they said, 'He has been very nice to us, very good on the set, very professional.' So I met with him and I liked him and I had a very nice experience working with him. He is a nice guy and a tremendous actor. He gave it his all and took direction and made contributions himself. I had no problem with him whatsoever. Recently he has asked me if I would come out and make a cameo in a film that he is going to direct. It's just a week's work. And I would do it, because I like him. I believe in him as a film-maker. I think he is serious.

SB: *Have you seen any of the films he has directed?*
WA: Yes, a couple of them. His latest film, *The Pledge*, I think is very good.

SB: *Can he play the guitar?*
WA: He never played the guitar before. We gave him lessons. We had a guy travelling with him. The guy who played the guitar in the movie gave him lessons.

SB: *Here you work with a new director of photography, Zhao Fei. How come you chose him? Had you seen his work with Zhang Yimou?*
WA: Yes, I had seen *Raise the Red Lantern* and some other film by Yimou and thought they were quite pretty and quite good. Zhao Fei showed great promise, and he is a wonderful cameraman. He doesn't speak a word of English. He had to have a translator, but it didn't bother me. I've worked with him on three pictures subsequently now.

SB: *Before the titles of* Sweet and Lowdown, *there is a short presentation of Emmet Ray in writing ('Emmet Ray: little-known jazz guitarist who flourished briefly in the 1930s . . .') to make us believe that he is a character from real life. Then you are the first in a row of connoisseurs of jazz who comment on his life and his career. This assumed documentary perspective offers you a great freedom in constructing the story.*
WA: Yes, it does. I like these loosely constructed stories, which are very tight at the same time. It gives me a chance to develop certain ideas I'm interested in and not just stick to a conventional plot line.

64   Allen directs Sean Penn in *Sweet and Lowdown*

SB: *Was this structure already there in 'The Jazz Baby', or did it develop in the rewrite?*

WA: No, this construction was already there in the original screenplay.

SB: *Emmet Ray is a compulsive thief and kleptomaniac, and not a very sympathetic character. Do you think it's more difficult to build a story around a character whom the audience might be less willing to identify with?*

WA: It is more difficult, because the audience has to get involved with the character in a certain way. And if they find the character too unlikable, it's hard, because you don't care what happens to him. So I was counting a lot on Sean's genius to make people interested. Because he brings with the performance a certain personality, a certain way of talking and looking, a way of making the character more complex, understandable.

SB: *One of the female characters tells Emmet she has never met a man who has his feelings so locked up. And his direct answer is, 'My feelings come out in my music.' Do you think this is a typical dilemma for the artist?*

WA: No, I don't. I think that was just a convenient line, maybe the worst line in the picture. (*Laughs.*) I don't think there is any generalization you can make about any of those things. There are artists who are full of feeling, and there are artists who are completely undisciplined. There are artists who work nine to five. There are artists that are family men, like Brahms. There are artists who are dissolute, like Gauguin or Charlie Parker. There is no formula for it.

SB: *In the young girl, Hattie (Samantha Morton), you introduced a mute character, which is quite extraordinary for somebody in a film of yours. How did you come upon the idea of having a non-speaking person in the film?*

WA: At first I thought of having her be deaf, so Emmet would play this beautiful music, but she couldn't hear it. But then it led to too many complications. What I wanted to have was a character like Harpo Marx, somebody very lovable who personified all the sweet things that Emmet was not. So I wanted to give her a handicap, where you never heard from her. A perfect person for him. He could just talk and talk about himself, and she would listen and listen and listen and think he was great.

sb:　*How did you find Samantha Morton?*

wa:　Juliet Taylor gave me a lot of video cassettes of different actresses, and as soon as I saw Samantha, in this little black-and-white movie she had done in England, I said, 'I think this is the one. I'd like to meet her.' And she came over. I met her, and I told her I would like her to play the part like Harpo Marx. And she said, 'Who is Harpo Marx?' and I realized how young she was. Then I told her about him, and she couldn't have been sweeter. Then she went back and saw the films.

sb:　*Samantha Morton shares that sweetness of Harpo in her portrayal. She also reminds me of an actress like Edna Purviance.*

wa:　Yes, she is that Chaplinesque heroine. Samantha has that naturally. And her character, Hattie, has this career as a silent-film actress as well.

sb:　*Both Sean Penn and Samantha Morton were nominated for Academy Awards for their performances, like so many actors in previous films of yours. Quite a few have won Oscars, such as Diane Keaton, Dianne Wiest, Mira Sorvino, Michael Caine and others. What do you think is the secret in your direction of them that makes them so good?*

wa:　There is no secret. I just hire good people. I mean, it's no feat to hire Sean Penn and have him get nominated for an Academy Award. He should be nominated practically every year. The same goes for the other actors I have worked with – Michael Caine or Dianne Wiest or Geraldine Page, Maureen Stapleton, Meryl Streep – all these incredible actors. It's easy. I hire someone like Judy Davis, and of course she gets nominated. If you are working with good people and you don't ruin them, they are going to be good. If you at random pick a picture that I have done – say *Crimes and Misdemeanors*. Who do I have there? I have Martin Landau, who is a terrific actor. Or Angelica Huston, who is as great. Or Mia or Alan Alda, who are very wonderful actors. And all these people turn in fine performances, because they are good.

sb:　*Throughout the film Emmet talks about Django Reinhardt, and at one point he says, 'I can't listen to him without crying.' Are there some film-makers you can't see without crying?*

wa:　There are always films that move me to tears, at certain parts of them and certainly at the endings. I can never watch the end of *The Bicycle Thief* or the end of *Citizen Kane* or the end of *The Seventh Seal* without tears in my eyes. Those films are always big emotional workouts.

65   Sean Penn and Samantha Morton in *Sweet and Lowdown*

sb: *What did you think of Django Reinhardt and his music?*

wa: He was a major genius. I have all his recordings, and I have listened to him my whole life. He is right up there with Louis Armstrong and Sidney Bechet and the great, great romantic virtuoso soloists of earlier jazz.

sb: Sweet and Lowdown *is set in and around Chicago and in California. But was anything at all shot in those places?*

wa: No, everything was shot right here in New York, within forty-five minutes from where I live. Even the Hollywood studio was also shot here.

sb: *Eventually Blanche (Uma Thurman) enters Emmet's life: this rich and spoilt young lady, who soon becomes his wife. She wants to become a writer and is very much an observer of life, making notes all the time and studying Emmet and commenting on his appearance and habits. Do you think the film-maker is an observer of life, or has to be?*

wa: I think you automatically have feelings about life. I mean, there are film-makers who make films with keenly observed details in them. And there are other film-makers who make perfectly wonderful films without the details, but they are thoughtful about life. They may not be observant visually, but intellectually they are observant about the life process, and they have something to say about that. I do think that any artist, any film artist, is giving you back his perceptions. When I talk about film-makers, I am only including the serious ones. Not the ones that grind out these movies that are opening every week in the United States, these Hollywood movies that are conceived totally in venality. I have no interest in them. I don't see them. I don't care about them and I don't take them seriously.

sb: *Does it ever happen that you get ideas for your stories from watching other people or eavesdropping on conversations? Can you, for instance, start fantasizing about people you might see in a restaurant?*

wa: Yes, absolutely.

sb: *Can you give any example of something like that which has led further, maybe into a scene in one of your films?*

wa: I always watch. Not consciously, but I always like to watch people in the street and in restaurants, and I invariably fantasize about them. I used to see a woman every morning when I went out for breakfast, like seven o'clock. The city would be quiet. And I always saw this woman, presumably on her way home, all dressed up.

SB: *In evening clothes?*

WA: Yes. And I've thought that would make a wonderful beginning to a movie. She is obviously on her way home, maybe from her boyfriend's house, I don't know. And then follow her for a couple of days. I have seen an attractive woman in the market buying food, and I've thought to myself, 'What an interesting way to meet someone.' This observation has occurred to me many times. I'll be home on a summer day like today, and it would be a weekend, like a Saturday, and everybody is out of town, the city is empty. I'll be home working and I want to get a beer or a sandwich or something. So I leave my house and I go to the store. I take a walk one block, and there is this other person, a woman, also getting something. And it's like we are the only two people in New York City. All our friends, everybody has gone away. I see her and she is pretty, and I walk after her a couple of blocks. And I notice she goes into a house. I quickly look at the doorbells, and there are five different names. So I ring every name, and she calls back. I say, 'I'm the person who was just buying the roast-beef sandwich in the store next to you, and would you like to go out for lunch or something?' She says, 'I just ate my sandwich.' So I say, 'You ate it very fast, you just bought it. Would you like to go to a movie or something?' Now, I have observed this phenomenon, so I wrote this scene into *Mighty Aphrodite*. That's how I was to meet Helena Bonham-Carter in the film. I shot the scene, all of it, with the ringing of the doorbells and calling her up, and the whole thing was based on experience – I mean, *fantasy* experience. But it all took so long in the movie, I had to cut it out. I didn't need to show so much of the past of Helena and myself. I learned that when I put the picture together. But that's only one example. There are many others that I could come up with.

SB: *Do you usually cut out a lot from your films?*

WA: Yes. Generally the first cut stops at about two hours, and the final version is never that. The final version is always closer to an hour and thirty minutes, an hour and thirty-five, an hour and forty-five tops. So I do cut out. And it's not just trims. Because you trim, trim, trim, and the day is over and you have cut a minute and a half or something. I cut, like I am telling you now, big blocks of material out. Of course, the trick is to be able to anticipate that and not spend money on shooting these scenes, but that's a very hard thing to do.

s B: *That was my second question. Have any of your producers ever said, 'You always cut away several scenes from your films. Can't you do that in the script?'*

w A: No, people have not demanded it, but they have suggested that I would be doing myself a favour. I would have more money to re-shoot parts of the film later. And all I can say is that it's easier said than done. Because the scenes looked good to me on the printed page. And they even look good when I shoot them or after I've put them in the film. It's just that when you see the whole flow, then it's a different story. And it's very hard to get the feeling of the flow, because many, many times those scenes that seem like a digression are fine. And they stay in the picture. What the producers have to know and what is a very, very unbearable truth about movie-making is that it's not an exact science. You could have made one movie or thirty movies, and it's still not an exact science. I have no problem cutting, though. I am not one of those directors who has problems parting with his material. I throw it away easily.

s B: *Towards the end of* Sweet and Lowdown *there is this farcical scene at the gas station, where you show three different versions of the incident. And you and two of the other narrators comment on it. Of course, the structure of the film with its semi-documentary style allows you to be a free agent in illustrating this. And I guess you like this kind of storytelling too, where truth and myth are exchangeable.*

w A: In this kind of story, it works fine, because there are so many legends about jazz musicians. You hear so many stories. You hear this version of some course of events, or that version of the same thing. So I wanted to include that structure in the movie, where there are different versions of the same story. This is very prevalent in jazz history. So much is oral history.

s B: *A very beautiful scene towards the end is when Emmet is seeing Hattie for the last time. Throughout the scene he brags about himself, and suggests that they should get together again. During his long speech you keep the camera on him all the time, but one has a very strong sense of her being there. Did you shoot this scene in any other way? Did you take any shots of her listening as well, so you would have an opportunity to crosscut, if needed, or to play it safe?*

WA: I went down there to shoot it, and I was going to show Emmet in one take and Hattie in another, and then later on decide where I wanted to be. But Sean was so great. I shot the whole scene in just one take. So when I was finished, I said, 'It's silly to do this again. You are never going to do it any better.' And I wondered if I should have a take on Samantha as well. I thought to myself, 'I may as well do it, because the light is so good. But I don't know if I really will be cutting to her later on, because Sean is so compelling.' So I made the take, and when we were editing the film, I cut a couple of times to her, just to punctuate. But I discovered that I didn't need these shots in the end. The whole situation was so expressively reflected through Sean.

SB: *Do you like to take risks when you are very certain about how a scene should be filmed? Or do you usually take some safe extra shots as well?*
WA: I don't need that. Once in a great while something is very, very complex, and if I am not completely secure, I say, 'Let's make a cut of that telephone or some other prop just in case.' But when it's clear that I have it and there is no doubt in my mind, I never look for easy options.

SB: *On* Sweet and Lowdown *you worked with a new editor, Alisa Lepselter. For more than twenty years you have been working with Susan A. Morse. How come you changed collaborator here?*
WA: Sandy Morse is an excellent editor and a wonderful person. But when Sweetland took over as production company, there were a lot of financial restrictions they put on, and Sandy was not comfortable with them. So after a few pictures she felt that it was not worth it for her, so she didn't want to remain with us any more. We have still remained quite friendly.

Small Time Crooks

SB: *How did you come upon the story of* Small Time Crooks?
WA: I read about some people who had a store next to a jewellery store, and they had made plans for the perfect crime. They dug a tunnel between the two stores, but they got caught while tunnelling through. So I have

these people who are planning to perform a great robbery, and they get themselves a store. Of course, this store has to be used for something, they have to sell something. So I have them selling cookies. And I thought it would be funny if the store then did better than their robbery. It just flowed very gracefully after that.

SB: *Here again is the classical story of 'the rise and fall', be it of a character or a family.*
WA: Yes, exactly.

SB: *This also gives you the chance to direct a comic look on different classes in society. Was this in the back of your mind when you constructed the story?*
WA: Yes, I only had half a story. What happens when they then become successful? I thought, 'My God, that's when the real fun begins, because then you have a real class conflict. You have these low-life people suddenly coming into a huge amount of money, and that would affect them.' And that gave me the development of the story.

SB: *It's like in the Marx Brothers' films, where Groucho invades and attacks the kind of people whom Margaret Dumont represents.*
WA: Yes.

SB: *Frenchy's (Tracey Ullman) ambitions are both very valid and superficial – her need for education and her craving to be someone, to belong to the seemingly more important part of society. But do you think that the only solution for her is to go back to the same life she lived before wealth struck her?*
WA: She should avoid extreme change. Her life should be a nice combination. My advice to lottery winners.

SB: *You don't see it as a defeat for her?*
WA: No, not when done sensibly. She was a little fanatic, but her impulses were OK.

SB: *In* Small Time Crooks *and your next film,* The Curse of the Jade Scorpion, *you abandoned your so-called 'Woody Allen' persona for rather more character roles. Was this by chance, or did you feel you wanted to escape for a while?*

66   Tracey Ullman, Allen and Hugh Grant in *Small Time Crooks*

WA: No, it's strictly by chance. In *Hollywood Ending*, I'm right back to the character I always play. When I did *Take the Money and Run* I had to play a bankrobber, a sort of a low-life character. Whatever the script demands, within my small limits, I do.

SB: *A very, very funny character in the film is Cousin May, played by Elaine May. I haven't seen her acting for a very long time. How come you chose her?*
WA: I have always loved her. I offered her a part in *Take the Money and Run*, my first movie, but she didn't want to do it. She has always been a brilliantly funny woman, who's been evasive over the years. It's hard to get her to do anything. In this case I sent the script to her, and two days later she answered, saying, 'Yes, I'd like to do this.' So it was fine. I mean, I had no problem at all, and of course she is great.

SB: *Did you know her at the time when you started as a stand-up comedian and she was doing the celebrated 'Evenings with Nichols and May' together with Mike Nichols?*
WA: I knew them both when they came on the scene. I have known them both slightly for decades. Slightly, not intimately. But yes, I saw them when they came to New York. They came from Chicago, as you probably know. We had the same manager, Jack Rollins. He discovered them. And once he brought them to New York, the world saw them. I used to see them up at the office of Rollins & Joffe. I used to see them in clubs in town. Our paths crossed many times.

SB: *Do you see or listen to any of the stand-up comedians of today? If so, what do you think about them?*
WA: They're all funnier and better than I was.

SB: *Do you think there is a difference in attitudes and jokes between male and female comedians?*
WA: Well, the females imitate the males except for Tracey Ullman and Elaine May and a few others.

SB: Small Time Crooks *reminds me to some extent of* Broadway Danny Rose. *The same kind of characters inhabit both films.*
WA: The characters in *Small Time Crooks* are less realistic. More cartoon-like.

SB: *You have two very beautiful scenes shot at sunset, one on the rooftop with you and Tracey Ullman, and another with you and Elaine May. How were they shot?*
WA: They were shot in one evening, working very fast.

The Curse of the Jade Scorpion

> The ugly curtain of reality will soon fall upon us.
> (From *The Curse of the Jade Scorpion*)

SB: *I saw* The Curse of the Jade Scorpion *as it opened here in New York, and I enjoyed it very much.*
WA: Where did you see it?

SB: *Downtown, in Loew's cinema on Second Avenue and 31st Street.*
WA: What time?

SB: *Four-fifteen.*
WA: Was there an audience?

SB: *It was about half-full.*
WA: Saturday or Sunday?

SB: *Friday. I left here at three after our meeting and went directly to see the film in the afternoon.*
WA: And were they laughing?

SB: *Yes, they were, very much. The film has very, very snappy dialogue.*
WA: That's really what it was about.

SB: *Also I think it has a very comic-book quality.*
WA: Right, even the title, the whole quality of it. That's why I wanted the big '1940' at the beginning, the numbers. I wanted it big and comic-book style, not realistic.

SB: *It brought another film to my mind, one that I think is quite under-rated,* Dick Tracy. *It is in quite another style, but there is a kinship.*
WA: Sure, because they are both comic-book films with the hats, and the coats and the cigarettes and all the props. *Dick Tracy* is much more stylized, though.

SB: *It also reminded me somewhat of the private-eye stories of* Radio Days.

WA: Yes. It has that kind of title, and that kind of dialogue. It is set in an era where people smoked cigarettes and drove to places at night to steal jewels, then came back to their apartments to find beautiful girls waiting for them. This is the stuff, not of real life, but of old movies and of old comic books, and that's what it is. It's meant to be a soufflé.

SB: Curse *also brought to mind the Bob Hope film* My Favourite Brunette, *where by sheer chance Hope's character has to act as a detective. Hypnosis has an important part there too. You talked before at one point about Bob Hope as a neglected talent.*

WA: I didn't say he was neglected, just not appreciated, considering how skilful he was. His films were so-so, but he was always very wonderful.

SB: *A character in the film says at one point, 'The ugly curtain of reality will soon fall upon us.'*

WA: You can see my real personality come through in that line. The truth is that we don't live in a hypnotic trance all the time, where we see things beautifully. The truth is that reality comes back, and it's not so pleasant.

SB: *Hypnotism is another way of producing fantasies. Through the hypnotist in the film you get a kind of 'film-within-the-film'.*

WA: Right, you get a different reality.

SB: *You've showed an interest in hypnosis in other films, such as* Oedipus Wrecks. *It's also present in your play* The Floating Lightball. *Have you ever considered turning that into a film?*

WA: No, I've never thought of doing anything with it. I wrote it for the Lincoln Center, just for the fun of it. It was a little idea I had, and I never did anything with it. I just let it be.

SB: The Curse of the Jade Scorpion *is a kind of comic mixture of film noir and screwball comedy. Looking back at the films of those genres from the forties, do you have any favourites among them?*

WA: Interestingly enough, I never liked screwball comedies – except for the interplay between the man and the woman who hated each other but wound up together at the end of the movie. Though you couldn't figure out how, because every word out of their mouths was an insult to each

67   Helen Hunt and Allen in *The Curse of the Jade Scorpion*

other. And that was frequent in the Claudette Colbert movies, in the Rosalind Russell movies, or in the movies with Robert Montgomery, William Powell, Carole Lombard, Katharine Hepburn or Spencer Tracy. I used to see them all the time. That part of screwball comedies I liked. I liked that verbal interplay. It was often quite remarkable. Most of the film noir ones are not very good, I think. Billy Wilder's *Double Indemnity*, of course, is a masterpiece. I don't count that film, because it's way above film noir. The best of the film noirs is probably Jacques Tourneur's *Out of the Past* with Robert Mitchum and Jane Greer. It's a beautiful film. But I only like moments in most of the noir films, special moments. They're 'B' films.

SB: *You mentioned Billy Wilder. I think you have a lot in common, in your mixtures of serious drama and light comedies. Do you have any other favourites of his films?*
WA: *Ace in the Hole* is very fine. I am a fan of his.

SB: *Of course, there's a lot of this kind of verbal interplay between you and Helen Hunt all through* The Curse of the Jade Scorpion.
WA: Yes, that was what I was going for.

SB: *How do you write dialogues like these? Do you usually write them in one go or does it happen that you leave them for a while and then come back to them?*
WA: I do them at once. But it's hard, because one line must grow out of the previous, and top it.

SB: *Do you sometimes come upon a good one-liner and then try to fit it into dialogue? Or do these one-liners just pop up while you're working on dialogue?*
WA: They come naturally. Once in a great while I can stick a preconceived one in, but usually it's a bad fit.

SB: *This is the third film on which you've worked with Zhao Fei as cinematographer, and both* The Curse of the Jade Scorpion *and* Sweet and Lowdown *are very rich in atmosphere. Did you have him see American films of the thirties and forties before the production of these two films?*
WA: No, I just told him what I wanted. When a cameraman like Zhao Fei or Sven Nykvist or Gordon Willis is given a period film, they are great. Everybody works magnificently on a period picture. The costume

designer becomes great. A production designer like Santo loves it. And the cameraman becomes great. It's when you give people a film in a contemporary setting that you get problems. They have to make this room look great and these clothes look great. Then you go out in the street, and there are parking meters and taxi-cabs and trucks and garbage trucks, and inside the house there are television sets. It's hard to make them look poetic and beautiful. But when you give your collaborators a period picture, everybody is thrilled. The costume people blossom like flowers, and so does the cameraman. So Zhao Fei was thrilled that two of the three films we made together were period films.

s b: *There was nothing specific you had to explain about the American background of the stories?*
w a: No, I told him what they were about, that *The Curse of the Jade Scorpion* was a comic detective story, and he understood that. If I had made the picture in black and white, I probably would have had him look at some pictures. But here I wanted his colour, and his lighting. He knew what I wanted from having done *Sweet and Lowdown*. There had been many mistakes on that film that we both made, and he learned what I liked. But there were times when he would show me a scene and I would say, 'It's not right at all, there are too many lights. It looks like an airport.' He was afraid I would say, 'Too dark, too dark, I can't see anything!' But I kept saying, 'No, no, it's too light!' and then he got it. So on *The Curse of the Jade Scorpion* he knew everything. We communicated through an interpreter, but there were no problems at all. Soon we didn't need the interpreter. You use the same few sentences almost all the time, as we're mainly talking about perspective and lighting. So after, say, the first month of shooting every day, he knew. If I said, 'This is too light,' he didn't have to ask the translator what I said. He already knew.

s b: *Do you think you will work with him again?*
w a: I will be happy to. Sometimes there might be a problem, because he does these big films in China and it takes him forever. I couldn't work with him on *Hollywood Ending*. I worked with Wedigo von Schultzendorff, a German cinematographer, whom I like very much. He has worked here a little bit, but mostly in Germany. I couldn't get one of my usual people, so he helped me out on this.

s b: *Dreamworks are presenting your two latest films. Are they also involved in the production of the films?*

wa: No, Dreamworks is just the distributor. *Small Time Crooks* and *The Curse of the Jade Scorpion* were made by my own production company.

sb: *And the producer of* Curse *is your sister, Letty Aronson. She has worked on a few of your previous films as executive producer. How did she happen to enter the movie business?*
wa: She used to work at the Museum of Television and Radio, and then she was interested in seeing what film would be like in the business sense. She worked at Sweetland for a while and she learnt about distribution and selling the films in Europe and all the nuts and bolts of production. So when Sweetland stopped making my films, she came over with me to my production company. So she deals with Dreamworks and with Europe.

sb: *Do you feel more comfortable working with her than with other producers?*
wa: She isn't a producer in the usual sense. She is at the business end. I've never had a producer in the conventional sense. I decide on the project. I decide on the script. No one knows about what the script is. I decide who I am going to use in it and what kind of a film it is going to be. There is no 'producing' to be done. It's business that has to be done. So I feel completely comfortable with her doing business. Of course, over the years I have also been comfortable with everyone I worked with. But I am completely comfortable with Letty, because she knows how to do the business. And she is family, so I know she is completely honest.

Hollywood Ending

> ALVY: I don't wanna live in a city where the only cultural
> advantage is that you can make a right turn on a red light.
> (From *Annie Hall*)

> It's about a neurotic film director who lives in New York.
> You see my limited range.
> (Woody Allen, quoted in the press
> kit for *Hollywood Ending*)

sb: *How did you come up with the idea of a blind film director?*
wa: I don't recall.

SB: *Have recent films produced in Hollywood been a kind of inspirational source for you in getting this idea?*

WA: Quite the opposite. Recent Hollywood films are uninspired nonsense.

SB: *Your extremely energetic performance in the first part of the film gives* Hollywood Ending *a very quick and effective pace, with your character's very swift and sudden changes in temper. Would you say that there is a connection between this performance and your early experiences as a stand-up comedian?*

WA: I can't say. I played it the way it was written and seemed most logical.

SB: *When you fire these temperamental outbursts, does it ever happen that your co-actor (like for instance Téa Leoni in the scene at the Café Carlyle) loses control and starts laughing?*

WA: Never.

SB: *One basic theme in your films is the conflict between the rational and the irrational. Other film-makers might make more comic points out of exploring irrational behaviour. But you seem to want to score more jokes from studying rational behaviour that at times becomes absurd . . .*

WA: I'm basically rooted in realism. Even when I'm being surreal I don't like to depart from reality.

SB: *The very energetic dialogue works almost as a verbal hand-held camera. Therefore I expected in the less talkative scenes a more moving camera to keep up and to continue the fast pace. But most of the scenes were shot in quite long and more steady takes. Had this anything to do with the fact that you were working with a new cameraman, who maybe wasn't yet used to your cinematic language?*

WA: In comedies – and *Hollywood Ending* is classic in form, it could have been done by Chaplin or Keaton – simplicity is important. Everything else bothers the comedy.

SB: *Did you get any ideas for the scenes with the Chinese photographer and his interpreter from your experiences working with Zhao Fei on your previous films?*

WA: Yes. We had an interpreter on those films and it was sometimes amusing.

SB: *The George Hamilton character spits on the word 'auteur', but Val Waxman and his film are in the end saved by the critical acclaim the film gets from critics in France. Is this a kind of belated appreciation of the reception of your work by critics and audiences all over Europe?*

WA: No. I was trying to draw Hollywood executives as I've experienced them. One trait is their disdain for the cultural respect given to films in Europe.

SB: *George Hamilton is in a way the quintessence of Hollywood: the movie hero, the womanizer. Were these qualities that made him a natural choice for the film?*

WA: Yes. Plus he's a good actor and very funny and creative.

SB: *Treat Williams is another unexpected choice of actor. How did you come to choose him?*

WA: He looked correct, and I've always liked him as an actor.

SB: *Téa Leoni would have been a perfect heroine for Hitchcock, I think – with her suave blonde looks and self-assurance.*

WA: I can't think of a director who wouldn't love her. She's got it all.

SB: *Since* Deconstructing Harry *your work has mainly consisted of light or more farcical comedy. Do you think that you will return to psychological drama or something similar one day? Would you like to?*

WA: It's just a coincidence that I've done a few light pieces in a row. I'm already on a different path.

SB: *In 2001 you directed a short film called* Sounds From a Town I Love, *which first aired on television. How did you come to make it?*

WA: It was a fund-raiser, a five-minute film for a benefit evening to raise money after September 11th, to which I contributed along with others.

SB: *Why did you choose to appear at the Academy Awards ceremony in March 2002?*

WA: Only to help New York. They were honouring New York films and I was willing to participate, for the city.

SB: *You then chose to go to Cannes in May 2002 for the screening of* Hollywood Ending *that officially opened the Festival.*

WA: Yes, it was to repay the French for years of support and affection.

68   Treat Williams, Téa Leoni, Allen and Debra Messing in *Hollywood Ending*

SB: *There seems to be a greater openness in your life now. You travel more. You seem to make yourself more available to people who want to discuss your work with you. I know that you usually don't want to comment on your private life, but do you think that the life you lead now with Soon-Yi and your children has influenced you into this new openness?*

WA: Only to the degree that Soon-Yi likes to travel and I like to make her happy.

Filmography

Directed by Woody Allen:

1969

Take the Money and Run
Producers: Charles H. Joffe, Jack Grossberg
Screenplay: Woody Allen & Mickey Rose
Cinematography: Lester Short
Production Designer: Fred Harpman
Editors: Paul Jordan, Ron Kalish
Editing Consultant: Ralph Rosenblum
Music: Marvin Hamlish
Production Assistant: Stanley Ackerman
Woody Allen (*Virgil Starkwell*), Janet Margolin (*Louise*), Marcel Hillaire (*Fritz*), Jacqueline Hyde (*Miss Blair*), Lonny Chapman (*Jake*), Jan Merlin (*Al*), Ethel Sokolow (*mother Starkwell*), Henry Leff (*father Starkwell*), Don Frazier (*psychiatrist*), Nate Jacobson (*judge*), Louise Lasser (*Kay Lewis*), Jackson Beck (*story-teller*).

1971

Bananas
Producers: Jack Grossberg, Charles H. Joffe
Screenplay: Woody Allen & Mickey Rose
Cinematography: Andrew M. Costikyan
Production Designer: Ed Wittstein
Editor: Ron Kalish
Music: Marvin Hamlish
Production Assistant: Fred T. Gallo
Woody Allen (*Fielding Mellish*), Louise Lasser (*Nancy*), Carlos Montalban (*General Emilio Molina Vargas*), Natividad Abascal (*Yolanda*), Jacobo Morales (*Esposito*), Miguel Suarez (*Luis*), David Ortiz (*Sanchez*), Renée Enriquez (*Diaz*), Jack Axelrod (*Arroyo*), Charlotte Rae (*Mrs Mellish*), Dan Frazer (*priest*), Dorthi Fox (*J. Edgar Hoover*), Sylvester Stallone (*tough guy*)

1972

Everything You Always Wanted to Know About Sex
(But Were Afraid to Ask)
Producers: Charles H. Joffe, Jack Grossberg
Screenplay: Woody Allen after the book by Dr David Reuben
Cinematography: David M. Walsh
Production Designer: Dale Hennesy
Editor: Eric Albertson
Music: Mundell Lowe
Episode 1, *Do Aphrodisiacs Work*: Woody Allen (*court jester*), Lynn Redgrave
(*queen*), Anthony Quayle (*king*); Episode 2, *What Is Sodomy?*: Gene Wilder
(*Dr Douglas Ross*), Elaine Giftos (*Mrs Ann Ross*), Titos Vandis (*Stavros Milos*);
Episode 3, *Why Do Some Women Have Trouble Reaching an Orgasm?*:
Woody Allen (*Fabrizio*), Louise Lasser (*Gina*); Episode 4, *Are Transvestites
Homosexuals?*: Lou Jacobi (*Sam Waterman*), Sidney Miller (*George*); Episode 5,
What Are Sex Perverts?: Jack Barry, Toni Holt, Robert Q. Lewis, Pamela Mason,
Regis Philbin (*as himself*), Don Chuy, Tom Mack (*footballer*); Episode 6, *Are the
Findings of Doctors and Clinics Who Do Sexual Research and Experiments
Accurate?*: Woody Allen (*Victor Shakapopolis*), Heather MacRea (*Helen Lacy*),
John Carradine (*Dr Bernardo*); Episode 7, *What Happens During Ejaculation?*:
Woody Allen (*a sperm*), Tony Randall (*operator*), Burt Reynolds (*switchboard
operator*), Erin Fleming (*Sidney girlfriend*), Stanley Adams (*stomach controller*),
Robert Walden (*a sperm*).

1973

Sleeper
Producers: Jack Grossberg, Charles H. Joffe
Screenplay: Woody Allen & Marshall Brickman
Cinematography: David M. Walsh
Production Designer: Dale Hennesy
Costume: Joel Schumacher
Editor: Ralph Rosenblum
Music: Woody Allen with the Preservation Hall Jazz Band & the New Orleans
Funeral Ragtime Orchestra
Woody Allen (*Miles Monroe*), Diane Keaton (*Luna Schlosser*), John Beck (*Erno
Windt*), Mary Gregory (*Dr Melik*), Don Keefer (*Dr Tryon*), John McLiam
(*Dr Agon*), Bartlett Robinson (*Dr Orva*), Chris Forbes (*Rainer Krebs*), Marya
Small (*Dr Nero*), Peter Hobbs (*Dr Dean*), Susan Miller (*Ellen Pogrebin*), Lou
Picetti (*master of ceremonies*).

1975

Love and Death

Producers: Charles H. Joffe, Martin Poll
Screenplay: Woody Allen
Cinematography: Ghislain Cloquet
Production Designer: Willy Holt
Costume: Gladys de Segonzac
Editors: Ralph Rosenblum, Ron Kalish
Music: Sergej Prokofieff
Woody Allen (*Boris Grushenko*), Diane Keaton (*Sonia*), Olga Georges-Picot
(*Countess Alexandrovna*), Jessica Harper (*Natasha*), Jack Lenoir (*Krapotkin*),
James Tolkan (*Napoleon*), Alfred Lutter III (*young Boris*), Lloyd Battista (*Don Francisco*), Frank Adu (*recruiting sergeant*), Harold Gould (*Count Anton*),
C. A. R. Smith (*Father Nikolai*), George Adet (*old Nehamkin*).

1977

Annie Hall

Producers: Charles H. Joffe, Robert Greenhut
Screenplay: Woody Allen & Marshall Brickman
Cinematography: Gordon Willis
Production Designer: Mel Bourne
Costume: Ruth Morley
Editor: Ralph Rosenblum
Music: 'Seems Like Old Times', 'It Had to Be You', 'A Hard Way to Go',
'Sleepy Lagoon'
Woody Allen (*Alvy Singer*), Diane Keaton (*Annie Hall*), Tony Roberts (*Rob*),
Carol Kane (*Allison*), Paul Simon (*Tony Lacey*), Shelley Duvall (*Pam*), Jane
Margolin (*Robin*), Colleen Dewhurst (*Annie's mother*), Christopher Walken
(*Duane Hall*), Donald Symington (*Annie's father*), Helen Ludlam ('*grandma*'
Hall), Mordechai Lawner (*Leo, Alvy's father*), Joan Newman (*Alvy's mother*),
Jonathan Munk (*Alvy, aged 9*), Ruth Volner (*Alvy's aunt*), Martin Rosenblatt
(*Alvy's uncle*), Hy Anzell (*Joey Nichols*), Marshall McLuhan (*as himself*).

1978

Interiors

Producer: Charles H. Joffe
Screenplay: Woody Allen
Cinematography: Gordon Willis
Production Designer: Mel Bourne
Costume: Joel Schumacher
Editor: Ralph Rosenblum
Music: 'Keepin' Out of Mischief Now', 'Wolverine Blues'

Kristin Griffith (*Flyn*), MaryBeth Hurt (*Joey*), Richard Jordan (*Frederick*), Diane Keaton (*Renata*), E. G. Marshall (*Arthur*), Geraldine Page (*Eve*), Maureen Stapleton (*Pearl*), Sam Waterston (*Mike*), Missy Hope (*young Joey*), Kerry Duffy (*young Renata*), Nancy Collins (*young Flyn*), Penny Gaston (*young Eve*), Roger Morden (*young Arthur*).

1979

Manhattan

Producers: Charles H. Joffe, Robert Greenhut
Screenplay: Woody Allen & Marshall Brickman
Cinematography: Gordon Willis
Production Designer: Mel Bourne
Costume: Albert Wolsky, Ralph Lauren
Editor: Susan E. Morse
Music: George Gershwin; 'Rhapsody in Blue', 'Love Is Sweeping the Country', 'Land of the Gay Caballero', 'Sweet and Low Down', 'I've Got a Crush on You', 'Do-Do-Do', ' 'Swonderful', 'Oh, Lady Be Good', 'Strike Up the Band', 'Embraceable You', 'Someone to Watch over Me', 'He Loves and She Loves', 'But Not for Me'
Woody Allen (*Isaac Davis*), Diane Keaton (*Mary Wilke*), Michael Murphy (*Yale*), Mariel Hemingway (*Tracy*), Meryl Streep (*Jill*), Anne Byrne (*Emily*), Karen Ludwig (*Connie*), Wallace Shawn (*Jeremiah*), Michael O'Donoghue (*Dennis*).

1980

Stardust Memories

Producers: Robert Greenhut, Jack Rollins & Charles H. Joffe
Screenplay: Woody Allen
Cinematography: Gordon Willis
Production Designer: Mel Bourne
Costume: Santo Loquasto
Editor: Susan E. Morse
Music: Dick Hyman; 'Tropical Mood Meringue', 'I'll See You in My Dreams', 'Tickletoe', 'Three Little Words', 'Brazil', 'Palesteena', 'Body and Soul', 'Night on Bold Mountain', 'If Dreams Come True', 'One O'Clock Jump', 'Sugar', 'Sweet Georgia Brown', 'Moonlight Serenade', 'Stardust'
Woody Allen (*Sandy Bates*), Charlotte Rampling (*Dorrie*), Jessica Harper (*Daisy*), Marie-Christine Barrault (*Isobel*), Tony Robert (*Tony*), Daniel Stern (*actor*), Amy Wright (*Shelley*), Helen Hanft (*Vivian Orkin*), John Rothman (*Jack Abel*), Anne de Salvo (*Debbie, Sandy's sister*), Joan Neuman (*Sandy's mother*), Ken Chapin (*Sandy's father*), Leonardo Cimino (*Sandy's analyst*), Louise Lasser (*Sandy's secretary*), Robert Munk (*young Sandy*), Sharon Stone (*girl on the train*), Andy Albeck, Robert Friedman, Douglas Ireland, Jack Rollins, Laraine Newman (*film*

company directors), Howard Kissel (*Sandy's manager*), Max Leavitt (*Sandy's doctor*), Renee Lippin (*Sandy's PR woman*), Sol Lomita (*Sandy's accountant*), Irving Metzman (*Sandy's lawyer*), Dorothy Leon (*Sandy's cook*).

1982

A Midsummer Night's Sex Comedy

Producers: Robert Greenhut, Charles H. Joffe
Screenplay: Woody Allen
Cinematography: Gordon Willis
Production Designer: Mel Bourne
Costume: Santo Loquasto
Editor: Susan E. Morse
Casting: Juliet Taylor
Music: Felix Mendelssohn
Woody Allen (*Andrew Hobbes*), Mia Farrow (*Ariel Weynmouth*), José Ferrer (*Leopold*), Julie Hagarty (*Dulcy Ford*), Tony Roberts (*Dr Maxwell Jordan*), Mary Steenburgen (*Adrian Hobbes*).

1983

Zelig

Producers: Robert Greenhut, Charles H. Joffe & Jack Rollins
Screenplay: Woody Allen
Cinematography: Gordon Willis
Optical effects: Joel Hyneck & Stuart Robertson
Animation: Steven Plastrik, Computer Opticals, Inc.
Production Designer: Mel Bourne
Costume: Santo Loquasto
Editor: Susan E. Morse
Music: Dick Hyman; 'I've Got a Feeling I'm Falling', 'I'm Sitting on Top of the World', 'Ain't We Got Fun', 'Sunny Side Up', 'I'll Get By', 'I Love My Baby, My Baby Loves Me', 'Runnin' Wild', 'A Sailboat in the Moonlight', 'Charleston', 'Chicago, That Toddlin' Town', 'Five Foot Two, Eyes of Blue', 'Anchors Aweigh'
Woody Allen (*Leonard Zeglig*), Mia Farrow (*Dr Eudora Fletcher*), John Rothman (*Paul Deghuee*), John Buckwater (*Dr Sindell*), Marvin Chatinover (*endocrinologist*), Stanley Sverdlow (*dietician*), Paul Nevens (*Dr Birsky*), Howard Erskine (*dermatologist*), Stephanie Farrow (*Sister Meryl*), Ellen Garrison (*old Dr Fletcher*), Sherman Loud (*old Paul Deghuee*), Elizabet Rothschild (*old Sister Meryl*), with Susan Sontag, Irving Howe, Saul Bellow, Dr Bruno Bettelheim, Professor John Morton Blum (*as themselves*).

1984

Broadway Danny Rose
Producers: Robert Greenhut, Charles H. Joffe
Screenplay: Woody Allen
Cinematography: Gordon Willis
Production Designer: Mel Bourne
Costume: Jeffrey Kurland
Editor: Susan E. Morse
Music: Dick Hyman; 'Agita', 'My Bambina' by Nick Apollo Forte
Woody Allen (*Danny Rose*), Mia Farrow (*Tina Vitale*), Nick Apollo Forte (*Lou Canova*), Sandy Baron, Corbett Monica, Jackie Gayle, Morty Gunty, Will Jordan, Howard Storm, Jack Rollins (*himself*), Milton Berle (*as himself*), Craig Vandenburgh (*Ray Webb*), Herb Reynolds (*Barney Dunn*), Paul Greco (*Vito Rispoli*), Frank Renzulli (*Joe Rispoli*), Edwin Bordo (*Johnny Rispoli*), Gina DeAngelis (*Johnny's mother, Mrs Rispoli*).

1985

The Purple Rose of Cairo
Producers: Robert Greenhut, Charles H. Joffe
Screenplay: Woody Allen
Cinematography: Gordon Willis
Production Designer: Stuart Wurtzel
Costume: Jeffrey Kurland
Editor: Susan E. Morse
Music: Dick Hyman; 'Cheek to Cheek', 'I Love My Baby, My Baby Loves Me', 'Alabamy Bound'
Mia Farrow (*Cecilia*), Jeff Daniels (*Gil Shepherd*), Danny Aiello (*Monk*), Irving Metzman (cinema director), Stephanie Farrow (*Cecilia's sister*), Dianne Wiest (*Emma*) and in the film within the film: Jeff Daniels (*Tom Baxter*), Edward Herrmann (*Henry*), John Wood (*Jason*), Deborah Rush (*Rita*), Van Johnson (*Larry*), Zoe Caldwell (*countess*), Eugene Anthony (*Arturo*), Karen Akers (*Kitty Haines*), Milo O'Shea (*Father Donnelly*), Annie Joe Edwards (*Delilah*), Peter McRobbie (*communist*).

1986

Hannah and Her Sisters
Producers: Robert Greenhut, Jack Rollins & Charles H. Joffe
Screenplay: Woody Allen
Cinematography: Carlo Di Palma
Production Designers: Stuart Wurtzel & Carol Joffe
Costume: Jeffrey Kurland
Editor: Susan E. Morse

Music: 'You Made Me Love You', 'I've Heard That Song Before', 'Bewitched', 'Just You, Just Me', 'Where or When', 'Concerto for two violins and orchestra' by Bach, 'Back to the Apple', 'The Trot', 'I Remember You', from 'Madame Butterfly' by Puccini, 'You Are Too Beautiful', 'If I Had You', 'I'm in Love Again', 'I'm Old-Fashioned', 'The Way You Look Tonight', 'It Could Happen to You', 'Polkadots and Moonbeams', 'Avalon', 'Isn't It Romantic'
Mia Farrow (*Hannah*), Woody Allen (*Micky Sachs*), Michael Caine (*Elliot*), Carrie Fisher (*April Knox*), Barbara Hershey (*Lee*), Lloyd Nolan (*Evan*), Maureen O'Sullivan (*Norma*), Max von Sydow (*Frederick*), Sam Waterston (*David Tolchin*), Dianne Wiest (*Holly*), Julie Kavner (*Gail*), J. T. Walsh (*Ed Smythe*), John Turturro (*writer*), Joanna Gleason (*Carol*), Tony Roberts (*Norman*), Daniel Stern (*Dusty*).

1987

Radio Days
Producers: Robert Greenhut, Jack Rollins & Charles H. Joffe
Screenplay: Woody Allen
Cinematography: Carlo Di Palma
Production Designer: Santo Loquasto
Costume: Jeffrey Kurland
Editor: Susan E. Morse
Music: Dick Hyman; 'Flight of the Bumblebee' by Rimsky-Korsakov, 'Dancing in the Dark', 'Chinatown, My Chinatown', 'Let's All Sing Like the Birdies Sing', 'I Double Dare You', 'You're Getting to be a Habit with Me', 'September Song', 'Body and Soul', 'In the Mood', 'Radio Show Times', 'Carioca', 'Tico, Tico', 'La Cumparsita', 'Frenesi', 'All or Nothing at All', 'The Donkey Serenade', 'South American Way', 'Maizy Doats', 'If You Are But a Dream', 'Begin the Beguine', 'Opus One', 'You and I', 'Paper Doll', 'Pistol Packin' Mama', 'If I Didn't Care', 'Schloff Mein Kind', 'I Don't Want to Walk Without You', 'Remember Pearl Harbor', 'Babalu', 'They're Either Too Young or Too Old', 'That Old Feeling', 'Lullaby of Broadway', 'American Patrol', 'Take the A-Train', 'The White Cliffs of Dover', 'Goodbye', 'I'm Getting Sentimental Over You', 'You'll Never Know', 'One, Two, Three, Kick', 'Just One of Those Things', 'You'd Be So Nice to Come Home To', 'Night and Day'
Seth Green (*Joe*), Julie Kavner (*Joe's mother, Tess*), Michael Tucker (*Joe's father, Martin*), Dianne Wiest (*Bea*), Josh Mostel (*Uncle Abe*), Mia Farrow (*Sally White*), Danny Aiello (*Rocco*), Jeff Daniels (*Biff Baxter*), Tony Roberts ('*Silver Dollar*' *MC*), Diane Keaton (*Monica Charles*), Wallace Shawn (*masked avenger*), Julie Kurnitz (*Irene*), David Warrilow (*Roger*), Hy Anzell (*Mr Waldbaum*), Judith Malina (*Mrs Waldbaum*), Woody Allen (*narrator*).

1987

September
Producers: Robert Greenhut, Jack Rollins & Charles H. Joffe
Screenplay: Woody Allen
Cinematography: Carlo Di Palma
Production Designer: Santo Loquasto
Costume: Jeffrey Kurland
Editor: Susan E. Morse
Music: 'On a Slow Boat to China', 'Out of Nowhere', 'Just One More Chance', 'My Ideal', 'What'll I Do', 'Who', 'I'm Confessin' ', 'Moonglow', 'When Day Is Done', 'Night and Day'
Denholm Elliott (*Howard*), Mia Farrow (*Lane*), Elaine Stritch (*Diane*), Jack Warden (*Lloyd*), Sam Waterston (*Peter*), Dianne Wiest (*Stephanie*), Rosemary Murphy (*Mrs Mason*), Ira Wheeler (*Mr Raines*), Jane Cecil (*Mrs Raines*).

1988

Another Woman
Producers: Robert Greenhut, Jack Rollins & Charles H. Joffe
Screenplay: Woody Allen
Cinematography: Sven Nykvist
Production Designer: Santo Loquasto
Costume: Jeffrey Kurland
Editor: Susan E. Morse
Music: 'Gymnopédie no. 3' by Erik Satie, 'Bilbao Song' by Kurt Weill, 'Suite for cello in D minor' by Bach, 'Equatorial' by Edgard Varèse, 'Perdido', 'You'd Be So Nice to Come Home To', 'Lovely to Look At', 'A Fine Romance', 'Make Believe', 'Symphony no. 4' by Mahler, 'Smiles', 'On the Sunny Side of the Street', 'Sonata for cello and piano, nos 2 & 3' by Bach, 'Roses of Picardy'
Gena Rowlands (*Marion Post*), Mia Farrow (*Hope*), Blythe Danner (*Lydia*), Sandy Dennis (*Claire*), Gene Hackman (*Larry Lewis*), Ian Holm (*Dr Kenneth Post*), John Houseman (*Marion's father*), Harris Yulin (*Paul*), Philip Bosco (*Sam*), Betty Buckley (*Kathy*), Martha Plimpton (*Laura*), Josh Hamilton (*Laura's boyfriend*), Margaret Marx (*young Marion*), David Ogden Stier (*young Marion's father*).

1989

Oedipus Wrecks (in *New York Stories*)
Producers: Robert Greenhut, Jack Rollins & Charles H. Joffe
Screenplay: Woody Allen
Cinematography: Sven Nykvist
Production Designer: Santo Loquasto
Costume: Jeffrey Kurland
Editor: Susan E. Morse

Music: 'I Want a Girl', 'Mother', 'Sing, Sing, Sing', 'In a Persian Market', 'I'll Be Seeing You', 'I've Found a New Baby', 'All the Things You Are', 'June in January'
Woody Allen (*Sheldon*), Mia Farrow (*Lisa*), Mae Questel (*mother*), Julie Kavner (*Treva*), Jessie Keosian (*Aunt Ceil*), George Schindler (*magician Shandu*), Marvin Chatinover (*psychiatrist*), Ed Koch (*Mayor of New York*).

1989

Crimes and Misdemeanours

Producers: Robert Greenhut, Jack Rollins & Charles H. Joffe
Screenplay: Woody Allen
Cinematography: Sven Nykvist
Production Designer: Santo Loquasto
Costume: Jeffrey Kurland
Editor: Susan E. Morse
Music: 'Rosalie', 'Dancing on the Ceiling', 'Taking a Chance on Love', 'I Know That You Know', 'English suite no. 2' by Bach, 'Home Cooking', 'Sweet Georgia Brown', 'I've Got You', 'This Year's Kisses', 'All I Do Is Dream of You', 'String Quartet no. 15 in G major' by Schubert, 'Murder He Says', 'Beautiful Love', 'Great Day', 'Star Eyes', 'Because', 'Crazy Rhythm', 'I'll See You Again', 'Cuban Mambo', 'Polkadots and Moonbeams', 'I'll Be Seeing You'
Carline Aaron (*Barbara*), Alan Alda (*Lester*), Woody Allen (*Cliff Stern*), Claire Bloom (*Miriam Rosenthal*), Mia Farrow (*Halley Reed*), Joanna Gleason (*Wendy Stern*), Anjelica Huston (*Dolores Paley*), Martin Landau (*Judah Rosenthal*), Jerry Orbach (*Jack Rosenthal*), Sam Waterston (*Ben, the rabbi*), Martin Bergmann (*Professor Louis Levy*), Jenny Nichols (*Jenny*), Stephanie Roth (*Sharon Rosenthal*), Anna Berger (*Aunt May*), Grace Zimmermann (*Ben's daughter*), Daryl Hannah (*Lisa Crosby*).

1990

Alice

Producers: Robert Greenhut, Jack Rollins & Charles H. Joffe
Screenplay: Woody Allen
Cinematography: Carlo Di Palma
Production Designer: Santo Loquasto
Costume: Jeffrey Kurland
Editor: Susan E. Morse
Music: 'Limehouse Blues', 'Breezin' Along with the Breeze', 'I Dream Too Much', 'Moonglow', 'La Cumparsita', 'The Courier', 'World Music', 'Caravan', 'I Remember You', 'Moonlight Becomes You', 'The Way You Look Tonight', 'Alice Blue Gown', Bach's 'Violin Concerto no. 1 in A major', 'Darn That Dream', 'Southern Comfort', 'Mack the Knife', 'Flight of the Foo Birds', 'Will You Still Be Mine?', 'O Tannenbaum'

Mia Farrow (*Alice*), Alec Baldwin (*Ed*), Blythe Danner (*Dorothy*), Judy Davis (*Vicki*), William Hurt (*Doug*), Keye Luke (*Dr Yang*), Joe Mantegna (*Joe Ruffalo*), Bernadette Peters (*muse*), Cybill Shepherd (*Nancy Brill*), Gwen Verdon (*Alice's mother*), Patrick O'Neal (*Alice's father*), Robin Bartlett (*Nina*), Julie Kavner (*interior designer*), Carolin Aaron (*Sue*), David Spielberg (*Ken*).

1992

Shadows and Fog

Producers: Jack Rollins & Charles H. Joffe
Screenplay: Woody Allen
Cinematography: Carlo Di Palma
Production Designer: Santo Loquasto
Costume: Jeffrey Kurland
Music: Kurt Weill, from *The Threepenny Opera*
Woody Allen (*Kleinmann*), Mia Farrow (*Irmy*), John Malkovich (*clown*), Madonna (*Marie*), Donald Pleasance (*doctor*), Kathy Bates, Jodie Foster, Lily Tomlin (*prostitutes*), John Cusack (*Jack*), Kate Nelligan (*Eve*), Julie Kavner (*Alma*), Fred Gwynne (*Hacker's pursuer*), Kenneth Mars (*magician*), David Ogden Stiers (*Hacker*), Wallace Shawn (*Simon Carr*), Philip Bosco (*Mr Paulsen*), Michael Kirby (*murderer*).

1992

Husbands and Wives

Producers: Robert Greenhut, Jack Rollins & Charles H. Joffe
Screenplay: Woody Allen
Cinematography: Carlo Di Palma
Production Designer: Santo Loquasto
Costume: Jeffrey Kurland
Editor: Susan E. Morse
Music: 'What Is This Thing Called Love', Mahler's 9th Symphony, 'That Old Feeling', 'Top Hat, White Tie and Tails', 'Makin' Whopee', 'The Song Is You'
Woody Allen (*Gabe Roth*), Judy Davis (*Sally*), Mia Farrow (*Judy Roth*), Juliette Lewis (*Rain*), Liam Neeson (*Michael*), Sydney Pollack (*Jack*), Lysette Anthony (*Sam*), Blythe Danner (*Rain's mother*), Ron Rifkin (*Rain's psychoanalyst*), Benno Schmidt (*Judy's ex-husband*), Jeffrey Kurland (*interviewer*).

1993

Manhattan Murder Mystery

Producers: Robert Greenhut, Jack Rollins & Charles H. Joffe
Screenplay: Woody Allen & Marshall Brickman
Cinematography: Carlo Di Palma
Production Designer: Santo Loquasto

Costume: Jeffrey Kurland
Editor: Susan E. Morse
Music: 'I Happen to Like New York', 'The Best Things in Life Are Free', 'The Flying Dutchman' by Wagner, 'Take Five', 'I'm in the Mood for Love', 'The Big Noise from Winnetka', 'Out of Nowhere', 'Have You Met Miss Jones', overture to 'Guys and Dolls', 'Sing, Sing, Sing', 'Misty'
Woody Allen (*Larry Lipton*), Diane Keaton (*Carol Lipton*), Alan Alda (*Ted*), Anjelica Huston (*Marcia Fox*), Jerry Adler (*Paul House*), Lynn Cohen (*Lillian House*), Ron Rifkin (*Sy*), Joy Behar (*Marilyn*), Melanie Norris (*Helen Moss*), Marge Redmond (*Mrs Dalton*), Zach Braff (*Nick Lipton*).

1994

Bullets Over Broadway
Producer: Robert Greenhut
Screenplay: Woody Allen & Douglas McGrath
Cinematography: Carlo Di Palma
Production Designer: Santo Loquasto
Editor: Susan E. Morse
John Cusack (*David Shayne*), Jack Warden (*Julian Marx, Rocco*), Chazz Palminteri (*Cheech*), Joe Viterelli (*Nick Valenti*), Paul Herman (*Maitre d'*), Jennifer Tilly (*Olive Neal*), Rob Reiner (*Sheldon Flender*), Stacy Nelkin (*Rita*), Dianne Wiest (*Helen Sinclair*).

1995

Mighty Aphrodite
Producer: Robert Greenhut
Screenplay: Woody Allen
Cinematography: Carlo Di Palma
Production Designer: Santo Loquasto
Music: Dick Hyman
Editor: Susan E. Morse
Woody Allen (*Lenny Weinrib*), Helena Bonham-Carter (*Armanda Weinrib*), Steven Randazzo (*Bud*), J. Smith-Cameron (*Bud's fru*), Mira Sorvino (*Linda Ash, Judy Cam*), Michael Rapaport (*Kevin*), Danielle Ferland (*Cassandra*), Jeffrey Curland (*Oidipus*), Olympia Dukakis (*Iocastes*).

1996

Everyone Says 'I Love You'
Producer: Robert Greenhut
Screenplay: Woody Allen
Cinematography: Carlo Di Palma
Production Designer: Santo Loquasto

Costume: Jeffrey Kurland
Editor: Susan E. Morse
Music: Dick Hyman
Edward Norton (*Holden*), Drew Barrymore (*Skylar*), Alan Alda (*Bob*), Goldie Hawn (*Steffi*), Julia Roberts (*Von*), Woody Allen (*Joe*), Tim Roth (*Charles Ferry*), Barbara Hollander (*Claire*), John Griffin (*Jeffrey Vandermost*), Itzhak Perlman (*himself*).

1997

Deconstructing Harry
Producer: Jean Doumanian
Screenplay: Woody Allen
Cinematography: Carlo Di Palma
Production Designer: Santo Loquasto
Costume: Suzy Benzinger
Editor: Susan E. Morse
Woody Allen (*Harry Block*), Judy Davis (*Lucy*), Elisabeth Shue (*Fay*), Richard Benjamin (*Ken*), Julia Louis-Dreyfus (*Leslie*), Kirstie Alley (*Joan*), Bob Balaban (*Richard*), Hazelle Goodman (*Cookie*), Demi Moore (*Helen*), Tobey Maguire (*Harvey Stern*).

1998

Celebrity
Producer: Jean Doumanian
Screenplay: Woody Allen
Cinematography: Sven Nykvist
Production Designer: Santo Loquasto
Editor: Susan E. Morse
Music: 'You Oughta Be in Pictures', 'Kumbayah', 'Fascination', 'I Got Rhythm', 'Will You Still Be Mine', 'Lullaby of Birdland', 'On a Slow Boat to China', 'Cocktails For Two', 'Soon', 'For All We Know'
Hank Azaria (*David*), Kenneth Branagh (*Lee Simon*), Judy Davis (*Robin Simon*), Leonardo DiCaprio (*Brandon Darrow*), Melanie Griffith (*Nicole Oliver*), Famke Janssen (*Bonnie*), Michael Lerner (*Dr Lupus*), Joe Mantegna (*Tony Cardella*), Winona Ryder (*Nola*), Donald Trump (*himself*), Charlize Theron (*super-model*).

1999

Sweet and Lowdown
Producer: Jean Doumanian
Screenplay: Woody Allen
Cinematography: Zhao Fei
Production Designer: Santo Loquasto

Editor: Alisa Lepselter
Music: The Dick Hyman Group play: 'I'll See You in My Dreams', 'Sweet Georgia Brown', 'Unfaithful Woman', 'Wrap Your Troubles in Dreams (and Dream Your Troubles Away)', 'Old-Fashioned Love', 'Limehouse Blues/Mystery Pacific', 'Just a Gigolo', '3 am Blues', 'All of Me/The Peanut Vendor', 'It Don't Mean a Thing (if it Ain't Got That Swing)', 'Shine', 'I'm Forever Blowing Bubbles', 'There'll Be Some Changes Made'; Benny Berigan and His Orchestra: 'Caravan' av Ellington, Sidney Bechet and Noble Sissie's Swingsters, 'Viber Mad'
Sean Penn (*Emmet Ray*), Samantha Morton (*Hattie*), Woody Allen (*himself*), Ben Duncan (*himself*), Daniel Okrent (*A. J. Pickman, Dan Moran*), Tony Darrow (*Ben*), Christopher Bauer (*Ace*), Constance Shulman (*Hazel*), Kellie Overbey (*Iris*), Darryl Alan Reed (*Don*), Uma Thurman (*Blanche*).

2000

Small Time Crooks
Producer: Jean Doumanian
Screenplay: Woody Allen
Cinematography: Zhao Fei
Production Designer: Santo Loquasto
Costume: Suzanne McCabe
Cutting: Alisa Lepselter
Music: 'With Plenty of Money and You', 'Stompin' at the Savoy', 'Could It Be Me?', 'Music Makers', 'Voices of spring waltzes "Frühlingstimmen" op. 410' av J. Strauss, 'Tequila', 'Cocktails for Two', 'The Modern Dance', 'Prelude in B Minor, op. 32, no. 10' by Rachmaninov, 'Mountain Greenery', 'Fascination', 'Zelda's Theme', 'Sarabande from suite no. 2 violoncello in D minor' av J. S. Bach, 'This Could Be the Start of Something Big', 'Lester Lanin Cha-Cha', 'Just In Time', 'Old Devil Moon', 'The Hukilau Song', 'Steady, Steady'
Woody Allen (*Ray Winkler*), Carolyn Saxon (*the candy salesman*), Tracey Ullman ('*Frenchy' Winkler*), Michael Rapaport (*Denny Doyle*), Tony Darrow (*Tommy Beal*), Sam Josepher (*the real-estate broker*), Jon Lovitz (*Benny Borkowshi*), Lawrence Howard Levy (*the dymamite dealer*), Brian Markinson (*the policeman Ken Deloach*), Elaine May (*May Sloan*).

2001

The Curse of the Jade Scorpion
Producers: Letty Aronson & Charles H. Joffe
Screenplay: Woody Allen
Cinematography: Zhao Fei
Production Designer: Santo Loquasto
Costume: Suzanne McCabe
Editor: Alisa Lepselter

Music: 'Sophisticated Lady', 'Two Sleepy People', 'Tuxedo Junction', 'How High the Moon', 'In a Persian Market', 'Flatbush Flanagan', 'Sunrise Serenade' Woody Allen (*C. W. Briggs*), Helen Hunt (*Betty Ann Fitzgerald*), Charlize Theron (*Laura Kensington*), Dan Akroyd (*Chris Magruder*), Elisabeth Berkley (*Jill*), Kaili Vernoff (*Rosie*), John Schuck (*Mize*), John Tormey (*Sam*), Brian Markinson (*Al*), Maurice Sonnenberg (*office clerk*), John Doumanian (*office clerk*), Peter Gerety (*Ned*).

2002

Hollywood Ending
Producers: Letty Aronson, Helen Robin & Stephen Tenenbaum
Screenplay: Woody Allen
Cinematography: Wedigo von Schultzendorff
Set Designer: Santo Loquasto
Costume: Melissa Toth
Editor: Alisa Lepselter
Woody Allen (*Val Waxman*), George Hamilton (*Ed*), Téa Leoni (*Ellie*), Debra Messing (*Lori*), Mark Rydell (*Al*), Treat Williams (*Hal*), Tiffani-Amber Thiessen (*Sharon Bates*), Anthony Arkin (*participant in audition*), Barney Cheng (*translator*).

2003

Anything Else
Producers: Letty Aronson & Helen Robin
Screenplay: Woody Allen
Cinematography: Darius Khondji
Production Designer: Santo Loquasto
Costume: Laura Jean Shannon
Editor: Alisa Lepselter
Woody Allen (*David Dobel*), Jason Biggs (*Jerry Falk*), Christina Ricci (*Amanda*), Fisher Stevens (*manager*), Anthony Arkin (*Pip's comic*), Danny De Vito (*Harvey*), KaDee Strickland (*Brooke*), Jimmy Fallon (*Bob*), Stockard Channing (*Paula*).

2004

Melinda and Melinda
Producer: Letty Aronson
Screenplay: Woody Allen
Cinematography: Vilmos Zsigmond
Set Designer: Santo Loquasto
Costume: Judy L. Ruskin
Editor: Alisa Lepselter

With: Will Ferrell, Vinessa Shaw, Radha Mitchell, Jonny Lee Miller, Chiwetel Ejiofor, Chloe Sevigny, Josh Brolin, Amanda Peet.

By other directors:

1965

What's New, Pussycat?
Director: Clive Donner
Screenplay: Woody Allen
Woody Allen (*Victor Shakapopolis*), Peter Sellers, Peter O'Toole, Romy Schneider, Capucine, Paula Prentiss, Ursula Andress, Edra Gale.

1966

What's Up, Tiger Lily?
Director: Senkichi Taniguchi
Screenplay & dubbing: Woody Allen, Frank Buxton, Len Maxwell, Louise Lasser, Mickey Rose, Julie Bennett, Bryna Wilson
Producers: Henry G. Saperstein, Woody Allen
Editor: Richard Krown
Music: Jack Lewis & songs from The Lovin' Spoonful
Tatsuya Mihashi (*Phil Moskowitz*), Mie Hana (*Terry Yaki*), Akiko Wakayabayshi (*Suki Yaki*), Tadao Nakamura (*Shepherd Wong*), Susumu Kurobe (*Wing Fat*), China Lee (*strip-tease dancer*).

1967

Casino Royale
Directors: John Huston, Ken Hughes, Val Guest, Robert Parrish, Joseph McGrath
Woody Allen (*Jimmy Bond*), Peter Sellers, Ursula Andress, David Niven, Orson Welles, Joanna Pettet, Deborah Kerr, Daliah Lavi, William Holden, Charles Boyer, John Huston, George Raft, Jean-Paul Belmondo, Barbara Bouchet, Jacqueline Bisset.

1969

Don't Drink the Water
Producer: Charles H. Joffe
Director: Howard Morris
Screenplay: R. S. Allen & Harvey Bullock after a play by Woody Allen.
Jackie Gleason, Estelle Parsons, Joan Delaney.

1972

Play It Again, Sam
Producers: Arthur P. Jacobs, Charles H. Joffe
Director: Herbert Ross
Screenplay: Woody Allen after his own play
Cinematography: Owen Roizman
Production Designer: Ed Wittstein
Editor: Marion Rothman
Music: Billy Goldenberg
Woody Allen (*Allan Felix*), Diane Keaton (*Linda Christie*), Tony Roberts (*Dik Christie*), Jerry Lacy (*Bogey*), Susan Anspach (*Nancy*), Jennifer Salt (*Sharon*), Joy Bang (*Julie*), Viva (*Jennifer, nymphomaniac*).

1976

The Front
Producers: Martin Ritt, Robert Greenhut, Charles H. Joffe
Director: Martin Ritt
Woody Allen (*Howard Prince*), Zero Mostel, Herschel Bernardi, Michael Murphy, Andrea Marcovici.

1987

King Lear
Written & directed: Jean-Luc Godard
Woody Allen (*Mr Alien, a fool*), Norman Mailer, Burgess Meredith, Molly Ringwald.

1991

Scenes From a Mall
Written & directed: Paul Mazursky
Woody Allen (*Nick Fifer*), Bette Midler (*Deborah Feingold-Fifer*), Bill Irwin, Daren Firestone, Rebecca Nickels, Paul Mazursky.

1997

Wild Man Blues
Director: Barbara Kopple
Producers: J.E. Beaucaire & Jean Doumanian
Photo: Tom Hurwitz
Cutting: Lawrence Silk
Woody Allen (*himself: clarinet*), Letty Aronson (*herself, Woody Allen's sister*), Soon-Yi Previn (*herself*), Dan Barret (*himself: trombone*), Greg Cohen (*himself:*

bass), Eddy Davis (*himself: the band leader, banjo*), Cynthia Sayer (*herself: piano*), Steven Schechter (*himself, jurist*), Simon Wettenhall (*himself: trumpet*).

1998

Antz
Directors: Eric Darnell & Tim Johnson
Screenplay: Todd Alcott, Chris Weitz & Paul Weitz
Producers: Brad Lewis, Aron Warner & Patty Wooton
Editor: Stan Webb
Music: Harry Gregson-Williams, John Powell
Woody Allen (*Z-4195, voice*), Dan Akroyd (*Chip, voice*), Anne Bancroft (*Queen, voice*), Jane Curtin (*Muffy, voice*), Danny Glover (*Barbatus, voice*), Gene Hackman (*General Mandible, voice*), Jennifer Lopez (*Azteca, voice*), Sylvester Stallone (*Weaver, voice*), Sharon Stone (*Prinsessan Bala, voice*), Christopher Walken (*Colonel Cutter, voice*).

The Impostors
Director: Stanley Tucci
Screenplay: Stanley Tucci
Producers: Beth Alexander & Stanley Tucci
Cinematography: Ken Kelsch
Editing: Suzy Elmiger
Production Designer: Andrew Jackness
Costume: Juliet Polcsa
Music: Gary DeMichele & Lisandro Androver
Oliver Platt (*Maurice*), Stanley Tucci (*Arthur*), Walker Jones (*Maitre d'*), Jessica Walling (*the attractive woman*), David Lippman (*Baker*), E. Katherine Kerr (*Gertrude*), George Guidall (*Claudius*), William Hill (*Bernardo*), Alfred Molina (*Jeremy Burton*), Michael Emerson (*Burton's assistant*), Woody Allen (*theatre director*).

2000

Picking Up the Pieces
Director: Alfonso Arau
Screenplay: Bill Wilson
Producer: Paul Sandberg
Cinematography: Vittorio Storaro
Editing: Michael R. Miller
Production Designer: Denise Pizzini
Costume: Marilyn Matthews
Music: Ruy Folguera
Woody Allen (*Tex Cowley*), Angélica Aragón (*Dolores*), Alfonso Arau

(*Dr Amado*), Brian Brophy (*CNN reporter*), Betty Carvalho (*Juana*), Enrique Castillo (*Grasiento*), Jorge Cervera Jr. (*Unojo*), O'Neal Compton (*Texas John*), Maria Grazia Cucinotta (*Desi*).

Company Man
Written/directed by: Peter Askin & Douglas McGrath
Producers: Guy East, Rick Leed, John Penotti & James W. Skotchdopole
Cinematography: Russel Boyd
Editor: Camilla Toniolo
Production Designer: Jane Musky
Music: David Nessim Lawrence
Paul Guilfoyle (*Constable Hickle*), Jeffrey Jones (*Senator Biggs*), Reathel Bean (*Senator Farwood*), Harriet Koppel (*typist*), Douglas McGrath (*Alan Quimp*), Sigourney Weaver (*Daisy Quimp*), Terry Beaver (*Ms Judge*), Sean Dugan (*Skull and Bones waiter*), Grant Walden (*an older man*), Nathan Dean (*young man*), Woody Allen (*Lowther*).

Cyberworld
(animated film)
Director: Colin Davies & Elaine Despins
Screenplay: Hugh Murray, Charlie Rubin & Steven Hoban
Producers: Steven Hoban & Hugh Murray
Animation: Jamie McCarter
Music: Hummie Mann
Jenna Elfman (*Phig, voice*), Matt Frewer (*Frazzled, voice*), Robert Smith (*Buzzed/Wired, voice*), Dave Foley (*Hank the Technician, voice*), Woody Allen (*Z-4195, voice, arkivfilm*), Sylvester Stallone (*Weaver, voice, archive film*), Sharon Stone (*Prinsessan Bala, voice, archive film*).

TV productions by Woody Allen:

1994

Don't Drink the Water
Teleplay: Woody Allen, after his own play
Producer: Robert Greenhut
Photography: Carlo di Palma
Cutting: Susan E. Morse
Production Designer: Santo Loquasto
Costume: Suzy Benzinger
Editor: Susan E. Morse
Ed Herlihy (*narrator*), Josef Sommer (*Ambassador Magee*), Robert Stanton (*Mr Burns*), Edward Herrman (*Mr Kilroy*), Rosemary Murphy (*Miss Pritchard*),

Michael J. Fox (*Axel Magee*), Woody Allen (*Walter Hollander*), Julie Kavner (*Marion Hollander, Mayim Bialik (Susan Hollander*)), Ed Van Nuys (*embassy clerk*), Skip Rose (*embassy clerk*), Leonid Usher (*policeman*), Stas Kmiec (*policeman*).

2001

Sounds From a Town I Love
Director: Woody Allen
Written by: Woody Allen
With: Marshall Brickman, Griffin Dunne, Hazelle Goodman, Bebe Neuwirth, Tony Roberts, Celia Weston.

Other appearances by Woody Allen:

1999

Light Keeps Me Company
(documentary)
Director: Carl Gustav Nykvist
Producer: Gudrun Nykvist & Carl Gustav Nykvist
Written by: Michal Leszcylowski & Carl Gustav Nykvist
With: Woody Allen, Bibi Andersson, Harriet Andersson, Richard Attenborough, Pernilla August, Ingmar Bergman, Tomas Bolme, Melanie Griffith.

2002

Last Laugh
(made for television)
Director: Jeff Mazzola
Written by: Denis Hamill
Producer: Andrew Charas
Cinematography: Michael Green
Editor: Jordan Mokriski
Music: Robert Santa
Ray Garvey (*John 'Murph' Murphy*), Vincent Pastore (*Harry Murphy*), Tony Darrow (*Uptown Donnie*), Sally Wheeler (*Victoria Worthington*), Danny Aiello (*himself*), Woody Allen (*himself*), Jackie Martling (*himself*), Jeff Mazzola (*himself*), Lorraine Mazzola (*herself*), Colin Quinn (*himself*).

Chronology

1935 Sunday, 1 December. Allan Stewart Konigsberg ('Woody Allen') is born. His parents are Martin and Nettie ('Cherry') Konigsberg from the Bronx, New York.

1938 Allen sees his first film, Walt Disney's animated *Snow White*.

1943 Allen's sister Letty is born.

1944 The Konigsberg family moves to Brooklyn.

1949 Allen enters Midwood High School.

1950 Allen starts playing the clarinet.

1951 16 years old, Allen performs in 'The Catskills' at Weinstein's Majestic Bungalow Colony. (Weinstein's is later mentioned in Allen's play *The Floating Light Bulb* and in the film *Broadway Danny Rose*.)

1952 'Woody Allen' is born when Allan Konigsberg decides to change his name and starts sending jokes to gossip columnists on New York papers.
25 November. Allen's first published joke turns up in Walter Winchell's column: 'Woody Allen says he ate at a restaurant that had OPS prices – over people's salaries.'
Allen sees his first Ingmar Bergman film, *Summer with Monika*.

1953 Allen starts working with David Alber, writing jokes after school for $20 a week.
June. Allen finishes his studies at Midwood High School.
Allen signs a five-year contract with William Morris Agency.

1954 19 years old, Allen meets Harlene Rosen.

1955 Allen moves to Hollywood to write for *The Colgate Variety Hour*.

1956 Allen marries Harlene Rosen at the Hollywood Hawaiian Hotel.
Summer. Allen and Harlene move to New York.
September. Max Liebman hires Allen to write for *Stanley*, a TV show with Buddy Hacket.

Starting in 1956, continuing for three summers, Allen writes a show during one week at Camp Tamiment Resort. He makes $150 a week.

1958 Sid Caesar hires Allen to write for NBC's *Sid Caesar's Chevy Show*. The show is broadcast on 2 November, and Allen and Larry Gelbart win the Sylvania Award for their scripts. They are also nominated for the Emmy Award for 1958–9.

1959 Allen begins psychoanalysis.

1960 At 25 years of age, Allen now makes $1700 a week, as a scriptwriter to *The Gary Moore Show*.

20 April. Allen's Broadway debut. The show *From A to Z* opens at the Plymouth Theatre. This show contained Allen's parody 'Psychological Warfare' and a Groucho Marx parody, both from his work at Camp Tamiment.

October. Allen gets the chance to try out a show at The Blue Angel nightclub. Rollins and Joffe take Woody upstairs at the Duplex in Greenwich Village, where he puts the finishing touch to his stand-up show. He performs it twice every evening, six days a week.

Allen meets Louise Lasser.

1961 June. Dick Cavett sees Allen at The Bitter End.

1962 Allen is a guest star in *The Ed Sullivan Show*.

Allen works as a scriptwriter for *The Tonight Show* under Jack Paars.

Allen and Harlene get a divorce.

1963 Allen guests several times on the TV show *Candid Camera*.

1964 March. Allen performs at Mr Kelly's in Chicago. His show that night is taped.

April. Allen makes $4000–$5000 a week on his stand-up shows.

July. Allen replaces Johnny Carson as a host for one week in his *Tonight Show*.

July. Colpix releases *Woody Allen*, Allen's first record album. He is nominated for a Grammy for the album. The winner is Bill Cosby's *I Started Out as a Child*.

1965 June. *What's New, Pussycat*, directed by Clive Donner from a script by Allen, is released by Famous Artists.

Fall. Colpix Records releases *Woody Allen, Volume 2*.

1966 20 January. Allen's comical short story 'The Gossage-Vardebedian Papers' is published in the *New Yorker*.

2 February. Allen marries Louise Lasser. The same night, in the middle of a giant snowstorm, he performs twice at the Royal Box in the America Hotel.

Spring. Allen finishes his play *Don't Drink the Water*.

September. *What's Up, Tiger Lily?*, an English variant of *Kagi No Kagi* (Japan 1964), is released by American International Pictures. Allen (and others) wrote a new script that was dubbed into the original film.

17 November. *Don't Drink the Water* opens on Broadway.

Woody is the guest host for the TV show *Hippodrome*.

1967 April. *Casino Royale* is released by Columbia Pictures.

1968 17 June. Allen starts shooting his first original film *Take the Money and Run*. The first scenes are shot at the San Quentin prison in San Francisco.

August. Allen performs at Eugene's (a cabaret the purpose of which was to collect money for Eugene McCarthy's presidential campaign).

His stand-up show is taped and is on *The Third Woody Allen Album*, Capital Records.

1969 12 February. Allen's play *Play it Again, Sam* opens at the Broadhurst Theatre.

19 August. *Take the Money and Run* is released by Palomar Pictures.

Allen and Louise Lasser get a divorce.

1970 Allen buys a duplex apartment on Fifth Avenue by Central Park East.

Spring. Allen writes a screenplay with the title 'The Jazz Baby' that he presents to United Artists, but does not produce at this time.

Allen hosts an educational programme for children, *Hot Dog*, which is broadcast on Saturday mornings.

1971 Together with Diane Keaton, Allen visits the New Orleans Jazz and Heritage Festival and takes part in a jam session in the French quarters. Allen remembers this trip as one of the highlights in his life.

Allen and his New Orleans Funeral and Ragtime Orchestra start playing every Monday night at Michael's Pub in New York City.

Getting Even is published by Random House.

Bananas is released by United Artists.

1972 5 May. *Play it Again, Sam* is released by Paramount Pictures.

August. *Everything You Always Wanted to Know About Sex . . .* is released by United Artists.

Allen finishes a six-week stand-up tour with a two-week performance at Caesar's Palace in Las Vegas. He makes $85,000 dollars in that fortnight.

October. Allen writes the play *Death*.

1973 18 December. *Sleeper* is released by United Artists.

1974 January. Allen begins work on the screenplay involving a murder story that he later uses in a partly edited form to write *Manhattan Murder Mystery*.

1975 11 June. *Love and Death* is released by United Artists.

The plays *Death* and *God* are published by Samuel French Inc.

Allen's book *Without Feathers* is published by Random House.

1976 United Artists release Woody's record *The Night-Club Years, 1964–1968*, a double album containing material from the albums *Woody Allen, Woody Allen, Volume 2* and *The Third Woody Allen Album*.

Inside Woody Allen, a comic strip drawn by Stuart Hample, is introduced in 180 papers in sixty different countries. The jokes were written by Allen and the strips were published for eight years until 1984.

10 May. The filming of *Annie Hall* begins and Woody now starts his collaboration with the film photographer Gordon Willis.

September. *The Front*, directed by Martin Ritt, is released by Columbia Pictures.

1977 21 April. *Annie Hall* is released by United Artists.

The thirty-minute documentary film *Woody Allen: An American Comedy*, written and directed by Howard Mantell, is released by Films for the Humanities Inc.

1978 Monday, 27 March. Allen wins Oscars for Best Director and Best Original Screenplay (with Marshall Brickman) for *Annie Hall*. Diane Keaton wins an Oscar (Best Actress) for her part in the same film.

On this historic evening, Allen plays the clarinet with the New Orleans Funeral and Ragtime Orchestra at Michael's Pub on Manhattan's East Side. Rumour has it he said, 'I couldn't let the boys down.'

2 August. *Interiors* is released by United Artists.

1979 25 April. *Manhattan* is released.

Fall. Allen meets Mia Farrow.

1980 27 April. Allen and Farrow have lunch at Lutèce and start their long relationship. *Side Effects* is published by Random House.

September. *Star Dust Memories* is released by United Artists.

Allen leaves United Artists for Orion Pictures, where he stays until 1991.

1981 27 April. Allen's play *The Floating Light Bulb* opens at New York's Vivian Beaumont Theatre.

1982 July. *A Midsummer Night's Sex Comedy* is released by Orion Pictures.

1983 *Zelig* is released by Orion Pictures.

1984 January. *Broadway Danny Rose* is released by Orion Pictures.

1985 March. *The Purple Rose of Cairo* is released by Orion Pictures.

Allen and Mia Farrow adopt a newborn baby girl from Texas. They name her Dylan O'Sullivan Farrow.

5 November. Allen starts shooting *Radio Days* in and around New York City.

1986 February. *Hannah and Her Sisters* is released by Orion Pictures.

February. As a protest against apartheid, Allen forbids his films to be shown in South Africa.

1987 30 January. *Radio Days* is released by Orion Pictures.

December. *September* is released by Orion Pictures.

Allen is chosen as one of ten honour members of the American Academy and Institute of Arts and Letters. He replaces Orson Welles.

Aged 52, Allen fathers his first biological child. Mia Farrow gives birth to a baby boy, whom they name Satchel O'Sullivan Farrow.

Hannah and Her Sisters is nominated for seven Academy Awards, Allen winning for Best Original Screenplay.

1988 Summer. Woody writes the first draft of *Crimes and Misdemeanours* at hotels in Stockholm, Copenhagen and Italy.

October. *Another Woman* is released in the US by Orion Pictures.

1989 March. The film anthology *New York Stories* is released by Touchstone Pictures.

October. *Crimes and Misdemeanours* is released by Orion Pictures.

1990 1 May. Martin Scorsese, Steven Spielberg, George Lucas and Sidney Pollack give a press conference at the Creative Artists Agency in Beverly Hills, California. They announce the founding of a film fund, an organization 'devoted to preserving the American film heritage'. Woody Allen, Stanley Kubrick, Francis Ford Coppola and Robert Redford are other distinguished members of the organization.

December. *Alice* is released by Orion Pictures.

1991 Paul Mazursky's *Scenes from a Mall* is released by Touchstone Pictures, the leading parts played by Allen and Bette Midler.

July. Allen flies to Italy to make a series of TV commercials for COOP, Italy's largest grocery chain. His fee is $2 million.

1992 12 February. The world première of *Shadows and Fog* in Paris.

13 August. Allen's custody dispute with Mia Farrow regarding the three children Moses Amadeus Farrow (14), Dylan O'Sullivan Farrow (7), and Satchel O'Sullivan Farrow (4 ½), breaks out.

September. Shooting of Allen's second film for TriStar, *Manhattan Murder Mystery*, begins.

18 September. His first film for TriStar, *Husbands and Wives*, opens in the US.

1993 11 May. *The Bunk Project*, a CD with Eddy Davis and New York Jazz Ensemble is released by BMG/Musicmasters. Allen plays the clarinet on the CD.

August. *Manhattan Murder Mystery* opens in the US.

27 September. Filming of *Bullets Over Broadway* begins in New York: this the first film that Allen makes for his friend Jean Doumanian's company Sweetland Films.

1994 4 April. Allen begins shooting the TV film *Don't Drink the Water*, after his own play from 1966.

3 October. Filming of *Mighty Aphrodite* begins.

October. *Bullets Over Broadway* opens in the US.

18 December. *Don't Drink the Water* is broadcast on the ABC network.

1995 6 March. Allen's one-act play 'Central Park West' opens in New York at the Variety Arts Theatre, part of a trilogy under the name *Death Defying Arts* with Elaine May's 'Hotline' and David Mamet's 'An Interview'. The show is performed 343 times.

11 September. The filming of *Everyone Says 'I Love You'* begins in Venice.

3 November. *Mighty Aphrodite* opens in the US.

1996 Spring. Allen and his New Orleans Funeral and Ragtime Orchestra tour in Europe.

April. Neil Simon's comedy *The Sunshine Boys* is broadcast on the US TV channel Hallmark Entertainment.

September. Filming of *Deconstructing Harry* begins.

6 December. *Everyone Says 'I Love You'* opens in the US.

1997 August. The filming of *Celebrity* begins in New York.

12 December. *Deconstructing Harry* opens in the US.

22 December. Allen and Soon-Yi Previn are married in Palazzo Cavalli in Venice. The ceremony is conducted by the city mayor Massimo Cacciari.

1998 17 April. Barbara Kopple's documentary *Wild Man Blues* opens in the US.

Summer. Allen breaks his long collaboration with agent Sam Cohn at ICM and moves to the William Morris Agency.

2 October. The animated film *Antz* opens in the US. Allen voices the ant Z-4195.

20 November. *Celebrity* opens in the US.

1999 Spring. Allen and Soon-Yi adopt a daughter, whom they name Bechet Dumaine, after the clarinettist Sidney Bechet.

3 December. *Sweet and Lowdown* opens in the US.

2000 February. Allen and Soon-Yi adopt their second daughter. She is named Manzie Tio, after Sidney Bechet's drummer Manzie Johnson.

19 May. *Small Time Crooks* opens in the US.

26 May. *Picking Up the Pieces*, directed by Alfonso Arau, premières on US TV.

Allen also buys a house on the Upper East Side of Manhattan and thereby leaves the penthouse he has lived in since 1970.

2001 11 May. It is made public that Allen is suing his friend Jean Doumanian, her partner Jaqui Safra and the company Sweetland Films. Allen contends that Doumanian has been keeping parts of the income from the eight films they made together during the 1990s from him.

5 August. *The Curse of the Jade Scorpion* opens in the US, Allen's first film to be distributed by DreamWorks.

20 October. Allen's short film about New York, *Sounds From a Town I Love* is shown on US TV in connection with the Concert for New York City, benefiting victims of the terror attacks of 11 September.

2002 24 March. Allen makes his first-ever appearance at the Academy Awards ceremony in Los Angeles, where he presents Nora Ephron's collage film *New York on Film Tribute*.

3 May. *Hollywood Ending* opens in the US.

15 May. Allen makes his first visit to the Cannes Film Festival, where *Hollywood Ending* is the gala opening film.

June. Allen begins shooting *Anything Else*.

June. Allen settles his case against Jean Doumanian after nine days of jury trial.

2003 27 August. *Anything Else* premières at the Venice Film Festival and opens in the US three weeks later.

Autumn. Allen begins shooting *Melinda and Melinda*.

Index